THE GREAT RIFT

THE GREAT RIFT

DICK CHENEY,
COLIN POWELL,
AND THE
BROKEN FRIENDSHIP
THAT DEFINED
AN ERA

JAMES MANN

HENRY HOLT AND COMPANY   NEW YORK

Henry Holt and Company
Publishers since 1866
120 Broadway
New York, New York 10271
www.henryholt.com

Henry Holt ® and 🯄® are registered trademarks of Macmillan Publishing Group, LLC.

Copyright © 2020 by James Mann
All rights reserved.
Distributed in Canada by Raincoast Book Distribution Limited

Library of Congress Cataloging-in-Publication Data is available

ISBN: 9781627797559

Our books may be purchased in bulk for promotional, educational, or business use. Please
contact your local bookseller or the Macmillan Corporate and Premium Sales Department at
(800) 221-7945, extension 5442, or by e-mail at MacmillanSpecialMarkets@macmillan.com.

First Edition 2020

Designed by Meryl Sussman Levavi

Printed in the United States of America

1   3   5   7   9   10   8   6   4   2

To my granddaughters, Emma and Phoebe.

May they live in a peaceful century.

CONTENTS

THE
GREAT
RIFT

PREFACE

He was, at the time, merely one of the American military's up-and-coming officers, a young general who had distinguished himself more for his talents in Washington than through commands in the field. Still, when General Colin L. Powell rose to deliver a speech at the Army War College in Carlisle Barracks, Pennsylvania, on May 16, 1989, he carried with him an unusual authority, conveyed by his having recently taken part in civilian events of surpassing importance.

Officially, Powell was the commander of U.S. Forces Command, which is responsible for all the U.S. troops stationed inside the United States. The post was less prominent than those of American commanders responsible for, say, the Middle East or Asia. But this job was merely a temporary placeholder for a rising star. During the previous two years Powell had served as the national security advisor to President Ronald Reagan, after having risen through a series of ever-more-important administrative jobs at the Pentagon and in the White House. He had played a leading role in organizing three summit meetings between Reagan and the Soviet leader Mikhail S. Gorbachev. Now, it was assumed, he was in line to fill a more exalted military post, such as army chief of staff. He was one of the few U.S. military leaders, if not the only one, who swapped friendly personal notes with ex-presidents, sitting presidents, and their wives.

In that spring of 1989, the world was in flux, in a way that seemed to benefit the United States. During Reagan's final six weeks in office, Gorbachev had given a far-reaching speech to the United Nations in which he announced that the Soviet Union would cut the size of its armed forces by half a million troops and that, in the process, it would withdraw six armored divisions from Eastern Europe. Gorbachev had said that the countries there could determine their own destinies; thus, the Soviet Union was forswearing the right to intervene at will in the affairs of its neighbors. With that speech, Gorbachev had gone beyond the mere rhetoric of change in Soviet foreign policy and had given substance to his words. It was now possible to imagine that after more than four decades, the Cold War might draw to a close.

Powell's message at Carlisle that day was that it was time for America to begin thinking about what would come next. He rejected the idea that Gorbachev's new policies were reversible. Though the old Soviet "bear" may be dying, Powell told the audience, "He's still a very formidable bear, and that we must never forget. But as a public and political matter our bear is wearing a Smokey hat and carries a shovel to put out fires."

Powell then posed the question that American leaders were just beginning to confront: "So what does this all mean for us? Remember the old saw *What will all the preachers do when the devil is dead?*"

* * *

That same month, the new secretary of defense, Dick Cheney, prepared a speech with a decidedly different outlook. Cheney, who had been White House chief of staff under President Gerald R. Ford and then served ten years in the House of Representatives, had taken charge of the Pentagon only two months earlier. It was a late, hurried appointment, made after the Senate had rejected President George H. W. Bush's first nominee, John Tower. During his first weeks on the job, Cheney had concentrated on learning his way around. En route to his first White House meeting, he got lost in the Pentagon basement. But by May 1989, when the new defense secretary was to deliver a speech at a Washington think tank, he was ready to give a detailed exposition of his views.

Cheney's views were essentially the opposite of Powell's. There was no need for far-reaching change, he argued in his speech. The Cold War was not over. "However genuine the reforms taking place in the Soviet Union, this is not the time to engage in a wholesale reworking of American defense policy," he asserted. He then took a step further, asserting that America would have to play a powerful role in the world even if the Cold War ended. Starting with World War II, he said, the United States had come to take the responsibility "for seeing to it that liberty and free government had a congenial home in the world." In other words, *"Our commitment to the exercise of global military power became not just a temporary expedient, but a permanent condition."*

* * *

As it turned out, the two speeches had little impact. In fact, Cheney's was never delivered. The White House rejected it as too hawkish. National Security Advisor Brent Scowcroft and his staff felt that it might interfere with the ongoing diplomacy with Moscow being pursued by Secretary of State James Baker. So, the speech lay in a file, unused.

Nor did Powell's speech in Carlisle get a much better reception. It was criticized from the opposite direction, for being too dovish. Scowcroft's deputy, Robert M. Gates, who for years had served as the CIA's leading Soviet analyst, telephoned Powell to say that the general shouldn't have been speaking in such broad terms about the Soviet Union. Senior military figures objected, too. "They said, 'What are you doing? The Soviet Union isn't dead. It's coming back,'" recalled Lawrence Wilkerson, Powell's speechwriter at the time.

The Cheney and Powell speeches are a stark illustration of the divergent viewpoints of these two men, who would eventually emerge as leading antagonists at the highest levels of the U.S. government. Over the following two decades, at the end of the Cold War and in its immediate aftermath, the United States reached the pinnacle of its power in the world. At first, it was accorded almost universal deference as the sole remaining superpower, a nation that could and did wield its economic and military power at will so as to shape the world in the ways it thought best. Then it overestimated its power, launching costly military ventures that proved spectacularly unsuccessful. After two decades, America began to pull back, no longer confident of its success or its power, no longer enjoying the instinctive deference of other nations. Eventually, in the presidency of Donald Trump, it actively cast off its role as leader of the international community.

Colin Powell and Dick Cheney were among the leading public figures of the post–Cold War era. They were close partners in the triumphs of the George H. W. Bush administration, riding together in victory parades after the end of the Persian Gulf War. They returned to office again in the George W. Bush administration, this time as adversaries favoring opposing visions of America's role in the world, as the United States embarked on its disastrous invasion of Iraq.

In their time, no other figures served so long at the top levels of American foreign policy as did Cheney and Powell. In the two decades between 1988 and 2008, Colin Powell served for nine years under four American presidents (Ronald Reagan, George H. W. Bush, Bill Clinton, and George W. Bush) as national security advisor, chairman of the Joint Chiefs of Staff, and secretary of state. Over the same period, Dick Cheney served for twelve years, as secretary of defense under George H. W. Bush and as vice president under George W. Bush. Even the two-term presidents of the post–Cold War era (Clinton, the younger Bush, and Barack Obama) held high office for only eight years apiece. Cheney and Powell had greater longevity at the top than any of them.

Powell was for a time so popular that many felt he could have been president, while Cheney was for a time so powerful that many thought that he *was*, effectively, the president. Powell's problem was that he could not find a home or a base in either of America's two political parties. He never fit comfortably into either of the two visions of U.S. foreign policy that dominated American electoral politics in those times, Democratic liberal internationalism and Republican neoconservatism. Cheney's problem lay elsewhere: He nestled snugly into the Republican Party, but he could never master the public side of electoral politics. Indeed, he seemed almost to revel in his own unpopularity, comforting himself with comparisons to Winston Churchill whenever he found himself advocating policies deemed unacceptable by the public at large.

There was no lack of irony here. Over time, Powell came to think of Cheney and Cheney's longtime associate and patron Donald Rumsfeld as politicians, whereas he, Powell, was not. He never ran for office. Yet Powell was the dynamic figure who could charm the crowds and the press, as

Cheney could not. Conversely, Cheney, although he himself held elective office, thought of Powell as the one who was by nature a politician, not a policy maker.

Powell was charismatic, while Cheney was aloof. Paul Wolfowitz, who worked with both men inside the Pentagon during the George H. W. Bush administration, recalled what happened when he traveled to the Middle East with them at the time of the 1991 Persian Gulf War. "Everywhere Powell would go, he was a rock star. The troops loved him, and vice versa, and he was good at it," he said. At one refueling stop, Wolfowitz was standing alone with Cheney outside the plane and noticed a small group of soldiers at a fence nearby. Wolfowitz had to walk over and ask, "Would you like to meet the secretary of defense?" When the soldiers said yes, Cheney ambled over and spoke cordially with them, seeming to enjoy it. "But it wasn't his instinct to go do that himself," Wolfowitz observed. "Powell would have been there in two seconds, without prompting."

Yet, curiously, when it came to public debate on the issues of the day, Cheney often seemed more comfortable operating in the spotlight than Powell. He would state his views, out front and forcefully. Powell preferred to operate behind the scenes, meeting with the key decision makers, seeking to persuade in private rather than in public. After the September 11 attacks and in the debates that led up to the invasion of Iraq, it was Cheney who thundered in television interviews and speeches to groups such as the Veterans of Foreign Wars. Richard Haass, who worked for Powell at the time, found himself spending less time than he'd expected on speechwriting. "Colin Powell wasn't inclined to give policy-laden speeches," he later wrote. "He much preferred more personal and less formal talks along the lines of those he honed during his years on the speaking circuit."

It is wrong to consider the two men lifelong rivals or enemies. On the contrary: only two months after their dueling speeches about the Cold War in the spring of 1989, Cheney went out of his way to select Powell as his candidate to serve as chairman of the Joint Chiefs of Staff, overcoming initial resistance from the White House, and it was this job that catapulted Powell to his prominence in post–Cold War America. The two men worked extremely closely together throughout George H. W. Bush's administration.

Powell and Cheney are remembered now as diminished figures because of the spectacular failure of the invasion of Iraq. Cheney was the most fervent proponent of military action. Powell never resigned or publicly dissented as the George W. Bush administration pursued that war. Yet their early triumphs and subsequent failures are a central part of the American narrative. It was the choices they made, together and separately, that helped set the course for America in the years following the end of the Cold War.

* * *

For years, a question has swirled around these men and the era in which they served. How and why did the country tumble from such optimism at the time of the Persian Gulf War and the collapse of the Soviet Union to the divisions, uncertainty, and diminished confidence that prevailed two decades later?

For Powell, the question centers on his role as secretary of state under President George W. Bush. To what extent did he oppose the Iraq War? Did he ever challenge President Bush? Why didn't he resign, or at least air his misgivings? How did he allow himself to be the public spokesman at the United Nations for accusations against Iraq that turned out to be untrue? Was he a lesser figure than he had seemed a decade earlier?

Concerning Cheney, the questions and theorizing have become a cottage industry. Above all, they focus on whether Cheney had somehow changed from the early 1990s, when he was widely portrayed as a calm, dispassionate, reasonable secretary of defense, to the early 2000s, when he was the truculent, implacable spokesman for conservative policies, above all for American military power and the right and necessity of using it.

In the years during and after the Iraq War, many popular explanations were offered for Cheney's behavior. They started with the medical: it was not uncommon to have heard at least secondhand of some cardiologist who claimed to "know" that Cheney's personality had changed because of his heart attacks or the operations to treat them—and that these changes were what had caused Cheney to become such a war hawk.

Other theories centered on his family and friends. Former president George H. W. Bush speculated that Cheney might have changed as a result of the influence of family members, specifically his wife, Lynne, and his daughter Liz. "You know, I've concluded that Lynne Cheney is a lot of the eminence grise here—iron ass, tough as nails, driving," the elder Bush told his biographer Jon Meacham.

Cheney offered a different explanation: that the world had changed with the September 11 attacks, and that his own thinking and conduct had changed in response to that event. When Brent Scowcroft voiced objections to a prospective war against Iraq, Cheney argued that Scowcroft had "a pre-9/11 mindset. . . . We were at war against terrorist enemies who could not be negotiated with, deterred, or contained, and who would never surrender. This was not the world of superpower tensions and arms-control agreements in which Brent had served."

A variant of this theory, common among foreign policy specialists, is that it was the anthrax attacks a few weeks after September 11 that solidified Cheney's hard-line views. "People who watched him said this is what changed him—it was not 9/11. It was the anthrax attacks. The vice president believed that this would be the beginning of a series of use of weapons of mass destruction against the United States," said Andrew Natsios, who served as a State Department aide under Powell. "That's when something switched in his mind and he became much more aggressive but also darker in his view of what was happening in the world."

Far less explored was the possibility that Cheney hadn't changed much at all: that he had always been more conservative and more tenacious than his former colleagues had recognized. What had changed was that as vice president, he had risen to a level of political authority where he could endeavor to put his views into effect.

It must be asked, finally, whether America itself had changed in these two decades from 1988 to 2008. What transpired in the United States and in the rest of the world to create a climate in which Dick Cheney's views would prevail over the principles that had held sway during the Cold War, principles that Colin Powell embraced? How did it happen that Dick Cheney and Colin Powell emerged on the same side of many of the debates that raged in the late 1980s and early 1990s, and on opposing sides in the early 2000s? That is the story this book means to tell.

PART ONE

INDISPENSABLE

1

USEFUL YOUNG MEN

I would spend nearly twenty years, one way or another, grappling with our experience in this country. And over all that time, Vietnam rarely made much more sense than Captain Hieu's circular reasoning on that January day in 1963. We're here because we're here, because we're . . .

—COLIN POWELL

I was of the opinion that the combination of Vietnam and Watergate had significant negative impact on the Presidency and in terms of the balance between Congress and the White House. . . . I thought Congress had infringed on executive prerogatives.

—DICK CHENEY

The early lives of Dick Cheney and Colin Powell possess some surprising similarities. Both men began their careers in the 1960s, when the Vietnam War was the preoccupying issue of the day. Both men began their ascent in Washington during the 1970s, as America struggled with the end of that war and its consequences.

As young men, Powell and Cheney gained prominence and were propelled forward not for their ideas or vision, but because of their skills at the less exalted tasks of organization and administration. Before they were political leaders, they were bureaucrats. Each started as an unusually talented staff aide; each proved adept at the basic task of getting things done for his bosses. Because of their fundamental competence, both Cheney and Powell attracted powerful, high-level mentors who would promote their careers in Washington for years to come.

But these similarities go only so far. Powell grew up in America's biggest city, Cheney in the sparsely populated mountain west. As he started his career, Powell was always trying to build a record for himself, to find ways in which he could stand out. Cheney, by contrast, was trying to overcome his own record, a police record, a legacy of his occasionally raucous youth. Each time Cheney was offered a new, more powerful job, he would feel compelled to confess to his indiscretions as a young man.

* * *

Powell was the older of the two, born in 1937, four years before Cheney. That age difference meant that Powell was old enough to harbor strong childhood memories of World War II, which the United States entered when he was four years old; Cheney could remember only the final year of the war and his father coming home. For Powell, the World War II memories lingered: decades later, he would sometimes be criticized for wanting to avoid small-scale wars and for seeking to conserve American troops for big wars of the sort that Dwight Eisenhower and Omar Bradley had fought.

As a grown man, Powell would be hosted by Queen Elizabeth at Buckingham Palace, dance with Princess Diana, own expensive Manhattan apartments, and become friends with tycoons such as Walter Annenberg. Yet no one ever questioned his humble origins or accused him of elitism. He was born in Harlem, the son of Jamaican immigrants, both of whom worked in the city's Garment District. The family eventually moved to the South Bronx, where Powell spent most of his childhood. He chose to go to City College of New York because its tuition was free, whereas New York University, which also accepted him, cost $750 a year.

At the prodding of his mother, Powell tried to major in engineering but quickly found it too hard for him. "A professor said to me, 'Imagine a plane intersecting a cone in space.' I said, 'I cannot imagine a plane intersecting a cone in space. I'm out of here,'" Powell recalled years later. He switched to geology, but soon began devoting most of his energy to another field in which he excelled: the military. He joined the CCNY branch of the Reserve Officers' Training Corps, loved it, and eventually became its cadet colonel, commander of the thousand-man regiment.

"The discipline, the structure, the camaraderie, the sense of belonging were what I craved," Powell said. "Race, color, background, income meant nothing."

He entered the army soon after his graduation in 1958. At first, he started down the predictable path of a young officer in peacetime, moving from base to base in the United States and Europe. But peace was not to last. In the mid-1950s, France had departed in defeat from its former colonies in Indochina, leaving behind a divided country in Vietnam. Communist North Vietnamese troops and guerrilla forces in the south sought to topple the pro-Western regime in South Vietnam and reunify the country, attracting support from the Soviet Union and China. The United States intervened to prop up the regime in Saigon, citing its Cold War policy of stopping the spread of communism. In the early 1960s, the administration of President John F. Kennedy began dispatching small numbers of American military advisors to South Vietnam; by the end of the decade, more than 500,000 American combat troops would be fighting there.

Colin Powell spent two tours of duty in Vietnam. The first was in 1962–63, the initial phase of the war, as the total American troop presence in Vietnam was being raised from three thousand to eleven thousand. At the time, ordinary Americans were so little aware of the country that when Powell first got his orders, his family had to look on a map to see where Vietnam was. Captain Powell served as an advisor to a South Vietnamese battalion far out in the jungle of the A Shau Valley, near the border with Laos, amid the insects, leeches, and Viet cong guerrillas. He once went a month without bathing, except for a quick splash in a stream. After six months there, spent largely on his own with the South Vietnamese troops, and frequently under fire, he was wounded when he stepped on a poisoned spike that went straight through his foot. He returned home from that tour with a Purple Heart and a Bronze Star.

Five years later, Powell was sent back, this time at the height of the war, a time when the morale of the American troops was flagging. Powell, now a major, served as executive officer of the U.S. Army's Americal Division and as its staff officer for operations and planning. During this second tour, a helicopter in which he was riding crashed; he suffered a broken ankle but managed to drag his commanding officer to safety. He was awarded a Legion of Merit.

The war turned out to be far costlier than America could tolerate. Younger Americans whose frame of reference is the U.S. invasion of Iraq in 2003 can scarcely imagine how much greater an impact the Vietnam War had on American lives, society, politics, the armed forces, foreign policy, intellectual life, and culture. More than 58,000 Americans were killed, nearly twelve times as many as in the Iraq War. By 1973, the United States had withdrawn all its forces; two years later, the South Vietnamese regime collapsed.

His Vietnam experience left Powell with a profound, instinctive mistrust of experts, abstractions, and technocratic solutions of the sort that officials in Washington had concocted to justify what turned out to be a futile military action. Powell had experienced the war up close, and he was convinced that the top U.S. political and military leaders in Washington had not understood the reality on the ground in Vietnam. In harboring such sentiments, he was hardly unique; millions of other Americans reacted to the war in the same way. But for Powell, Vietnam also amplified the anti-intellectual tendencies he had already harbored earlier in his life. He belittled "slide-rule prodigies" such as Secretary of Defense Robert McNamara, who had regularly proclaimed that America was winning the war.

"Deep thinkers . . . were producing printouts, filling spreadsheets, crunching numbers, and coming out with blinding flashes of the obvious, while an enemy in black pajamas and Firestone flip-flops could put an officer out of the war with a piece of bamboo dripped in manure," he later wrote. "Experts often produce more data than judgment."

The war also left Powell with a sense of anger at the injustices of the military draft. Young men from wealthy or middle-class backgrounds received draft deferments while the poorer and less educated were shipped off to Vietnam. (Among the millions who obtained deferments was a young man from Wyoming named Dick Cheney.) Powell disparaged the way America was fighting a war for which it had little enthusiasm. "We were in a war against an enemy who believed in his cause and was willing to pay the price, however high," he later wrote.

For all these reasons, Powell developed strong views about the ways

America should and should not go into battle. The United States should not have gone into a "half-hearted, half-war" in Vietnam, he later wrote. War should be "the politics of last resort," he argued, and the United States should go to war only with strong public support. But once America did go to war, it should set clear goals, mobilize its resources, and go in to win.

Over the following three decades, Powell would repeatedly find himself confronting these same questions about how and when America should go to war. He would play a role in the creation of new guidelines for American policy makers, seeking to ensure that America never again fought a military conflict the way it had in Vietnam.

* * *

Dick Cheney's childhood was, if anything, too stable, instilling a desire for movement, upheaval, and disorder. His father's parents had wandered around the Great Plains, their lives subject to the vicissitudes of drought, recessions, and bank failures. Seeking to avoid a similar fate, his father took a job with the U.S. Soil Conservation Service, held it for three decades, settled in Wyoming, and was pleased to retire on a federal pension. Cheney grew up in Casper, where he was an All-State football star at Natrona County High School, served as president of the student council, and began to date his future wife, Lynne Vincent, the state champion baton twirler. "He was very popular, very involved. And smart, but—he's never been the kind of smart that is flashy," said Dave Gribben, who went to high school with Cheney and later worked for him.

After graduating from high school in 1959, Cheney began a period of instability, insobriety, and intermittent wildness that lasted for several years. Most of his fellow graduates went on to the University of Wyoming or to nearby Casper College, but a Yale alumnus living in Wyoming had encouraged Cheney to apply to his alma mater. At the time, Yale's student body was composed mostly of students from the Northeast, often from elite schools. The active recruitment of public high school graduates from states such as Wyoming was part of an effort to expand Yale's geographical diversity. Cheney won admission and entered Yale, but he soon discovered that he didn't fit in—except with a small group of friends who, in his own words, "shared my belief that beer was one of the essentials of life." At the end of his freshman year, the Yale administration asked him to take a year off. He did, but after returning, he continued to receive poor grades and disciplinary warnings and finally dropped out of Yale again, this time permanently.

Returning west, Cheney went to work as a lineman, stringing cable and power lines and operating equipment for construction crews as he moved from job to job in Wyoming, Colorado, and Utah. He lived in roadside motels and unwound at night in local watering holes, drinking beer, sometimes with shots of bourbon. He was arrested for drunk driving in late 1962 and again less than a year later. On the second occasion, he woke up with a hangover, in jail.

By Cheney's own account, this was something of a conversion experience. He decided to stay away from the bars and to go back to school. He returned to college at the University of Wyoming, mostly because he was a resident of the state and, thus, the university was obliged to accept him, despite his poor grades. There, he turned into a serious student.

To some extent, the demeanor and affect for which Cheney would be known later in life (the deep voice, the cool assurance, the extreme gravity and sobriety, the aura that everything has been foreseen and is under control) can be viewed as a reaction to this chaotic period in his youth. The arrests for drunk driving became a record he felt compelled to explain at various stages in his life. When he was being considered for a top job in the White House, during the administration of Gerald Ford, Cheney disclosed the arrests, saying he didn't want the president to be surprised. The issue went to Ford himself, who ordered that Cheney be hired. A quarter century later, when George W. Bush offered him the vice presidency in the summer of 2000, Cheney again felt obliged to confess, to Bush and his political advisor Karl Rove, the drunk-driving episodes of his youth. (At the time, Cheney did not know that Bush was concealing a similar arrest in his own past, one that would become public just before Election Day.)

Cheney finished his undergraduate degree at Wyoming and went off to the University of Wisconsin for graduate school in political science, together with his wife, Lynne, who was also a graduate student. In 1966, they had their first child, Elizabeth. Cheney had received a 2-S student draft deferment while attending college; after his daughter was born, he was given another deferment, as a parent with dependents. Two years later, as the war was reaching its peak, he turned twenty-seven and was no longer eligible for the draft.

Cheney subsequently admitted to an overall sense of detachment from the war and the issues it raised. "As a general proposition, I was supportive in those days, I think, of the Johnson administration policy," he observed in one interview. "I didn't spend a lot of time thinking about it. . . . From my personal standpoint, it wasn't a traumatic event at the time." He went on to say, repeatedly, that if he had been called up, he would have gone. (He had been, in fact, briefly classified as 1-A and was thus, theoretically, eligible for the draft in his days of drifting after leaving Yale, but the war was in its earliest stages then, and there were few call-ups.)

Two decades after the war, during his confirmation hearings to become secretary of defense, Cheney told the Senate Armed Services Committee, "I had other priorities in the '60s than military service." It was a statement that did little to endear him to those serving in the military or to Vietnam veterans, some of whom wrote angry letters to their local newspapers. In the early 2000s, at the time of a new war in Iraq, opponents of the war brought up that Cheney quote again, with renewed anger.

* * *

When Colin Powell returned home from his second tour in Vietnam in 1969, his family urged him to get out of the army. By this time, he already had a family; he had married his wife, Alma Johnson, in 1962, and they already had two young children. Powell overcame his family's objections by telling them that if he stayed in and made the rank of lieutenant colonel, he could retire at age forty-one with a 50 percent pension. They went along, and he was indeed promoted to lieutenant colonel a year later.

He enrolled in graduate school, itself a traditional stepping-stone for a young military officer. But at the army's prodding, he took an unusual path, pursuing an MBA at George Washington University, rather than the more typical military path of enrolling in an international relations program to study strategy and policy. "I was more interested in business than in just getting a soft policy degree," he later explained.

After two years, his master's degree in hand, Powell was assigned to a staff job at the Pentagon. While working there in late 1971, he was given an opportunity that would become of profound importance to his career. His army superiors handed him a form and instructed him to apply to the White House Fellows program, in which fifteen promising young people from various fields, viewed as future leaders, were assigned to work for a year as special assistants to senior White House staff, Cabinet secretaries, and other top officials. Army leaders were eager to get more military officers into the program. Powell sent in his application, one of fifteen hundred submitted that year, and was chosen as a White House fellow for the year 1972–73.

Powell had to decide where in Washington he would spend his year. He was first sounded out about the FBI, but the idea didn't appeal to him. He interviewed with the secretary of housing and urban development, George Romney, but that job seemed too limiting. Finally, he went to work for one of the least glamorous agencies in the federal government: the Office of Management and Budget. Once again, his instinct for doing what was practical worked out spectacularly well for him. At the time, the director of OMB was Caspar Weinberger, a California lawyer who had worked for Governor Ronald Reagan and who would later become secretary of defense. Weinberger's deputy at OMB was Frank Carlucci, himself a future national security advisor and secretary of defense.

Carlucci was especially important for Powell's career. He had served on the panel that selected Powell as a White House fellow, and he hired Powell to spend his fellowship year at the budget office. Powell was assigned to an office across the hall from Carlucci. Years later, Carlucci would recall that he found Powell to be a quick study, a hard worker, easygoing but forceful when he needed to be. "He had the diplomatic finesse to say no without alienating people," Carlucci said.

The civilian contacts Powell made during his year as a White House fellow would prove invaluable for him. In the early 1980s, when Weinberger became secretary of defense, Powell would work as his military assistant. A few years later, when President Reagan appointed Carlucci to be his national security advisor, Carlucci would pick Powell to serve as his deputy. After Carlucci moved to the Pentagon to succeed Weinberger as secretary of defense, Powell would rise to become national security advisor. And when Dick Cheney took over from Carlucci at the Pentagon, Carlucci would recommend strongly that Cheney name Powell as chairman of the Joint Chiefs of Staff.

Jim Webb, a future U.S. senator who clashed regularly with Powell when both men served in the Pentagon during the Reagan administration, said that he thought Carlucci "created Colin Powell." That seems more than a little unfair to Powell, whose own extraordinary talents propelled him forward. But Webb's acid comment says something about the long, close mentor-pupil relationship between Frank Carlucci and Colin Powell.

* * *

Like Powell, Dick Cheney first moved to Washington in the late 1960s. Before long he, too, developed a close working relationship as an aide to a high-level mentor— one who would over time become even more important to Cheney's career than Carlucci was for Powell's.

In 1968, while still a graduate student at Wisconsin, Cheney came to the nation's capital on a fellowship from the American Political Science Association. The fellows were assigned to work for individual members of Congress. Cheney interviewed with a young congressman from Illinois, Donald Rumsfeld, but after a short time, Rumsfeld brusquely dismissed him, saying, "This isn't going to work." It was "one of the most unpleasant experiences of my life," Cheney later recalled. "The truth is I flunked the interview." Instead, he settled in the office of Wisconsin congressman Bill Steiger.

The following year, President Richard Nixon brought Rumsfeld into his administration, appointing the congressman to head the Office of Economic Opportunity, the antipoverty agency created in the Johnson administration. Rumsfeld asked Steiger for advice about running the agency. Cheney noticed the request for help on Steiger's desk and spent a weekend writing a memo with thoughts on how to organize and staff OEO. The memo made its way to Rumsfeld, who a few weeks later called Cheney to offer him a job.

Cheney began as the agency's head of congressional relations but was soon moved to a new position, as Rumsfeld's special assistant, with a desk outside Rumsfeld's office. Because Rumsfeld also had a separate title as special assistant to the president, Cheney was given a second office along with Rumsfeld in the West Wing of the White House. When the FBI screened him for the White House job, the two drunk-driving arrests turned up. Rumsfeld asked Cheney about them and then decided to ignore them, winning Cheney's everlasting gratitude.

It was Rumsfeld's style to issue orders and to receive information at one remove through his special assistant. Cheney became Rumsfeld's instrument and gradually began to take on an importance of his own. In these early days of the Nixon administration, Frank Carlucci was serving as Rumsfeld's deputy at OEO. He later said he learned quickly that the way to get things done at the agency was to go to Cheney, who was discreet and effective. "When you gave something to Dick, it happened. It got done," Carlucci said.

The Rumsfeld-Cheney relationship proved to be one of Washington's most enduring high-powered partnerships. When Rumsfeld left OEO after a year and a half and moved to the White House as a full-time domestic policy advisor to the president, he took Cheney with him. When Rumsfeld later was named director of Nixon's Cost of Living Council, Cheney became his assistant director.

In those early years, by his own acknowledgment, Cheney was entirely subservient to Rumsfeld. At White House meetings, Cheney got to see the president—but only in the role of flipping charts when Rumsfeld made presentations. Their personalities could not have been more different: Rumsfeld was brash and aggrandizing, Cheney laconic and subdued. Rumsfeld was cosmopolitan, sophisticated, and well-traveled; Cheney had hardly traveled at all.

Cheney was the more conservative and partisan of the two, perhaps reflecting his Wyoming roots. Rumsfeld, who in Congress had been a moderate Republican, maintained a variety of Democratic friends, some of whom he had met on Capitol Hill. One of them was Allard Lowenstein, a leading liberal congressman from New York. In 1970, seeking to fend off a challenge by a Republican who portrayed him as a dangerous radical, Lowenstein obtained a statement from his old friend. It wasn't an outright endorsement, but Rumsfeld attested to Lowenstein's personal qualities. The Republican opponent asked the White House to get Rumsfeld to issue a retraction. Rumsfeld turned the matter over to Cheney, who issued a strong statement of support for Lowenstein's opponent. "Cheney was focused more on the need to elect Republicans to Congress than on my friendship with Al," Rumsfeld later wrote. Lowenstein lost the seat and was furious with Rumsfeld; their friendship never recovered.

Cheney grew increasingly interested in Republican politics, and in 1972 he had preliminary talks with the Nixon campaign about joining the Committee for the Re-election of the President, nicknamed CREEP. Rumsfeld's appointment to run the Cost of Living Council came through at just this time, and Cheney elected to go with Rumsfeld instead. He was lucky; CREEP became deeply enmeshed in the Watergate scandal, and two of CREEP's leaders, including the official who had sought to recruit Cheney, went to prison. Virtually everyone working at the organization was tarred by association with it.

After Nixon won reelection, Rumsfeld, whose relationship with the rest of the White House staff ranged from testy to miserable, eagerly accepted an appointment as the U.S. ambassador to NATO, based in Brussels. Rumsfeld again asked Cheney to serve as his assistant, but this time Cheney declined. He had little interest in leaving the country. Instead, he left the government and went to work with some old friends at an investment advisory service.

As Cheney later acknowledged, he was lucky to leave the Nixon administration when he did. The Watergate scandal soon snowballed into a continuing series of investigations by a special prosecutor and in Congress, ensnaring many officials who worked for Nixon. "I watched the absolute destruction of a number of colleagues," Cheney reflected a quarter century later.

Cheney learned an early lesson from Watergate: to minimize the use of memos and records of what you are doing. "I worked for Don Rumsfeld, and Don and I survived and prospered in that environment because we didn't leave a lot of paper laying [sic] around," he said. "It's unfortunate from the standpoint of history, but I did not want to leave a lot of tracks around."

* * *

Following his year as a White House fellow, Colin Powell returned to the army. He was given a more traditional assignment as commander of a battalion for the Eighth Army in South Korea.

He could not know it, but that year in Korea, 1973–74, turned out to be Powell's last overseas posting for more than a decade. He would spend practically the rest of his army career inside the United States, mostly in Washington assignments. The White House fellowship had marked him within the military as a rising star, one who could work at the highest levels of government.

His army superiors came to see him as an officer who knew how to do business with top civilians. Conversely, civilian leaders saw Powell as someone who could translate to the military what the civilians wanted, and do so in ways that the uniformed leaders could understand. These qualities stood out inside Washington.

After Korea, Powell was selected for another prestigious posting, a year of study in military strategy at the National War College. He read the military classics in the field—Alfred Thayer Mahan on sea power, Carl von Clausewitz on war. He took Clausewitz's principles and applied them to his own experience in Vietnam: Clausewitz had written, for example, that political leaders must set the specific objectives for a military conflict and that a war must have public support. Powell concluded that Vietnam had failed on both counts.

In the 1970s, the army was in flux, in its leadership and in the composition of the troops. Vietnam had demonstrated that America's older generation of officers was too often flawed, inflexible, and limited—stuck in a mentality of body counts, predictable tactics, and stilted briefings. Those problems pointed to the need for new, more adaptable leaders.

Meanwhile, the army itself was changing. The Vietnam-era military draft had served to increase political opposition to the war, as young Americans and their families came to question the need for the military conflict for which they were to be called up. The draft had also intensified debates over the equity of a system in which middle-class and wealthy Americans often got deferments while the poor did not. After years of controversy, the Nixon administration abolished conscription and instituted an all-volunteer army. By the mid-1970s, the army found itself with new kinds of recruits: better-educated young men and women, with at least a high school education, who had chosen to be in the military and often planned to make a career there.

Amid these other post-Vietnam changes, the army was seeking to increase the number of black officers. During the war, racial tensions had boiled to the surface within the army. One factor was simply the impact of developments in the United States in the 1960s, from the civil rights movement to the Black Power movement. But there were also racial issues specific to Vietnam, ranging from tangible day-to-day conflicts among the American troops to the awkward fact that the United States was fighting its war against a nonwhite population. ("I ain't got no quarrel with them Viet Cong," the heavyweight boxing champion Muhammad Ali had declared in refusing to comply with his own draft notice.)

The percentage of black enlisted men in the army was rising rapidly. In 1973, 18 percent of the enlistees in the U.S. Army were black; by 1980, the figure was 33 percent. The percentage of black officers was far lower; over the same period, it rose from 4 percent to 7 percent.

Military and civilian leaders were under pressure to increase the number of black people in leadership positions, and Powell was a very attractive candidate. Not only could he bridge the divide between military leaders and civilians, but he could also talk with ease across the racial divide, as whites and blacks alike tended to feel comfortable with him. In 1977, Jimmy Carter, a former Southern governor and a strong supporter of civil rights, was elected president. He appointed Clifford Alexander, a Washington lawyer, to be the first African American secretary of the army. Alexander tripled the number of black generals during his tenure, including a promising young colonel named Colin Powell.

Powell never sought to deny or downplay that he had benefited to some extent from affirmative-action policies. Indeed, throughout his career, he regularly and strongly supported the concept of affirmative action to help overcome the legacy of discrimination and slavery—more so, in fact, than other prominent black officials. (Years later, when the George W. Bush administration took a position against affirmative action before the U.S. Supreme Court, Powell quickly made public his disagreement. Bush's national security advisor, Condoleezza Rice, another high-ranking African American, initially gave some carefully qualified support to the president's position before reversing course and saying she supported the general concept of taking race into account for college admissions. When asked about Rice's hesitant stand a few days later, Powell said simply, "Finally!")

Yet affirmative action cannot suffice to explain Powell's speedy rise or his continuing attractiveness to his white superiors. His winning personality, ambition, and well-concealed guile were also crucial factors. He understood instinctively how to handle race in such a way that the issue seemed to melt away.

In the mid-1990s, in an interview with the African American historian Henry Louis Gates Jr., Powell explained concisely the way he handled the issue of race. "One, I don't shove it in their face, you know? I don't bring any stereotypes or threatening visage to their presence," he said. "Two, I can overcome any stereotypes or reservations they have, because I perform well. Third thing is, I ain't that black."

That phrase, "I ain't that black," seemed at first to be simply a lighthearted reference to skin color. On other occasions, though, Powell gave the words a broader cultural meaning: He stood apart from many American blacks because of his Jamaican background. Blacks in Jamaica, he explained, "were also brought from Africa as slaves, but they lived under a British system, where slavery was different—and was abolished earlier. And the British provided education and a civil service in which ex-slaves could advance. That didn't exist in this country, where blacks were systematically deprived of every opportunity, of education, of any suggestion they could be anything more than second-class people."

In 1977, soon after Jimmy Carter took office, the new national security advisor, Zbigniew Brzezinski, ran across Powell's résumé and sought to recruit him onto his staff to oversee defense programs. Powell flew to Washington from Fort Campbell, Kentucky, where he was serving as a brigade commander for the 101st Airborne. But after an interview, he turned Brzezinski down. He didn't want to leave his command assignment early, he said. He wanted to stay with the troops.

In his autobiography, Powell alluded at one point to another factor. He said he told Brzezinski, "This work you're describing isn't me. I don't know anything about it." However, one of Brzezinski's closest aides,

William Odom (a Soviet specialist who later served as director of the National Security Agency), would recall that Powell had given a different, more explicit explanation. "He said, 'I know I can't do that kind of analytical work.'" Even then, Powell's self-image was that of a doer, not an idea man.

A few months after that interview, as Powell's tour as brigade commander was coming to an end, he was offered another Washington assignment: to work inside the Pentagon as an executive assistant to John Kester, a senior civilian aide to Secretary of Defense Harold Brown. At the time, Powell was hoping for a promotion within the 101st Airborne. This time, however, army superiors made it clear that they wanted him to take a Washington job. The army chief of staff sent word through an intermediary that Powell should accept the offer from Kester. The position could give the army an edge in the perennial turf wars among the services.

These two decisions, turning down Brzezinski and then working inside the Pentagon, would chart the future course for Powell's career. First, despite his repeated protestations that he wanted to stay in regular army commands, all the forces at work (and perhaps Powell himself, semiconsciously) were propelling him toward Washington. His White House fellowship ensured that his résumé went to the top of the pile whenever a new, high-ranking official in Washington was looking to hire an aide or assistant. At the same time, his own superiors saw the usefulness in having him working for top civilian decision makers. His job with Kester would lead to a series of other Washington positions.

Powell's own choices then determined the nature of the Washington jobs he got and the skills he developed. Powell didn't want, or he thought he might not be able to do, the sort of "analytic work" carried out at the National Security Council. He shunned the world of abstractions, ideas, and policy formulations. Instead, he gravitated toward day-to-day operations, to questions of what was practical and effective. He was especially talented at these administrative tasks, even if he himself didn't consider them particularly important. Vietnam was still fresh in his mind. When an assistant secretary of defense wrote Kester to pass on congratulations to Powell for improvements in the Blue Room, a Pentagon dining facility, Powell scrawled on his own copy of the memo: "News Bulletin: Former dashing hard and courageous jungle fighter finds new career as a friggin' mess officer."

Over the following years, Powell would learn the ways and rhythms of Washington. He would come to understand the inner workings of the federal government as well as anyone else in the nation's capital, with the possible exception of Dick Cheney.

2

THE QUIET CONSERVATIVE

O n August 8, 1974, U.S. ambassador to NATO Donald Rumsfeld was on vacation, sitting on a beach in Saint-Tropez, when
he glanced at that morning's *International Herald Tribune*. The paper
informed him that President Nixon was on the verge of resigning from
office. Rumsfeld, an old friend and congressional colleague of Vice President Gerald Ford, decided that he needed to get back to Washington as
soon as possible. As NATO ambassador, Rumsfeld enjoyed certain privi-
leges, including the use of military aircraft. He arranged for a plane to
take him from Nice to London early the next morning, where he caught
a Pan Am flight to Washington, arriving on the afternoon Ford was
sworn in as president.

Waiting to greet him at Dulles Airport was Dick Cheney. Rumsfeld
had asked an aide in Brussels to let Cheney know not merely that he was
returning, but also what flight he was on. Also waiting for Rumsfeld at
the airport was a message from Ford, asking him to take charge of a
four-man transition team for the new president. As a White House car
ushered them back to Washington, Rumsfeld asked Cheney to work for
him again, at least temporarily. Cheney quickly accepted. It had been
only eighteen months since Cheney left the White House for his friends'
investment advisory company, but he was ready to return to government
service and to Rumsfeld's side.

For a short time, it seemed conceivable that Rumsfeld might even become vice president, filling the position that the new president had just vacated. Ford's close aide Bryce Harlow put together a list of three possible candidates: Nelson Rockefeller, George H. W. Bush, and Rumsfeld. Although Rumsfeld claimed he never took the possibility seriously, he filled out the paperwork necessary to be considered.

Ford chose Rockefeller on the grounds that he was an older, establishment figure with international credentials. But the president also said he believed that the two younger runners-up, Bush and Rumsfeld, were the future of the Republican Party. That offhand remark by Ford, perhaps made casually to soothe the two disappointed candidates, turned out to have long-term implications: Bush and Rumsfeld went on to become enduring political rivals.

With his family still in Brussels, Rumsfeld stayed temporarily at Cheney's home in Northern Virginia. Rumsfeld and Cheney watched on television as Rockefeller left New York with three jets full of staff aides and family to fly to Washington. Rumsfeld turned to his host. "You know, damn it, Cheney, that's the problem," he joked. "There's Rockefeller with all those airplanes and all that money and all those staff people, and all I've got is you!"

Less than six weeks later, Ford decided to replace a leading holdover from the Nixon White House, Chief of Staff Alexander Haig, with Rumsfeld. In turn, Rumsfeld once again appointed Cheney as his assistant. At the time, Cheney was thirty-three years old.

* * *

The Ford administration was brief and, by outward appearances, relatively inconsequential, at least by comparison with the turbulent Nixon era. Yet the Ford years proved to be of profound importance for the individuals involved in it, for the issues they confronted, for the factional fights in which they engaged, and for the ideological battles that emerged over the future of the Republican Party. The Ford administration served almost like a freshman dormitory for officials arriving for the first time at the top ranks of government, Republican leaders who would go on to serve at higher levels in subsequent administrations: Dick Cheney, George H. W. Bush, Donald Rumsfeld, Brent Scowcroft, James Baker, Alan Greenspan, and Paul O'Neill, among others.

Cheney operated at the center of the maelstrom, responsible above all for day-to-day operations. At first, his formal title was simply assistant to Donald Rumsfeld; before long, he obtained the more important-sounding rank of deputy chief of staff. In both cases, his function was the same: to do whatever was needed, however menial. He was tied to Rumsfeld as if he were the junior partner in a buddy movie. Rumsfeld himself, not customarily given to self-deprecation, later admitted that in the White House he himself sometimes functioned as a high-level factotum, with Cheney at his side. "No assignment was too small if it eased the burden on the President," he recalled. "We weren't always saving the world." One job that took several days, for example, was to find the right curtain to keep the sun off President Ford's neck in the Oval Office.

Still, Rumsfeld was White House chief of staff, taking part in high-level meetings, while most of the trivial and time-consuming tasks fell to Cheney. Early on, as Rumsfeld was about to move into the West Wing office previously occupied by Haig and, before him, H. R. Haldeman, aides discovered a locked safe in a cupboard. No one knew if it contained something relevant to Watergate or some other Nixon scandal. "Don Rumsfeld indicated that he wanted the safe removed before he began work," Cheney wrote in a memo for the files. Rumsfeld also insisted on obtaining a receipt proving that the safe had been transferred out of his custody. It fell to Cheney to spend hours arranging with the Secret Service and the White House counsel's office to have the safe moved to a special vault in the Executive Office Building and then blown open a couple of days later. It was empty.

Cheney was given the apt Secret Service code name "Backseat." Memos in the Ford Presidential Library contain evidence of the concerns that took up his time as deputy chief of staff: which saltshakers were to be used at congressional breakfasts, how the White House plumbing got fixed, which names were on the White House Christmas card list.

Before long, the Rumsfeld-Cheney duo became locked in intramural struggles within the Ford White House, battles that presaged the more bitter factional struggles in which Cheney and Rumsfeld would participate three decades later. Bureaucratic infighting seemed to accompany Rumsfeld in whatever job he took on, in part because he was so prone to engaging in turf wars and so often sought to cut down other powerful figures. During the Ford years, their leading adversaries were Vice

President Rockefeller and Secretary of State Kissinger, who was simultaneously serving as national security advisor. Rockefeller had been Kissinger's original political patron, before Rockefeller in effect turned him over to Richard Nixon after Nixon won the 1968 presidential election. By the mid-1970s, it was Kissinger who had the greater power and stature, because of his foreign policy initiatives under Nixon.

Ford's early inclination was to give Kissinger free rein. On the first day of the new administration, shortly after Rumsfeld and Cheney had driven in from Dulles Airport, Ford met with his fledgling staff and gave them instructions. He told them to review everything concerning the operations of the White House, the Cabinet, and the budget process. However, Ford went on to say that the new team should "stay out of the national security area. The NSC, State, Defense, they're off limits," Cheney recalled.

Once Rockefeller was confirmed as vice president by Congress in December 1974, he began to involve himself in the full range of international and domestic issues. Rumsfeld and Cheney toyed with the idea of trying to hem Rockefeller in and to limit his focus by giving him specific authority over a particular part of the government—for example, by asking Ford to appoint him to serve simultaneously as a Cabinet secretary. The idea never went anywhere, but it caused Cheney to begin thinking about the role and authority of the vice president, a subject to which he would return on several occasions.

One of the many skirmishes with Kissinger involved the final days of the Vietnam War. Throughout Ford's first year in office, Rumsfeld and Cheney viewed themselves as responsible for the president's political interests, including the need to make sure that he could win the 1976 presidential election. Their view was that Ford needed to show that he, and not Kissinger, was in control of U.S. foreign policy, and also to demonstrate that Ford was in touch with public opinion. Kissinger, by contrast, was always nervous about the public mood, which could get in the way of his two major initiatives: détente with the Soviet Union and rapprochement with China.

As North Vietnamese troops were making their way toward Saigon in April 1975, the White House speechwriters, who were under the supervision of Rumsfeld and Cheney, inserted a paragraph into a presidential speech in New Orleans saying bluntly that the Vietnam War was over. "Today, America can regain the sense of pride that existed before

Vietnam," said Ford. "But it cannot be achieved by refighting a war that is finished as far as America is concerned." The speech gave recognition to the American mood that it was time to move on. Kissinger was irate; no one had shown him an advance text of the speech, and he complained that it had complicated the task of getting American and South Vietnamese personnel out of the country.

In the summer and fall of 1975, after Ford had been president for a year, the balance of forces shifted against Kissinger. Ford felt more secure in his own judgments and less inclined to defer to his secretary of state on all foreign policy questions. With an election year approaching, former California governor Ronald Reagan was positioning himself to challenge Ford for the Republican presidential nomination, and Ford needed to be ever more careful about the rising power of conservatives within the party. The Republican right was beginning to criticize Ford's foreign policies in general and Kissinger in particular.

That fall, the maneuvering and power struggles inside the White House reached a climax. In October, Rumsfeld and Cheney sent Ford a biting memo, some forty pages long, bluntly describing the problems. They urged him to seize control of his own administration and to make the changes they argued were necessary to win the 1976 election. The administration was a mess, they said, with haphazard decision making, warring agencies, and an abundance of leaks. "Be Presidential—act like you are President," the memo read. Rumsfeld and Cheney were willing to name names: "The bulk of the problems involve [White House counselor Robert] Hartmann, the Vice President and Kissinger," they wrote.

Nor was the memo shy about urging a more powerful and controlling role for the White House chief of staff, the job that happened to be occupied by Rumsfeld. He should be considered the president's top assistant. "The President would instruct the staff that the top assistant is in charge and will be backed up so that he doesn't have to waste his time horsing around," Rumsfeld and Cheney argued. In an attempt to show that they weren't merely seeking power for themselves, Rumsfeld and Cheney each submitted a letter of resignation, appended to the memo, for Ford to accept if he chose. (In this, they were borrowing a tactic of their rival Kissinger, who on several occasions had threatened to resign if he didn't get his way.)

Ford had different ideas. Rumsfeld and Cheney were suggesting that he give some officials in the administration more power within their existing jobs and others less. Instead, Ford decided to order a far-reaching shake-up of the jobs in his administration. He had been considering it for some time; one precipitating factor, unrelated to the Rumsfeld-Cheney memo, was his desire to get rid of Secretary of Defense James Schlesinger, whom Ford found arrogant and disrespectful. The president went on from there to reshuffle top jobs throughout his administration, an action that became known as the "Halloween Massacre."

Heading all the changes was the announcement that Vice President Rockefeller would not be on the Republican ticket with Ford in 1976. Ford also took the job of national security advisor away from Kissinger, while retaining him as secretary of state. He named Brent Scowcroft, Kissinger's deputy, the new national security advisor. (Scowcroft then voluntarily gave up his commission in the air force because he believed it would be a conflict for an active-duty military officer to serve as national security advisor and thus have dual loyalties to the American president and to his military superiors.) Ford replaced CIA director William Colby with George H. W. Bush, who had been serving as head of the U.S. liaison office in Beijing. He appointed Elliot Richardson to head the Commerce Department. Finally, he appointed Rumsfeld as his new secretary of defense and elevated Cheney to the job Rumsfeld was vacating, White House chief of staff.

In a particularly awkward moment, Cheney found himself in the odd position of having to persuade Rumsfeld, his longtime boss, to take the Pentagon job. Rumsfeld wasn't sure he wanted to leave the White House, where he had just asked for more power and where his antagonists Rockefeller and Kissinger were about to be cut down several notches. Rumsfeld was still balking when, with the pending changes not yet announced, Ford left Washington for a meeting in Florida with Egyptian president Anwar el-Sadat. Cheney went on the plane with him. En route, word came that news of the administration shake-up was beginning to leak. Ford ordered Cheney to get in touch with Rumsfeld in Washington and urge him to take the Pentagon job. "I leaned pretty hard on Don to say yes, and he finally relented," Cheney later wrote.

* * *

As White House chief of staff, Cheney had for the first time reached the top level of the U.S. government. He was not subservient to Rumsfeld, or to anyone else besides the president; he was, at the age of thirty-four, running the White House and, through it, the entire administration. It had been only twelve years since he woke up in a jail cell in a remote western town, an itinerant worker recovering from his second drunk-driving arrest. And he and Lynne continued to live in an unimposing home in an unimposing neighborhood in Northern Virginia. "Really, they lived very modestly, and they had no money then to speak of," recalled Jeane Kirkpatrick, then a Georgetown University political scientist, who had gotten to know the Cheneys; her husband, Evron, also a political scientist, had given Cheney help in applying for internships in congressional offices.

Cheney's new status as White House chief of staff took some getting used to, both for him and for others in the administration. A few weeks after the administration shake-up, President Ford visited China. The advance team for the trip had given Cheney, as White House chief of staff, a bigger bedroom at Diaoyutai, the Chinese guesthouse, than the one assigned to Kissinger. Cheney's room was also closer to the president's bedroom. Kissinger, who viewed the relationship with China as his own preserve and was never one to ignore any symbols of rank or status, erupted in fury. Recalling the incident many years later, Cheney offered a typically laconic analysis: "Henry didn't like that."

Cheney's rise had been truly remarkable, and while it was undeniable that he had been propelled upward by his long relationship with Rumsfeld, that factor by itself would not have sufficed had Cheney not impressed others, including Ford, with his attributes. He was, above all, a trustworthy aide; when asked to take care of something, he got it done. In that respect, he was strikingly similar to Powell.

Then there was his manner. In Washington, Cheney had developed a persona that was the opposite of (and was designed to overcome) the erratic young man he had once been. He dressed in gray suits, white shirts, and dark ties, without the slightest hint of color or flash. He was, above all, calm and low-key. Nothing seemed to excite or surprise him. He was succinct, never expansive. He was not charismatic; indeed, he was anti-charismatic.

He avoided any subjects that seemed too personal—whether he was dealing with the president, with subordinates, or with adversaries. The first time Rumsfeld stayed at the White House for a presidential trip and let his deputy Cheney travel on his own with Ford, Rumsfeld asked the president afterward how Cheney had done. "Dick is great!" Ford told Rumsfeld. "He comes in, he's got ten items to cover, he covers them and he leaves."

Cheney seemed to suggest that whatever he did was merely what was required. His watchword could have been the famous line from *The Godfather*: "It's not personal, it's strictly business." By his own admission, he became so adept at firing people that others would turn this unpleasant task over to him; he fired Ford's agriculture secretary, social secretary, and campaign manager, among others. "My method was direct: no hints, cold shoulders or slow, agonizing departures," he later wrote. "Those were not good for anyone—neither the president nor the person being fired. Anyone failing to serve the president's interests, intentionally or not, simply needed to move along."

Above all, Cheney possessed that distinctive deep voice, the sound of gravitas and self-assurance he would employ in one high-level job after another. It was a voice that seemed to function almost as a seductive gas, soothing and winning over the people who run America from day to day: business executives, professionals, the Chamber of Commerce, CEOs, shopkeepers. Cheney's voice conveyed, more than anything else, a sense of prudence, the idea that everything was under control, that all options had been considered and all possibilities taken into account, that whatever decision had just been made (or was about to be made) was the right one, the one any sober-minded, cautious executive would make. It would take years, indeed decades, for Americans to catch up to the fact that sometimes this wasn't true, that sometimes Cheney's voice conveyed only a false prudence.

* * *

It's important to determine Cheney's political views in those days and assess where he stood on the political spectrum during the Ford administration, if only to form a judgment as to whether the Dick Cheney of the George W. Bush administration had changed since his early days. "Dick Cheney I don't know anymore," asserted Brent Scowcroft in 2005, three decades after the two men had worked side by side in the Ford White House. Scowcroft was putting forward what might be called the myth of the moderate Cheney.

It is not difficult to surmise why Scowcroft (and others) misperceived Cheney to be a moderate or a centrist in those early days. One reason was Cheney's low-key, businesslike, pragmatic style. He seemed so non-confrontational in approach that others simply assumed he agreed with them more than he in fact did.

A second reason was the factional politics of the mid-1970s within the Republican Party. Gerald Ford, Cheney's boss, was a relatively moderate Republican, increasingly under attack from Ronald Reagan, a strong conservative. Simply by virtue of his White House job, Cheney was on the Ford side of the Ford/Reagan divide within the party during that period.

Third, even as Cheney rose from Rumsfeld's deputy to become White House chief of staff, he continued to define his task narrowly, concentrating on daily operations and steering clear of questions involving larger policy or ideology. "My job as chief of staff was process and administrative and making sure the trains ran on time," he explained.

Cheney subsequently admitted that in the Ford years he had strong views but often kept them hidden. At the time, he considered it more important to make sure the president got all the opinions and policy options from others in the government than to seek to advance his own viewpoint. He gave an example: If the chief of staff became known as a strong advocate of cutting the Pentagon's budget, then he would get along less well with the secretary of defense, with whom he needed to work from day to day; moreover, the defense secretary might accuse the White House chief of staff of trying to shape the papers going to the president and the people he saw. (Cheney's example was entirely hypothetical, particularly because, during his long career, cutting the defense budget was not something he generally wanted to do.)

"I was careful not to have people know what my views might be on some of those issues, because I felt it would inhibit my capacity to function in a way that had integrity in terms of the operations of the White House," he said. Whether a White House chief of staff needs to be so inhibited is debatable; what matters is that the way Cheney construed his role as chief of staff helps explain why his colleagues thought of him as more of a moderate or centrist than he was.

Nevertheless, on several occasions Cheney has acknowledged that he was more right-wing than those around him in the Ford White House. "I think you'd have to describe me as probably more conservative than most of my colleagues in the Ford administration on most issues," he reflected in one oral history interview in 2000. "I was more conservative philosophically than a lot of my colleagues around the Ford administration," he said on another occasion. Even at the time, his colleagues certainly got a sense of where he stood, despite his reluctance to voice opinions. "Whenever his private ideology was exposed, [Cheney] appeared somewhat to the right of Ford, Rumsfeld, or, for that matter, Genghis Khan," Robert Hartmann, Ford's longtime aide and White House counselor, wrote a few years later.

Indeed, for those who cared to probe deeper, there were ample signs of Cheney's conservative outlook and instincts. One example was the controversy over whether Ford should meet with Soviet dissident Aleksandr Solzhenitsyn, who had gone into exile in the United States. In July 1975, the AFL-CIO hosted a dinner in Solzhenitsyn's honor in Washington. Members of Congress urged Ford to welcome the novelist and Nobel Prize winner to the White House, but Kissinger argued against doing so, on the grounds that it would undermine American relations with the Soviet leadership and Kissinger's ongoing policy of détente. Cheney, then still deputy chief of staff, wrote a memo questioning the wisdom of refusing to see Solzhenitsyn.

"My own strong feeling is that the President should see Solzhenitsyn," Cheney wrote. "I think the decision not to see him is based upon a misreading of détente. . . . It does not mean that all of a sudden our relationship with the Soviets is all sweetness and light." Signing agreements with the Soviet Union "does not imply also our approval of their way of life or their authoritarian government," Cheney asserted. He argued that if Ford's goal was to negotiate an arms-control agreement with the Soviet Union, then "I think that ratification will be easier to achieve if the President is in good shape with the conservative wing of the Republican Party." Cheney's memo didn't persuade Ford, who decided not to meet with Solzhenitsyn.

Cheney also disagreed with the Ford administration's efforts to negotiate a treaty returning the Panama Canal to Panama. This issue had seemed relatively minor until Ronald Reagan seized upon it in his speeches. "We bought it. We built it. We paid for it. And we intend to keep it," he told Republican audiences, to considerable effect. In this case, Cheney wrote no memos trying to change Ford's views, but he later acknowledged that "I hadn't agreed with President Ford on the canal." In the fall of 1977, a year after they had all left office, Ford and Kissinger testified before Congress in support of the Panama Canal Treaty, but Cheney came out in opposition, thus publicly disagreeing with a policy of the administration in which he had served.

* * *

Cheney's general skepticism about the value of détente and his opposition to the Panama Canal Treaty were in line with standard conservative positions, and they had deep historical roots in the Republican Party, dating back to the days when its leaders opposed American participation in the League of Nations. But there was another set of issues regarding which Cheney became a leading conservative not because of his party's positions in the past, but as a direct result of his experiences in the Ford administration. They involved questions of executive power.

In 1973, historian Arthur M. Schlesinger Jr. had published his book *The Imperial Presidency*, arguing that the powers of modern presidents had vastly increased beyond what the founding fathers envisioned, and that Congress's role had correspondingly declined. The book was itself a reflection of disenchantment with presidential power, specifically with regard to sending American troops to Vietnam during the Kennedy and Johnson administrations and in perpetuating the war under Richard Nixon.

Early efforts by Congress to restrict U.S. participation in the Vietnam War had failed. But in 1973, overriding a veto by Nixon, Congress passed the War Powers Act, which set new restrictions on a president's war-making powers. It required a president to notify Congress within forty-eight hours after sending American troops into a military conflict and to withdraw those forces within sixty days unless Congress granted a specific authorization for the use of military force.

Then, as the Vietnam War was winding down, the Watergate scandal and Nixon's resignation intensified Congress's efforts to limit presidential power. The 1974 midterm elections, held only months after Ford was sworn in, ushered in a new group of younger, more liberal Democratic congressmen, sometimes called the "Watergate babies." Bolstered by these new members, Congress enacted a series of new, often unprecedented restrictions on the president's authority in foreign policy. Throughout late 1974 and early 1975, it refused to appropriate new aid for South Vietnam. Ford's request for $722 million was still pending when the Saigon government finally collapsed in April 1975.

Vietnam was merely the most prominent issue, not the only one, for which Congress asserted a new, more powerful role. Congress cut off military aid to Cambodia. It imposed an embargo on arms shipments to Turkey (at the time, an unprecedented limitation on sales of military equipment to a NATO ally). It barred the use of any funds to influence the outcome of the civil war in Angola, effectively ending a covert program aimed at counteracting the Cuban forces fighting there. Ford found himself beset by one congressional restriction after another, most of them responses to past or potential exercises of presidential power.

Cheney, first as Rumsfeld's deputy and then as White House chief of staff, looked on as Kissinger fought most of these congressional battles, seeking to fend off restrictions on his own foreign policy. When it came to the CIA and the intelligence community, however, Cheney took on the larger role of a participant.

It seemed almost inevitable that Cheney would be driven to take an interest in intelligence issues and that Rumsfeld would naturally delegate intelligence issues to him. Cheney was, above all, discreet. He cut a low profile. He did not relish publicity or drama. He knew how to keep secrets. If he had been required to work somewhere on the front lines of American foreign policy, as a diplomat, a soldier, or a spy, he would almost certainly have chosen to be an intelligence agent. The title that Thomas Powers gave to his biography of CIA director Richard Helms, *The Man Who Kept the Secrets*, could easily have applied to Cheney.

In Ford's early days as president, Congress was beginning to impose limits on the CIA as part of its larger effort to assert greater control over U.S. foreign policy. In 1974, it required the president to report all covert intelligence operations to congressional committees, laying out in writing what was called a "finding" explaining why such operations were important to America's national security.

At the end of 1974, the *New York Times* published a groundbreaking article by Seymour Hersh, laying out the details (collected by the CIA itself) of a series of secret U.S. intelligence operations, ranging from covert funding operations to assassination plots. In response, Ford set up a commission headed by Rockefeller to investigate the abuses, and both houses of Congress launched special committees to conduct their own investigations.

Cheney became a leading coordinator within the White House for dealing with these investigations. His memos and handwritten notes show him struggling to find ways to respond to Congress while still keeping secret the U.S. government's most sensitive information. One technique he considered, for example, was to have covert operations discussed only in hypothetical, rather than concrete, specific terms. Another was to make claims of executive privilege for some of the documents. When the staff of the Rockefeller Commission was drafting its report, Cheney edited it, removing some of the most sensitive disclosures about the history of CIA assassination plots and toning down language that called some of the agency's actions unlawful.

Cheney also favored direct action against the news media. When the *New York Times*'s Seymour Hersh reported in the spring of 1975 that U.S. intelligence agencies had secretly tried to lift a sunken Soviet submarine off the seabed in the Pacific Ocean, Cheney was put in charge of formulating the Ford administration's response. His own handwritten notes show that he considered the possibility of bringing criminal charges against Hersh and also of obtaining a warrant to search Hersh's apartment. No such action was taken against the journalist—Cheney was merely exploring the possibilities—but the episode demonstrated Cheney's instinct for taking strong action to protect intelligence secrets and his close involvement in intelligence issues even in the early stages of his career.

Eventually, the investigations of the Ford era resulted in a series of reforms that opened the way for congressional oversight of the intelligence community. The Senate and the House created intelligence committees to monitor the CIA and other intelligence agencies, and these commit-tees took the lead role in overseeing covert operations. Cheney, who had initially sought to limit congressional investigations of the CIA, would a few years later became one of the senior members of the House Intel-ligence Committee and therefore one of the Republican officials most knowledgeable about intelligence, thus ultimately benefiting from the changes he hadn't thought necessary.

* * *

In the summer of 1975, Cheney was brought into the early efforts to organize Ford's reelection campaign. When Cheney became chief of staff that fall, he became the principal point of contact (other than the president himself) with Ford's political apparatus. In that role, Cheney personally groomed and promoted a young Houston lawyer named James A. Baker III, who was working at the time in a second-level job at the Commerce Department. "Dick is the guy that pulled me out of obscurity," said Baker. It was the beginning of a close friendship; over the years, the two men would frequently go on backpacking trips into the mountains of Wyoming, and they would later serve in the Cabinet together. Baker was moved to the campaign in 1976, where he was put in charge of working with the delegates for the Republican convention, and he became Ford's campaign manager for the fall campaign. Thus, by Ford's final year in office, Cheney was working side by side with what would become the nucleus of the future George H. W. Bush administra-tion: Scowcroft (at the National Security Council), Baker (at the reelec-tion campaign), and Bush himself (at the CIA). If George H. W. Bush's administration seemed like an unusually close-knit group, the bonds they had formed during the Ford years were the reason for it.

In the campaign, there were once again plenty of signs that Cheney was more conservative than the rest of the Ford team. He not only sought to placate or preempt the Reagan forces, but also showed considerable sympathy for them. He later acknowledged that a couple of weeks before the 1976 Republican National Convention, he went to Camp David to try to persuade Ford to accept Reagan as his running mate. Ford rejected the idea.

At the convention, the conservative wing of the party mounted a new challenge to Ford in the form of a proposed plank to the Republican platform that called for "Morality in Foreign Policy." The provision, introduced by Senator Jesse Helms of North Carolina, was abstractly worded, but it was an all-but-explicit attack on Kissinger and his foreign policy of détente. It would put the Republicans on record as favoring a foreign policy without "secret agreements" of the sort for which Kissinger was well known. The plank said that the United States should face the world "with no illusions about the nature of tyranny" and singled out Solzhenitsyn for special praise.

Kissinger, outraged, insisted that Ford strongly oppose the inclusion of this language; he was supported by Rockefeller and Scowcroft. But Cheney urged Ford to let the language be included in the platform without a fight, and Ford's political advisors sided with Cheney. They reasoned that if they fought the Morality in Foreign Policy plank, it could galvanize conservative support for Reagan on the convention floor and turn into a symbolic battle that Ford might lose. Cheney argued, pragmatically, that it was no good to take a stand on principle if it jeopardized Ford's chances of winning the nomination.

"We took a dive on that issue," Cheney recalled in an interview years later. "We just went down and accepted the platform on a voice vote. Nobody ever cared or paid any attention to it; platforms aren't very important anyway, once the fight's over with." It was simply domestic politics, in Cheney's telling—yet his earlier memo urging the president to meet with Solzhenitsyn showed that he had considerable sympathy with the conservatives and the wording they successfully inserted into the Republican platform.

All the accumulating tensions at the top echelons of the Ford team boiled over at the convention. At one point, as Rockefeller was addressing the convention, offering what was essentially his swan song as vice president, the microphone failed. Rockefeller believed that Cheney had cut him off, although Cheney insisted then and afterward that he had had nothing to do with what was a technical failure. Those at the convention witnessed a show, right beneath the speaker's platform, with Rockefeller pointing and screaming at Cheney, who was, in the vice president's eyes, the symbol of high-level opposition to his own role as the leading liberal Republican. Cheney as usual downplayed questions of ideology or principle and insisted his handling of Rockefeller was just routine business. "My job was to do what the President needed to have done," he explained.

All these political efforts were for naught. In the minds of many voters, Ford was still weighed down by the burden of his association with Richard Nixon; he had been Nixon's choice for vice president and, after Nixon's resignation, had issued him a formal pardon. Ford had further harmed his campaign with a fumbled assertion during a presidential debate that "there is no Soviet domination of Eastern Europe." Afterward, it fell to Cheney to persuade Ford to issue a retraction, even though Ford was reluctant to do so.

It wasn't enough; the Democratic challenger, Jimmy Carter, narrowly won the election. Among the swing voters and independents who voted for the Democrat was a young army colonel named Colin Powell, who was serving with the 101st Airborne division in Fort Campbell, Kentucky. "After the ordeal of Watergate, the country needed a fresh start," Powell explained many years later, but he would vote for the Republican candidate in the next seven presidential elections. Needless to say, Cheney, a loyal Republican, voted for Ford, for whom he had worked so hard. Two months later, after Carter was sworn in, Cheney and Rumsfeld and their wives went off for a vacation in Eleuthera, in the Bahamas. Even outside work, they were becoming close friends.

Cheney later played a role in one remarkable effort to revive the Ford administration, or at least some semblance of it. It came four years later, at the 1980 Republican National Convention. Ronald Reagan had already won the party's nomination and was trying to decide upon a running mate. For a time, Reagan and his aides seriously considered the idea of putting Ford on the ticket as the vice-presidential nominee. This led to a hurried, intense negotiation over the terms of such an arrangement. Several veterans of the Ford administration, Cheney among them, gathered hurriedly to explore what was briefly called a Ford "co-presidency" with Reagan. Ford, who was himself less enthusiastic about the idea than others such as Henry Kissinger, set extremely tough terms: Along with the title of vice president, the Ford team also asked that he be given extraordinary power over foreign policy and the budget. He was to be chairman of the National Security Council, to have veto power over the choice of secretary of state, and to choose the national security advisor. Reagan finally balked, and Ford himself concluded that the arrangement wouldn't work.

Cheney had already begun to think about the role of a vice president when he and Rumsfeld sought to rein in Nelson Rockefeller during the Ford administration. Taking part in the negotiations over a possible Reagan-Ford ticket caused him once again to address these questions: What could a vice president do? What sort of powers should a vice president be given or assume? Did a vice president have to be as weak and impotent as many of the occupants of the office had been? This subject was to prove of direct relevance to Cheney's future.

* * *

In the 1970s, America sought to put behind it the failure of the Vietnam War, which not only cost 58,000 American lives but also caused a profound loss in the country's confidence. In Washington, young leaders such as Colin Powell and Dick Cheney who conveyed a quiet self-assurance and efficacy played an important role in restoring a sense that the country still had a bright future and could deal with its problems.

Both men were swept up in these efforts to recover from Vietnam, yet it is important to note how different they were, in their experiences and in the lessons and the institutions on which they focused their efforts. They were, in fact, reacting to different aspects of the war.

Powell was shaped indelibly by the war itself, in which he served two tours of duty. He developed a passionate resentment toward the "slide-rule commandos" in Washington who didn't understand the war and the "flabby thinking" at the top levels of the military. He devoted his efforts to restoring a single, large American institution: the U.S. Army. And in turn, others within the military came to see the promotion of Powell as a way to keep the military abreast of the times and to renew its strength.

Cheney had had no direct experience in Vietnam, which was strikingly remote from his own life. Even his opinions about the war were distant and dispassionate; he had not opposed the war but had never been a strong advocate for it, either. He would always say afterward (in the fashion of a careful politician) that he would have served in the war if he had been called.

Rather, Cheney's passion was directed at the negative impact he felt the Vietnam War had had on the American presidency; in his view, Congress had intruded on the authority of the White House and, more broadly, the executive branch of government. As a result, Cheney's efforts concentrated on restoring and augmenting presidential power in Washington.

What this meant was that in some circumstances, Powell and Cheney would find themselves in tune with each other. There would be times when the causes of restoring American military power and restoring the authority of the presidency went hand in hand. But Powell also believed that America could sometimes preserve its military power by not using it too often or indiscriminately; and Cheney did not feel the same passion on that question as he did about presidential power. Indeed, there would be times when these two men's causes would come into conflict.

3

CLIMBING THE LADDER

Although Colin Powell and Dick Cheney had started their careers as staff aides and gatekeepers for powerful Washington officials, during the presidency of Ronald Reagan each began to emerge as a figure of stature in his own right, developing the ideas and the principles he believed would prevent another disaster like Vietnam (although each of them defined that disaster differently). They remained focused on different problems and different institutions—Powell on reviving the military, Cheney on restoring the power of the presidency.

Inside the Pentagon, Powell had moved up in 1979 from his job as military aide to John Kester to another position, as aide to Deputy Secretary of Defense Charles Duncan, Kester's boss. In the process, he was also promoted to the rank of brigadier general. Before long, through the force of his personality, his charm, and his easygoing demeanor, he began to make connections of the sort that would prove invaluable throughout his career. He sat in on high-level meetings at the Pentagon, traveled around the world with Duncan, and went out drinking with him in Washington. His ability to make friends among the influential was uncanny. He played racquetball regularly with a young Saudi prince named Bandar bin Sultan, whom he had met during a trip to Saudi Arabia and who had come to Washington for his studies; years later, Prince Bandar would be the Saudi ambassador to the United States, perhaps the most well-connected diplomat in Washington for a generation, and a central figure in the Persian Gulf War.

When President Carter appointed Duncan to be secretary of energy, Duncan took Powell with him to the Energy Department for a few months. But Powell soon returned to the Pentagon to work as military assistant for Duncan's successor as deputy secretary, Graham Claytor. Powell kept insisting that he wanted to return to the regular army and an assignment in the field, even worrying from time to time that too close an association with Washington would harm his military career. Yet senior civilian leaders in the Pentagon kept offering him jobs as their military aide, and his superiors in the army encouraged him to accept these offers. Having Powell working under these top civilian leaders served the army's institutional interests, which were to protect itself in the never-ending struggles with the other military services; in the army's logic, if Powell didn't accept a job as a military aide, that position might go to the navy or the air force.

In this string of assignments as a military aide, Powell learned how the game was played in Washington, how things got done and why they didn't. The passages in his memoir covering these years could serve as a user's guide for Washington operators and insiders. "You staked out your turf the way tigers do when they urinate on trees," Powell noted. "Your scent had to be stronger than someone else's or you would be elbowed aside." In large-scale meetings where everyone was called on for their opinions, Powell observed, "The only ones who spoke at length were those who did not understand the game. I always had plenty to discuss . . . , but not before a crowd."

Despite his strong ties to the Carter administration's Pentagon team, Powell voted for Ronald Reagan in 1980. He had been unhappy with Carter's defense cuts; he was also distressed by Iran's seizure of American hostages and by the failed military mission to rescue them. After Reagan won, Powell was surprised to discover that he possessed even closer personal ties to the new Reagan appointees at the Pentagon than to the outgoing Carter team.

Reagan's choice for defense secretary was Caspar Weinberger, who had been director of the Office of Management and Budget when Powell worked there as a White House fellow. Pentagon officials gave Powell the job of escorting Weinberger into the building for his first tour of his new office. The new defense secretary told Powell he remembered him and was happy to see him again.

Powell still held the title of senior military assistant to the deputy secretary of defense—meaning that once the Reagan team took office, he would be working for his third deputy secretary. Shortly after Reagan's inauguration, Powell discovered who would occupy that office: Frank Carlucci, who had served as Weinberger's deputy at OMB. Like Weinberger, Carlucci remembered Powell from his days as a young White House fellow. In fact, Powell recalled, "I knew Carlucci a little better than Cap [Weinberger]." Weinberger and Carlucci both looked on Powell as someone they could trust, someone who could help them learn their way around the Pentagon. "Just call me Frank," Carlucci told Powell when they resumed their acquaintanceship in 1981. It was the start of what would become a close partnership.

Like his predecessors, Carlucci found Powell to be an exceptional military aide. Civilians in the Pentagon "depend on the military aide for advice, they use him for their eyes and ears," Carlucci explained. "If you're off there on your own, you'll be snookered every time." Powell was a master at the job. "He didn't hesitate to give advice," Carlucci recalled. Moreover, Carlucci found that Powell could deal with the military services, telling them what the civilians wanted, without undercutting his standing as a career army officer.

* * *

It was in the late winter of 1981, in the earliest days of the Reagan administration, when Powell first met a new colleague named Richard Armitage, the distinctive character who would become his close working partner and, eventually, his best friend for life.

Armitage was a former Republican campaign aide and Southeast Asia specialist whom Weinberger had met during the transition. He looked and sounded like no one else in Washington: he had a raspy voice and a mammoth chest, the result of years of weightlifting. Like Powell, he was a Vietnam veteran, in his case a graduate of the Naval Academy who had served three tours of duty in the war. Whereas Powell was in the regular army, Armitage had been an irregular, a special operations specialist. He opted out of duty on a navy destroyer offshore and chose instead to work on land alongside the Navy SEALs, eventually serving as an advisor to a South Vietnamese ambush team and accompanying it on nighttime raids. After his three military postings, he had returned to South Vietnam, this time as a civilian. He spoke the language and loved the country. At the end of the war, he led a special mission to get American equipment and South Vietnamese personnel out of the country before the government collapsed. He had been the sole American representative leading a flotilla of ships carrying twenty thousand South Vietnamese refugees to the Philippines.

Those years had left Armitage with intense, often bitter feelings. He believed the United States had betrayed its South Vietnamese allies. In one interview, he said that the 1973 peace settlement in which the Nixon administration had agreed to withdraw U.S. forces from Vietnam was "akin to getting a lady pregnant and leaving town. . . . I thought we were a runaway dad."

On Armitage's first visit to the Pentagon, he and Powell bonded almost immediately. "We were both Vietnam vets," Armitage said years later. "And we were both kind of excited about the possibility of the Reagan defense buildup." Over the next six months, the two men began working closely together. Weinberger put Armitage in charge of U.S. defense policy in Asia, while Powell continued to work for Carlucci. By this juncture, however, Powell was determined to get an assignment outside Washington, to prove that he was not merely a political general. Within six months, he persuaded Carlucci to let him go, and he accepted a new military assignment as an assistant division commander at Fort Carson, Colorado.

* * *

In the fall of 1977, Wyoming's lone congressman, Teno Roncalio, a Democrat, announced that he would not run for reelection. Dick Cheney quickly decided to run for his seat in the 1978 midterm election. When Cheney started to campaign, reporters and public officials asked him why he was running for such a lowly job. Not long before, he had been serving as White House chief of staff, supervising the entire Ford administration. Wouldn't it be a comedown to serve as a freshman congressman?

Cheney had a ready answer. "When you're in a staff job, you're never yourself," he told one reporter. "It's humbling—you're just somebody's hired gun—and even if that somebody happens to be the president of the United States, there's not much you can do on your own. Congress is different. You're responsible for your own decisions. You act for yourself." From his viewpoint, the real Dick Cheney was the one who ran for office on his own, not the one who was appointed to various positions.

During that first congressional campaign, the most serious obstacle Cheney confronted was his health. Though he was only thirty-seven, he suffered a heart attack in June 1978. After a brief hospitalization he returned to his campaign, making light of the incident by joking that he had formed a group called Cardiacs for Cheney. His Democratic opponent alluded gingerly to Cheney's failure at Yale by labeling him a curious sort of carpetbagger, someone who didn't want to be there: "Wyoming has always been Cheney's second choice," said the opponent's campaign manager. "When he ran into difficulty in college, he came back to Wyoming." The ploy didn't work; Dick and Lynne possessed more than enough Wyoming roots, and enough friends in the state, to withstand such attacks.

In the 1978 election, the Republicans picked up fifteen seats in the House of Representatives, including Cheney's. The Democrats were still the majority party, as they had been for decades, but younger Republicans were beginning to challenge the status quo. The freshman class of Republicans arriving in January 1979 included a young history professor from the Atlanta suburbs, Newt Gingrich, who would soon display a willingness to provoke showdowns not only with the Democrats but with the Republican hierarchy as well.

Cheney's operating style could not have been more different from Gingrich's. He was determinedly restrained and tight-lipped, just as he had been in the White House, avoiding direct confrontation wherever possible, staying cool where Gingrich was hot, behaving more like a business executive than a firebrand. Once, when Gingrich called for the public censure of two Republicans accused of misconduct, Cheney grumbled that Gingrich was putting the Republicans "through the wringer" and was being simply a "pain in the fanny."

While Gingrich was attacking the House Republican leadership, Cheney gravitated toward it. The senior Republicans in the House, such as

Minority Leader Bob Michel, viewed Cheney as a natural recruit, largely because of his experience in the executive branch; his White House years meant that Cheney was knowledgeable on a range of issues, from budgets and taxes to foreign affairs to domestic programs. By his second term in the House, he was elected chairman of the Republican Policy Committee, the fourth-ranking position in the leadership.

As always, he preferred to operate behind the scenes, gravitating toward issues that were more complex than attention-grabbing. He gave remarkably few floor speeches, only a handful a year. Most members of Congress hire a speechwriter on their staff; Cheney chose not to do so because the job seemed unnecessary. Reporters covering Capitol Hill regularly turned to him for calm, thoughtful-sounding quotes about how Congress was doing or how presidents were faring there.

Yet, while Cheney was not a flamethrower like Gingrich, he was usually just as conservative on the issues, and sometimes even more so. On foreign policy, he voted against the Panama Canal Treaty that Ford and Kissinger had helped negotiate and Carter had finalized, against a proposal for a freeze on nuclear weapons, and against imposing sanctions on South Africa's apartheid regime. On domestic issues, he became a staunch opponent of gun control, the Equal Rights Amendment, and federal funding for abortion. He frequently voted against legislation to protect the environment. When the states of Nebraska, Utah, New Mexico, and Wyoming all refused to provide a home for MX nuclear missiles, citing environmental objections, Cheney arranged for the weapons to be based in Wyoming, over his home state's objections. At one point, when the *Washington Post* described him as a moderate, Cheney instructed an aide, "Will you please call the *Washington Post* and tell them I'm a conservative? Don't they ever check my voting record?"

Indeed, Cheney and Gingrich became good friends, and years later Cheney would speak of their relationship as a partnership. "Our relationship was useful in maintaining some degree of peace among the Republicans in the House," he wrote. "For the leadership I served as a bridge to the younger, more aggressive members. For Newt I provided knowledge of which lines he shouldn't step over if he didn't want to get in a pile of trouble."

There was one particular set of issues where Cheney staked out a strong position and never wavered: presidential power. Throughout history, American politicians have tended to favor expansive authority for whichever branch of government they happened to be serving in at the time, supporting congressional power during their time on Capitol Hill, executive power when they served in the executive branch. Presidents Harry Truman, Richard Nixon, and Lyndon Johnson all displayed this tendency. Not Cheney: he was unusual in that even while serving in Congress, he championed strong presidential powers and a more constrained view of legislative authority. In his later years, these views were mistakenly attributed to the Iran-Contra scandal of the late 1980s, when Cheney sought to limit a congressional investigation of the Reagan administration. But his views go back to his earliest days in Congress, when his experiences in the Ford White House were fresh in his mind.

In 1984, Cheney laid out these views in a little-noticed article called "U.S. Foreign Policy: Who's in Charge?" The article, published in an academic journal, was written as an abstract argument, not prompted by any specific event or controversy, and it provides a remarkable overview of his thinking on the powers of the presidency. In it, Cheney attacked in detail what he perceived to be the congressional intrusions on presidential authority in the post–Vietnam War era: the War Powers Act, the limitations on arms sales, the restrictions on covert action by the CIA. More broadly, he debunked "the concept of the so-called imperial presidency" that had held sway in the 1970s. "The 'imperial' presidency is, in my view, a myth that evolved out of the frustration of the Vietnam situation and the disillusionment of Watergate," he wrote. Cheney argued that blame for the problems of that era should be laid at the feet of Lyndon Johnson and Richard Nixon, rather than ascribed to any larger defect in the constitutional arrangements between Congress and the executive branch. "What happened, unfortunately, is that congressional reaction to those events resulted from the erroneous conclusion that the problem was fundamentally with the system and that, because of this, the system had to be changed to allow Congress more power and the executive branch less," he observed.

Cheney's conclusion was sweepingly dismissive of congressional efforts. "I just basically disagree with those who think we need additional restrictions on the president's conduct of foreign policy," he asserted.

"We do not need further restrictions. We need a president who is free to successfully use the tools at his command."

* * *

Colin Powell managed to stay out of Washington for nearly two years, in postings at Fort Carson and Fort Leavenworth, before he was summoned back. In early 1983, Caspar Weinberger's senior military aide was leaving, and he needed a replacement. What better candidate could there be than Powell, whom Weinberger already knew and who had served as military assistant to three deputy secretaries of defense? Powell told Weinberger he didn't want the job, but once again his superiors in the army were pleased at the prospect of gaining a seat inside the Office of the Secretary of Defense. "We haven't had an Army man in that spot since I left in 1976," said General John Wickham, who was about to become army chief of staff.

The three years Powell spent as Weinberger's assistant would be the launching pad for his career at the top levels of the U.S. government. By that point, he already knew his way around the Pentagon, how it operated on the inside, and how it interacted with the rest of Washington. Now he was working for a defense secretary whose weaknesses matched up well with Powell's strengths. Though Weinberger had enjoyed close ties to Reagan since their days in California and was experienced in the ways of Washington, he was a remote figure, dogged in his views and not easily approachable. Moreover, where other secretaries of defense had a civilian aide on staff to help manage their lives, Weinberger had done away with that job, leaving his military aide to handle everything. The result was that once Powell joined Weinberger's staff, others in the Pentagon quickly learned that, whenever possible, they should take their business to Powell. "When you talked to Weinberger, you had the feeling you were talking to a strange guy," recalled Lawrence Korb, who was in charge of manpower issues at the Pentagon. "With Powell, he was a regular guy, he would take care of things." Robert Kimmitt, the executive secretary at the National Security Council, found himself talking to Powell as often as two or three times a day, calling him for anything related to the Defense Department. "Colin even then was a guy who could just get things done," Kimmitt said.

Inside the Pentagon, Powell operated through an informal network of friends—above all through his partnership with Armitage. By 1983, when Powell returned, Weinberger had set up a system in which one of his assistant secretaries, Richard Perle, was in charge of dealing with the Soviet Union and arms control, while a second assistant secretary, Armitage, was responsible for the rest of the world, especially Asia and the Middle East. Armitage managed to build up his own network of associates and followers, not just inside the Pentagon but at other agencies, too. Insofar as possible, he did business in Washington by employing the same informal style with which he'd operated in the military. He would spend Saturday mornings at the Pentagon, wearing a gym suit and baseball cap, smoking a cigar as he dealt with business left over from the workweek.

In those days, Armitage was arguably the higher-ranking, more powerful figure, but rank didn't matter when he and Powell worked together. Both arrived at the Pentagon in the early hours of the morning to check the cables coming in from overseas. Soon after Armitage settled in for the day, he would call Powell to find out what was happening, what Weinberger was doing or thinking, what had landed on his desk. "Rich always checked the traps every morning—he was a wonder to behold, an intelligence-gathering device," recalled Karl Jackson, a Southeast Asia specialist who worked for Armitage. Powell relied on Armitage in a similar fashion.

As a result, it seemed to many inside the Pentagon that, at least when it came to daily operations, Armitage and Powell were the true powers running the Defense Department. They sometimes sought advice together from older, more experienced officials. Frank Carlucci recalled that after he left the Pentagon in 1983, Powell and Armitage sometimes came to his house in Northern Virginia for help in trying to figure out how best to deal with Weinberger on one issue or another.

The Powell-Armitage team was not always popular with other senior Pentagon officials. Jim Webb, who served as an assistant secretary of defense and then as secretary of the navy in the Reagan years, came to admire Powell personally. "He was as good with people as anyone I've ever met. And he's good at politics," said Webb. Nevertheless, he came to dislike the Powell-Armitage team-up and to resent the power the two wielded. "They know how to play the game," he said. "They've got a tight network." There was always an inner circle, and you were either part of it or you were not, said Webb, who was not.

Webb also noticed that Powell was reluctant to take a stand on issues. When Weinberger asked for Powell's views on what should be done, Powell would sometimes answer that such matters were above his pay grade.

Webb's observation notwithstanding, Powell was beginning to formulate some views on military issues, particularly on the fundamental question of how and when military force should be used. As a soldier in the field and as a military staff aide, he had the task of executing the decisions made by civilian leaders. But now he was beginning to take part in the decision making, both within the army and, at Weinberger's side, among civilian leaders.

Shortly before he moved to Weinberger's office, Powell had been part of a small group of senior officers appointed by the army chief of staff to study the role of the army over the coming years. One recommendation was that the military needed to win some victories and thereby counteract the impact of recent fiascos, such as the failed 1980 mission to rescue the American hostages in Iran. In short, the military should pick its battles more wisely and score some victories that would restore the nation's confidence.

In a larger sense, this was the fundamental underlying dynamic of the 1980s: the search to restore the quality and reputation of the American military. While Powell was working as Weinberger's military assistant, another overseas catastrophe prompted American officials to add a component to their set of ideas about how to recover from Vietnam: the notion that in the future the United States should avoid putting troops into conflict in murky circumstances where it was unclear that they could win.

Disaster struck with the bombing of a U.S. Marine barracks in Lebanon. For more than a year, the marines had been stationed near the Beirut airport to serve as a stabilizing force as rival Lebanese armies and militias maneuvered for control of the country. On October 23, 1983, a truck bomb destroyed the barracks and killed 241 marines—the largest number of American military deaths in a single day since World War II. It was Colin Powell who received the middle-of-the-night phone call with news of the bombing, which required him to wake up and inform Weinberger. Powell was then obliged to call the secretary of defense again and again in the following hours with updates on the death count.

Within months, Reagan withdrew the marines from Lebanon, but the impact of the Beirut disaster did not stop there. It profoundly affected American thinking about the stationing of forces overseas. Why had the marines been sent to Lebanon in the first place? Weinberger and the Joint Chiefs of Staff had objected to the deployment, but the State Department and National Security Council had wanted them there. Afterward, this debate was replayed with greater intensity: in the Pentagon, many officials believed that American troops should be reserved for major wars, not used for lesser, ancillary foreign policy operations.

Among those holding this view was Powell. His commentary on American policy during this period is reminiscent of his anger at Robert McNamara's "slide-rule commandos" during the Vietnam War. This time his anger was directed at the State Department rather than the civilians in the Pentagon. "I was developing a strong distaste for the antiseptic phrases coined by State Department officials for foreign interventions which usually had bloody consequences for the military, words like 'presence,' 'symbol,' 'signal,' 'option on the table,' 'establishment of credibility,'" he wrote in his memoir. "What I saw from my perch in the Pentagon was America sticking its hand into a thousand-year-old hornet's nest with the expectation that our mere presence might pacify the hornets." American policy makers should not place lives at risk, he argued, "until we can face a parent or a spouse or a child with a clear answer to the question of why a member of that family had to die. To provide a 'symbol' or a 'presence' is not good enough."

With his lawyerly cast of mind, Weinberger decided to formalize this line of thinking with a new set of rules. In the spring of 1984, he drafted guidelines for deciding when American forces should or should not be sent overseas. The White House prevented Weinberger from announcing these rules until after the presidential election, on the grounds that they might be interpreted as an acknowledgment that Reagan had been wrong to send the marines to Lebanon in the first place. They were finally unveiled in a postelection speech by Weinberger to the National Press Club.

America should not send its combat forces overseas unless vital national interests were at stake, Weinberger said. U.S. leaders should send forces abroad only as a last resort, after all other options had been exhausted. American leaders should be prepared to send the troops and firepower necessary to win a war, not merely enough to hold ground or preserve a stalemate. The mission should have clear military and political objectives, and American policy makers should regularly review the mission to make sure it was meeting those objectives. Finally, Weinberger said, the mission should have the support of the American people.

These rules reflected an attempt to stave off another Beirut bombing, but more important, they represented an effort to stave off a much bigger disaster like the Vietnam War. It had been less than a decade since the end of that war, and many of the principles Weinberger enunciated were clearly written with Vietnam in mind.

At the time, these principles were known as the Weinberger rules. Over the following decades, as Powell rose to one top-level job after another, the ideas set down by Weinberger would more commonly be known, in modified form, as the Powell doctrine.

Powell himself never set down on paper any version of a "Powell doctrine." That was characteristic of him: he instinctively avoided doctrines, theories, rules, or anything that smacked of an academic exercise. In his memoir, published in 1995, he said he thought Weinberger's rules had been too "explicit"; he had been concerned that putting the ideas into writing would give adversaries a chance to find loopholes.

But in a second book, written nearly two decades later, Powell acknowledged that there were "similarities" between the Weinberger rules and what later became known as the Powell doctrine. He underscored once again the importance of clear objectives, public support, and the use of "decisive" force. (Powell said he preferred the word *decisive* to *overwhelming*, although others would frequently describe the Powell doctrine as calling for the use of overwhelming force.)

During Powell's time as military aide to Weinberger, there was one other episode that would, indirectly, have far-reaching consequences for his future career. In the fall of 1983, only days after the Beirut bombing, American forces were dispatched to the Caribbean island of Grenada to oust a regime that was threatening American medical students there.

The military operation succeeded within weeks, in that sense satisfying the desire for a clear-cut American military triumph.

But the Grenada operation also revealed serious problems in the way the military services failed to communicate with one another. Dick Cheney, who was part of a bipartisan congressional delegation sent to Grenada, later explained it this way: "The Army guy on the beach can't talk to the ships at sea, so he's using his AT&T credit card to call Fort Bragg, so they can put him in touch with the Navy in the Pentagon, so they can talk to the guy off the coast. Serious screw-ups."

In the aftermath of Grenada, Congress sought to fix these deficiencies through the Goldwater-Nichols Act, which streamlined the military chain of command and fostered greater cooperation among the various services. Among its provisions, Goldwater-Nichols also enhanced the authority of the chairman of the Joint Chiefs of Staff. Neither Powell nor Cheney, who was one of the cosponsors of the legislation, could know that within a few years they would become the first chairman of the Joint Chiefs and the first secretary of defense, respectively, to operate entirely within this new chain of command, and that Powell in particular would benefit immensely from the power given to the chairman by the new law.

Powell was originally supposed to serve as military aide to the secretary of defense for two years, but Weinberger convinced army leaders to let him stay longer, and so he remained in the job for a third year. Finally, in 1986, he was allowed to leave to serve as commander of the army's V Corps in Germany. It was to be his last overseas posting before he became swept up into Washington for good.

* * *

After the 1984 elections, as congressional leaders were organizing a new session of Congress, Dick Cheney was given a new position. At the recommendation of House Minority Leader Bob Michel, Speaker of the House Tip O'Neill appointed him to the House Intelligence Committee.

It seemed like a natural assignment, one that perfectly fit Cheney's personality and interests. The intelligence committee does most of its work in secret. It reviews the work of American intelligence agencies, approves funding for covert operations, and authorizes the use of new technologies and techniques. Most of its work is out of the political limelight;

members are rarely able to call a press conference or otherwise tell the public the details of what they are doing or learning. For many congressmen, these limitations (no press, no publicity) would seem inhibiting, but not for Cheney. Indeed, if one had to write a job description that would have attracted him, this was it.

Cheney went at the job with relish. By his own description, he loved spending hours poring over classified material, sitting in the secured room inside the Capitol set aside for members to read or hear intelligence reports and information. He also made a habit of visiting CIA headquarters, in Northern Virginia. He took pride in being one of the first civilians to see the Stealth fighter plane.

Cheney was not the ranking Republican on the intelligence committee, but he soon became the Republican congressman whom officials in the intelligence agencies or the White House sought out whenever they had something important to discuss. "I met with Cheney to ask his advice on how to deal with the White House and Congress," recalled Robert Gates, who served as acting CIA director in 1987. "He was the only member of Congress I consulted."

Many of the interests and much of the operating style that Cheney would display throughout the rest of his career were developed when he was a member of the intelligence committee. "He had a voracious appetite for intelligence in all forms. He was interested in, you know, raw stuff," reported Aaron Friedberg, a Princeton professor who would later serve on Cheney's vice-presidential staff nearly two decades later. Condoleezza Rice would write, not admiringly, that Cheney was "given to personally sifting through raw intelligence data (not assessments that have been analyzed, checked for credibility, and integrated with other intelligence, but undigested information coming straight from the field)."

During his four years on the House Intelligence Committee, Cheney hired David Addington, a young staff aide whom he came to like, trust, and rely upon so much that he would bring Addington along from one job to another for two decades, in government and in private life. Addington had previously worked as a lawyer for the CIA under Director William Casey, at a time when American intelligence operatives were running their most aggressive, adventurous operations to challenge Soviet power—in Central America, in Afghanistan, and even inside the

Soviet Union itself. The CIA needs lawyers for two reasons: to find ways to keep secrets and to provide legal justification for its operations. Addington proved adept at both.

In 1984, Addington, then twenty-seven years old, joined the staff of the House Intelligence Committee, where he and Cheney would soon become involved in efforts to prevent the Democrats on the committee from restricting American intelligence operations in Central America, including the provision of money and support for the Contra rebels seeking to overthrow Nicaragua's left-wing Sandinista regime.

The two men thought alike on a range of issues. Addington, like Cheney, was eager to prevent congressional restrictions on presidential power. And like Cheney, he was quiet, low-key, and discreet. But he added a quality that Cheney hadn't often displayed: he was combative. Addington was willing to wage bureaucratic battles head-on, and when he did, he was determined to win.

Over time, he became almost a part of Cheney's own personality—his tough side, his hard edge. Addington had been trained in the ways and thinking of a clandestine service, and he instinctively brought this mentality to dealings with Congress and the public. He not only reinforced Cheney's instincts and views, but also provided the ideas and memos needed for legal justification.

Even aside from his work on the intelligence committee, Cheney was becoming ever more closely intertwined with the nation's national security apparatus, the nexus of the defense, military, and intelligence agencies established during the Cold War. He was a leading participant in the intensely secretive "continuity of government" exercises that the Reagan administration carried out so that the United States could maintain effective political leadership during a nuclear war. The goal was to make sure that the Soviets couldn't use a nuclear attack to "decapitate" the U.S. civilian command structure and paralyze America's ability to respond.

Under plans dating back to the 1950s, if nuclear war broke out, the president, vice president, and other American political leaders were to be taken to huge underground bunkers outside Washington. But by the 1980s, as nuclear weapons became more powerful and their targeting more accurate, there was concern that the big, fixed bunkers themselves might not survive. Instead, the Reagan administration practiced taking teams of about forty to sixty government officials to different sites around the nation, where they would rehearse how to keep the U.S. government and armed forces running during a nuclear war.

Cheney was included in this clandestine program not because of his role in Congress or on the House Intelligence Committee, but because he was a former White House chief of staff. Others who had served in top positions in the executive branch, such as Cheney's former boss Donald Rumsfeld, also took part. The participants, who would disappear from their jobs and families for three days at a time, would board a plane in the middle of the night at Andrews Air Force Base, outside Washington, and fly to some discarded military base or abandoned elementary school, where they would practice a variety of tasks: how to communicate with submarines, how to protect the water supply, and so on.

Many aspects of this continuity-of-government program were shut down or suspended in the early 1990s, after the end of the Cold War, but some core functions were preserved. The participants in the 1980s exercises remembered what they had rehearsed. Those rehearsals were still in Dick Cheney's mind on September 11, 2001.

* * *

Cheney's years in Congress gave him the opportunity to travel more frequently overseas. He had never set foot abroad while growing up in Wyoming. He left the United States for the first time in 1970, when President Nixon included Rumsfeld in a delegation to the funeral of Egyptian president Gamal Abdel Nasser, and Rumsfeld asked Cheney to accompany him. Cheney, then nearly thirty years old, didn't even possess a passport at the time. Instead, he had to get a letter vouching for him from the U.S. embassy in Cairo.

On the House Intelligence Committee, he began to travel more frequently. On one of his trips, he visited the Khyber Pass and spoke with leaders of the Afghan mujahideen, the rebel forces who were fighting the Soviet Union with the support of the United States. He also met with President Muhammad Zia-ul-Haq of Pakistan.

In the fall of 1986, Cheney and other members of the committee made a trip to the Middle East. On the way home, the delegation stopped in Frankfurt, where the congressmen paid a visit to the headquarters of the

U.S. Army's V Corps. There, Cheney was introduced to the corps com-mander, Lieutenant General Colin Powell, who gave the visitors a briefing on the army's plans for defending against a Soviet invasion. Powell and Cheney also talked more generally about the changes taking place around the world.

Powell later said that he had been struck by the incisive nature of Cheney's questions. "I recognized that I was in the presence of an excep-tional mind," he wrote in his memoir. Cheney, too, said that he had been impressed by Powell. It was the first time the two had ever met.

4

"YOUR BUDDY, COLIN"

T hroughout Colin Powell's time as a rising army officer, his superiors tended to extend his tours of duty inside Washington and
cut short his assignments in the field. True to form, Powell's posting as
a corps commander in Germany lasted barely five months in late 1986
before tumult in Washington caused him to be called back. He claimed
he didn't want to return, and by all appearances, his disappointment was
genuine.

The Washington upheavals stemmed from the Iran-Contra scandal.
On November 1, 1986, a Lebanese newspaper revealed that the United
States had been secretly selling arms to Iran, its adversary, in an effort
to win the release of American hostages in Lebanon. Later that month,
President Reagan confirmed that some of the profits from these arms
sales had been used, also secretly, to finance the Contra rebels in Nicaragua. Thus, the administration had been violating two separate laws, one
barring arms sales to Iran and the other prohibiting support for the Contras; in addition, the transactions with Iran flouted Reagan's frequently
stated policy of refusing to bargain for the release of hostages. In short
order, Congress set up a special committee to investigate the affair, and
the Reagan administration appointed a special prosecutor to pursue possible violations of the law.

Reagan fired his national security advisor, John Poindexter. To take his place, the president chose Frank Carlucci, who had served not only as deputy secretary of defense but also, before that, as deputy director of the CIA. Carlucci had long-standing relationships with Secretary of State George Shultz and Secretary of Defense Caspar Weinberger, whose intense personal antipathy toward each other had been one of the chronic malfunctions of the Reagan administration.

Carlucci also happened to be Colin Powell's leading mentor and patron. After being offered the job of national security advisor, Carlucci got on the phone to Germany and asked Powell to come back as his deputy. Powell demurred, saying he wanted to stay in Germany. Leaving would hurt his army career, he told Carlucci. He said he would take the job only if the president called him personally. Reagan telephoned a few days later to urge Powell to come work with Carlucci at the NSC, and Powell agreed. As he later noted in his memoir, when the president asked him, "I had no choice."

It is worth pausing here to note how, in Powell's rise in Washington during the 1980s, each step flowed smoothly from the previous one, so that it seemed a natural progression—and yet, at the same time, each step brought something fundamentally new. After serving as military aide for three straight deputy secretaries of defense, Powell saw it as a small step to serve as Weinberger's military aide—and yet that job meant that he was running the office of a leading Cabinet secretary, sitting in on daily meetings and discussions at the top level of American foreign policy. So, too, after Powell had served as the military aide for Carlucci as deputy secretary of defense and for Weinberger as secretary of defense, it didn't seem such a big step for him to take the job of deputy national security advisor under Carlucci. And yet in many ways, it was. Powell would now be working for the first time in an established civilian job. He would now be operating not only outside the military command structure but outside the Pentagon entirely—by its very nature, the National Security Council treats the Defense Department as just one of America's foreign policy agencies, alongside the State Department, the CIA, the Treasury Department, and various other bureaucracies.

Most important, in his new job Powell was no longer working as a military aide to a top civilian, but as someone with a civilian title all his own. He enjoyed unparalleled proximity to others at the top levels of political power. While the deputy national security advisor has only a very small office in the West Wing of the White House, Powell found himself sharing a bathroom with the vice president of the United States, George H. W. Bush, and formed a close relationship with him during this period. (Sharing a bathroom, Powell later observed, "will dictate a certain degree of familiarity.")

Powell didn't entirely realize it at the time, but the move to the NSC marked him for future leadership positions, both military and civilian. Looking back, he would recognize the significance of what had happened. When Henry Louis Gates Jr. interviewed Powell in the mid-1990s for a book on African American men, Powell told him, "If it hadn't been for Iran-Contra, I'd still be an obscure general somewhere. Retired, never heard of."

* * *

At the beginning of 1987, as Carlucci and Powell started their new jobs, the Reagan administration was at its nadir. The president had replaced the top leaders of the National Security Council staff, and he would soon fire his White House chief of staff. Congress and a special prosecutor were starting their investigations, and the press was reporting that the president was remote and seemed almost dazed. *Time* magazine published a cover story on Reagan that asked, "Can He Recover?" Policy initiatives were stalled or frozen—understandably so, given that one of the policies the president had been pushing, the secret opening to Iran, had failed so spectacularly. "The government damn near collapsed," Powell would later recall.

As usual, Powell did his homework before starting the job. Robert Kimmitt, who had been a senior staff member on the National Security Council earlier in the Reagan administration, recalled that Powell called him from Germany with a series of questions about how the NSC operated and what changes could be made.

As soon as they arrived in the West Wing, Carlucci and Powell moved quickly to establish control. They put out orders: There was to be no more "freelancing" of the sort carried out by Colonel Oliver North, the prime mover on the NSC for the Iran-Contra initiatives. There were to be no surprises, either; everything was to be okayed by them before-hand, and everything was to be clearly documented.

Powell put to good use the organizational skills he had learned over the years. Meetings had a fixed agenda, and participants were not allowed to waver too far from it. The sessions started on time, stayed generally on point, and ended on time, with Powell summarizing the consensus on the participants' decisions and recommendations. William Burns, who had recently joined the National Security Council staff as a young Middle East specialist, was immediately impressed by the changes Pow-ell imposed. "I was the lowliest note taker in the room," Burns said. "He [Powell] ran as orderly a meeting as I've ever seen. People had a chance to express their views."

One specific job Carlucci gave Powell was to review all the nation's covert intelligence operations. The aim, Powell later explained, was "to satisfy ourselves that each one of them rested on the basis of law, that they made sense and could stand the test of a *Washington Post* revela-tion." Those last words were telling: later in his career, Powell's critics would complain that he cared too much about press coverage, but at this point, in early 1987, Reagan's presidency was on the edge of collapse and couldn't have survived further revelations of intelligence abuses.

Another task Carlucci delegated to Powell was to manage the com-plex, arcane issue of arms control negotiations with the Soviet Union. "Frank didn't have a great passion for arms control. It kind of bored him," Powell recalled. "And so most of the arms control, I did." It was therefore left to Powell to chair the interagency meetings at which the Reagan administration's positions were thrashed out.

This was no small task. Washington had been locked in internal bickering over arms control for years, with conservatives opposed to any agreements. Those debates were all the more intense during the Reagan administration. Powell did not have to handle the top-level wrangling between Shultz and Weinberger, much of which was handled by Carlucci. But one or two levels down, the battles were just as intense. The meetings Powell chaired would often include Frank Gaffney, an ultraconservative Pentagon official then working on Soviet issues (who, decades later, became an apostle of anti-Islamic policies); Rozanne Ridgway, a State Department official who pressed fervently for arms control and engagement with the

Soviet Union; and General Edward Rowny, who had been a leading opponent of arms control agreements since the early 1960s. "Those were the most fun meetings I've ever chaired in my life," Powell said sardonically in an interview many years later. "Because everybody believed in something that was diametrically opposed to what someone else in the room believed. It was my job to straighten it all out."

In 1987 the focus of arms control efforts was being narrowed down to the idea of negotiating a treaty with the Soviet Union to ban intermediate-range nuclear missiles, which were considered destabilizing to the security of Europe. During the course of that year, a deal was reached and signed; in the Intermediate-Range Nuclear Forces Treaty, the United States and the Soviet Union for the first time agreed to eliminate an entire class of nuclear weapons.

The driving forces behind this treaty were Reagan and Shultz. By 1987 they had decided that Soviet leader Mikhail Gorbachev was different from his predecessors and a potential agent for change inside his country; overriding objections from American conservatives, they decided to do business with him. In the historic summit at Reykjavik in October 1986, Reagan had discussed with Gorbachev the far-reaching possibility of abolishing all nuclear weapons. When the two leaders failed to reach such an agreement, American military officials were relieved, because their strategy and war plans were linked to nuclear weapons. The treaty on intermediate-range missiles was a lesser substitute. Reagan gave it his backing, and Powell discovered in his meetings that U.S. military leaders were not as intensely opposed to the idea as they had been to Reagan's more sweeping proposals at Reykjavik. "The Joint Chiefs didn't fight, particularly," Powell said. "It was a way to save money by giving up some of this stuff."

As deputy national security advisor, Powell also found himself at the center of another epic struggle within the Reagan administration, this one over what eventually became Reagan's famous speech at the Berlin Wall. In this case, the battle lines were not the Pentagon versus the State Department, but rather, the State Department versus Reagan's speechwriters. This time, the State Department was the loser.

Dealing with Reagan's speechwriters was a novel experience for Powell. He was far more accustomed to the familiar battles between hawks and doves within the foreign policy bureaucracy. On his very first day as deputy national security advisor, he had sought to tone down a presidential speech drafted by Reagan's principal speechwriter, Anthony Dolan, suggesting that it was too shrill. Dolan countered with a diatribe, telling Powell how little he knew about speechwriting.

The brouhaha over the Berlin Wall speech broke out in the spring of 1987, a few weeks before Reagan was scheduled to visit West Germany. One of the younger speechwriters, Peter Robinson, had drafted a speech in which Reagan would call upon Gorbachev to tear down the wall. State Department officials, led by Ridgway, attempted to remove the line from the speech, arguing that it was too much of a challenge to Gorbachev and might undercut his position atop the Soviet leadership.

For a time, Powell and his aides on the National Security Council staff supported the State Department, suggesting blander language: "It's time for the Wall to come down." Robinson, the speechwriter, and Reagan's communications director, Thomas Griscom, recalled a meeting in Griscom's office at which Powell raised objections to the speech.

Years later, Powell insisted that he had merely been carrying forward the objections of State Department officials, including Shultz. "I think George had serious reservations that we might be too much putting our fingers in Gorbachev's eyes, when we were trying to build a relationship," he explained. Indeed, Powell was also sending messages to State Department officials that they should rein in some of their opposition to the speech. When Ridgway asked that the speech be completely rewritten, Powell sent her a note to give up that battle: "Roz— . . . At this point, we need to work from this draft, as opposed to a completely new draft. Colin."

In the end, Reagan gave his own approval for the speech his writers had drafted, and he delivered what became one of the most remembered lines of his entire presidency: "Mr. Gorbachev, tear down this wall."

* * *

As the congressional committees assigned to investigate the Iran-Contra affair were beginning to organize themselves, the Republican leadership in the House of Representatives chose a familiar figure to serve as the ranking member on their committee: Dick Cheney.

By this juncture, Cheney was clearly the rising star among Republicans in Congress. He maintained the image of a pragmatist, yet his voting record was profoundly conservative. A tally by *Congressional Quarterly* in 1987 found that Cheney "consistently voted with the 'conservative coalition' of Republicans and Southern Democrats," and was, in fact, even more partisan in his voting patterns than the two Republican leaders, Trent Lott and Bob Michel. An accompanying profile of Cheney perfectly captured his operating style: "Cheney's natural habitat is behind the scenes. If he faces any problem, it is that he operates so far behind the scenes that some in the rank and file do not know him well." His presence on the House's Iran-Contra Committee would give him greater prominence. In fact, it accomplished that purpose fairly quickly: only a few months later, Cheney was promoted to chairman of the Republican Conference, the third-ranking position in the leadership.

The Iran-Contra investigations appeared at first glance to require Congress to focus upon specific factual questions: who sold arms to Iran; what promises were given about the release of American hostages; who in the White House authorized the transactions; who authorized the diversion of funds to the Contras? But soon after the House committee convened, Cheney served notice that he would be concentrating on something entirely different, a question not of fact but of principle: how to preserve presidential power and the prerogatives of the executive branch of government.

Throughout his time in Congress, Cheney held a special allure for certain kinds of Washington columnists. His solemnity and air of detachment conveyed the message that he was above the petty, short-term concerns of ordinary politicians. His background in political science, his experience as White House chief of staff, and his interest in political institutions made him irresistible for columnists seeking a perspective that would go beyond the daily news reports.

So it was that on Sunday, February 8, 1987, the *Washington Post* published a column by David Broder, the serious-minded journalist frequently described as the dean of the Washington press corps. Broder passed along to readers the concerns voiced to him by Dick Cheney. The principal objective of the Iran-Contra investigations, Cheney asserted, was to protect the power and privilege of the president of the United

States. Cheney was upset by reports that Reagan might turn over to congressional investigators some of his own notes about dealing with Iran. If the president were to make foolish concessions and release this sort of information, he could end up weakening his office and presidential authority. "I'm worried," Cheney told Broder, "that no one in the White House is concerned about the next president and his prerogatives."

* * *

It turned out that one of the people whose activities came under investigation in Iran-Contra was Colin Powell. As the military aide to Caspar Weinberger, he had been among the few officials in the Reagan administration who had been personally aware of the secret arms sales to Iran as they were taking place.

Powell was doubly removed from any direct culpability for the decisions at issue in Iran-Contra. As secretary of defense, Weinberger had made it clear to the White House and National Security Council from the outset that he was intensely opposed to the arms sales and, indeed, to any sort of dealings with Iran. Moreover, Powell was not himself a decision maker but merely Weinberger's assistant.

Yet the situation was a bit more complicated. Despite his opposition, Weinberger (and Pentagon aides, including Powell) had helped execute the arms transfers. Weinberger was in some jeopardy for having failed to tell Congress about activities that were illegal. He would also eventually come into further jeopardy for having failed to tell Congress about daily notes he kept that could have been used as evidence.

On April 17, 1987, members of the House and Senate Intelligence Committees formally interviewed Powell about Iran-Contra. Powell, accompanied by two lawyers from the National Security Council, testified that he did not remember or "had no recollection of" some of the events in question. He chose his words carefully, in an apparent effort to avoid saying anything that would harm Weinberger.

Powell gave another round of testimony two months later, but he was not called to testify at the public hearings that summer. Five years later, Lawrence Walsh, the special prosecutor appointed to investigate Iran-Contra, asserted in his final report that Powell's testimony had been "at least misleading" and "hardly constituted full disclosure," but concluded that what Powell had done did not warrant prosecution. It turned out that Weinberger had in fact kept detailed daily notes of his activities, and he was indicted for having lied to Congress about these. However, before Weinberger went to trial, President George H. W. Bush would grant him a pardon.

On November 17, 1987, the two congressional Iran-Contra committees issued their final report. The Democratic majority concluded that in providing arms to Iran and in the diversion of funds from those sales to the Nicaraguan contras, the Reagan administration had operated with "secrecy, deception and disdain for the rule of law." However, the Republicans, led by Dick Cheney, filed a lengthy dissent with an entirely different viewpoint.

The 155-page minority report was vintage Cheney, a full exegesis of the ideas he had been developing since the 1970s. He had brought David Addington, the onetime CIA lawyer, from the House Intelligence Committee onto the House's Iran-Contra Committee to assist him. In the Cheney-Addington perspective, the principal malefactor in Iran-Contra had not been the Reagan administration, nor the president, nor any of the individuals who carried out the operations (e.g., Oliver North, John Poindexter). Rather, the transgressor was the Congress of the United States, for trying to take power away from the executive branch of government.

Cheney's minority report said the Democratic majority in Congress "rested their case upon an aggrandizing theory of Congress's foreign policy powers that is itself part of the problem." Even if those who perpetrated Iran-Contra had flouted laws passed by Congress, the report went on, those laws should never have been passed. "Unconstitutional statutes violate the rule of law every bit as much as do willful violations of constitutional statutes," the report said. The laws Congress had enacted to place limits on the executive branch actions on Nicaragua and on Iran "resulted directly from an ongoing state of political guerrilla warfare over foreign policy between the legislative and executive branches."

Nor did the minority report shy away from specifying when the relationship between Congress and the executive branch had gone awry: "The boundless view of Congressional power began to take hold in the 1970s, in the wake of the Vietnam War." The report mentioned the War

Powers Act and the investigation of the CIA by the Church Committee, the investigation that Cheney himself had sought to restrict when he
served in the Ford White House.

Where the Democratic majority had recommended changes in the
way the White House and National Security Council operated, Cheney's
minority report recommended changes in Congress. There should be a
"secrecy oath" for members of the House and Senate Intelligence Committees, the report argued, and fewer members of Congress should be
notified about covert operations.

In short, the Republican minority's report on Iran-Contra was a
road map to Dick Cheney's thinking about presidential power, one that
he would carry forward for the next twenty years.

* * *

By the fall of 1987, the stage was set for the final act of the Reagan presidency, and Colin Powell would find himself at center stage.

It was becoming clear that Reagan was moving toward a new arms
control agreement with Gorbachev and that, in general, the president had
begun to accept George Shultz's arguments that Gorbachev represented
a new kind of Soviet leader. Reagan was turning against the hawks inside
his own administration who had portrayed Gorbachev as merely a new
face for the same old Soviet policies. Richard Perle, the Pentagon official
who had tenaciously opposed arms control agreements, left the administration in May 1987. That same month, another leading conservative,
CIA director William Casey, suddenly died; his replacement was William Webster, a centrist.

In early November, Weinberger, the most high-ranking and implacable hawk in the administration, announced that he was stepping down
as secretary of defense, citing his wife's poor health as the reason. Reagan and his new White House chief of staff, Howard Baker, decided that
Frank Carlucci, the national security advisor, should move to the Pentagon as Weinberger's successor.

Carlucci's departure would leave the job of national security advisor open. During his presidency, Reagan had already established a clear
pattern in personnel choices: when senior positions became vacant, he
often promoted from inside, elevating the number-two official to the top

job. Two previous deputy national security advisors, Robert McFarlane and John Poindexter, had been promoted to national security advisor. As Carlucci's deputy, Powell had established himself as both efficient and popular, and his supporters included not only Carlucci but also Howard Baker, George H. W. Bush, and George Shultz. Like Weinberger and Carlucci, Shultz had known Powell since their days at the Office of Management and Budget in the Nixon administration, and he had become a strong booster. "As deputy [national security advisor], Powell had proved to be extraordinarily knowledgeable, and gifted intellectually," Shultz later wrote. Thus it was not a surprise when Reagan chose Powell to serve as the sixth (and final) national security advisor in his administration.

There was one awkward impediment, however. Powell was still a lieutenant general in the U.S. Army, and he had no intention of resigning from the military to take the civilian job of national security advisor. He was not absolutely required to do so, but this was a sensitive subject: the final report of the Senate and House Iran-Contra committees, issued in the same month as Powell's appointment, had specifically recommended that the job of national security advisor not be held by a military officer. (The congressional committees clearly had in mind the unhappy precedent of Poindexter, a vice admiral who retained his navy post while serving as national security advisor during the Iran-Contra affair.)

Moreover, there was another obstacle: a federal law prohibited a military officer from holding a top-level civilian position. That law had been waived from time to time: Alexander Haig had been permitted to take the job of Richard Nixon's White House chief of staff without resigning from the army, and the law had been waived again for Poindexter. Nevertheless, the concept of preventing dual loyalties—in theory, at least, a military officer serving as national security advisor would owe allegiance both to the president and to his military superiors—had some prominent adherents, such as Brent Scowcroft, who had decided voluntarily to give up his air force commission when he became national security advisor in 1975.

Worse, another one-time supporter of this principle had been Colin Powell. A few weeks earlier, in an interview with the *New York Times*, Powell had defended the idea that military officers could work as staff members on the National Security Council, but he thought the top job of national security advisor should be held by a civilian.

Powell powered through this obstacle with his usual charm and his good-natured disdain for abstractions. Asked by reporters about the recommendation of the Iran-Contra Committee for a civilian national security advisor, he told them to "search your morgues" for the *Times* article in which he had said the same thing. Why was he taking the job, then? reporters asked. "That's a good question!" Powell replied. Then he gave a more serious answer. "The President should be free to select whoever he thinks is best able to perform that role," he said. If Reagan wanted to appoint him, Powell said, "I did not think it was my position to disagree with him and tell him he shouldn't appoint me to the position. And I'm flattered and honored that he's done so."

This answer skirted the questions concerning divided loyalties and military involvement in civilian affairs. Those issues were not merely theoretical ones for Powell, who made clear he still had ambitions for his military career. He himself would acknowledge, more than a decade later, that he had been fudging the issue. "I just took the best excuse and said, 'Well, it's up to the president. He has no problem. Why should I have a problem?'"

The excuse sufficed. Underneath it all, Powell knew he enjoyed the friendship, support, and goodwill of all the key figures in the Reagan administration. It remained an open question for the future how he would fare inside an administration where his charm wouldn't count so much and where his colleagues would view him with suspicion or hostility.

* * *

Colin Powell's ascent to national security advisor represented more continuity than change within the Reagan White House. As Carlucci's deputy, Powell had frequently stood in for his boss, briefing the president and chairing interagency meetings. The two men thought in similar fashion about the issues. Powell simply moved into the larger West Wing office that Carlucci had occupied.

Yet, when it came to image and press coverage, the promotion meant a dramatic change for Powell. He was no longer a second in command, as he had been in his string of Washington jobs over the previous decade; rather, he was at the top level of the national security apparatus. His new title made him a public figure, not just an insider, and he became a natural subject for newspaper profiles and television interviews.

Much of the public interest centered on his race. Carl T. Rowan, an African American columnist who had served in the Kennedy and Johnson administrations, wrote: "To understand the significance of Gen. Powell's elevation to this extremely difficult and demanding post, you must realize that only a generation ago it was an unwritten rule that in the foreign affairs field, blacks could serve only as ambassador to Liberia and minister to the Canary Islands. The view was that they were unwelcome in Europe, Latin America, the Far East."

Within Reagan's newly constituted national security team, Powell was not the dominant figure; Shultz was. Shultz had spent most of the Reagan administration battling with Weinberger, Casey, and various White House aides, but his rivals were now gone, and his views on foreign policy generally held sway. One of Powell's tasks was to end the constant friction between the State Department and the Pentagon. Given his own considerable experience at the Pentagon and his close ties to Carlucci, the new defense secretary, he managed that task with ease.

Every morning at 7 a.m., Powell, Shultz, and Carlucci would meet in Powell's West Wing office for fifteen or thirty minutes to talk about what had happened overnight and what needed to be done that day. The meetings were Shultz's idea, and the rules were strict: no note takers and no deputy or assistant secretaries, no substitutions of any kind. If one of the three men was out of town, there was no meeting.

On the surface, these sessions were simply an effort at good government, a matter of coordinating the bureaucracy. But there was a larger purpose to these daily sessions: the three men were making as many decisions as possible on Reagan's behalf, without actually having to involve the president. "If the three of us agreed, that was it," Carlucci later explained. "Reagan was past the point where he could intervene in the system. We worked it that way for over a year." Powell explained the meetings more delicately: "I would never ever characterize it as me, Frank and Shultz *making* the decisions," he said. "But we made it easier for him [Reagan] to make decisions. I would never usurp the authority of the president. I don't think we ever did anything that he did not agree with."

By many accounts, Reagan had started to slip mentally from time to time during his final two years in office. He was not diagnosed as having

Alzheimer's disease until 1994, five years after he left the White House, and there is no sign that he had the disease during his presidency. However, by early 1987 his domestic advisors were concerned enough about how inattentive and detached he was becoming that they researched the possibility of invoking the Twenty-Fifth Amendment, which would have enabled the vice president to take over.

Asked directly in an interview years later whether Reagan was losing his faculties during those last two years, Carlucci paused, sighed, and replied, "He slowed down." When asked the same question, Powell responded, "The last year [of his presidency] he was starting to have some trouble. I don't know that he had Alzheimer's. I don't know when Alzheimer's starts. But there were a few times in that last year when he looked like he wasn't quite as focused as he should be."

As the national security advisor, Powell was the foreign policy official with the closest proximity and greatest access to the president. It was therefore an increasingly important aspect of his job to manage Reagan amid his increasing disengagement. Powell emphasized that during that period, Reagan was able to make a forceful, quick decision when one was needed. In an intense debate over Panama policy, when Vice President Bush proposed a policy that could have required the use of force, Reagan personally turned him down. When a skirmish broke out between American naval vessels and Iranian gunboats in the Persian Gulf and the Pentagon sought permission for the marines to enter Iran's territorial waters, Powell went into the Oval Office to ask Reagan for approval. The president listened carefully to the details and said, "Right, go ahead and do it."

Still, day in and day out, Reagan remained distant from daily events. Powell accepted the president's isolation as a fact of life and put the best face on it: it meant, he thought, that Reagan trusted his aides and was letting them handle routine decisions. "I'd go and see the president, and I'd have some terrible problem, a huge fight between State and Defense over something, or State and Treasury, and I'd start to describe the problems to the president, why it is causing us all this distress," Powell explained. "And he was listening to me, but he wasn't paying all that much attention to me." He continued: "He would kind of look over my shoulder as I was laying out my woes to him, and after my five minutes or so of laying out this terrible problem, he would interrupt me, and say something like, 'Colin, Colin, the squirrel's finally picked up the nut that I left out in the Rose Garden.' Holy cow! And it bothered me, and Frank, for the first few weeks, until I realized, what the guy was saying to me was, 'Colin, the problem you're telling me about, sounds terribly interesting, and it certainly is a problem, and if you wish me to hear about it, I'm a gentle soul, I'll listen to you—but Colin, you're the one I hired to solve this problem. And so, when you have one that I really need to get involved in, I will. But until then, I will listen to you, it's a pleasant morning, you're a pleasant fellow, but I'm watching the squirrels pick up the nuts I put out there."

Powell admired Reagan and, at the same time, protected him. In the end, he concluded, almost reverentially, "He always was somewhere above the rest of us. And people thought that was a weakness. But it wasn't. The weakness was when he didn't have people underneath him who could properly use the confidence that he placed in them."

* * *

It was during this period that Colin Powell started to transact business on a regular basis with Dick Cheney. It was a natural outgrowth of their respective jobs. As national security advisor, Powell needed to forge decent relations with Capitol Hill. Cheney was a senior Republican on the House Intelligence Committee, the ranking Republican on the Iran-Contra Committee, and a rising star in the party's leadership.

Powell sometimes went directly to Cheney on sensitive subjects. "You mentioned today at staff that you were meeting Thursday on a private matter with Dick Cheney," one of Powell's aides, Alison B. Fortier, wrote him in the spring of 1988. "I would like to ask that you raise briefly with him one business issue: South Africa sanctions." At the bottom of this printed memo, Powell had scrawled a brush-off reply: "ABF, Didn't get to it. CP."

What was this "private matter" between Powell and Cheney? There is no answer in the files. It could have been something related to Iran-Contra, though that seems unlikely; the committees had filed their report months earlier. The special prosecutor, Lawrence Walsh, was continuing his investigation, but Cheney had no influence over that. Rather, the secret meeting between Powell and Cheney almost certainly involved legislation then pending on Capitol Hill that would have imposed new restrictions on the CIA. That spring, in the wake of Iran-Contra, Congress was considering several bills that would have set out tighter rules for covert intelligence operations. The principal measure would have required the president to notify Congress within forty-eight hours of the start of any covert action. Reagan and the White House were trying to head off enactment of these new curbs (and, later that spring, Powell said in public that Reagan would veto the bill). Cheney was not only a senior Republican on the House Intelligence Committee but also, in general, a determined opponent of congressional limits on presidential power. When Powell, as national security advisor, looked for someone in Congress to help kill the proposed new limits on the CIA, Cheney was the obvious candidate.

Powell and his aides were dealing with Cheney and his staff, particularly David Addington, concerning specific "black" programs. "Dave Addington says that the DOD Authorizers have not solved the 908 program problem," an aide reported in a memo. Project 908 was the name for the clandestine continuity-of-government program the Reagan administration had carried out to guarantee presidential succession during nuclear war. "I am not read into this program. I know however that Dave has spoken to Colin about this."

In the course of doing business, Powell and Cheney also began swapping personal notes that testify to their developing friendship. Cheney had suffered a second heart attack in 1984 and a third one in the summer of 1988. "Dear Dick, I was sorry to hear that you are a little under the weather," Powell wrote Cheney that summer. "I look forward to your speedy recovery and return to the battlefield." Cheney replied two weeks later that he was bored at home and "looking forward to resuming my schedule—maybe even getting a little fishing in. . . . Your thoughtfulness means a great deal to me."

* * *

By far the most important task Powell confronted as national security advisor was to guide Reagan through his final three meetings with Gorbachev: one in Washington in December 1987, one in Moscow five months later, and a final one, brief and hastily arranged, during the presidential transition in December 1988.

For these summits, Powell had to fill several duties at once, dealing with the president to prepare him for his discussions with the Soviet leader; with Nancy Reagan concerning the ceremonial aspects of the summits; and with the federal bureaucracy concerning the complex issue of arms control. With his blend of interpersonal skills and bureaucratic sophistication, Powell was at his best in handling events like these.

Reagan and Gorbachev's first two summits had been on neutral ground, at Geneva and Reykjavik. By late 1987 they were ready to upgrade to reciprocal summits in each leader's home country. The Reagans were eager to take Gorbachev on a late-November grand tour throughout the United States. Nancy Reagan was pressing hard to have the Soviet leader come to their ranch in Santa Barbara. "She's already bought the groceries for Thanksgiving," Powell joked to Shultz. "Gorbachev's going to the ranch whether he wants to or not." In the end, Gorbachev turned down all these ideas and announced that he would be visiting only Washington.

During their preparatory sessions, Powell found that Reagan was sometimes more interested in the personal aspects of the meetings than in the issues that would be raised. The president's California friends had given him a set of cufflinks to give to Gorbachev that showed men beating swords into plowshares, the symbol of peace. Reagan broke up Powell's private presidential briefing sessions to talk about the cufflinks. "He said, 'When do you think I ought to be giving him the cufflinks?'" Powell recalled in an interview years later. "I would say, 'Mr. President, he's going to be talking about SS-18s [missiles], he's going to be talking about throw weights.' 'Yeah—when do you think I ought to give him the cufflinks?'"

Meanwhile, Powell helped orchestrate meetings between American officials and their Soviet counterparts, some of them groundbreaking. When Vladimir Kryuchkov, the head of the KGB's foreign operations, appeared in Washington ostensibly to arrange security for the summit, Powell telephoned Robert Gates, the CIA's deputy director and its leading expert on the Soviet Union, to arrange a small dinner for him with Kryuchkov. It was, at the time, the highest-level meeting ever held between the CIA and the KGB.

Ultimately, Powell's preparations paid off, and the Washington summit went smoothly. Not all of it was cufflinks and pleasantries, however. At a state dinner for Gorbachev, Nancy Reagan had seated the Soviet leader next to her and, on the other side of her, a leading Republican congressman, Dick Cheney. Seizing the opportunity, Cheney began to grill Gorbachev about whether he still thought communism was a workable system. He also asked the Soviet leader how he had risen to the top. "I came away from the evening thinking he wasn't as serious a reformer as some believed," Cheney wrote.

Reagan's trip to Moscow in the spring of 1988 required even more elaborate preparations. Once again, Powell was responsible for coordinating policy issues in Washington and dealing with the president's set of priorities. One particular problem Powell confronted was that Reagan wanted to talk to Gorbachev about religion, not only the idea of religious tolerance but also belief in God. Reagan had seized upon some offhand comments by Gorbachev (e.g., "God be with you") as signs that he might be in some way a closet believer. "We had to talk to him [Reagan], I had to spend a lot of time on this," Powell recalled. "I had to tell the president, 'Don't see this as an expression of religious faith. It's almost idiomatic. He's not ready to get down on his knees for you.'" Despite Powell's efforts, once in Moscow, Reagan did in fact try to talk to Gorbachev about a belief in God. But the transcripts of the meeting show that as Reagan persisted, Gorbachev kept trying to change the subject, until the meeting finally came to an end.

Nevertheless, the Moscow Summit was a success. Reagan gave Gorbachev the most important words of endorsement he could have imagined. As he was standing in Red Square, reporters asked the American president if he still considered the Soviet Union to be an "evil empire," the phrase he had famously used five years earlier. "No," replied Reagan. "I was talking about another time and another era."

* * *

In every presidency, there are ill-conceived ventures that are put forward but then left on the drawing board. In September 1988, Ronald Reagan once again tried to engage in secret diplomacy with Iran to win (or, rather, buy) the release of American hostages who were being held in Lebanon. He did this, astonishingly, less than two years after the Iran-Contra scandal erupted and ten months after the congressional Iran-Contra committees issued their final report and, so far as was known, laid the matter to rest.

Reagan was entering the last autumn of his presidency. The 1988 presidential campaign between Vice President George H. W. Bush and

Governor Michael Dukakis of Massachusetts was in its final weeks. There is no indication that Bush was involved in the effort to free these hostages; Reagan may have concluded on his own that such a release could help Bush—or, more likely, politics aside, he may simply have been making one last try to accomplish the same goal that the Iran-Contra initiative earlier in his presidency had failed to achieve.

On September 13, 1988, Reagan met with Powell. According to Powell's handwritten notes of the meeting, the subject the president wanted to talk about was "Iran." Reagan "wants to talk about a better relationship," Powell wrote.

"We have billions," Reagan told Powell, apparently referring to Iran's frozen assets in the United States. Reagan thought the United States should work through a neutral country, a third party, "so it doesn't look like we're doing it or making the offer." In his scenario, a third party "asks them to use all their influence to release all hostages." (Asked about these notes and about Reagan's evident interest in a deal with Iran, even after the Iran-Contra scandal, Powell replied thirty years later, "The President was musing to me. And I took down his musings. But I can assure you it never went anywhere. It didn't result in any policy changes.")

The presidential archives also show that at roughly the same time, at least one of Reagan's old California cronies was overseas working on a release of the hostages. On September 28, two weeks after Reagan and Powell spoke about Iran and the hostages, a man named Fred Gottfurcht called Powell at the White House. Gottfurcht was a Southern California developer and investor whom Reagan had known for many years. He told Powell he had been in Paris for more than a week dealing with Iranian interlocutors. Powell wrote, "According to Fred, the Iranians claim that four of the hostages are in Iran and could be released immediately. However, they say the remaining five will be in Iran by October 7 and all can be released at that time."

Powell wanted no part of this. Reagan and Gottfurcht, whether independently or together, seemed to be flirting with the same sort of operation that had nearly brought down Reagan's presidency once before—precisely the kind of activities that Powell and Carlucci had been brought to the White House to stop. It is not clear what Powell told Reagan at the time, but his rebuke to Gottfurcht could not have been blunter.

"I again told Fred that I did not wish to be involved in this matter, and the White House most definitely should not be involved," Powell wrote. All the unofficial channels to Iran, however well meaning, "are doing nothing but cause confusion," he went on. "I again encouraged him to retire from these endeavors." He ended the conversation by telling Gottfurcht "that the only thing I would be interested in is if he had the hostages in hand. Otherwise, I do not wish there to be any linkage between his efforts and the White House."

To Reagan's good fortune, the public never found out about the president's effort to revive the secret Iran diplomacy. Instead, historians usually judge Reagan's final two years in office to be among the most successful of his presidency, for two reasons: Reagan recovered from Iran-Contra, and his summitry with Gorbachev laid the groundwork for the end of the Cold War.

Both these judgments are well founded, but they leave out some important facts. First, a faltering Reagan was helped through the Gorbachev summits by his advisors. And second, Reagan never really abandoned his attempts to pay for the release of American hostages through back-channel diplomacy with Iran. Instead, he was surrounded by a new team of White House advisors who squelched his continuing efforts.

Colin Powell played a central role in reviving the Reagan presidency and ensuring that the historical verdicts on Reagan would be largely flattering. In this instance, the might-have-beens were all negative ones: The Soviet diplomacy might have gone awry because of Reagan's lack of focus. Reagan might have wandered into another trading-for-hostages mess. Or he might have stumbled in some other way, enough to be judged unable to carry out his duties. Thanks to the protection of Powell and other aides, none of these things ever came to pass.

* * *

Powell had tried to stay as far away as possible from George H. W. Bush's presidential campaign, even though he had begun to develop a personal relationship with the vice president. For Powell, foreign policy and politics were separate enterprises, never to intersect. At one point, Bush tried to persuade a young Middle East expert on the National Security Council, Dennis Ross, to work for his presidential campaign; Bush had been impressed by Ross on one of his trips overseas. Powell threw cold water on the idea. "He counseled me against leaving to work for Bush," Ross recalled. "He wasn't anti-Bush. But he was saying, 'Look, why do you want to go do that? It's politics!'"

Although Powell was speaking to Ross as an employer seeking to prevent one of his staff members from leaving, his words also reflected his deeper sense that politics was something best left to others. He had been imbued since his ROTC days at City College with the idea that military officers should stay out of politics; his years on the National Security Council had not changed that view.

But despite his expressed disdain for politics, 1988 marked the first of several presidential campaigns in which Powell was mentioned as a possible candidate. On a network news program early that year, Howard Baker, the White House chief of staff, had included Powell's name on a list of possible vice-presidential running mates for Bush, and a few columnists had picked up the idea. George F. Will wrote that Powell was "bright as a new nickel." While some people said the nation's racism would count against him, Will countered, "They are underestimating the country and the capacity of boldness by a conservative party to have a constructive effect." This was a train of thought that would emerge from time to time throughout the 1990s—that putting Powell on the ticket could demonstrate that the Republican Party was tolerant and inclusive on racial issues. There were several problems with this idea, but the first was that Powell wasn't a politician.

The talk ended in the summer of 1988, when Bush chose Senator Dan Quayle of Indiana as his vice-presidential nominee. Nevertheless, the episode demonstrated something else about Powell: though he had only recently become a public figure, he was a much larger presence than that fact might suggest. He was easily the most prominent African American in the Reagan administration, and he was carrying out his job with evident success. He was frequently seen standing alongside the president of the United States or conducting briefings at summit meetings. Years later, many Americans would believe that Powell burst forth into the nation's consciousness as chairman of the Joint Chiefs of Staff. But that wasn't quite right: he had already attracted intense press coverage and public attention while working for Reagan.

After Bush defeated Dukakis that November, questions immediately arose about what Powell, then fifty-one years old, would do next. Bush spoke briefly with Powell about the idea of being included in the new administration. "They offered me a job at CIA as a deputy or director, I don't even remember now, and deputy secretary of state," Powell recalled.

However, this would have been awkward in several ways. While Bush and Powell got along well personally, there was considerable friction between the outgoing Reagan team and the incoming Bush team. Moreover, Bush wanted to set his own course on foreign policy. He had argued during the campaign that Reagan had been too willing to believe that Gorbachev represented change in the Soviet Union; Bush had suggested that he might take a more hawkish stance than Reagan had in his final years, and Powell had played a leading role under Reagan. Above all, even apart from policy considerations, Powell would have been a problematic presence on the new Bush team simply because he was the outgoing national security advisor.

Powell cast the Bush overtures aside. He had decided to keep his position as an active-duty army officer when he took the position as national security advisor. Now he wanted to return to the army. After checking with his superiors to make sure they still wanted him back and finding that they did, Powell accepted an offer to become commander in chief of the U.S. Forces Command, which is in charge of the nearly one million troops stationed inside the United States. In the process, he became a four-star general. Writing two decades later, he called that promotion "one of the happiest days of my life."

Even this decision to return to military life attracted attention and was accorded larger cultural significance because it was so different from what outgoing administration officials generally do. *The Economist* published a story about Powell's return to the army with the title "Not Selling Out." The piece pointed out that Powell could have commanded hundreds of thousands of dollars a year in the private sector or on corporate boards. "America's celebrity culture places an ever-higher value on Washington big shots," the magazine noted. Powell did not have the self-image of a Washington big shot, at least not yet. But he was becoming one.

* * *

During Powell's final weeks in the White House, he received the usual phone calls and letters from people he had come to know, saying good-bye and wishing him well. One of these was from his friend Dick Cheney. By Cheney's account, he called Powell during the transition "and expressed the hope that we would have the opportunity to work together at some point in the future." That perhaps sounded formulaic, the sort of words anyone might use in saying good-bye to an outgoing colleague. Cheney's words would take on more significance the following year.

Powell reciprocated with warm words for Cheney. The 1988 elections had ushered in a new Congress, and in its earliest days the House Republicans promoted Cheney to be the House minority whip, the second-ranking position in the leadership. On December 21, Powell scrawled a handwritten note to Cheney. "Dear Dick," it read. "Belated but sincere congrats on your new position. A superb selection which I *know* will not only benefit your party but also those committed to good government and to all Americans.

"Your buddy, Colin."

PART TWO

FORTY-ONE

5

APPOINTMENTS

W hen George H. W. Bush was sworn in as president on January 20, 1989, neither Dick Cheney nor Colin Powell was part of his administration. Powell was settling into his new position as commander of the U.S. Army Forces Command in Atlanta, while Cheney was beginning his new job as House minority whip.

In assembling his team, Bush had relied heavily on a different network of Republicans from that which had come to Washington with Ronald Reagan eight years earlier. The leading members of the Bush administration were more traditional Republicans, with inside credentials and closer ties to the moderate wing of the party. Some had worked for the Ford administration, in which Bush himself had served as CIA director. Bush appointed Brent Scowcroft, Ford's national security advisor, to take the same job in his White House. He appointed James Baker, the manager of Ford's 1976 campaign and Bush's close friend from Texas, to be his secretary of state; Baker had also served as Reagan's chief of staff and secretary of the treasury. For secretary of defense, Bush appointed another figure with years of Washington experience, former senator John Tower of Texas, who had served as chairman of the Senate Armed Services Committee.

However, this lineup had to be altered in the earliest days of the new administration. Tower had been unpopular with some of his Senate colleagues, and he had been recently divorced. Allegations emerged of his excessive drinking, his womanizing, and his links to defense contractors. On March 9, less than seven weeks after Bush was sworn in, the Senate voted 53 to 47 to reject Tower's nomination. It was the first time in history that the Senate had turned down a Cabinet appointment by a new president in his first months in office.

Bush was suddenly confronted with the need to name someone to run the Pentagon, and to do so quickly. "When we got shot down on John Tower, we needed a secretary of defense very badly. This was already March, and we just couldn't make policy with a big gap there," Scowcroft recalled. "So, we needed somebody fast. That to me meant that it had to be somebody from the Congress—because otherwise we'd go through these long hearings and so on. And then I automatically went to Dick Cheney. And we looked at—to be fair, we looked at a list of possibles from Congress, from both Houses. But Dick was my very first choice, and I think he was pretty close to the president's first." Bush recalled that he wanted Cheney not only because he was a member of Congress likely to win quick confirmation but also because of his personal qualities. "He had a reputation for integrity and for standing up for principles and, at the same time, for getting along with people," Bush said.

For Bush, "getting along" was of paramount importance. He and Scowcroft could be confident that Cheney would fit in well with the new team. Scowcroft had worked alongside Cheney in the Ford White House, and Baker had been friendly with him since Ford's 1976 presidential campaign.

Neither Bush nor Scowcroft considered Cheney too conservative for this team. To them, a "conservative" meant someone who had been on the Reagan team, or at least on the Reagan side of the bitter Ford/Reagan divide in the 1970s. Cheney didn't qualify in that way, even though, on issues such as the Panama Canal Treaty and welcoming Aleksandr Solzhenitsyn to the White House, he had been in fact more in tune with Reagan than with Ford. So, too, in the congressional politics of the 1980s, a "conservative" usually meant Newt Gingrich or one of his upstart supporters. As a member of the Republican leadership, Cheney didn't seem to qualify in that way, either, though he was in fact closer to Gingrich than many realized.

Even before Tower's nomination was formally rejected, Bush and Scowcroft had begun talking about Cheney as a possible replacement. On the morning of the Senate vote, Scowcroft called Cheney and asked him to come to the White House, ostensibly to discuss what to do next. By the time Cheney got there, the Senate had formally rejected Tower. Scowcroft asked Cheney who he thought should be the next nominee.

Cheney's first suggestion was that Bush should bring back Donald Rumsfeld, his old boss, who had already served as defense secretary. This suggestion was to become the beginning of a ritual: over the years, whenever a high-level position opened up in a Republican administration, Cheney was likely to suggest Rumsfeld for it, and conversely, Rumsfeld would suggest Cheney.

In fact, Cheney was not alone in suggesting Rumsfeld as a replacement for Tower; others included him on a short list of possible nominees. However, Bush had no interest. Rumsfeld had been his political rival since the mid-1970s, when Gerald Ford proclaimed Bush and Rumsfeld to be the two young rising stars of the Republican Party. More recently, Rumsfeld had tried to run against Bush for the Republican presidential nomination for president in 1988 before dropping out; after quitting, Rumsfeld had endorsed Senator Bob Dole on the eve of the New Hampshire primary. The rivalry had led to personal antipathy between the two men as well. Bush wrote in his diary that Rumsfeld was "unacceptable, because Baker doesn't like him and I worry about his game playing, and I think Brent does, too." Other presidents at other times might experiment with the concept of a "team of rivals," but George H. W. Bush was decidedly not among them.

At their White House meeting on the day of Tower's defeat, after casting aside the suggestion that Rumsfeld be the next nominee, Scowcroft bluntly asked Cheney, "What about you? Would you consider it?" Cheney asked for time to think about it overnight. "I obviously had a promising career in the House, which I had to give up to go do this," Cheney later explained. His goal had long been to become the Republican leader in the House of Representatives, and as the whip, he was only one step from that goal. But he calculated that it would be four more years before Bob Michel, the Republican leader, stepped down. At the same time, Cheney was excited at the prospect of running the Pentagon and attracted to the idea of working alongside Scowcroft and Baker, both of whom were close friends. When he discussed the offer with his wife, Lynne, that night, "it wasn't a close call," Cheney later said. As if to reinforce his thinking, Baker called to lobby for him to accept.

The job hadn't been formally offered to Cheney yet; he was supposed to decide for certain whether he would accept the job if offered before he spoke with the president. The following morning, he told Scowcroft he would do it if asked. In a meeting with Bush later that day, the two men talked about impending issues such as arms control. But Cheney also felt compelled to bring up his past: he reminded Bush that he hadn't served in the military, that he'd twice been kicked out of Yale, and that he'd been arrested twice for driving under the influence. That last confession seemed necessary because alcohol had played a role in Tower's failure to win confirmation. Bush told Cheney he didn't think any of this history would be an impediment to confirmation. Shortly after the interview, Bush phoned Cheney on Capitol Hill to offer him the job. Cheney quickly accepted.

Senator Sam Nunn, the Georgia Democrat who chaired the Senate Armed Services Committee, agreed to handle Cheney's arrest record discreetly by raising the subject only in a closed session of the committee, at which Senator John Glenn of Ohio asked Cheney how he had managed to "clean up his act." Cheney told him, "I got married and gave up hanging out in bars." That exchange was sufficient for the committee, and both the committee and the full Senate went on to approve Cheney's nomination.

His career in the House came to an end—happily so, from Cheney's point of view. Despite his earlier reverence for the institution, despite the fact that he had studied Congress's role in American history in graduate school and had even written a book about the Speakers of the House, after Cheney left Congress, he came to regard it mostly with disdain, viewing it as an obstacle to be avoided whenever possible.

* * *

In his first days at the Pentagon, Cheney made two crucial personnel decisions.

The first was to move forward with a choice initially made by John

Tower a few weeks earlier: to appoint Paul Wolfowitz to be undersecretary of defense for policy, the third-ranking position in the department.
In most administrations, the job of deputy secretary, the number two
position, goes to a specialist on management and budgets, so that for
policy questions, the undersecretary serves as the top civilian advisor to
the secretary of defense.

Wolfowitz had been associated with the neoconservative movement
that had blossomed in Washington during the 1970s in opposition to
détente and arms control with the Soviet Union. He began his government career working for the hawkish Democratic senator Henry Jackson and then served in the Reagan administration as a State Department
official and an ambassador to Indonesia.

Wolfowitz had been approached about two jobs in the incoming
Bush administration. James Baker suggested he join the State Department as assistant secretary for Europe, while an aide to Tower tried to
recruit him for the Pentagon. Undecided, Wolfowitz sought counsel from
several people, including Colin Powell, whom he had come to know during the Reagan years. Powell advised Wolfowitz to take the State Department job; Baker was the sort of person, Powell said, who would never
forgive you if you turned him down.

Wolfowitz tentatively decided to heed that advice. He told associates,
including Powell's close friend Richard Armitage, that he had decided to
go to the State Department. Then he abruptly changed his mind. Wolfowitz knew Baker operated through a small, tight circle of close aides, and
he was afraid he would be excluded from it. Instead, he accepted the offer
from Tower. Cheney in turn decided he wanted to keep Wolfowitz,
although in theory he could have chosen someone else. The close-knit
conservative network played an indirect role: Cheney and Wolfowitz had
a close mutual friend in Kenneth Adelman, another conservative whom
Cheney had known as a colleague under Rumsfeld in the Nixon years.
"I'd met Paul socially previously at the Adelmans, . . . and knew him by
reputation," Cheney once said in explaining the decision to retain Wolfowitz.

Once he began working at the Pentagon, Wolfowitz helped recruit
onto his staff several other foreign policy experts with credentials comparable to his own: They tended to be book-smart, though not always

street-smart, good at thinking in abstract terms about policy issues, often from academic backgrounds but also with experience in Washington. Above all, they were hawkish on foreign policy issues, with an expansive view of America's role in the world. I. Lewis (Scooter) Libby, who had served as Wolfowitz's assistant at the State Department in the Reagan years and took on a similar role in the Pentagon, joined Wolfowitz's staff, as did Eric Edelman, Stephen Hadley, and Zalmay Khalilzad. All of them would play important roles under Cheney inside the Pentagon, and they would become an informal network of close colleagues when Cheney returned to government as vice president more than a decade later.

Cheney's second personnel decision was much more important but, at this stage, still preliminary. The four-year term of Admiral William Crowe as chairman of the Joint Chiefs of Staff would expire in September. Scowcroft had talked to Crowe about his possibly staying on the job for at least another two years, but Crowe was lukewarm on the idea. Cheney was even less enthusiastic: he wanted to install his own chairman. He also knew whom he hoped to appoint: Colin Powell, the new friend he had acquired over the last two years of the Reagan administration.

"I made the decision the afternoon the President announced my appointment that if I could, I wanted to get Colin for my chairman of the Joint Chiefs of Staff," Cheney recalled in an oral history. Within days, Cheney went to see Frank Carlucci, his predecessor, to talk about decisions and problems he would likely face as secretary of defense. During their talk, Cheney broached the idea of appointing Powell as chairman of the Joint Chiefs. Carlucci liked the idea. This was hardly a surprise, given that he had long been Powell's strongest supporter in Washington. The Joint Chiefs appointment didn't need to be made until the summer, and Cheney meanwhile needed to persuade Bush and Scowcroft to support his decision.

In these first two personnel choices, Wolfowitz and Powell, Cheney set into motion a dynamic that would characterize his four years in the Pentagon and, later on, the first four years of the George W. Bush administration: the tension between a group of hawkish civilian experts and a more cautious military leader, one who was tradition-minded, centrist, and conventional in his thinking, but who was also vastly more dynamic and charismatic than any of the civilians.

* * *

Colin Powell remained distant from this Washington maneuvering. During the George H. W. Bush administration's early months, he was in Atlanta, getting accustomed to his new job as commander of FORSCOM, as the U.S. Army Forces Command was known inside the army. After two years working inside the White House, he had returned to military life, but despite his efforts to blend in, Powell was hardly an ordinary general. He was the only military commander who had also served as national security advisor. When he happened to be in California in early 1989, he paid a visit to President Reagan "just to see how he was doing," as he explained in one letter. In late March, after the ceremony in which Powell received his fourth star, Reagan sent him a congratulatory note. When Powell's first grandson was born, he received another note of congratulations, this time from President Bush, who added a postscript: "Dick Cheney says that fourth star looks mighty nice on you, Colin." For good measure, in April the First Lady, Barbara Bush, scrawled a handwritten note to Powell admonishing him on his formality in addressing her as "Mrs. Bush": "If you don't call me Barbara, I'll kill you. Get permission from your mother! Love, Barbara." No other military leader of the modern era could come close to Powell when it came to friendly ties with America's political leaders.

Still, if Powell harbored any short-term ambitions for his next step after FORSCOM, they centered on his becoming the army chief of staff, the highest-ranking officer in the army. Powell valued that job for its intrinsic merits, but the position became even more attractive in the spring of 1989 because of developments involving his close friend Richard Armitage.

Armitage had been one of the leading figures in the Pentagon during the Reagan years. Carlucci, the outgoing secretary of defense, had lobbied for Armitage to be appointed undersecretary for policy in the new Bush administration, but that job went to Wolfowitz, leaving a residue of animosity between him and Armitage. Then, in April, Armitage was nominated to be secretary of the army. This raised the prospect that

Powell and Armitage could team up once again as army chief of staff and secretary of the army, the senior military and civilian positions in charge of the largest military service. "He and Rich had this idea that Rich was going to be selected secretary of the army, and he was going to be chief of staff," recalled Lawrence Wilkerson, who had just joined Powell's staff as a speechwriter. "And they had this kind of plan—it was in rough form— that they were going to take to the army and crack the whip. They were going to majorly reform the army."

This idea fell through when Texas businessman H. Ross Perot, who had clashed with Armitage during the Reagan administration, launched an intensive drive against his nomination. Armitage went to Cheney to ask if he was prepared to fight hard to win a battle in the Senate over the nomination, but the defense secretary was cool and noncommittal. "I don't know," Cheney told him. Sensing that Cheney didn't want to spend political capital on a personnel fight in his first months in office, Armitage withdrew his name from consideration, and the dreams of a Powell-Armitage combine at the top of the U.S. Army vanished.

* * *

By the spring of 1989, the Bush administration was grappling with the question of how to deal with Mikhail Gorbachev and the Soviet leadership. During the 1988 presidential campaign, Bush had taken the position that Reagan and Secretary of State Shultz had become too enamored of Gorbachev and that a tougher line toward the Soviet Union was warranted. This was more than mere domestic political posturing; it reflected the views of many within the Washington foreign policy establishment, including Brent Scowcroft and Robert Gates, for years the CIA's leading Soviet analyst.

Still, even the doubters were obliged to acknowledge the significance of the speech that Gorbachev had delivered to the United Nations at the end of 1988, in which he announced that the Soviet Union would withdraw six armored divisions from Eastern Europe and would cut the size of its armed forces by half a million troops. It was hard to imagine a more tangible symbol of fundamental change.

Gorbachev's actions served as the backdrop to Colin Powell's speech to the Army War College in May 1989. Through that speech, Powell was reminding others in the army that as national security advisor, he had done business face-to-face with Gorbachev. This was not mere showmanship or one-upmanship on Powell's behalf; he had a serious point to make, an unpopular one at that, at least for the audience he was addressing. He was saying that the army needed to be ready for major changes. The Cold War was ending. America's adversary of the past four decades was no longer so adversarial. Hence the question Powell raised: "What will all the preachers do when the devil is dead?"

Wilkerson, who had helped draft this unusual address, recalled that Powell was consciously seeking to demonstrate that he intended to be a voice in national debates about the future of American national security. "He was telling me, 'I'm not your everyday general. I've been the national security advisor to the president of the United States. I was there; I looked into Gorbachev's eyes. The Cold War's over, and I'm going to start talking about that,'" said Wilkerson.

Back in Washington, Cheney most certainly did *not* agree with Powell's view that the Cold War had ended. He repeatedly warned his colleagues that any ideas about dramatic changes in America's defense posture were premature. In the text of the major speech he prepared to give that May, the speech the White House stopped him from delivering, Cheney had written, "We hear that world politics is undergoing a fundamental change, that the Soviet threat has diminished, if not totally evaporated, and that in response to all this we must reshape our strategy for keeping the peace and securing our national interest." This was, in fact, a summation of Powell's view, and Cheney went on to reject it. "Hopes, however, cannot rule defense policy," his speech continued. "And there are a great many reasons why we should maintain the policy that has brought us to [this] point."

In light of this difference of opinion over the significance of Gorbachev, it may seem odd that Cheney was laying the groundwork to appoint Powell as chairman of the Joint Chiefs of Staff. But the contradiction diminishes when one considers that their disagreements about Gorbachev seemed of less importance than their general agreement on other issues that mattered more to them. The Democrats on Capitol Hill, who held a majority in both the House and the Senate, were beginning to talk about far-reaching cuts in the defense budget, and neither Cheney nor Powell was willing to go along with the kind of cuts the Democrats envisioned.

Moreover, ideology counted far less for Cheney at this point than the long-standing friendships and relationships that had been developed over the years. He was conservative, but he was also a member in good standing of the Ford administration's informal alumni association. It is difficult to overestimate the sense of togetherness that prevailed among the top officials of the George H. W. Bush administration. Bush, Scowcroft, Baker, and Cheney were old colleagues, and from the start they found ways to minimize or suppress many of their internal disagreements. Indeed, the attraction of working again with Bush, Baker, and Scowcroft had been part of the reason Cheney decided to leave Congress and take the job of defense secretary in the first place.

There was "almost a kind of sociology" to the togetherness of the Bush team, observed Dennis Ross, Powell's former National Security Council staffer, who was now a senior aide to Baker at the State Department. Scowcroft, Baker, and Cheney met for breakfast every Wednesday; Cheney and Baker vacationed together in Wyoming; and President Bush actively fostered and insisted upon this internal harmony. "One thing to understand about Bush Forty-one is that he *hated* the open bureaucratic warfare and the ongoing struggle [in the Reagan administration] between Weinberger and Shultz, preceded by Weinberger and [former Secretary of State Alexander] Haig," said Ross. "He just hated that. And he sort of laid down the law that it wasn't going to happen in his administration." Ross recalled that Bush said, quite bluntly, that "these are the rules, you know: we're going to work together—we can have differences, but we're going to work together. And if you expose differences, you're out."

In retrospect, it seems significant to note which alumnus of the Ford administration was *not* part of this team: Donald Rumsfeld. His absence undoubtedly had an impact on Cheney throughout the George H. W. Bush presidency; it was the only administration in which Cheney served where his close ties to Rumsfeld were not a factor. Indeed, by Rumsfeld's own subsequent account, Cheney stayed away from him during those years. Even though, as defense secretary, he had the same job that Rumsfeld had held under President Ford, Cheney didn't consult with his longtime mentor. "He may have been sensitive to President George H. W. Bush's attitude toward me, and kept his distance," Rumsfeld later wrote.

Powell, of course, was not part of the old Ford team, but independently, Cheney had gotten to know him during the late Reagan years, and Bush had worked alongside him in the West Wing. It seemed clear that he would easily fit in.

* * *

If there was any hesitation about Cheney's request to appoint Powell as chairman of the Joint Chiefs, it came from the president and, particularly, Scowcroft.

"Someday, I think it should be Colin Powell, but I don't think he's quite ready," Bush wrote in his diary. "He needs to have a big and more visible command in the Army. . . . But Cheney wants him, and I love the guy." Bush also worried he might be setting a bad precedent by appointing a chairman who had just served as national security advisor—perhaps sending a message to military leaders that the route to the top was to serve in the White House. There had already been a bad example in the previous decade, one upsetting to the military hierarchy: Alexander Haig had gone to work for Henry Kissinger in the Nixon White House as a lieutenant colonel and returned to the army a four-star general.

Scowcroft had similar concerns, and a few others. "To jump him over so many general officers could cause resentment," he explained years later. "The other thing, he had not had true Joint experience, and I thought it would be great for him to go and be NATO Supreme Allied Commander for a couple of years before he became Chairman." But Scowcroft had other reasons for his reluctance to elevate Powell, stemming from his personal experience and beliefs. In 1975, Scowcroft had chosen to give up his military career when he became national security advisor. Powell had not done that when Reagan appointed him to the same job in 1987.

Cheney believed that Scowcroft had still another, unstated reason for not wanting Powell as chairman of the Joint Chiefs: he did not want his immediate predecessor as national security advisor to be taking part in the top-level decision making of the new Bush administration.

Meanwhile, Cheney's civilian advisors were also nervous about the appointment. They believed that Powell was impressive and charismatic and, for that reason, could pose problems for the secretary of defense. Wolfowitz told Cheney directly that as good as Powell was, he might prove to be hard to control, and he suggested that perhaps Cheney shouldn't go ahead with the appointment. In the face of all these objections, Cheney was unshaken and determined. "Cheney wanted Colin Powell very hard," Scowcroft recalled.

Still dubious, Bush asked Cheney to visit Powell at his new command in Atlanta and get a better sense of him up close: Was he fitting back into the military, or was he essentially a political general who would engender resentment from other officers? Was he ready to be chairman of the Joint Chiefs, despite his relative youth? Cheney used the pretext of an inspection visit of the Central Command and Special Operations Command in Tampa and of FORSCOM in Atlanta to stop in to talk with Powell over lunch at Fort McPherson.

"I didn't ask him about the job, I didn't tell him I was thinking about him for the job," Cheney recalled years later. "Just that I was in the area, wanted to stop in, spend some time." Powell, one of the most politically attuned leaders the military has ever produced, was not fooled for a minute. "I was fairly sure Cheney had not stopped in Atlanta only for a briefing on FORSCOM training," he later wrote. But, he said, "my message to him was that I was content where I was." If there was any doubt, those last words confirm that Powell, too, was treating their conversation as a job interview.

Cheney was satisfied. "It was clear that this was a guy who loved the U.S. Army, who had no qualms at all about moving back in the U.S. Army," he decided. "It was my judgment based on that conversation that in fact this would fly and that we wouldn't get into difficulties in terms of having a lot of resistance [within the army] to it."

Cheney returned to Washington, reported his impressions to the president and to Scowcroft, and again said that he wanted Powell as chairman. They approved, and Bush announced the appointment in early August. Just as when Powell had been appointed national security advisor twenty months earlier, his nomination as chairman of the Joint Chiefs of Staff won an outpouring of praise from across the political spectrum: Benjamin Hooks, the executive director of the NAACP, hailed the choice, as did Barry Goldwater, now retired from the Senate, but still a leading conservative.

Powell won confirmation in the Senate without a single dissenting vote and was sworn in as chairman on October 1, 1989. Cheney had gotten the man he wanted.

6

THE FIRST INVASION

Colin Powell's first few weeks as chairman of the Joint Chiefs of Staff were rocky, not because of his own failings or Dick Cheney's, but because of slipups within George H. W. Bush's administration. Years later, Bush's team would come to be regarded as an unusually experienced, smooth-working, tightly knit group. In the fall of 1989, however, there was still a lot of learning on the job. Cheney and Powell found themselves confronted with two separate crises involving the potential use of American force. On both occasions, there were serious problems, delays, and miscommunications. In one of the two, Powell managed to save the day.

The first crisis involved Panama, and it erupted with an attempted coup d'état during Powell's first days as chairman. The question that had plagued U.S. officials for several years had been what to do about the Panamanian strongman, General Manuel Noriega, who had been effectively the country's dictator since 1983. He had been linked to the brutal murder of one political opponent and the beatings of many others; had nullified the results of an election earlier that year; was involved in drug trafficking; and had been indicted by two grand juries in Florida on drug and money-laundering charges.

Bush harbored unusually strong feelings about Noriega, as Powell had discovered when he was national security advisor. In the spring of 1988, the Reagan administration had tried to find a way to persuade Noriega to give up power, hoping to replicate its earlier success in convincing President Ferdinand Marcos to leave the Philippines. Powell and Secretary of State Shultz had worked out a prospective deal in which the drug trafficking charges against Noriega would be dropped if he left Panama. Vice President Bush had vigorously opposed this arrangement, arguing that it would show a lack of commitment to prosecuting drug traffickers. Powell recalled years later that he had rarely seen Bush so animated. "He keeps arguing with the president about it, he keeps chewing me out about it, this is bad, this is wrong," Powell said.

After Reagan rejected Bush's pleas, the proposed deal fell apart for other reasons, and Noriega remained in power. In early 1989, after Bush became president, he ordered an increase in preparations for military intervention in Panama. That summer Dick Cheney further paved the way by replacing the U.S. military commander responsible for Panama, General Fred Woerner. Bush and Scowcroft had approved this decision in advance; Woerner had been resisting the administration's plans for a military buildup, and it was widely believed that, as James Baker later put it, the general "had developed a severe case of 'clientitis' with Noriega." Cheney, who prided himself on being able to fire people with as few words as possible, had called the general in and said, "Fred, the President has decided to make a change. . . . It has nothing to do with you or your performance. You did everything that we wanted you to do. It's political. It's just political."

In light of this history, it is astonishing that when Major Moisés Giroldi of the Panamanian Defense Forces launched a coup against Noriega in early October, the Bush administration was paralyzed with uncertainty over what to do. But that is exactly what transpired.

Powell had been on the job for only a day when he was woken in the middle of the night to the news that an attempted coup d'état was imminent. Powell woke up Cheney, who in turn alerted Scowcroft. Yet over the next two days, the administration held back from taking any action. U.S. officials weren't sure that the coup would succeed or that Giroldi was worthy of American support. They sought guarantees that Noriega would be turned over to the United States, but Giroldi refused.

The coup attempt began on October 3, when Giroldi and his supporters seized Noriega, but the Panamanian leader was able to phone other military units for help, and within a few hours he had persuaded Giroldi to surrender. The coup not only failed but seemed to strengthen Noriega's position.

It had been, in Powell's words, a "debacle." For weeks afterward, members of Congress and the press criticized the administration's inaction. "Panama Crisis: Disarray Hindered the White House," the *New York Times* reported on its Sunday front page. David Boren, the chairman of the Senate Intelligence Committee, rejected the administration's excuses. These attacks stung because the Bush team knew it had performed poorly; years later Scowcroft would admit, "We *were* sort of Keystone Kops."

"I did not find this an auspicious start, but I had learned a few things already," Powell later wrote, one of which was that "Cheney was cool and solid" in a crisis. Over the following weeks, Scowcroft responded by setting up a new group called the Deputies Committee, consisting of the number two officials from all the national security departments and agencies, to meet regularly and coordinate quick, unified responses across the government. Meanwhile, at Powell's urging and with strong support from Bush, the new American military commander, General Max Thurman, began updating and refining the plans for a military intervention.

* * *

The second crisis during Powell's early weeks on the job involved another attempted coup d'état, this time in the Philippines. In this case, the target was not a leader the United States wanted to get rid of, but one it wanted to keep in power: President Corazon Aquino, one of America's most important friends in East Asia.

In early December, rebellious Philippine Army troops seized an air base outside Manila and threatened to attack the presidential palace. Aquino pleaded for American help, specifically for the U.S. Air Force to bomb the rebels. In Washington, senior State Department officials urged that the bombing be carried out. "We've got to do something, we've got to keep her in power, we have to use power to keep her in power," argued Lawrence Eagleburger, the deputy secretary of state.

But Powell balked, and Cheney backed him up. Bombing the rebels' airfield would likely mean deaths, injuries, and property damage, which would be blamed on the United States. Explaining his thinking years later, Powell used language similar to his early anger at Washington while he was a soldier in Vietnam: "The State Department probably pictured a neat, surgical strike," he wrote. "I envisioned anxious young pilots flying their first combat missions, not precision-tooled automatons." Powell told his colleagues, "I can guarantee you that the Filipinos are going to blast us at their funerals, no matter which side we hurt." He reminded them that some in the Philippines still resented the United States as the former colonial power there.

Instead, working with the American military commander, Powell came up with a different solution, called an "air cap": the United States sent F-4 Phantom jets from Clark Air Base to fly over Manila, and particularly over the rebel airfield, with instructions to show they meant business and would shoot down any planes that tried to take off. Karl Jackson, then an Asia specialist for Scowcroft, later said the air cap conveyed a simple message to rebel pilots: "You fly, you die." Once the American planes were overhead, the Philippine rebels backed down, and the coup ended in failure. Powell's gambit had worked.

Still, the process by which the Bush administration arrived at this successful result was nowhere near so neat and clean. The attempted coup had started just as the president and Scowcroft were traveling to Malta for a summit meeting with Mikhail Gorbachev. In their absence, Vice President Dan Quayle went to the White House to summon a National Security Council meeting. But Cheney refused to come. He pointed out that as vice president, Quayle had no legal authority to give orders: he argued that the vice president was not in the formal chain of military command, which flowed from the president to the secretary of defense to American military commanders. What Quayle was labeling a National Security Council meeting wasn't even a valid one, Cheney said.

The result of this contretemps was that while Quayle was in the White House Situation Room calling Bush and Scowcroft on Air Force One to get their approval, Cheney was separately making calls to them from his home. Meanwhile, both he and Quayle were also phoning Powell at the military command center inside the Pentagon. The situation was every bit as disorderly as the Bush administration's efforts two months earlier to deal with the coup in Panama. This time, luckily, the outcome was better.

In retrospect, this episode had two important longer-term consequences. It may at first glance seem ironic that Cheney, who would go on to become the most powerful vice president in modern American history, would have objected to Quayle's assertion of authority as vice president during the Philippine crisis. The irony is real, but the relationship between Cheney's views on the vice presidency in 1989 and his views after 2001 may be more complicated: the dispute with Quayle may have concentrated Cheney's mind on the vague legal authority of the vice president so that, when he took office in 2001, he sought and obtained from President George W. Bush much greater power than Quayle could ever have envisioned for himself.

The second consequence was subtler and more indirect. Within the Bush inner circle, the handling of the Philippine crisis helped crystallize the perception of Quayle as an outsider, too eager to assert himself in internal policy deliberations and to seek attention from the conservative wing of the Republican Party.

Quayle later boasted that he had played the decisive role in putting down the coup. Powell would ridicule that assertion as self-aggrandizing. "Some of us remember the incident a little differently," he scoffed. Even worse for the vice president, Bush recorded in his diary at the time that he was becoming "thoroughly annoyed" at Quayle. During this same period, the vice president was also letting it be known to right-wing columnists that he thought the administration was too soft in its dealings with the Soviet Union. While others in the administration such as Cheney and Gates remained skeptical of Gorbachev, Quayle was the most conservative of all of them, sometimes suggesting that Gorbachev's reforms might be merely a trick to delude the United States into letting down its defenses. "Quayle has to go out and shore up the right wing," Bush told his diary. "I find this disturbing."

Quayle's efforts also shed light on how Cheney managed to become so fully accepted within George H. W. Bush's national security team despite his strong conservative views. Here, the contrast between Cheney and Quayle provides part of the answer. In those years, Cheney was generally a team player, whereas Quayle was less so. Quayle was, clumsily, trying to buttress his standing with the political right, but Cheney wasn't thinking about domestic politics at all; he had happily given up the need for political campaigning when he left Congress for the Pentagon.

In fact, when it came to politics and ideology, Quayle's presence in the Bush administration helped to normalize Cheney. Cheney wasn't seen as the right-winger inside the administration; Quayle was. Many years later, Cheney's former colleagues, including Scowcroft and President Bush himself, would express surprise at Cheney's hard-line positions during the George W. Bush administration. But Cheney's beliefs hadn't changed much; instead, he held greater power and his views attracted greater attention under the younger President Bush than under his father.

* * *

By December, the Bush team and the U.S. military were fully prepared for military action in Panama. Given the slipshod response to the failed coup two months earlier and the biting criticism the administration had received, it would not have taken much to provoke an American intervention to topple Noriega. "All of us vowed never to let another such opportunity pass us by," Secretary of State Baker would recall.

Administration officials had been laying plans for how to intervene if there were another coup attempt. That didn't happen; Noriega had brutally eradicated all opposition within the military. Nevertheless, he soon gave Bush and his top aides the chance they were seeking. In mid-December, Panamanian soldiers killed a U.S. Marine and, in a separate incident, beat up a navy officer and groped his wife. Beyond the general interest in protecting the Panama Canal, Bush could now claim to be protecting American lives. He convened his top national security officials to decide what to do. Although previously American military leaders had been reluctant to go to war in Panama, Powell was now strongly in favor. "There will be a few dozen casualties if we go," he told Bush at the decisive meeting. "If we don't go, there will be a few dozen casualties over the next few weeks, and we'll still have Noriega."

But questions remained: how to intervene, and with how much force? Here Powell played the crucial role. One possibility under consideration was a tight, lean military operation to snatch Noriega and take him out of Panama. Powell argued against this on the grounds that merely getting rid of Noriega wouldn't solve the problems in the country. The entire Panamanian military was corrupt, and someone similar to Noriega might seize power, he warned. Instead, the United States needed to dismantle and remake the country's armed forces; it should also be prepared to install a new government, led by the winners in the democratic election that Noriega had nullified. Powell argued that the United States could accomplish these objectives only with a massive military intervention.

His proposal for overwhelming force was, of course, in line with the principles Caspar Weinberger had set down while Powell was serving under him four years earlier. According to Richard Armitage, the original planning had called for one division in the operation, but Powell chose to deploy two instead. "He put in another division because he didn't know what we were going to find outside of Panama City," Armitage explained. "And his feeling was [it was] a lot easier to get them [the extra troops] home than it would have been to get them down there."

Powell emerged as a strong hawk on Panama, a role that would contrast with his more cautious stance on the use of force in later disputes, notably over Iraq. He was aware that before he took over as chairman of the Joint Chiefs, the civilians in the Bush administration, including Scowcroft and Cheney, had been irritated at the military's reluctance to use force in Panama; that was why Woerner had been replaced. Powell had also seen firsthand how strongly Bush wanted to get rid of Noriega.

There was no serious opposition to military intervention among others at the top levels of the administration, either. There was some debate at lower levels, however, about whether the incidents involving the U.S. soldiers in Panama provided sufficient justification for an American invasion. One of the few skeptics was Paul Wolfowitz, Cheney's top civilian advisor, who wasn't convinced that the death of one soldier and the assault upon another soldier and his wife amounted to a "smoking gun." During one meeting in Cheney's office, when one of Wolfowitz's aides raised questions about the military operation, Powell mocked him for being too timid.

The military plan had been given the code name Operation Blue Spoon. It called for the ouster and replacement not just of Noriega but of the entire Panamanian Defense Forces. At the last minute, Powell's top military aides decided that "Blue Spoon" was too arbitrary and undignified a name—one of the planners said it sounded like a pornographic movie—and therefore, hurried discussions commenced to choose a new name. Someone jokingly suggested "Operation Just Because," reflecting the underlying reality that the Bush administration had been waiting to use force to get rid of Noriega and that the stated reasons for the operation were secondary. After the kidding ended, they settled on Operation Just Cause.

Bush approved the plans at a final White House meeting, and Just Cause commenced in the early hours of December 20, 1989, with nearly 27,000 U.S. troops taking part in the operation (of these, 17,000 were dispatched to Panama to join nearly 10,000 already there). It was the first deployment of any kind since the invasion of Grenada six years earlier and, more to the point, the largest deployment of U.S. forces overseas since the Vietnam War. The invasion went relatively smoothly and succeeded quickly. Noriega at first disappeared and then, four days later, amid a massive manhunt, took refuge in the Vatican's embassy in Panama.

Having heard that Noriega hated rock music, the U.S. military for a time blasted heavy-metal music at a deafening volume outside the embassy, to the point where the papal nuncio and Vatican officials complained. Powell ordered that the music be turned off. Finally, two weeks after the start of the invasion, Noriega surrendered and was flown to Florida, where he was arrested and eventually convicted of drug charges. He would spend the next two decades of his life in prison. As Powell had predicted, the casualties in Operation Just Cause were relatively light: 23 American soldiers killed and 325 wounded. Several hundred Panamanians died.

* * *

The Panama operation marked the apotheosis of Colin Powell, the point where he began to emerge as the most powerful chairman of the Joint Chiefs of Staff in American history. There were several reasons for this, stemming not only from his personal strengths but also from bureaucratic and institutional changes.

Powell was the first chairman of the Joint Chiefs to go to war following the reforms of the Goldwater-Nichols Act. That law, passed three

years earlier to help ease frictions among the military services, strength-
ened the power of the chairman by making him the principal military
advisor to the president and secretary of defense. It was no longer necessary for the chairman to put together a consensus, or to offer a least-
common-denominator opinion reconciling the varying views of the
army, navy, air force, and marines. Instead, the chairman's opinion was
decisive. Moreover, Goldwater-Nichols gave the chairman full control
over the Joint Staff, the more than fifteen hundred military officers working on planning and operations inside the Pentagon. Previously, this
staff had worked for the four service chiefs collectively; now, when the
Joint Staff worked up plans for a military operation, it no longer had to
consult laboriously, one by one, with each individual service.

In practical terms, this meant that Powell was no longer required to
give each of the military services at least a little of what it wanted. In the
Panama invasion, the U.S. Army was given an overwhelmingly dominant role; it had 22,000 soldiers taking part, while the other military services together had a total of 5,000. When the marine commandant asked
for the inclusion of marine amphibious units, Powell simply turned him
down. He had the power to do that, whereas his predecessors had not.

Curiously, over the years, as historians and military scholars have
pointed to the role of the Goldwater-Nichols Act in amplifying the power
of the chairman, Powell has insisted otherwise. His argument rests on
other language in the statute saying that the chairman is still merely an
advisor to the president and secretary of defense, who are the decision
makers. Under this reading, the military commanders in the field did not
report to Powell, but to Bush and to Cheney. In practice, it didn't work
that way: Cheney signed an order, at Powell's request, that all instructions from Cheney to the commanders or messages from the commanders to Cheney go through Powell as chairman of the Joint Chiefs. "No
one [of the military commanders] would dare go see the secretary [of
defense] without coming to see me first, and telling me later what he
talked about," Powell explained.

Powell regularly attributed the power he wielded as chairman to
Cheney's support for him. "I was empowered not by [the Goldwater-
Nichols Act] but by Dick Cheney, to be his partner in helping him run
the Pentagon," he said. "Nothing in the law said he had to listen to my

advice, had to hear it if he didn't want to, or couldn't take his advice from the guard at the desk." The only thing the new law had done, Powell maintained, was to make the process inside the military work more smoothly. Summing it up more than a quarter century later, Powell said that Cheney "gave me enormous influence."

Whatever the impact of the new law, Goldwater-Nichols was only one component of Powell's augmented power. The rest was personal, stemming from his political talents inside the administration and his skill in public appearances. Panama was the first American war to be covered after the arrival of cable television news. Remembering the impact of negative news coverage during the Vietnam War, Cheney and Powell chose to dominate the news about Panama by giving regular briefings on how the war was going. Cheney, by nature closemouthed and reticent, let Powell take the podium for large portions of the briefings. Powell had the confidence and the sense of humor to make the most of this situation. In one memorable exchange, soon after Noriega went into hiding at the beginning of the invasion, a reporter asked what might happen if Noriega remained at large. Powell pointed out that the Panamanian strongman had already been "decapitated" from the Panamanian leadership, and then noted drily that it had been years since Noriega had lived in the jungle. "He's used to a different kind of lifestyle, and I'm not sure he would be up to being chased around the countryside by Army Rangers, Special Forces, and light infantry units," he quipped. Since Vietnam, American military leaders had come across in public as stiff and careful. Powell was telegenic, relaxed, and pithy.

Throughout the operation, Cheney and Powell worked extremely closely. The two men could often be found monitoring events together in the Pentagon's National Military Command Center. Before the invasion, Cheney had told Powell that he wanted as much information as possible, from as many sources as possible; Powell should not try to limit information flowing to the defense secretary or polish it into a clean, neat package. (Here, Powell was getting a taste of Cheney's career-long preference for raw, undigested intelligence.) Powell complied with this request without complaint, and Cheney was satisfied. Inside the Pentagon, Cheney asked probing questions of Powell; at the White House, he explained what Powell and other military leaders were doing and backed them up.

Powell complained during the Panama operation about the intrusion of civilian leaders into decisions that he felt should be left up to the military, a sore point with U.S. military leaders dating back to Vietnam. His criticism was directed not at Cheney but at Scowcroft, the national security advisor. Thus, the personal relationships within the George H. W. Bush administration on Panama were almost the opposite of the way they would emerge thirteen years later, at the time of the Iraq War: on Panama, Powell was aligned with Cheney and at odds with Scowcroft. At one point early on, Scowcroft urged Powell to destroy Panama City's broadcasting tower so that it couldn't be used by Noriega's allies for propaganda purposes. Powell thought the tower was ultimately harmless and should be left for use by the democratically elected government that would take Noriega's place. At another point, Scowcroft pressured Powell to order U.S. troops to rescue some American reporters trapped by the fighting.

"Scowcroft was making me crazy. They [White House officials] started to get deeply involved in Panama," Powell acknowledged years later. "We had to sort of say, 'Guys, take a deep breath. Don't call me every time you see something on television or a reporter calls you. Give us some time.'" The tension between the two men may have been amplified by the fact that each one knew enough to question the decisions of the other: Powell had served in Scowcroft's job as national security advisor; Scowcroft, in turn, was the only one of Bush's top advisors who had spent most of his career in the military.

Overall, though, the Bush team worked together smoothly; there were no miscommunications of the sort that had emerged over the previous three months. That was the first and most immediate impact: the operation was a success, and the result was to increase greatly the confidence of the entire foreign policy team, including Cheney, who had never served in the military, and Powell, who had been on the job for only three months. Cheney viewed Panama as the point where the Bush administration learned and practiced how to send American troops into battle. Panama was "the right thing to do, I don't have any doubts about that at all," he reflected years later. "But I have to say, I think it also was very important because it gave us the opportunity to go through the process of using force, and that was very important later on. . . . The only way to learn it is to do it."

* * *

Another, much broader impact was that Panama represented a clear military victory, easing the sense of defeat that had lingered in the United States since Vietnam. To be sure, America had "won" when it sent troops to Grenada a few years earlier, but that was such a small and short operation, with barely a quarter as many troops, that it hardly counted. "In breaking the mind-set of the American people about the use of force in the post-Vietnam era," Secretary of State Baker wrote, "Panama established an emotional predicate that permitted us to build the public support so essential to the success of Operation Desert Storm thirteen months later."

For Powell in particular, Panama confirmed the wisdom of the lessons he had drawn from Vietnam. "Have a clear political objective and stick to it," he wrote. "Use all the force necessary, and do not apologize for going in big if that is what it takes. Decisive force ends wars quickly and in the end saves lives. Whatever threats we faced in the future, I intended to make these rules the bedrock of my military career."

Still, it remained unclear to what extent these lessons would apply elsewhere in the world. After all, the Panama crisis had taken place in Latin America, where the United States had declared a special interest in guiding the course of events since the Monroe Doctrine; and not merely in Latin America but in Panama, where the United States possessed a clear security interest in protecting the Panama Canal. Would the United States be so willing to employ force in, say, the Middle East, or Europe or Asia, where other powers might become more closely involved?

There was another, related factor that could have made Panama a unique case, perhaps an exception to what might happen elsewhere: the Panamanian Defense Forces were no challenge at all. It was clear that if the United States used enough force, it would achieve an easy victory. "With Powell, he had to know it was doable. And he knew Panama was doable," said Lawrence Wilkerson, Powell's longtime aide. "Later, with Iraq, he was not sure."

7

A MUCH BIGGER WAR

During the last two months of 1989, while Dick Cheney and Colin Powell were preparing for and carrying out the successful invasion of Panama, historic changes were unfolding elsewhere in the world—changes that would carry vastly greater impact for the two men, for the U.S. military they oversaw, and for America's role in the world.

On November 9, 1989, East Germans burst through and began tearing down the Berlin Wall, the symbol of the divisions of the Cold War. Despite urgent appeals to Moscow by East German leaders, Soviet president Mikhail Gorbachev did not intervene. Instead, he instructed them to avoid the use of force, and thus paved the way for the collapse of the East German regime. Over the following weeks, there were successful uprisings to topple the Communist governments in Czechoslovakia, Bulgaria, and Romania, along with changes at the top in Poland and Hungary. By the end of the year, the Soviet Empire in Eastern Europe had all but disappeared, replaced by a collection of new leaders, all of them anti-Communist and most of them eager to move toward democracy.

At the same time, the relationship between the United States and the Soviet Union was rapidly changing. When George H. W. Bush became president, he and his new administration had viewed Gorbachev as, above all, a competitor, taking a more dubious view of the Soviet leader than the outgoing Reagan administration. An early memo from Brent Scowcroft to Bush was called "Getting Ahead of Gorbachev." The memo argued that Gorbachev's new foreign policies and his reduction in the size of the Soviet armed forces were aimed at weakening NATO resolve and winning greater diplomatic support for Soviet policies around the world. "He is very good; we have to be better," Scowcroft told Bush.

Bush held his first summit meeting with Gorbachev in Malta in early December 1989, amid the upheavals in Eastern Europe. By then, it was clear that Gorbachev not only sought but desperately needed a new, accommodating relationship with the United States in order to proceed with reforms at home. The Bush team's earlier skepticism about Gorbachev melted away. The Soviet leader became not an adversary but something of a partner, and the United States entered into a new, more collaborative relationship with the Soviet Union. Baker began to seek deals with Gorbachev and Soviet foreign minister Eduard Shevardnadze to settle conflicts in various corners of the world, from Afghanistan to Angola to Germany.

For the Pentagon, the impact of these changes was sweeping. Cheney and Powell would spend their remaining three years in office trying to come to grips with the consequences. The Cold War was indeed coming to an end, as Powell had said two years earlier. That, in turn, raised immediate questions about the future of the U.S. defense budget and American troop deployments overseas. Immediately after the fall of the Berlin Wall, Democratic leaders in Congress began calling for a "peace dividend," in which funds previously devoted to defense could be redirected to domestic programs. That December, James Sasser, the chairman of the Senate Budget Committee, spoke of "this unique moment in world history" and "the dawn of the primacy of domestic economics." Former secretary of defense Robert McNamara, one of the architects of the Vietnam War, testified before Sasser's committee that the reduced threat from the Soviet Union meant that the three-hundred-billion-dollar defense budget could be cut by half over the next decade.

The changed relationship with the Soviet Union had a subtler impact on American military strategy and the Weinberger-Powell doctrine regarding the use of force. It opened new possibilities: if the United States now found itself with more troops than it needed in Germany, then some of those troops would be available for use elsewhere.

Powell had helped foster the doctrine of using overwhelming force (or, as he called it, "decisive force") to resolve any conflict in which the United States found itself. But in practice, this doctrine had not been applied much, except in Panama—that is, on America's home turf of the Western Hemisphere. Farther from home (the Middle East, Europe, Asia), other rules came into play, among them the doctrine of "limited war." Since the end of World War II, the United States had held back from wielding all the power at its disposal, because of the fear that the Soviet Union (or, in East Asia, China) might intervene and possibly escalate a local conflict toward direct confrontation and even nuclear war. But with the easing of the Cold War, such fears were drastically reduced, allowing for new opportunities for American action, including the application of overwhelming force.

* * *

During the first half of 1990, Cheney and Powell were preoccupied with drafting new budgets and plans for scaling back the armed forces. Under pressure from Congress, they realized that they needed to respond to the dramatic changes in Eastern Europe and to the considerably reduced threat from the Soviet Union. Their goal was to come up with a blueprint that would satisfy congressional demands for a peace dividend yet leave the Pentagon with most of its existing capabilities.

Of the two men, Powell was certainly the more willing to proceed with cutbacks. He had been talking about this subject since the spring of 1989, well before he became chairman, when he had delivered the speech that asked, "What does the preacher do when the devil dies?" A month after becoming chairman of the Joint Chiefs and a few days before the fall of the Berlin Wall, he began jotting notes to himself about the sorts of reductions he wanted to accomplish during his tenure: scaling back the army by 30 percent, from 760,000 to 525,000; and cutting the number of American troops in Europe by more than two-thirds, from 300,000 to between 75,000 and 100,000. "These levels would be tough to sell to Cheney," he acknowledged to himself.

Yet, in the context of the politics of this period, Powell and Cheney were not at odds with each other. Rather, they were allies, in battles where the adversaries were the liberal Democrats in Congress, who sought even more drastic reductions at the Pentagon. Near the end of 1989, Cheney summoned the service chiefs to his office and told them to come up with proposals for cutbacks. If we don't do it ourselves, somebody will do it to us, he told them. Recalling this period a decade later, Cheney said he was trying "to find some way to keep this thing from coming unraveled on us. . . . 'Peace dividend, peace dividend,' we heard that over and over again."

Both Cheney and Powell had historical precedents in mind that they wanted to avoid. "Cheney was worried that as the Cold War was ending, the United States, as it had done after World War I, after World War II, after Korea, and to some degree after Vietnam, would overcorrect," said Eric Edelman, one of Cheney's civilian advisors. "And that it would draw down too deeply. And that it would be very hard then to come back from it."

Powell drew similar comparisons. Testifying before the House Budget Committee in early 1990, with Cheney at his side, he reminisced about his days as a battalion commander after the end of the Vietnam War, "when I only had 30 percent of my officers and 60 percent of the troops I was allowed. The equipment didn't work. . . . Let's not go through a demobilization. Let's not put us on a ski slope that sends us back into the days of hollow armed forces." Powell was particularly eager to avoid cuts in the army, the service where he had spent his career. Indeed, his aide Lawrence Wilkerson recalls that Powell's mantra during this period was "Save the army."

Cheney and Powell worked so closely together that they became almost a tag team. They traveled around the country telling defense manufacturers to prepare for reductions as the Cold War was winding down. In congressional hearings, the two men didn't even have to coordinate their testimony, because each knew what the other would say: Cheney would talk about the overall policy concerning defense cutbacks and then would turn the podium over to Powell, who would talk about the military aspects of the cuts. "We never even had a piece of paper in front of us. We just knew each other so well," Powell said years later.

Cheney delegated his top civilian aides to work with the military to restructure the armed forces and to create a set of principles to guide the cutbacks. Powell worked closely with Undersecretary of Defense Paul

Wolfowitz and his deputy, Lewis (Scooter) Libby. Eventually, they came up with a blueprint and got White House approval for it. The president was set to announce the plans at a gathering of the Aspen Institute, in Colorado, on August 2, 1990. It was to be a gala occasion, with British prime minister Margaret Thatcher in attendance and with Powell and Baker standing alongside Bush to underscore the importance of the president's announcement. In the prepared text of his speech, Bush was set to declare, "The cold war is now drawing to a close" and to propose a "rational restructuring" of America's armed forces, "an orderly reduction, not a fire sale." The Pentagon released a new strategy paper envisioning that America's armed forces could be cut back from 2.1 million to 1.6 million over five years.

In fact, Bush did deliver that speech, but nobody paid much attention. Other events had intervened.

* * *

To the American public, Iraq's invasion of Kuwait came out of the blue. To Cheney, Powell, and other senior officials in Washington, it did not; they had worried for a long time about such a possibility. When the Iran-Iraq War ended in 1988, Iran was prostrate, no longer able to provide any military counterbalance to Iraq's million-man army. At the same time, Iraq itself was left with a huge war debt it had little ability to repay. American officials grew concerned that Saddam Hussein might seek to use his army to exert power elsewhere in the Middle East.

Throughout most of the 1980s, it had been American policy to help Iraq against revolutionary Iran. But after the Iran-Iraq War ended, some American strategists began to argue that the United States should switch direction and try to keep Saddam Hussein in check either by covertly strengthening Iran or by building up America's own forces in the region.

Cheney first was drawn into this issue during his early months as secretary of defense. Admiral William Crowe, Powell's predecessor as chairman of the Joint Chiefs of Staff, had issued a new statement of U.S. defense policy that reduced the importance of protecting the Persian Gulf. Crowe's logic was that the ongoing changes in the Soviet Union had greatly lessened the possibility of a Soviet invasion of the Persian Gulf, a longtime American concern. Cheney disagreed, contending that there could still be a threat to American interests in the Gulf from some other country.

"Do you defend the Saudi peninsula, the Arabian peninsula?" he explained years later. "At one point, Crowe wanted to drop that off." Cheney waited until Powell had replaced Crowe and then revised what Crowe had written, restoring the emphasis on the Persian Gulf. "We insisted on identifying Saudi Arabia as a strategically vital part of the world for us, and something we had to defend," Cheney said.

In the summer of 1990, Cheney began to get urgent warnings from Israel about Saddam Hussein's military ambitions. In clandestine meetings, Israeli defense minister Moshe Arens, accompanied by the head of Mossad, Israel's intelligence service, and the director of Israeli military intelligence, warned Cheney that Saddam's agents were trying to buy nuclear weapons technology that would make Iraq a threat not only to Israel but also to Saudi Arabia and Kuwait. This was an early example of what was to become an extremely close relationship between Israeli officials and Dick Cheney. Arens and other Israeli leaders would be in regular contact with Cheney over the following months.

By late July, American intelligence agencies began reporting that Iraqi troops and tanks were moving toward the border with Kuwait. In the early morning hours of August 2, the invasion began. The Bush administration scrambled to figure out how to respond. At the first, hurried meeting of the National Security Council that morning, after the CIA had finished its overview of the invasion, Bush asked what had been the reactions from Iran and Israel. "Arens is saying, 'I told you so,'" Cheney answered.

* * *

Now, after the Iraqi invasion of Kuwait, America's ever-warmer relationship with Gorbachev and the Soviet Union became vital. For all the actions that the United States and other countries took over the next eight months, nothing was as important as what did *not* happen: the Soviet Union did not intervene to support Iraq.

At the height of the Cold War, any American action against a Soviet client in the Middle East would have raised the risk of Soviet military intervention. The Soviet Union had been Iraq's leading arms supplier in the 1980s, providing it with more than $23 billion in arms, including Scud missile technology. The Soviets also helped Iraq develop its oil industry. But the Bush administration recognized that the dynamics had changed. On the day of the Iraqi invasion, Baker happened to be overseas, meeting with Shevardnadze. They negotiated a joint U.S.-Soviet statement condemning the Iraqi aggression, which the two men announced, side by side, at Moscow's Vnukovo airport. The world's two superpowers were now working at least loosely on the same side, in the heart of the Middle East. Baker would later call this "the day the Cold War ended." He pointed out that when Gorbachev acquiesced to the fall of the Berlin Wall and the collapse of communism in Eastern Europe, these were "essentially passive reactions to an inexorable tide of events." This time, on Iraq, the Soviet Union was actively joining the United States to denounce a former Soviet ally.

The new partnership with the Soviets thus made it conceivable for the United States to contemplate the use of force against Saddam Hussein, and even to think of using overwhelming force. The issue then became: what should the Bush administration do? To that question, Colin Powell and Dick Cheney had different answers. Iraq marked the point where the viewpoints between the two men began to diverge, even if the public was not aware at the time.

* * *

Any examination of the different ideas Powell and Cheney held in the lead-up to the Persian Gulf War has to start with the legacy of Vietnam. That war had taught different lessons to military and civilian leaders. Powell was reflecting the military reaction to Vietnam; Cheney, the response of many civilian leaders.

After Vietnam, military leaders were convinced that one of the primary reasons for America's failure was that the generals and admirals had been too acquiescent to civilian leaders such as President Lyndon Johnson and Secretary of Defense Robert McNamara without telling the civilians what was feasible and without asking them to specify the goal or mission of American forces. Powell fully embraced this line of thinking. "As a midlevel career officer, I had been appalled by the docility of the Joint Chiefs of Staff, fighting the war in Vietnam without ever pressing the political leaders to lay out clear objectives for them," he recalled.

Since Vietnam, the U.S. military had engaged in only relatively small conflicts such as Grenada and Panama. Iraq was different: it had a battle-hardened army of a million men. If the Bush administration was going to contemplate military action against Iraq, Powell was determined to ask questions and to do so early. Richard Haass, an aide to Scowcroft who took part in these deliberations, would later write of Powell, "His formative years were in Vietnam, and he took with him a suspicion of civilians who cooked up ideas that got a lot of young men and women in uniform killed."

Cheney's thinking served as a counterpoint to Powell's, reflecting the attitudes of civilian leaders who came to believe that the U.S. military had become too cautious. In some ways, this was merely a part of Cheney's own distinctive viewpoint, developed when he was Gerald Ford's chief of staff: that the United States needed to restore the executive power weakened by Congress in the wake of Vietnam. But the idea that military leaders had become reluctant to use force extended well beyond Cheney. Bush and Scowcroft had reflected the same thinking when they authorized the replacement of General Woerner before the invasion of Panama. Moreover, in the months leading up to the Gulf War, Cheney and Scowcroft formed a bond in talking about "our reluctant generals."

Cheney argued that the United States couldn't allow Saddam Hussein to seize permanent control of Kuwait, because Iraq would then control 20 percent of the world's oil reserves. Even worse, it would then be in a position to threaten Saudi Arabia, which, together with Kuwait, could give Saddam control of nearly half the world's reserves. "Initially we should sort this out from our strategic interests in Saudi Arabia and oil," he told his colleagues in the initial meetings after the invasion.

In this emphasis, Cheney was not alone. Bush and Scowcroft held similar beliefs, although in public they tended to emphasize other rationales, such as preserving international borders and protecting international law. At the time and for years afterward, all the top leaders of the Bush administration would insist that the Gulf War was not about oil. But in the immediate aftermath of the invasion of Kuwait, the subject of oil dominated the administration's discussions.

Cheney had additional reasons for endorsing a military response to Saddam Hussein that were more closely linked to his own long-standing views. One was his perpetual concern about America appearing weak.

"Saudi Arabia and others will cut and run if we are weak," he told the National Security Council at its first meeting after the invasion. Another was his concern about Iraq acquiring weapons of mass destruction. Here, the Israelis played a leading role in alerting Cheney to this danger. On August 9, one week after the invasion of Kuwait, Moshe Arens wrote to Cheney, "We are very concerned with Iraqi threats to use CW [chemical weapons]." Indeed, in Cheney's mind, the issues of oil and weapons of mass destruction were intertwined: new oil revenue from Kuwait could enable Saddam Hussein to buy new weaponry, including nuclear weapons and missiles, Cheney scrawled on a notepad during one of the Bush team's early meetings.

These differences between Cheney and Powell emerged in the first days after the Iraqi invasion and would persist for months. Powell began to wage a quiet battle of ideas, against not just Cheney but also the White House. At first, while acknowledging the strategic importance of Saudi Arabia, he questioned whether it was worth going to war over Kuwait and whether Americans would be willing to support such a war. At a meeting with Cheney and Wolfowitz immediately after the invasion, Powell asked, "Wait a minute, it's Kuwait. Does anybody really care about Kuwait?" At the first National Security Council meeting soon afterward, he put it somewhat differently: "Should we put out a strong redline on Saudi Arabia as a vital interest?" he asked. "I think there is no choice." What Powell was suggesting was that Kuwait would have been outside that "redline."

Bush clearly rejected the line of thinking about abandoning Kuwait when he issued his warning a few days after the Iraqi invasion: "This will not stand, this will not stand, this aggression against Kuwait"—a fervent declaration that caught Powell by surprise. "Had the President just committed himself to liberating Kuwait?" he remembered wondering. "Did he mean to do it by diplomatic and economic pressure, or by force?"

In those early days, Powell warned his colleagues that getting Iraqi troops out of Kuwait would be much more difficult than any American military operation since Vietnam. "This is harder than Panama and Libya," he said. "This would be the NFL, not a scrimmage." He argued that deploying troops to defend Saudi Arabia, rather than trying to dislodge Iraq from Kuwait, would be "the most prudent option."

Cheney was irked at these arguments, and he soon delivered an icy rebuke. "Colin, you're Chairman of the Joint Chiefs," he told Powell after that first NSC meeting. "You're not Secretary of State. You're not the National Security Adviser anymore. And you're not Secretary of Defense. So stick to military matters." Cheney told Powell he wanted to hear not policy discussions or diplomatic advice, but concrete military options.

Bush and Scowcroft decided to send an emissary to Saudi Arabia to persuade the kingdom of the necessity of accepting U.S. troops on its soil. The original plan had been to send Scowcroft and Powell, but Cheney argued successfully that he should be the one to go instead of Scowcroft; as the secretary of defense, he was the official responsible for American deployments. Then, having won that argument, Cheney argued against including Powell on the trip because he felt that Powell had been too hesitant in the discussions about military options. He brought General Norman Schwarzkopf, the head of the U.S. Central Command, in place of Powell. On Cheney's trip, the Saudis agreed to allow American forces on their soil, and within hours, with Bush's approval, Cheney ordered American F-15 warplanes to Saudi Arabia.

Over the following weeks, through the end of September, Powell continued to question the idea of going to war against Iraq to expel its troops from Kuwait. His quiet campaign did not rest solely on opposition to the use of force. Rather, he had an alternative strategy to offer, one that he hoped could resolve the crisis without military action. It was the classic strategy of containment, a version of America's Cold War strategy against the Soviet Union: to prevent Saddam from going any farther than Kuwait, to strengthen America's alliances against Iraq, and to apply sanctions and other economic pressure that might, over time, force Iraq to yield.

In an effort to enlist the support of Secretary of State James Baker, Powell placed a call in September to Dennis Ross, who was in charge of policy planning at the State Department. Powell and Ross knew each other well; Ross had worked on Powell's staff when Powell was Reagan's national security advisor. "Can you arrange a private meeting for me with Baker?" Powell asked Ross. "I want this [meeting to be] kind of outside the system. Can you do that?" Ross asked what he wanted to talk about. Powell laid out his arguments, first to Ross and then subsequently to Baker. "It was about 'Why do we want to go to war with Iraq? Isn't containing good enough?'" Ross recalled in an interview years later. "He was saying, 'We should be really mindful of what we are getting into. And what it's going to take to do it.'" Ross said that Baker heard Powell out but wasn't willing to go along or accept his arguments because he was completely loyal to Bush and felt that the president had already committed himself to liberating Kuwait.

In suggesting a strategy of containment, Powell could find no allies at the top levels of the Bush administration, but in September a member of Cheney's staff, Zalmay Khalilzad, wrote a paper for Cheney titled, "The Case for Containment." Khalilzad, a civilian Middle East specialist who had been an aide to Paul Wolfowitz during the Reagan administration, found himself working "in parallel" with Powell, preparing papers on the subject of containment, though Powell was obviously of vastly higher rank and status than Khalilzad.

"The argument for containment was: Saddam has taken over a small part of the oil, so to speak—important but not vital. The Saudis need us now, very badly. And we can go sit on Saudi oil, and do a containment of Saddam like we did of the Soviet Union," Khalilzad explained. "And eventually, they're going to collapse, and we can squeeze them. But meanwhile, we've got the bigger piece of the pie [in Saudi Arabia]."

Still, while Khalilzad was thinking along the same lines as Powell, there was a difference: Khalilzad was a policy planner, responsible only for giving Cheney options. Containment was merely one of two options he gave his boss. A second paper laid out the case against containment and in favor of military action.

Not surprisingly, Khalilzad found that Cheney was inclined toward war. Bush and Scowcroft had already made clear they didn't want to accept the Iraqi occupation of Kuwait, and Cheney himself was arguing for military action from the outset. "No non-military action is likely to produce any positive result," he had written in notes to himself the day after the invasion. "U.S. military power—the only thing Hussein fears." The key to success would be America's "determination to use whatever force is necessary."

This debate over going to war never got heated; in fact, it was remarkably civil. When Powell continued to urge a containment policy, Cheney decided to let him make the case directly to the president. In the last week of September, he brought Powell to the White House, and Powell laid out his arguments to Bush, pointing out that the United States could keep troops in Saudi Arabia while relying on economic sanctions to force Saddam Hussein to pull his troops out of Kuwait. Bush listened, but told Powell, "I really don't think we have time for sanctions to work." Instead, the president asked for more military planning for an invasion of Kuwait.

Powell's private appeal to Bush was not made public at the time. After the episode came to light a year later, well after the end of the war, Powell was accused of having been a "reluctant warrior." Acknowledging this criticism in his memoir, he was not at all defensive. Reluctant warrior? "Guilty," Powell said. "War is a deadly game, and I do not believe in spending the lives of Americans lightly. My responsibility that day was to lay out all the options for the nation's civilian leadership."

Former officials of the George H. W. Bush administration have pointed to this meeting, where Powell laid out the case against war directly to Bush, as a classic example of how collegial the discussions were during that administration: although Cheney and Powell disagreed, Cheney went out of his way to make sure Powell's views were not minimized or suppressed. That is certainly true, but Cheney admitted years later that while he wanted the president to hear Powell's arguments, his motives weren't entirely lofty. "I didn't want Powell to be able to say, after the fact, that we hadn't listened to him," he wrote.

For several weeks after that Oval Office meeting, it remained theoretically possible for the administration to switch strategies or even pursue both of them; the troops flooding into Saudi Arabia would have been necessary for a defensive policy of containment as well as for an invasion. But by the end of October, in another White House meeting, Powell and Cheney told Bush it was time to choose. Cheney pointed out that the forces sufficient to defend Saudi Arabia, about 250,000 in all, were now in place; however, offensive action against Iraq would require a much bigger buildup. Powell said that, as a matter of logistics, he needed to know whether to plan on rotating the American forces already in Saudi Arabia or to get more troops in the pipeline to send. "We are at a fork in the road," he told the president. Bush chose to continue plans for offensive action and to order what amounted to a doubling of the forces already in place.

* * *

Apart from the question of war or sanctions, the Bush administration was also trying to decide upon its military strategy if it were to attack Iraqi forces in Kuwait. On this question, too, significant tensions emerged between Cheney and Powell.

Powell allowed Schwarzkopf, his military commander in the Middle East, to take the lead in drawing up the war plan. Schwarzkopf, who had at first been preoccupied with defending Saudi Arabia, drew up a quick plan for offensive action into Kuwait. It called for a head-on attack against the Iraqi forces, which could incur high numbers of casualties. When Powell presented Schwarzkopf's plan to Bush and Scowcroft, the response was negative. "It was a terrible plan," Scowcroft would recall. "It called for a frontal assault, right up to the Iraqi strength. What role Powell played, I honestly don't know, but he submitted it on behalf of Schwarzkopf."

Nor did Cheney like it. In fact, he had an alternative plan, drawn up by his civilian advisors without Powell's knowledge, which laid out an operation to send American troops into the vast deserts west of Baghdad. Cheney presented this plan to Bush and Scowcroft while Powell was on a trip to Saudi Arabia. Thus, the low-level intrigue during these months was two-sided: Powell was quietly going around Cheney to officials such as Baker, urging a strategy of containment; and Cheney was going around Powell to the White House, to come up with a war plan. Upon returning to Washington and finding out about Cheney's meeting, Powell told Schwarzkopf, "I better not go out of town anymore."

But Bush and Scowcroft didn't approve Cheney's proposal, either. They were concerned that bringing American troops into Iraq, even into the vacant desert, could spark chaos inside the country, arouse fears of an attack on Baghdad, and thus jeopardize the support of crucial allies such as Turkey and Saudi Arabia, which did not want to see the breakup of Iraq. Powell saw another specter as well: Vietnam. Henry Rowen, the Pentagon civilian official who had come up with the ideas underpinning Cheney's plan, said that Powell "obviously didn't want to be there [inside Iraq] at all. . . . It looked like a dry version of Vietnam: that if you went in, you would never get out."

After this flurry of initial, conflicting war plans, Schwarzkopf went back to the drawing board and came up with an approach that satisfied everyone. It became known as the "left hook," in which American and allied forces would carry out a flanking maneuver around the Iraqi forces in Kuwait to encircle them. The operation was eventually to be named Desert Storm.

The left hook was going to be a much bigger operation than originally envisioned, meaning that the United States would need more troops, more planes, and more equipment. On this larger question, Cheney and Powell were united: Cheney had accepted and embraced Powell's views about the importance of large-scale, decisive military force.

For Powell, the idea of overwhelming military force was, of course, in line with the ideas set down by Caspar Weinberger years before, and the concept had worked very well in the Panama operation. But in planning for war with Iraq, a new wrinkle emerged: some senior officials viewed Powell's talk about the necessity for overwhelming force as driven by his overall support for containment, rather than war. "Colin Powell never wanted the Gulf War, never wanted to prosecute it, never wanted to go forward, never wanted to do anything that he loves taking credit for now," recalled John Sununu, who was then the White House chief of staff. "He came to George Bush to frighten him, in my opinion, my word, out of making the decision to go in."

Sununu's comments may be viewed skeptically, because he was not a foreign policy specialist, and as a conservative, he tended to be critical of Powell. But Robert Gates, an admirer of Powell who served as Scowcroft's deputy national security advisor, put forward a strikingly similar view. "My experience with the military over the years," he later said, "has been that they are so accustomed, after Vietnam, to civilians wanting to use military force that any time a President demands a contingency plan to consider, the military puts together a force that is so overwhelming that the President will balk at the cost and at the disruption and everything else and not do it."

Gates recalled that after the military was asked to draw up a plan not merely for defending Saudi Arabia but also for attacking Iraqi forces in Kuwait, Powell came to the White House with a series of requests. He asked to move the army's VII Corps, the heart of NATO's defense, out of

Germany and into Saudi Arabia. He asked for six aircraft carrier battle groups, more than the United States had ever put in a single theater of action. Beyond that, Gates said, there was what he called the "poison pill": Powell said Bush would have to activate both the National Guard and the Reserves.

Cheney supported Powell's proposals. In general, when it came to questions of broad military strategy, the defense secretary relied heavily throughout this period on Powell's advice and views. "He's my principal military advisor, and we spent a lot of time together, we spent a lot of time talking about these kinds of issues," Cheney later recalled. One of the debates before the Gulf War was whether, as some within the air force were suggesting, the United States could defeat Saddam Hussein with air power alone and thus avoid having to use ground forces. Powell, steeped in the army's land war traditions, believed that the war could not be won without boots on the ground. Cheney was persuaded. "One of the views that he had expressed that I came to share was that we could not count on the Air Force to win the war," Cheney reflected years later. In similar fashion, Cheney also accepted Powell's logic for the use of overwhelming force. If skeptics such as Sununu viewed Powell's series of requests as a way of heading off plans for war, Cheney viewed them differently, as a means of winning the war.

To everyone's surprise, Bush said yes to all of Powell's far-reaching requests. "To the day I die I'll never forget, Bush pushed his chair back, stood up, looked at Cheney and said, 'You've got it. Let me know if you need more,' and walked out of the room," Gates recalled. "Cheney's jaw dropped. Powell's jaw dropped. Cheney looks at Scowcroft and says, 'Does he know what he just authorized?' And Brent smiled and said, 'He knows what he just authorized.'"

Richard Haass viewed Powell's approach during this period as something of a trade-off: Powell would go along with war if Bush and Scowcroft waged it under Powell's rules and conditions. "The price for winning Powell's support for military intervention was agreeing to his marshalling enormous manpower and firepower, to assign the military objectives they could readily understand and carry out, and to refrain from micromanaging them in the field," Haass later wrote. "It seemed a fair price and good policy to boot."

* * *

On most of the decisions leading up to the Gulf War, Cheney was allied closely with Bush and Scowcroft in the White House—indeed, more so than Powell. When Cheney favored going to war rather than relying on economic sanctions, he was as much following as leading the president and his national security advisor, who had been hawks from the earliest days after the invasion of Kuwait. So, too, with the original war plan calling for a frontal assault: Cheney's negative reaction was fully in tune with that of Bush and Scowcroft in the White House.

There was one issue, however, where Cheney found himself isolated in dissent. As the additional American troops were flowing into Saudi Arabia for an offensive war against Iraq, Bush decided he wanted to obtain a congressional resolution supporting military action. This was to be by far the biggest American military action since Vietnam, and he did not want there to be claims afterward that Congress had not authorized the war or had been deceived into approving it.

Cheney was against seeking congressional authorization. He said he was worried that the Democratic Congress might say no. "Once you had 500,000 troops in the desert and Saddam in Kuwait, you couldn't go to Congress and have them vote no and say, 'Okay, bring everybody home,'" he would later argue. "That was just unacceptable."

Yet these practical considerations were not the only ones, as Cheney later acknowledged. He had come to hold a dark view of Congress, the institution he had once revered and originally come to Washington to study, the place where he had once been in line to become minority whip. "The way the Congress was going to view the operation was whether you won or not and how well it went," he grumbled. "They'd cover their fannies whichever way it went." Over the years, those working alongside or under Cheney came to recognize his continuing reluctance to go to Congress, whether to ask for authorization for actions or to inform it of what was happening in the executive branch. "If it had anything to do with Congress, he didn't want to have anything to do with it," Powell said years later.

Cheney summed up his accumulated cynicism about Congress in two terse sentences. In explaining why Bush was willing to ask for congressional approval for the Gulf War while he was not, Cheney said, "The difference between me and the President was that he only served two terms [in Congress]. I served five."

Despite Cheney's fears, Congress did approve the use of force, and Cheney would acknowledge that, in hindsight, Bush had been right. The congressional debate over the Gulf War turned out to be of high quality, he admitted. Moreover, getting approval from Congress "did a lot to boost public support, confidence," he said. "I was wrong to argue against going up [to Congress]."

* * *

It is difficult to reconstruct now the sense of tension, fear, and dread in America in the weeks leading up to the Gulf War, not just among ordinary citizens but even more so among their leaders, including Dick Cheney and Colin Powell.

Objectively, the United States seemed to be in an extremely advantageous position. It had vastly superior troops and technology. Moreover, it had the support of a broad range of allies in Europe, Asia, and the Middle East. Many of these countries had sent troops to fight alongside the Americans, and others, such as Japan, had made significant financial contributions. Yet against this array of strengths lay the specter of Vietnam, the knowledge that a quarter century earlier, America had gone to war with confidence and technological superiority against a backward nation—and had been forced to withdraw years later, after more than fifty thousand American deaths.

Many feared that this history could repeat itself. Senate majority leader George Mitchell and Speaker Tom Foley of the House delivered to Bush a letter signed by eighty-one Democrats arguing that military action against Iraq would be "catastrophic—resulting in the massive loss of lives—including 10,000–50,000 Americans." Inside the Bush administration, the predictions of American deaths were much lower, but estimates of between 1,000 and 3,000 deaths were commonplace. "We thought the numbers would be in the thousands, but the low thousands," said Powell.

Even Cheney, normally so cool, tough, and hard-hearted, was affected by the shadow of Vietnam. The Bush administration decided to launch military action on the evening of January 16, 1991, starting with an intensive air campaign. Early that morning, Cheney and his wife, Lynne, paid a quiet visit to the Vietnam Veterans Memorial, accompanied only by security officials. They stood there silently, bowing their heads in prayer. "I wanted a very stark reminder of what happens when you screw it up," he would say years later. He thought it was the obligation of civilian leaders to give American soldiers "a clear mission and the resources to prevail." Those words were as clear a statement as one could imagine of what he thought the Powell doctrine should require of civilian leaders.

* * *

Powell was better positioned than anyone else to know that by 1990, the American military was no longer the troubled, disorganized force that had fought in Vietnam. He had spent most of his adult life seeking to improve the U.S. Army. If America's civilian leaders were nervous about how the military would do in a conflict with Iraq, Powell had greater reasons for confidence than they did.

And so, starting in November and December, Powell turned into a hawk. Once Bush had rejected his suggestion that they rely on economic sanctions rather than military action, once it was clear that the president was determined to go to war, Powell identified himself with the cause of winning that war.

This was a striking change, particularly for those working inside the Pentagon who had observed how assiduously Powell had campaigned for a policy of containment. "It was a rough transition, inside the building," said Powell's aide Lawrence Wilkerson. It seemed for a time as though Powell "was trying to play both ends against the middle" by opposing the war and then leading the way to it. Nevertheless, Wilkerson noted, Powell's fluidity was the sort of character trait that earlier American military leaders had also displayed: "Marshall was adept at it, Eisenhower was adept at it."

* * *

The Gulf War commenced with an intensive air campaign that lasted more than a month. From the start of the conflict, Cheney and Powell began holding regular briefings at the Pentagon. There, Cheney regularly turned the podium over to Powell, allowing his chairman ample time and scope to dominate the proceedings in a way that no other chairman of the Joint Chiefs had ever been able to do, or has since. Years later, one former Bush administration official, Undersecretary of State Robert Kimmitt, pointed out that subsequent presidents and defense secretaries became leery of appointing a chairman of the Joint Chiefs who might be as charismatic as Powell. That was one reason that General David Petraeus never became chairman, Kimmitt believed.

The Gulf War briefings were regularly televised. Cable news, primarily CNN, was just coming into its own, allowing Americans to follow the conduct of a war minute by minute, in real time. The Pentagon news conferences became part of popular culture: in one *Saturday Night Live* skit, a reporter asked, "What time in the morning are you going to attack?"

For Powell, this was the role of a lifetime. For years he had excelled at all of Washington's inside operations: dealing with top officials, working the bureaucracy, learning when to push an issue and when not. Now, with tens of millions of Americans looking on, the Gulf War gave him a chance to make use of all his talents: his skill at the podium, his excellent voice, his humor, and his down-to-earth way of speaking. Powell had briefed the press during the invasion of Panama, but that war was short and its outcome certain. By contrast, the Gulf War went on much longer, six weeks in all, and during much of that time, Americans remained fearful of heavy casualties. Throughout, Powell was the man to watch. He knew how to explain what the military was doing and to do so in pithy, memorable ways that would appeal to a national audience. He could speak the language of the elites, but also the argot of the street. (Once, a few years later, describing his strategy of employing decisive force, Powell phrased it this way: "I believe in the bully's way of going to war: I'm on the street corner. I got my gun. I got my blade. *I'ma kick yo' ass.*")

A week after the air campaign began, Powell, dressed in full uniform with Cheney at his side, delivered to a televised news conference a line he had drafted, refined, and honed beforehand: "Our strategy to go after this [Iraqi] army is very, very simple. First, we're going to cut it off, and then we're going to kill it."

* * *

The day after the start of the air war, Iraq fired Scud missiles at Israel. At first, there were reports that the missiles contained chemical weapons. This was to prove the most serious complication to American strategy in the Gulf War: after the Scuds began landing in Tel Aviv and Haifa, Israel sought permission to respond by attacking Iraq. If it did, the war would widen and, at the same time, America might lose the support of many Arab governments in the Middle East.

Cheney played a leading role in dealing with these missile attacks and, more broadly, with Israel. He was more preoccupied than Bush, Scowcroft, or Powell with the concern that Iraq would use weapons of mass destruction, and he was more willing to support Israel's positions.

Iraq had used chemical weapons in its recent war with Iran. When Pentagon officials began preparing for an operation to push Iraqi troops out of Kuwait, they feared that Iraq would use chemical weapons again—or, perhaps, biological agents. "We spent quite a bit of time worrying about bugs and gas" in preparing for the Gulf War, Cheney would recall. American troops were issued protective suits and masks. In addition, the Bush administration gave Iraqi officials a series of warnings, through Secretary of State Baker and others, that if Iraq used poison gas or germ warfare, all restraints on America's means of fighting the war would be thrown off. "Obviously we weren't going to use chemical or biological agents," Cheney said. "The threat clearly was that we'd use, or threaten to use, nuclear weapons."

Cheney, moreover, was willing to go further than his colleagues, not only to threaten the use of nuclear weapons, but also to contemplate and lay out plans for actually using them. He asked Powell's Joint Staff to begin planning for how the United States would respond to chemical weapons attacks. "I want to know how many tactical nuclear weapons will it take to destroy a division of the Iraqi Republican Guard," Cheney asked, according to his own subsequent account. "Here's your [Iraqi] divisions laid out there. You come back and tell me how many nukes."

Powell's own view on weapons of mass destruction, then and throughout his career, was that of a professional military officer: he tended to minimize and deemphasize the threat because, in practical terms, the weapons could rarely be used. "It's become a hysterical acronym—oh my god, weapons of mass destruction," Powell reflected at one point. "Chemicals are not a weapon of mass destruction unless you can get a whole bunch of people in an enclosed place. Biological weapons are the worst, but they're probably the most difficult to use. Nukes are of course a weapon of mass destruction, but I can list as many countries that have given them up as those who have tried to pursue them. . . . They can't be used. It would be suicidal."

When Cheney wondered how many tactical nuclear weapons were needed to destroy an Iraqi Republican Guard division, Powell resisted giving an answer, before finally coming back with a number: seventeen. "Colin really didn't want to give me those numbers," Cheney said. Nevertheless, he went on, "I was perfectly prepared, if I thought it had made sense, to recommend that we consider the use of tactical nuclear weapons if he [Saddam Hussein] had done it [used chemical weapons]."

The focus of these prewar discussions was the use of chemical weapons against American troops. Once the war started and Iraq began firing Scuds at Israel, the issue was raised anew, in a different context: what if Iraq were to use chemical weapons against Israel?

Moshe Arens, the Israeli defense minister, got on the phone to Cheney, with whom he remained in daily contact throughout the war. Israel wanted to launch a counterstrike and, in effect, join the coalition's military campaign against Iraq. Cheney, alone among the senior Bush administration officials, would have supported Israel's request and paved the way for it to attack Iraq. "The big problem is how to keep Israel out, and it is going to be almost impossible," Bush wrote in his diary on January 17, 1991. "Cheney wants to let them go, and go fast. Get it over with."

The president rejected Cheney's recommendation to support Israel's entry into the war. It turned out, after a few hours, that the Iraqi Scuds launched against Israel were carrying conventional warheads, not chemical weapons. Bush successfully appealed to Israeli prime minister Yitzhak Shamir to refrain from the counterattack that could have changed the course of the Gulf War. Instead, the United States supplied Israel with Patriot missile batteries to shoot down the Scuds. The United States also launched an air campaign, not always successful, to find and destroy the mobile missile launchers in Iraq's western desert.

The war proceeded without Iraq using chemical weapons, but this aspect of the Gulf War was to have a lasting impact on Cheney. His attention had been drawn to the subject of weapons of mass destruction in Iraq. He would not forget. It was an issue to which he would return, over and over again, in the next two decades.

* * *

When it came to more conventional military questions during the Gulf War, Cheney and Powell were closely allied with each other—or, to put it more precisely, Cheney let Powell make decisions and then backed him up. Powell anticipated problems and brought them to Cheney.

In fact, it sometimes happened that in administration debates, Cheney and Powell were on one side and Bush and Scowcroft on the other. After the air war had gone forward for more than a month, with the principal installations of Baghdad and other cities in ruins, a decision needed to be made on the timing of the planned ground war. Bush and Scowcroft wanted it soon; Cheney and Powell, backing up Schwarzkopf in the field, pleaded for more time. "Gosh darn it, I wish Powell and Cheney were ready to go right now," Bush wrote in his diary on February 18.

Finally, on February 23, the ground campaign began. Within four days, the Iraqi forces were in a rout, rapidly surrounded and retreating in chaotic fashion from Kuwait back into Iraq.

8

DECIDING NOT TO
GO TO BAGHDAD

With Iraqi troops encircled and in flight, President George H. W. Bush made a historic decision that is widely known but not so well understood. He summoned his closest advisors and decided to stop the war, allowing Saddam Hussein's forces to proceed with their retreat from Kuwait back into Iraq. The American troops and their allies had been in position, if ordered to do so, to proceed to Baghdad, possibly installing a new leadership for the country. Bush chose not to take this course. Colin Powell and Dick Cheney were full participants in this decision.

Over the years, a series of misconceptions has arisen, both about the decision itself and about each of the two men's roles in it. It is sometimes argued that Powell played the decisive role in it or that his thinking determined the outcome. This is not true. It is also sometimes claimed that Cheney, as the most hawkish member of Bush's inner circle, favored going to Baghdad before the end of the war, or else that he subsequently regretted the decision not to do so. This is not true, either. Powell and Cheney not only approved of Bush's decision but also shared many of the broader assumptions, attitudes, and emotions of the president and the other senior officials who gathered in the Oval Office on February 27, 1991.

During the war and the run-up to it, the Bush team had become so close-knit that they referred to themselves as the Gang of Eight: Bush, Vice President Dan Quayle, Scowcroft, Gates, Baker, Sununu, Cheney, and Powell. "Bear in mind there was a kind of groupthink," said Dennis Ross, a senior aide to Baker. "There's a group dynamic when you take a very small group that meets all the time that goes through a period of incredible emotional stress."

Why did they decide not to go to Baghdad? With the benefit of hindsight and relying on interviews, memoirs, and archives, one could find four separate rationales—the two reasons that they regularly talked about, a third one that they spoke of much less often, and a fourth, more amorphous and more emotional reason that underlay all their other thinking. The four components of the decision were: (1) military tradition and honor; (2) diplomacy and international law; (3) Middle East geopolitics and strategy; and (4) the need to overcome the legacy of Vietnam with a clean victory.

Military Tradition and Honor

At the time, the reason most frequently cited for stopping the war could be called the "Highway of Death" argument. America and its allies had already captured roughly seventy to eighty thousand Iraqi prisoners. Tens of thousands more Iraqi soldiers, encircled, disorganized, and often separated from their units, were streaming along the highway from Kuwait to Basra, in southern Iraq. It would have seemed unchivalrous and out of character with military tradition to slaughter them.

It is Colin Powell who is most closely identified with this view—and indeed, at the time, it was Powell who most forcefully articulated this argument to his colleagues in the Bush administration. "As a professional soldier, I honored the warrior's code," Powell later wrote. He said he told Bush, "We don't want to be killing for the sake of killing, Mr. President."

Other members of the Bush team described Powell as especially impassioned in making this argument—suggesting, at the same time, that they did not feel as strongly as he did. Baker remembered Powell saying, "We're killing literally *thousands* of people." Robert Gates recalled, "It really bothered Powell. I think it bothered Colin a lot more than it bothered some of the rest of us. And Colin . . . essentially said, 'This is turning from a military conflict into a rout and from a rout into a massacre, and the American army does not do massacres.'"

This feeling was not Powell's alone; Cheney would later recall that Bush himself was sympathetic to the "Highway of Death" argument. "General Powell and the president were particularly concerned that we not ask our young soldiers to continue to fire upon an enemy that seemed to be retreating in defeat," he later wrote.

Powell's sense of military honor was deeply felt. The problem with attributing the decision to end the war to this factor, however, is that it was not enough by itself to tip the scales. Even Powell was also motivated by other factors, and this was even truer of Bush and the rest of his advisors.

Diplomacy and International Law

The second reason Bush and his aides regularly gave for not going to Baghdad was that it would have violated the terms on which the war had been fought. The objective of the war, reaffirmed over and over since the previous August, had been to get Iraqi troops out of Kuwait. Not only was this the American war aim, but it was also the basis on which the United States had put together its broad coalition against Iraq. Other countries, particularly those in the Middle East, would not have signed on if they had known the war in Iraq would lead to internal chaos or a breakup of the country. Furthermore, the resolution by the UN Security Council that gave international legitimacy to the use of force was based on the assumption that it was intended only to reverse Saddam Hussein's invasion of Kuwait.

It was Bush who articulated this rationale most frequently. Like Powell's sense of military honor, it was sincere, not feigned. Bush's ethic was that not of a soldier, but of a statesman; he didn't want to break the promises he'd made. "Our stated mission, as codified in U.N. resolutions, was a simple one—end the aggression, knock Iraq's forces out of Kuwait, and restore Kuwait's leadership," he later wrote. "To occupy Iraq would instantly shatter our coalition, turning the whole Arab world against us, and make a broken tyrant into a latter-day Arab hero."

Cheney agreed with this idea that the war had limited objectives. "There was never a serious debate about whether or not we ought to go to

Baghdad," he said later. "At the time, we all agreed we'd done what we set out to do. It was time to stop the operation."

Middle East Geopolitics and Strategy

The third reason was less exalted than stopping the killing or following international law: Bush and his advisors were also motivated by hard-nosed calculations about the balance of power in the Middle East. Put simply, having defeated Iraq, they did not want to leave the country so weakened that it could no longer pose a counterweight to Iran.

Iran and Iraq had already fought a long, bloody war. In its later stages, the United States had decided to support Iraq because it feared the rising power of Iran. These sorts of balance-of-power considerations were then temporarily put aside after Iraq's invasion of Kuwait, but now, with Iraq at the moment of defeat, the question of how to contain Iran reemerged. Many years later, explaining the decision to stop the war, Powell would acknowledge, "There was something called Iran right next door, that they [Iraq] had fought for eight years. We're going to hand it [Iraq] to Iran because these guys don't have the capacity to defend themselves?" Powell said America wanted "to leave Baghdad enough power to survive as a threat to an Iran that remained bitterly hostile towards the United States."

Bush administration officials did not talk much about these strategic calculations in public, but they figured prominently in the internal decision making to stop the war. One vivid description of what happened comes from a participant inside the room the day Bush called for a halt to hostilities. The meeting had been called on short notice, and Quayle couldn't attend. Instead, the vice president's seat at the table was occupied by his principal foreign policy advisor, Karl Jackson.

Jackson said that Bush dominated the session. The president began by saying, "Militarily, we can go on to Baghdad. But if we do, we will be forced to run it [Iraq] and deal with the divisions among Kurds, Shia and Sunni. Given our own beliefs, we will need to turn power over in a democratic election. Since the Shia are the majority, this will mean yielding power to the friends of our enemies, Iran. Now, is there something here I don't understand?"

No one spoke up to disagree, Jackson says. Reflecting on that decision in the wake of the American invasion of Iraq in 2003, Jackson said he was astonished: in retrospect, he said, "The president got everything right that the subsequent team got wrong. He absolutely understood that Iraq was this giant termite pile into which we should not throw a rock."

But Bush and his team did not get everything right. He and his advisors, including Cheney and Powell, operated on the assumption that Saddam Hussein could not survive as Iraq's leader after the military defeat. They believed that some new Iraqi leader would emerge, perhaps a military strongman. That assumption proved wrong. With Saddam Hussein still ruling the country, Iraq would continue to challenge American efforts to craft a "Goldilocks" solution for a country that was weakened but not too weak.

Over the following decades, Cheney and Powell would reaffirm that the decision not to go to Baghdad at the end of the Gulf War was the right one. Neither man voiced any regrets. However, each would concede in retrospect that it was a fair question whether perhaps the United States had decided to end the war a bit too hastily. Iraq survived the Gulf War with most of its Revolutionary Guard intact, and many hundreds of Iraqi tanks and armored vehicles were permitted to return to Iraq undamaged. Continuing the war for even a day or two longer might have prevented this from happening.

"It is a legitimate criticism, or a debatable criticism, to say you should have kept beating up on the Revolutionary Guard," Powell reflected. "More of them got out than perhaps should have been the case." Cheney, too, would later acknowledge that there had been confusion about what was happening on the ground at the time the Gulf War was ended, and that "this led to calling a halt before the escape routes into Iraq had been blocked. . . ." He also admitted that "there were arguably some misjudgments at the end of the war," but insisted somewhat defensively that "you would be hard-pressed to argue that they fundamentally altered the strategic landscape."

The Legacy of Vietnam and the Need for a Clean Victory

This brings us to the fourth, broader factor in the Bush team's decision to end the war when it did: the legacy of Vietnam and the intense desire for a clean American victory.

The Bush team was in no mood to get bogged down in messy details as the Gulf War was ending. Bush and his top aides had been under stress for more than six months since the invasion of Kuwait, as Dennis Ross observed. They had taken the risk of going to war, rather than relying on a strategy of containment and of using American forces only to protect Saudi Arabia. They had made the decision to attack in the face of predictions of large numbers of casualties. Now they were at the moment of victory, and they were eager to seize it.

Moreover, in their minds, the war was about something larger than Iraq: it was about restoring America's sense of self-worth and its view of itself as a force for good in the world. They wanted a simple victory to a quick war, one that would serve as a contrast to Vietnam, where the United States had been bogged down in a years-long stalemate while America became ever more torn apart.

As the Gulf War was nearing an end, the president took the lead in drawing these comparisons. "Vietnam will soon be behind us," Bush wrote in his diary the day before he decided to end the Gulf War. "It's surprising how much I dwell on the end of the Vietnam syndrome. I felt the division in the country in the 60s and 70s. . . . I remember the agony and the ugliness, and now it's together. We've got to find a clean end, and I keep saying, how do we end this thing?"

Powell was saying virtually the same thing. During the Oval Office meeting at which the decision was made to stop the war, Ross recalls Powell saying, "It's great to win one, isn't it? We kicked the Vietnam syndrome." On the day after the war ended, Bush made these feelings public, declaring in a Washington speech, "It's a proud day for America. And, by God, we've kicked the Vietnam syndrome once and for all!"

For Powell, the triumph in the Gulf War served to help restore the reputation of the American military, which had been a preoccupation throughout his own career. For Cheney, the victory served as a demonstration of renewed American strength abroad and at home, including public support for the armed forces. "There was a palpable sense that their magnificent performance had restored a feeling of pride we had lost in Vietnam," he later wrote.

In the face of this profound sense of relief among Bush and his top advisors, the administration's second- and third-level officials discovered that their bosses were not particularly receptive to thinking too deeply about policy options or details that might complicate the narrative of a clean victory. "They didn't want to hear because it was time to celebrate," recalled Zalmay Khalilzad, who was working as an aide to Cheney.

The starkest example was the controversy over Saddam Hussein's use of his helicopters. Before the war, Bush had given a speech encouraging Iraqis to overthrow Saddam Hussein, and immediately after the Gulf War ended, Shia forces in southern Iraq and Kurds in the north rose up in rebellion. At the time of the cease-fire, General Schwarzkopf had gone along with a request by Saddam Hussein to use Iraq's helicopter gunships once again, ostensibly for humanitarian purposes and to transport Iraqi officials around the country. Instead, within days after the war was declared over, the gunships regained by Saddam's army began to attack the Shia and Kurds.

In Washington, Dennis Ross and Paul Wolfowitz argued that Saddam Hussein should be stopped, all the more so because the Shia and Kurds seemed to be responding to Bush's earlier appeals. The two men believed that the United States should use force, if necessary, to ground the Iraqi helicopters.

"Both of us were feeding into our respective guys, me to Baker and him [Wolfowitz] to Cheney, pushing hard on this," Ross said. They failed. No one in the top ranks of the administration was in favor of interfering with Saddam's helicopters. "There was no dissent in the meeting," Ross recalled. "Not Cheney. Everybody agreed. The thrust of the argument was that we don't want to get sucked in. And I remember very vividly Powell's arguments that we have a neat, clean victory, we don't want to do anything that raises questions about that."

This dispute over the helicopters may have helped give rise to the mistaken belief that Cheney wanted American troops and their allies to go on to Baghdad at the end of the Gulf War. But the push for military action against the helicopters had come from Wolfowitz and Ross, not Cheney; and the action they proposed was not to go on to Baghdad, but to stop the postwar slaughter of the Shia and Kurds. In any event, Cheney rejected the idea. The available evidence shows that on all the issues relating to the termination of the Gulf War, he was fully in agreement with Bush, with Powell, and with others in the top ranks of the administration.

* * *

As it turned out, the American public was just as eager to celebrate the Gulf War victory as were Bush and his advisors. While Panama had turned the spotlight briefly on Cheney and Powell as symbols of an American military triumph, the Gulf War did so on a vastly greater scale. Panama had required fewer than thirty thousand troops; the Gulf War had involved more than five hundred thousand, including Reserves.

Once again, it was Powell who more easily captured the nation's attention and adulation. He was the Pentagon leader who wore the uniform, the one with the personal touch, the wit, and the outgoing, relaxed manner. Cheney was not one to rise to the occasion; even in triumph, he remained reserved and taciturn. Powell's voice could at times convey the sense that he was a man off the streets, lucky enough to have risen. Cheney's deeper, self-assured voice conveyed authority, the notion that he was in charge, but also that he was at a distance, that he always possessed more information than ordinary citizens and had difficult, important decisions to make.

On June 10, 1991, Cheney and Powell rode in a ticker tape parade through the streets of New York City, receiving the sort of adulation previously accorded to Charles Lindbergh, Dwight Eisenhower, Douglas MacArthur, and the Apollo astronauts. The two men were placed in convertibles in a procession up Lower Broadway, along with thousands of troops just back from the Gulf. Cheney rode in the first car, along with his wife, Lynne, and their daughter Liz. In the middle of the procession, sitting in a 1959 white Buick convertible, sat Powell and his wife, Alma; behind them, in a third car, were Schwarzkopf and his wife. More than six thousand tons of ticker tape and ten thousand pounds of confetti were distributed for the celebration, along with red, white, and blue balloons. "It's a great day to be back home in New York!" Powell exclaimed, reminding everyone of his roots in Harlem and the Bronx—and in the process, doing nothing to dispel budding speculation about his potential as a political candidate.

* * *

There were lessons to be learned and conclusions to be drawn from the Gulf War, and both Powell and Cheney would find themselves writing, speaking, and reflecting on the war for years to come.

Powell, not surprisingly, often emphasized the importance of the use of overwhelming force and of carefully tailored, specific objectives, correcting the errors of Vietnam. Writing in *Foreign Affairs* the year after the Gulf War ended, he offered thoughts that would seem sad and prophetic fifteen years later: "The Gulf War was a limited-objective war. If it had not been, we would be ruling Baghdad today—at unpardonable expense in terms of money, lives lost and ruined regional relationships. The Gulf War was also a limited-means war—we did not use every means at our disposal to eject the Iraqi Army from Kuwait. But we did use overwhelming force quickly and decisively."

For his part, Cheney reflected that the Gulf War took place at a time when American troops were at a peak in training and readiness. "You'd send them [U.S. soldiers] to the desert, there's nothing else for them to do but train. There sure as hell aren't any dens of iniquity to hang out in over there in Saudi," he recalled years later. The war had also succeeded, he said, because it was relatively quick, there had been minimal casualties, and the financial contributions of more than fifty billion dollars from allies such as Japan had made it surprisingly cheap. "Frankly, we got somebody else to pay for it," Cheney quipped. Those factors had made the Gulf War different from Vietnam, and Cheney believed that future American defense planning should bear in mind the need to keep casualties low and get the war over as rapidly as possible.

Cheney was willing to admit that there had been a few negative aspects in the Bush administration's handling of the war. "If there was a weakness there, we hadn't done a lot of planning for what happens after the war," he said.

* * *

Amid the celebrations, there were signs that the narrative was not over; there were portents of another war to come.

After the war ended, Cheney placed a call to David Ivry, the senior Israeli defense official who in 1981 had served as commander of the Israeli Air Force when Israel had bombed Iraq's nuclear reactor at Osirak. At the time of the raid, a decade before the Gulf War, the United States had officially condemned the Israeli attack. But Cheney now told Ivry he wanted to thank him for Osirak. "Without Israel's courageous action we may well have had to face a nuclear-armed Saddam Hussein in 1991," he said. That phone call underscored Cheney's close and continuing relationship with Israeli defense officials, and it showed that the Gulf War had, if anything, only intensified his focus on stopping Iraq from developing nuclear weapons.

Meanwhile, only days after the end of the Gulf War, Zalmay Khalilzad received a call from Bernard Lewis, a well-known Middle East scholar at Princeton University. Lewis said he had just met with some interesting Iraqi exiles, and he thought that the top levels of the Bush administration should hear what they had to say. The Iraqis were led by a former mathematician and banker named Ahmed Chalabi.

Khalilzad tried to arrange a meeting. The State Department strongly objected, on the grounds that any meeting between Chalabi and Pentagon officials would raise suspicions that the United States was trying to arm the Iraqi opposition. Still, the exiles won support in Congress, and Khalilzad was soon authorized to meet with Chalabi.

That was merely the beginning of a battle over Chalabi and the Iraqi exiles, a struggle that, a decade later, would lead to intense, passionate disagreements between the State Department and the Pentagon, and between Powell and Cheney. Out of the ruins of one war with Iraq grew the seeds of another.

9

THE SOVIET COLLAPSE

T he happy faces in the victory parade were genuine; the Gulf War had deepened the personal bond between Dick Cheney and Colin Powell and helped lay the groundwork for a friendship that would endure through the remainder of the decade.

When they had joined the George H. W. Bush administration, there were strong institutional reasons for the two men to make an effort to work well together. During the last years of the Reagan administration, it had been commonplace for the secretary of defense and the chairman of the Joint Chiefs of Staff to appear at top-level meetings, each with his own separate view, analysis, or policy recommendation. "OSD [the Office of the Secretary of Defense] had a position, JCS [the Joint Chiefs of Staff] had a position," Cheney recalled in one interview a decade later. "Lots of times they were at odds, in conflict. I didn't want that. Colin Powell and I worked hard to avoid it. . . . We tried to get our own act together internally in the Department of Defense." The two men arranged to meet in Cheney's office at 5 p.m. each afternoon to go over what had happened that day and what should be done moving forward. If Cheney was taking part in some other afternoon meeting and the time approached 5 p.m., he would tell others, "Let's wrap this up. I don't want to keep the chairman waiting."

But from that starting point, the working relationship evolved into something more. By the accounts of both men, expressed frequently during their years at the Pentagon and at various points through the 1990s, they came to like and admire each other. Cheney described their relationship in those years as "very close," and so did Powell. "Cheney was my boss, but we were very close personal friends," he reflected in the late 1990s. Even two decades later, after all the frictions of the Iraq War, Powell's description of their time together in the George H. W. Bush administration hadn't changed much. "Dick and I were friends," he said. "We had a great relationship in the Pentagon."

Cheney talked to Powell over a direct phone line between their two offices, and Powell stopped by Cheney's office, often several times a day. The daily five o'clock meeting came to be supplemented by more informal sessions later in the evening. "We were pretty close and we would talk late at night," Powell said on another occasion. The subjects of their conversations extended beyond defense issues to people and politics. In the early stages of the 1992 presidential campaign, the two men privately agreed that the Bush reelection effort wasn't going well and wondered whether something was the matter with Bush.

On the military issues that cropped up during the Gulf War, Cheney not only supported Powell but often ran interference for him with the White House, with civilian authorities, and with the press. With his years of army training, Powell understood far better than others the significance of the change from the weeks of air war against Iraq to the introduction of ground forces. The air war, with its precision strikes, had been, among other things, a great television show, almost like a video game. "Ground war ain't air war," Powell told Cheney. "It's ugly, it's dirty, and you're liable to see pictures coming out of some kid laying halfway outside of a tank on fire. He's burning. It's very ugly." He wanted Cheney to limit press access to the initial stages of the ground war. He also wanted him to prevent civilian leaders (meaning, among others, those in the White House and National Security Council, including Bush and Scowcroft) from asking too many questions too quickly and from pestering the military with queries about how many people were killed or wounded in this or that operation. "Cheney understood it beautifully," Powell said. "And, in fact, he held the press off for a while, until it became too hard to do, and when it was going so well and we weren't seeing these kinds of images."

Cheney was similarly impressed by Powell's personality and abilities. After the Gulf War ended, Cheney's aide Zalmay Khalilzad was assigned the task of supervising the official multivolume Pentagon report about the Gulf War: what had worked, what hadn't, what roles the various military services had played. The report was to include an introduction under Cheney's name. Khalilzad recalled that Cheney ordered him to revise the draft of this report several times to give greater credit to Powell. "The secretary felt that we hadn't quite captured the unique, historic, unbelievable role that Colin Powell had played in this period, with the war," Khalilzad said. At one point, in frustration after the third or fourth try, Khalilzad let his frustration out when Cheney said that the words still didn't quite capture what he wanted to say. "Why doesn't he [Cheney] write it up himself?" Khalilzad muttered.

Cheney didn't, and Khalilzad finally satisfied him. A comparison between the interim report to Congress and the final report shows that the following passage was added, under Cheney's name: "We were fortunate in this precedent setting time . . . to have a Chairman with the unique qualities of General Colin Powell. General Powell's strategic insight and exceptional leadership helped the American people through trying times and ensured our forces fought smart. He drew upon all of our capabilities to bring the necessary military might to bear."

* * *

Yet all was not quite so serene. Though Cheney and Powell developed a close personal rapport, there were hints of discord, the seeds of the acrimony that would burst into the open a decade later. Here, the tensions were not between Powell and Cheney, but between Powell and the civilians working in the Pentagon under Cheney. These frictions were themselves a reflection of the two leaders' underlying differences in style and outlook.

When he became secretary of defense, Cheney had decided to retain Paul Wolfowitz as undersecretary for policy, the job for which John Tower had originally picked him. Wolfowitz was (accurately) labeled as a neoconservative, associated with the movement of former Democrats who came to question the underpinnings of liberalism and who eventually lined up behind Ronald Reagan. But in practical terms, what counted far more was simply that Wolfowitz was a foreign policy hawk who consistently favored tougher policies in dealing with the Soviet Union. Once Wolfowitz was on the job in the Pentagon, he began bringing onto his staff a collection of other foreign policy specialists with similarly hawkish views and, often, similar backgrounds. These included I. Lewis (Scooter) Libby, Wolfowitz's protégé and closest aide; Eric Edelman, a Foreign Service officer and Soviet specialist; Zalmay Khalilzad; and several other prominent conservatives. Many of them had academic training in various foreign policy disciplines, such as nuclear strategy. Meanwhile, separate from Wolfowitz's team, Cheney had also brought onto his personal staff David Addington, the former CIA lawyer he had met while serving on the House Intelligence Committee, who had his own deeply conservative views on secrecy, intelligence operations, and the power of the executive branch. The indirect consequence of Cheney's personnel choices was that while he and Powell were closely aligned on day-to-day operations, when it came to longer-term questions, they were not.

The civilian advisors were trained in theory, policy options, and abstract issues, and their jobs and assignments at the Pentagon usually involved addressing such questions. In contrast, Powell was dedicated to the concrete problems on the agenda, whatever those might be. To him, *abstraction* was almost a dirty word: it reminded him of Robert McNamara and the Vietnam War era, when, as a foot soldier, Powell had railed against the "slide-rule prodigies" in the Pentagon.

Powell and his aides sometimes joked to one another about Cheney's conservative aides. One particular target was Addington, whose views and secretive style made him stand out. "We called him 'Weird David,'" recalled Lawrence Wilkerson. "We couldn't associate the more rational, pretty strategic-thinking secretary of defense with this guy, who we thought lived to bring the Constitution out of his inner pocket and talked about how the executive power was the ultimate and be-all of everything."

In his memoir, written soon after leaving the Pentagon, Powell described the Pentagon's policy staff under Wolfowitz as "a refuge of

Reagan-era hard-liners." He went on to describe how one day, as he and Cheney were debating an issue of nuclear planning, Cheney said, "Not one of my civilian advisors supports you."

"That's because they're all right-wing nuts like you," Powell retorted.

In Powell's account, this was all lighthearted banter and in good humor: he wrote that he was kidding, and that Cheney laughed. They moved on, until the following decade, when the dynamics remained similar but the humor had vanished.

Just as Powell held disparaging views of Cheney's aides, they in turn developed unflattering opinions of him. Their misgivings took shape as he came to acquire an ever-greater stature in the press and with the public in the wake of the Panama operation and the Gulf War. Cheney's aides complained that Powell cared too much about public opinion and his own image, that he spent too much time cultivating the press. A year after the Gulf War, *Washington Post* reporter Bob Woodward published an inside account of the prewar debates, revealing to the public for the first time how Powell had argued initially for a policy of deterrence rather than war. To those in Cheney's entourage, Powell's views were not news, but they saw the Woodward revelation as another example of Powell courting the press, seeking to cover his tracks (in case the prosecution of the war went badly) and to shape the public narrative to his own advantage.

Many of Powell's differences with the Cheney aides were at root political. The Cheney staffers were conservative, and they felt that Powell always seemed to come down wherever mainstream public opinion happened to be at any particular moment, invariably embracing the moderate, establishment-oriented views of the Council on Foreign Relations or the newspaper editorial pages. "Powell, for all his many considerable virtues—and he really does have a lot—has a very strong instinct to stick with the conventional wisdom," said Eric Edelman, who was working on Soviet policy in the Pentagon under Wolfowitz. "I would defy people to find places in his career where he's very orthogonal to conventional wisdom."

But beyond that, Cheney's civilian aides also pointed to a shortcoming in Powell's generally powerful leadership skills, one that the general's own friends and even Powell himself would occasionally acknowledge:

he did not care much about ideas or strategic vision. What Powell cared about was being effective in the task at hand—getting the immediate job done, motivating his troops, working the bureaucracy, winning public support. "I think his one Achilles' heel is, he doesn't really have strong analytic powers," said Edelman. Some of Powell's own aides, while admiring of their boss, came to similar judgments. "He was probably the most prepared individual for crisis and circumstance that I've ever met in my life—tactically prepared. Not much of a strategist," observed Wilkerson.

Indeed, no one described this aspect of Powell's character better than Powell himself. "I don't like think tanks. And I don't like study groups," he asserted. "What people forget is I'm not an academic. I didn't steep myself in this stuff [policy and strategy] for thirty-five years. I was a soldier. I have views, but they are the views of—not an ideologue, but what I was trained to be, and that's a problem solver. You see problems, and you attack them. You see hills, and you take them. You analyze how to take a hill, or how to solve a problem, and then you go about solving it—either frontally, or in flank attacks, or better yet, you slip on them at night and hit them in the head. And you take the hill. So, I'm a problem solver."

Powell's extraordinary skills in managing the tasks at hand, even the biggest ones, made him an invaluable asset to the Bush administration. But his lack of interest in debates on ideas and strategy would lead to frictions with Cheney and his staff on other kinds of issues, ones that touched on America's future role in the world.

One set of issues concerned the Soviet Union, Russia, and the transition from one to the other.

* * *

Once or twice a month, on Saturday mornings at 9 a.m., a group of about twelve to fifteen senior defense and intelligence officials would gather in a conference room at the Pentagon for a continuing informal seminar on events in the Soviet Union. The meetings were a way of trying to think and learn about what was happening under Mikhail Gorbachev's leadership. In the Reagan years, Secretary of State George Shultz had held similar weekend meetings, and Dick Cheney decided to continue the tradition. Prominent Soviet experts from academia or elsewhere outside the government would be invited to take part.

The underlying questions the participants addressed went to the heart of American defense policy: How should the United States respond to the diminishing threat from the Soviet Union? What threats to the United States remained from what was left of the old Soviet apparatus? But the meetings did not address any specific, immediate policy questions involving, say, line items in the defense budget or troop deployments.

Cheney liked these sessions so much that he kept asking for more of them. "Let's round up the usual suspects and have another Saturday morning session on the Soviet Union," he would often tell his aides. Powell had considerably less interest in these strategy sessions. Fritz Ermarth, a longtime Soviet expert and the chairman of the National Intelligence Council, recalled that Powell would drop by the Saturday sessions from time to time but wouldn't stay long. He would sit for fifteen minutes or so, then get up and quietly depart. As Powell said, he didn't like study groups.

As events inside the Soviet Union unfolded in 1990 and 1991, the focus of debate in Washington changed. The Bush administration had come into office preoccupied with how to deal with Mikhail Gorbachev and whether his reform program would or could succeed. But as the reforms began to falter and Gorbachev came under attack from political rivals, new questions arose: Should the United States lend support to Boris Yeltsin, Gorbachev's principal challenger? Should the United States go even further and support the breakup of the Soviet Union?

On these issues, Cheney emerged as the strongest voice within the administration on one side of the debates. From the start of his tenure as defense secretary, he had minimized the importance of Gorbachev's reforms and warned against giving him too much American support. He took it upon himself to play the role of the administration's in-house skeptic and continuing hawk. "I . . . had the strong feeling that as Secretary it was my responsibility, more than anyone else in the administration, to make certain we didn't give away the store," he said. "There were going to be enough other people out there who were arguing that this was the new day, the Cold War is over, we can dismantle the defense budget and take down the force." It was one of his "obligations," Cheney said, "to make sure that there was a voice somewhere in the Administration saying, 'Hey, wait a minute. Let's make sure this is for real before we walk down that road.'" Most of his arguments were with President Bush and Secretary of State Baker, who had come to favor a strong American relationship with Gorbachev.

There were times when Cheney's consistently hawkish positions led him into twisting positions and swerving rationales. In the early days of the administration, he warned that the United States needed to avoid cutting the defense budget because Gorbachev would take advantage and revive Soviet power to threaten the United States. Later, as it became clear that this was not Gorbachev's intention, Cheney maintained that the United States needed to preserve the defense budget because Gorbachev could be replaced by another Soviet leader who "could reverse military course decisively." Later still, Cheney would argue that the United States needed to maintain its defenses in case the Soviet leadership grew so weak that it lost control of the country.

Cheney's critics inside the administration felt that he was giving Gorbachev too much credit for Machiavellian plans or designs that he didn't have. "There was always some suspicion [by Cheney]—which was, in hindsight, a little crazy—that Gorbachev was going to somehow steal a march on us and surprise us and take the initiative, whereas in hindsight he [Gorbachev] was just making stuff up as he went along," said William Burns, a Soviet specialist working in the State Department.

By the early months of 1991, Bush administration officials began to contemplate a once-unimaginable possibility: that the Soviet Union might be on the way to collapse. By that time, the CIA was reporting that Gorbachev was losing control rapidly and that a shift of power was underway from the Soviet Union to the various republics. Yugoslavia, meanwhile, was already falling apart; nationalist movements had won elections in the republics of Serbia, Croatia, Bosnia, and Slovenia.

Zalmay Khalilzad attended an interagency meeting as Cheney's representative to discuss what was unfolding in Yugoslavia. The deputy secretary of state, Lawrence Eagleburger, who chaired the session, observed that if Yugoslavia disintegrated, "the next thing you know, people will be talking about the disintegration of the Soviet Union." Khalilzad, who was not a Soviet expert, suddenly began paying close attention. He went back to the Pentagon and wrote a memo to Cheney reporting what had been discussed and adding his own conclusion that the United States should be watching for possibilities to help foster the breakup of the Soviet Union.

On June 12, 1991, the first direct elections were held for the position of president of Russia, still a component republic of the Soviet Union. Yeltsin, who had emerged as a critic of the Communist Party leadership and a strong proponent of democratic change, won easily. When Yeltsin visited Washington a week later, he received a careful reception at the White House, but a warm welcome at the Pentagon.

"Cheney treated him like royalty," Wolfowitz recalled. "We took him all over the [Pentagon] building. The two things that impressed him the most were the department stores in the concourse and the long aisle that had nothing but reporters' offices." At a meeting in Cheney's office, the defense secretary asked Yeltsin about rumors that the Soviet leadership might seek to increase the defense budget. Even Cheney's aides privately admitted the reports were implausible on their face, but Yeltsin went far beyond simply denying them. "Increasing the Soviet defense budget would be a crime against the Russian people, who have already suffered enough under seventy years of communism," he replied. Nothing Yeltsin said could have been more pleasing to Cheney, who by that time was looking for opportunities to undermine the Soviet leadership. "For Cheney, the breakup of the Soviet Union was devoutly to be wished," recalled Wolfowitz.

Bush and Baker continued to support Gorbachev. For the president, this was in part an outgrowth of his emphasis on personal relationships and diplomacy: Bush had established a bond with Gorbachev and was not going to undercut him. The secretary of state had his own reasons for supporting the Soviet leader. In a nighttime conversation over drinks aboard his plane as he flew into Moscow in late July, Baker mused to a reporter, "They say I'm sticking too long with Gorbachev. Well, I'm getting good deals from Gorbachev. I got a good deal on Afghanistan, I got a good deal on Angola, I got a good deal on Cambodia, I'm getting good deals on arms control. And when I stop getting good deals, maybe I won't stick with Gorbachev."

Washington's policy disagreements remained unresolved until, on

August 18, 1991, a group of hard-liners from the Soviet military and security apparatus mounted an attempted coup d'état against Gorbachev. Virtually all the administration's senior officials were off on vacation and had to rush back to Washington—Bush from the family summer compound in Kennebunkport, Maine; Baker from his ranch in Wyoming; and Cheney from a fishing trip in British Columbia. In those first hours after the news broke, they tried to determine whether the coup would succeed and what to say publicly about it.

Bush's initial statement was cautious and guarded, in part because he and his aides thought the coup in Moscow might succeed and that he would have to deal with its leaders. However, the intelligence community began reporting that the coup wasn't going well. Within the Pentagon, Cheney's civilian aides were pressing for a strong condemnation of the coup. When Deputy National Security Advisor Robert Gates prepared a statement that criticized the coup as illegitimate, Stephen Hadley, a Pentagon staffer who was representing Cheney, pointed out that Gates's draft didn't include the word *condemn*, and he argued strongly that it be added. Hadley's effort succeeded, and as a result, the United States became among the first major powers to condemn the coup. The American statement, in turn, gave important support to Yeltsin and to the Russians demonstrating against the coup on the streets of Moscow.

The Soviet hard-liners' putsch soon failed, and Gorbachev returned to Moscow. Over the following two months, a new debate emerged within the Bush administration over the extent to which the United States should support the formal dissolution of the Soviet Union. Was it in America's interest for the country to break apart completely, or should Washington try to encourage the retention of a strong central authority in Moscow, even as the Soviet republics were given more autonomy?

In these debates, Cheney once again took the hardest line in favor of a breakup. At the highest levels of the Bush administration, it was "Cheney against the field," recalled Gates. "Cheney was the most aggressive participant, saying, 'The breakup of the Soviet Union is in our interest.'" This was, effectively, the final round in the decades of Washington debates over U.S. policy toward the Soviet Union. It proved all but meaningless, as events were moving faster than anyone could control. By the last two months of the year, not only Yeltsin in Russia but also the leaders of

Ukraine and several other Soviet republics had effectively declared their independence. On December 25, 1991, Mikhail Gorbachev resigned, and the Soviet Union passed out of existence.

* * *

Colin Powell was not a leading protagonist in the Gorbachev-versus-Yeltsin debates. Indeed, there had been little doubt where he stood on Gorbachev's importance. During the first year of the administration, the main argument had been whether Gorbachev represented something different for the Soviet Union or whether he was merely a new face for the same old Soviet regime. Powell believed strongly that Gorbachev was a genuine agent of change, a belief stemming from Powell's having served as Ronald Reagan's national security advisor and having dealt firsthand with the Soviet leader. "He had looked into Gorbachev's eyes, and had not seen his soul but he had seen that the Soviet Union was truly dead," Lawrence Wilkerson recalled. In that sense Powell had been not only on the other side of the argument from Cheney, but also well ahead of Bush and Scowcroft, who had come to the White House believing that Reagan had become too enamored of Gorbachev, before coming around to a similarly positive view.

But on the later issue of whether to push for a breakup of the Soviet Union—that is, the urgent question that arose in 1990 and 1991—Powell generally took a backseat. "Colin Powell came down somewhere in the middle of the debate," said Gates. "He said he wanted to see the dissolution of the old Soviet Union, but wasn't sure that meant 'sixteen republics walking around.'"

Powell's passivity may have been a consequence of the rebuke he had received from Cheney after questioning the idea of going to war with Iraq. ("You're not the Secretary of State. You're not the National Security Advisor anymore. . . . So stick to military matters.") Powell seemed to embrace the message when it came to the Soviet Union. He became involved in discussions about military questions such as the command-and-control of Soviet nuclear weapons, but not in discussions about the pros and cons of supporting Yeltsin or a breakup of the Soviet Union. He was merely the chairman of the Joint Chiefs of Staff; America had just fought its biggest war since Vietnam, and Powell was involved in working out the aftermath, such as getting the troops home. The Soviet future was a subject for Cheney, not so much for him.

* * *

The skirmishing within the administration over support for Gorbachev once again manifested itself in frictions between Cheney's civilian advisors and Powell.

Cheney's principal policy advisor for the Soviet Union, working directly under Wolfowitz, was Eric Edelman, a Foreign Service officer and Soviet specialist who had served in the U.S. embassy in Moscow during Gorbachev's early years. Edelman was a hawk. Like Cheney, he was wary of Gorbachev, favored strong support for Yeltsin, and thought that the breakup of the Soviet Union would carry strong benefits to the United States, for example, by reducing the supply of manpower for a Russian army.

In the fall of 1991, Cheney and Powell scheduled a series of briefings in the National Military Command Center to keep abreast of the latest developments in the Soviet Union. Powell may not have been an especially strong proponent of preserving a closer relationship with Gorbachev, but Edelman certainly perceived him as in that camp. "Powell was really much closer on that issue to Baker and to the people around Baker, and he was not happy with what I was telling Cheney," Edelman recalled years later. At one of the briefings, Edelman, sitting in the rear of the room, began to raise a series of leading questions that showed strong support for the dissolution of the Soviet Union: Would there really be chaos, or was that fear exaggerated? Would Soviet nuclear weapons fall into the hands of crazy Ukrainian nationalists? The Pentagon briefer said that these scenarios were unlikely—as Edelman knew he would, given that he and the briefer had rehearsed the question-and-answer routine beforehand.

Powell was furious at this gambit, so much so that a few days later, Wolfowitz told Edelman, "You know, you really pissed off the chairman in that briefing." Powell had gone directly to the secretary of defense, asking him to exclude Edelman from future briefings. But Cheney replied that Edelman had not said anything inaccurate about events in the Soviet Union and that he wanted Edelman to be there. When Edelman arrived at the next briefing, there was a seat for him not in the rear of the room, but at the front, with his nameplate on the table.

Edelman was profoundly grateful. "I had this enormous loyalty to Cheney after that," he said. "I had it before then, but I really had it after that. Because it would have been easy—I was so junior and so dispensable—it would have been very easy to throw me under the bus."

10

CHENEY'S BLUEPRINT

In the spring of 1991, in the wake of America's triumphant victory in the Gulf War, Colin Powell joked about the increasingly secure position in which the United States had found itself. "I'm running out of demons. I'm running out of villains," he said in one interview. "I'm down to Kim Il Sung and Castro." It was the sort of pithy quote that raised eyebrows among Cheney's civilian advisors, who were wary of Powell's mainstream views and of anything that might lead to an erosion in public support for the defense budget.

Yet, by the early months of 1992, after the formal dissolution of the Soviet Union, even Cheney, the ultimate hawk, was saying essentially the same thing, though in less catchy language. "The threats have become remote, so remote they are difficult to discern," the defense secretary testified to the House Armed Services Committee. But he immediately added a thought that was distinctly his own and could not be found in Powell's thinking: "That's a very desirable situation, *one we should work to maintain* [emphasis added]." Those words suggested an active role for the United States to stave off potential competitors.

* * *

With the collapse of the Soviet Union, the United States found itself in search of a new strategy to establish America's role in a post–Cold War world.

For more than four decades, Pentagon officials had addressed themselves to the threat of all-out war with the Soviet Union. That meant the U.S. military needed not only to protect the United States and its allies from nuclear or missile attacks, but also to stop a Soviet invasion of Western Europe. In an interview he gave during the relative calm of the mid-1990s, Cheney described the thinking that had long held sway in the Pentagon: The United States had needed to be ready to dispatch a large number of troops with little warning. "Our planning assumptions said you've got to be prepared to deal with a Soviet lead force of a hundred divisions," he said. "And you've got to have ten divisions there within ten days of a decision to mobilize." With the dissolution of the Soviet Union, Cheney went on, "All the assumptions that had driven defense planning over the past forty years had gone out the window." The United States "could operate on the assumption that we would have enough warning time before there was a global threat."

In early 1992, Cheney's aides set about trying to write a new strategy. The timing was dictated in part by a bureaucratic necessity: every two years, the Pentagon is required to draft or update a formal statement of its strategy, called the Defense Planning Guidance (DPG), a document that serves as the basis for budgets, deployments, military programs, and the many other nuts-and-bolts decisions that need to be made from week to week. The breakup of the Soviet Union gave Pentagon officials an opportunity to draft something new, rather than a standard boilerplate document.

The job of writing this guidance was assigned to Zalmay Khalilzad, working under Paul Wolfowitz and Lewis (Scooter) Libby. The three of them held brainstorming sessions and sought out ideas from prominent defense intellectuals, among them Richard Perle, a leading neoconservative, and Albert Wohlstetter, a University of Chicago professor who had served as a mentor to both Wolfowitz and Perle. It was a fairly likeminded group; virtually all these men had been prominent hawks during the Cold War.

Khalilzad synthesized the ideas from their meetings, produced a draft, and began to circulate it for comment. It was so early in the process that neither Wolfowitz nor Libby had a chance to read or comment on it. Nevertheless, the draft leaked, and in early March it was summarized on the front page of the *New York Times* under the headline "U.S.

Strategy Plan Calls for Insuring No Rivals Develop: A One Superpower World: Pentagon's Document Outlines Ways to Thwart Challenges to Primacy of America."

Khalilzad's paper began with the uncontested proposition that with the collapse of the Soviet Union, the United States had emerged as the world's only superpower. It went on to argue that America should continue to play that dominant role well into the future. By itself, the idea might not have caused much controversy, but Khalilzad's draft then said that the United States should actively seek to "prevent the reemergence of a new rival." It maintained that America should block "any hostile power" from dominating any of the most important economic regions of the world: Western Europe, East Asia, and the Middle East. Moreover, Khalilzad left open the possibility that the potential rivals could include not just Russia and China, the heirs to the legacy of the Cold War, but also any of the "advanced industrial nations." Throughout the late 1980s and beginning of the '90s, there had been a wave of books, columns, and articles predicting that Japan and Germany, then the rising economic powers, might reemerge as rivals to the United States, and Khalilzad's paper seemed to countenance that possibility.

This draft of the Defense Planning Guidance was notable in several respects. First, it laid out a rationale for maintaining relatively high defense budgets in the absence of specific or immediate threats to the United States. Khalilzad later explained that he was seeking to find a way to break away from "threat-based thinking" in justifying defense budgets. Cheney and his civilian advisors had been arguing that the United States should not repeat the mistakes it had made after each of the two world wars, when America had demobilized its forces too quickly, causing problems that led to future wars. Cheney had made this historical argument the centerpiece of a speech he gave at Pearl Harbor in December 1991, on the fiftieth anniversary of the Japanese attack. "Pearl Harbor showed us that failing to be ready to fight brings a high price," he said.

Second, Khalilzad's draft emphasized the importance of democracy and political freedom. This may have seemed like merely a continuation of America's thinking during the Cold War, but in the 1990s, it meant support for democracy not only in Central Europe but also in Russia, Ukraine, and the other former Soviet republics, and the text made that explicit. Moreover, it suggested that the United States and NATO should have some sort of security or defense relationship with at least some of these former Soviet republics. In that sense, the DPG of 1992 was a forerunner to the thinking that led, during the Clinton administration, to the expansion of NATO.

Third, Khalilzad's draft reflected a distinct wariness about America's allies, particularly Germany and Japan. These countries should not be allowed to stray from the existing alliances (NATO and the United States–Japan Security Alliance) to the point where they could develop their own independent military capabilities. The United States did not want to see the "renationalization of defense" in Germany and Japan, in the words of Eric Edelman.

Fourth, the draft focused almost entirely on the problems that could be caused by other nation-states. It said little about transnational issues or the problems that could be caused by nonstate actors, such as terrorist groups. Years later, well after the September 11 attacks, some of Cheney's former advisors would acknowledge this defect. "If anything, the document can be faulted for not sufficiently anticipating the danger of Islamic extremism, state failure and terrorism," Edelman observed in 2011.

Finally, Khalilzad's draft gave short shrift to the notions of collective security and multilateralism. It never mentioned the United Nations. It said that while America might operate in some instances through its existing alliances, the United States might also in other cases act through "ad hoc assemblies" of nations. Those words were a precursor to the phrase used by the George W. Bush administration a decade later: that the United States would act with the support of a "coalition of the willing."

Above all, the focus of Khalilzad's draft was on the importance of America preserving its status as the world's most powerful nation and preventing any challengers from emerging. America's role would be one of "primacy," and the United States would work actively to maintain that primacy for as long as possible.

Not surprisingly, as soon as the draft leaked, it touched off a furor, not only in the press and with America's allies but even inside the Bush White House. Brent Scowcroft rejected it from the start. "That was just nutty," he said. "I read a draft of it. I thought, 'Cheney, this is just kooky.' It didn't go anywhere further."

At the time, the 1992 presidential campaign was in its early stages, with Bill Clinton seeking the Democratic nomination. Clinton said that the Pentagon draft report was "one more attempt" by Pentagon officials "to find an excuse for big budgets instead of downsizing." Officials in Western Europe were even less pleased. A French official asked why the Bush administration was developing a strategy "to keep Europe down." Amid the public controversy, even Wolfowitz briefly began to distance himself from the draft his subordinate had written. "He didn't want to be associated with it," Khalilzad said.

Then Cheney intervened. Although it had been drafted by Khalilzad, the report accurately reflected Cheney's views. At a meeting in his office, the defense secretary told Khalilzad, "You've discovered a new rationale for our role in the world. I read the document last night and I think it is brilliant." However, Cheney ordered that the draft be rewritten in a way that would place greater stress on alliances and would deemphasize the theme that America should act to undermine potential competitors.

The job of rewriting went to Libby. He adjusted wording that had seemed too provocative, but also introduced a few new concepts that filled out the notion of American primacy. The United States should seek to "shape the security environment" in each region, the new draft read, a phrase that reinforced the notion of America continually and actively operating to preserve its preeminence. Most important, Libby's new draft stated that the United States should seek to preserve its "strategic depth." It should remain so much more powerful than any other country that the leaders of other nations would not even try to compete with the United States, or would bankrupt themselves if they ever tried. Libby believed that with these new phrases, he had in subtle ways toughened, rather than weakened, the original draft.

The revised version was released to the press in the spring of 1992. Libby's careful euphemisms successfully turned around the press coverage; news stories at the time suggested that the problems with the earlier draft had been overcome. But the new draft did not win over Scowcroft or Bush. Not only did the White House decline to endorse the document, but officials there were not even willing to schedule a meeting to discuss it. Some of Cheney's aides believed that one reason had to do with domestic politics: President Bush's aides did not want the

Cheney-led strategy to become a continuing target for Clinton and the Democrats in the 1992 campaign. But even apart from political considerations, the Bush White House was composed of pragmatists who were not inclined to engage in grand strategy or what Bush himself called "the vision thing."

Instead, the new strategy became Cheney's own. In January 1993, in the final days of the administration, the DPG was put into declassified form and formally released under the name of the secretary of defense, with the title "Defense Strategy for the 1990s: The Regional Defense Strategy." It did not carry the imprimatur of the Bush administration as a whole; nor was it signed by Powell as chairman of the Joint Chiefs of Staff. It was strictly the product of Cheney and his civilian advisors, and it endures as the fullest expression of Cheney's vision for how America should approach the world after the Cold War.

In the years since this document became public, Cheney's closest aides, notably Wolfowitz and Edelman, have argued that the ideas in the DPG were not new and that they represented merely commonplace views in Washington in the period after the Soviet collapse. "Far from being an extreme strategy developed by a small group of Defense Department officials, the DPG not only reflected the consensus thinking of the first Bush administration but became generally accepted defense policy under President Clinton," Wolfowitz wrote in one academic paper. Edelman maintained that these were "basically unexceptional principles that everyone, including [subsequently] the Clintonites, agreed with."

Such claims are true in a few specific ways, but wrong in a broader sense. It is true that the Clinton administration later accepted the idea that the United States would act as the world's sole superpower; Bill Clinton and his secretary of state, Madeleine Albright, chose the phrase "indispensable nation" as their version of this idea. Clinton also did not consider himself bound by the United Nations or by principles of collective security; he chose to use military force in the Balkans without seeking UN approval. He also decided to expand NATO to the countries of Central and Eastern Europe, in much the way Cheney's document had envisioned.

However, Wolfowitz's claim that the Cheney strategy reflected "the consensus thinking" of the first Bush administration ignores the fact that George H. W. Bush's White House, over a period of nearly a year, refused to endorse what the Pentagon officials had written. The original intention had been to draft an administration strategy, not a Cheney strategy. Moreover, the Cheney DPG conveyed an emphasis on American military power and a de-emphasis on the role of alliances, neither of which was embraced by others in the Bush administration. Cheney's strategy gave lip service to the importance of alliances, but always with the qualification that alliances worked only when they followed American leadership. In the final three months of the Bush administration, Lawrence Eagleburger, the outgoing secretary of state, put together a memo on America's future role in the world that was strikingly different from the Cheney strategy. Rather than warning of rival powers, it emphasized problems caused by the fact that existing states were falling apart.

The assertions by Wolfowitz and Edelman that the ideas in their revised Defense Planning Guidance document were not new are also inaccurate or misleading. In fact, the declassified memos from the Pentagon's files about the Cheney-approved version of the DPG include a long, detailed summary laying out in detail the many "new policy directions" the DPG contained. The list starts with the notion that the United States should "preclude" hostile, nondemocratic domination of Europe, East Asia, and the Middle East, and that the United States should form a "security community" with new democracies from the former Soviet Union. Among the other "new policy directions" is a specific mention of American unilateralism: the report says that future U.S. presidents will need to act with force "in cases where very few others are with us."

* * *

It is curious that such an important Defense Department document as the one finally issued under Cheney's name would not bear the imprint or endorsement of the chairman of the Joint Chiefs of Staff. Indeed, logic suggests that Powell should have been directly involved. The drafting of the new defense strategy took place entirely within the Pentagon, and the authors were consulting with Powell's aides on the Joint Staff. The cover memo that circulated with Khalilzad's draft lists Powell as the most prominent recipient. One of the main purposes of the new strategy was to help determine military deployments, and Powell had both an interest and a direct stake in those decisions. Moreover, he had already worked closely with Cheney and Wolfowitz in the decision making over how to deal with congressional pressure to cut back and reshape the military.

Yet Powell's hands are nowhere to be seen on the DPG. He did not sign the final version issued to the public by Cheney as he was leaving office. He did not appear to sign any of the earlier drafts, either. He did not mention the report in his memoir, even though he covered almost every other public controversy that arose during his time as chairman of the Joint Chiefs.

It has been speculated that it was Powell, or people working for him on the Joint Staff, who leaked the early draft of the report, thus setting off the public controversy from which he then remained aloof. The first news story, based on Khalilzad's original draft, said that the document's source was "an official who believes this post–cold war strategy debate should be carried out in the public domain." Years later, Khalilzad noted pointedly that the document "was reviewed extensively within the Pentagon bureaucracy, particularly by the Joint Staff, which reported to Powell." In an interview, he was more explicit: he believed the leaker was Powell himself. He had no proof, he said, but he had been told of Powell's role in leaking it at the time by other senior Pentagon officials. (Powell responded that he had no idea who leaked the document, but he speculated that it might have been Wolfowitz or someone else on his staff. "It can't just be someone who wanted to shoot it down. It could be someone who wanted to puff it up," he said.)

Whether Powell leaked the report or not, the controversy helps to illustrate the different roles of Cheney and Powell, and also the larger dynamics within the Bush administration during its final eighteen months. On the surface, everything was harmonious. America had just won its stunning victory in the Gulf War, the Soviet Union had crumbled, and George H. W. Bush was running for reelection on the strength of his record on foreign policy. Inside the Pentagon, Cheney and Powell were close working partners—not just because of their collaborative roles in the wars in Panama and Iraq, but also because of their shared mission in preventing the Democratic Congress from cutting the defense budget too much or too fast.

Nevertheless, beneath the surface, there were growing disagreements over policy and philosophy. These tended to play out not as disputes between Cheney and Powell, but as disputes pitting Cheney and his civilian advisors against Bush, Scowcroft, and Baker and their staffs. The tension had first materialized over how to handle the Soviet collapse, where the mistrust between the Cheney team and the rest of the administration was intense. The debate a half year later over Cheney's strategy for the post–Cold War world, with its strong emphasis on American military power, represented a revival of this same internal struggle, with similar participants: Cheney and his civilian team developed the new strategy, but Scowcroft in the White House and Baker's State Department refused to endorse it.

Powell did not directly engage in these skirmishes, but his other actions and his record suggest that his sympathies lay with Bush, Scowcroft, and Baker, and in opposition to Cheney and his aides. The ideas expressed in the Cheney-endorsed DPG, of ensuring American primacy by precluding the emergence of rivals to American power, do not seem like principles Powell would have embraced.

But Powell did not openly oppose the ideas, either. He viewed himself as a manager and executive, not a thinker or long-term strategist. His job was to run the military, and he chose to let others, including the American public, decide questions of long-term strategy. The *Times's* description of the person who leaked Khalilzad's draft—an official who believed the debate over strategy after the Cold War ought to be carried out in public—could easily have described Powell.

One way or another, what had started out as the Defense Planning Guidance for the Bush administration as a whole became instead the "Regional Defense Strategy" issued by Cheney alone. The final document would not attract much attention because it was not released until the administration's final days in office. The Cheney strategy, a vision of America that emphasized its military power, would sit, virtually unnoticed, for eight years.

11

DEPARTURES

During the later stages of the Gulf War, even before the United States and its allies had completed their victory, a *New York Times* story listed both Colin Powell and Dick Cheney as potential Republican presidential candidates for 1996. Both men were also said to be possible vice-presidential nominees for President Bush if he were to replace Dan Quayle on the ticket in 1992. The article's author, White House correspondent Maureen Dowd, reported that "General Powell and Mr. Cheney are hailed on Capitol Hill, as one Republican lawmaker put it, as 'the most effective combination we've seen in this country since Babe Ruth and Lou Gehrig.'"

This was the narrative that prevailed throughout the final two years of the Bush administration. Cheney and Powell were the administration's shining lights. The internal conflicts over Russia policy and over the DPG were largely hidden from public view. America was swept up in the sense of triumph that followed the Gulf War, and Cheney and Powell were more closely identified with the military victory than anyone else in the administration.

Their reputations were at a peak, their services in demand. In late 1991, when Bush decided to replace John Sununu as his White House chief of staff, Cheney was briefly under consideration to succeed him.

But Cheney wasn't interested in returning to the job he had held six-teen years earlier, in the Ford administration. The new chief of staff, Sam Skinner, lasted only half a year before stepping down, and when he did, Cheney was once again at the top of the list of possible replace-ments. Brent Scowcroft called Cheney to ask if he wanted the job. Cheney declined. "If the president had asked me directly, I would have done it," he later admitted, "but I'm glad that he got Jim Baker to do it instead."

Meanwhile, Powell's name was repeatedly put forward for vice presi-dent. Several Republican politicians proposed that Bush dump Quayle and choose Powell as his running mate; he would have been the first person of color on any major-party ticket. These suggestions came from inside the administration, too. In the spring of 1992, Secretary of State Baker asked one of his senior aides, Dennis Ross, to come up with ideas for some dramatic move that could improve Bush's chances for reelec-tion, and Ross specifically suggested putting Powell on the ticket. Noth-ing came of it because Bush was unwilling to replace Quayle. At the same time, Bill Clinton and the Democrats were also trying to enlist Powell as a vice-presidential nominee. Clinton's friend and advisor Vernon Jor-dan approached Powell to ask if he was interested in serving as Clin-ton's running mate. Powell said no; he had no interest in running against Bush.

That summer, as the Republican National Convention drew near, another name came up as a possible vice-presidential nominee: Dick Cheney. George W. Bush, the president's oldest son, recommended to his father that he should drop Quayle and replace him with Cheney. "Dad said no," recalled the younger Bush. "He thought the move would look desperate and embarrass Dan." It would not be the last time George W. Bush entertained the prospect of Cheney as vice president.

* * *

Reflecting years later on the unusual mood in America in 1992, a year after the Gulf War, Dick Cheney observed, "We'd had a hell of a suc-cess. What do you do after you've done the ticker tape parade on Broad-way? . . . You know, what's the encore? Of course, what happened was that the focus shifted to a large extent, I think, off national security and defense kinds of issues and onto domestic issues."

That year, Powell and Cheney became involved in one more searching foreign policy debate: whether the United States should intervene to
prevent ethnic cleansing in Bosnia. Once again, the two men were on the
same side of the issue. They opposed the use of force, rejecting arguments
by the State Department and some members of the National Security
Council that military action was warranted. In their opposition, however, Powell and Cheney took slightly different paths. The debate over
Bosnia brought forth from Powell strong views that went to the essence
of his mind-set, and from Cheney, separate arguments that went to the
heart of his core beliefs.

The problems in Bosnia arose as an outgrowth of the breakup of
Yugoslavia. In the republic of Bosnia-Herzegovina, a referendum in
February 1992 produced an overwhelming vote for independence. In
response, Bosnian Serb soldiers and militias began attacking the Bosnian Muslim population in what would become a protracted campaign
of "ethnic cleansing." The Serb forces also began to attack international
relief missions. By July, European leaders were urging Washington to
send troops to help stop the violence.

Baker and Scowcroft supported U.S. military action, if only for the
limited purpose of delivering humanitarian relief and supplies in Bosnia. The issue went before a meeting of the president's national security
team, one that Baker later called "one of the most spirited I had ever
attended as Secretary of State." Cheney and Powell adamantly opposed
even a limited, short-term use of force. Cheney told reporters that the
United States "cannot be the policeman of the world. We have to make
critical judgments about when it is in our interest to intervene and when
it isn't." Instead, the Bush administration tentatively decided to help
finance relief missions, but not to send troops. The debate was revived
that autumn, however, after new reports of atrocities. British prime minister John Major appealed to President Bush to approve limited air strikes
that would stop the Bosnian Serbs from shelling the city of Sarajevo.

By this point, the continuing calls for U.S. military action were
beginning to alarm Colin Powell. For him, the idea of intervening in
Bosnia sparked memories not only of Vietnam in the 1960s, but also of
the terrorist bombing that killed marines in Beirut in 1983. He felt that
such an intervention would run afoul of the principles he and Caspar

Weinberger had developed to determine when American troops should be sent into battle. In Bosnia, there was no clearly defined mission and no sense of whether limited military action would accomplish U.S. objectives or fall short, leading to calls for deeper military involvement.

In late September, Powell launched what amounted to a public campaign against even a limited American intervention or surgical air strikes in Bosnia. "As soon as they tell me it is limited, it means they do not care whether you achieve a result or not," he said in one newspaper interview. "As soon as they tell me 'surgical,' I head for the bunker." His comments brought forth a denunciation by the *New York Times* editorial page. "Missions are seldom as well defined as generals would like," the editorial read. "When Americans spend more than $280 billion for defense, surely they ought to be getting more for their money than no-can-do." The editorial concluded that Bush should tell Powell what President Lincoln had told General George McClellan: "If you don't want to use the Army, I should like to borrow it for a while."

These words infuriated Powell, and he sat down and wrote an impassioned response. He obtained formal approval from Cheney to publish it and then sent it off to the *Times*, which ran it as an op-ed piece four days later, under the headline "Why Generals Get Nervous." Powell first cited the successful military operations for which he had been responsible in Iraq, Panama, the Philippines, and elsewhere. However, he went on, "military force is not always the right answer. If force is used imprecisely or out of frustration rather than clear analysis, the situation can be made worse. . . . When the desired result isn't achieved, the situation can be made worse."

Some of Powell's arguments were open to question. Experts on the Balkans pointed out that Bosnia wasn't like Vietnam, which had a well-trained, determined Communist Party and army that had been fighting for many years; the Serb irregular forces, by contrast, were weekend warriors trying to grab more land. But Powell's views held sway, and the Bush administration stayed out of Bosnia.

What attracted little public attention at the time, but stands out far more in hindsight, was the stunning nature of the public role Powell was assuming in this campaign against involvement in Bosnia. This was the chairman of the Joint Chiefs of Staff, a military leader, essentially telling civilian leaders and the American public not to go to war. He was running roughshod over long-established principles of civil-military relations. The chairman of the Joint Chiefs of Staff is supposed to be the principal military advisor to the president, but in the past and in the future, that military advice was given in private, not in the op-ed pages.

Nevertheless, throughout these debates, Cheney supported Powell; he, too, opposed action in Bosnia. "We were in total agreement, and we thought it was a bad idea" to send U.S. forces there, Cheney later said. Before long, he began to raise some arguments of his own against intervention. He told reporters that he was concerned that the United States could not work easily in a coalition with its allies. "We're constrained to some extent by virtue of the fact that we're operating as part of an international coalition," he said. It was an early version of an argument he would make years later: that America should seek to preserve its own unilateral freedom of action, rather than being hemmed in by the needs or different interests of its allies.

* * *

As the 1992 presidential campaign drew to a close, Powell and Cheney speculated privately during their after-hours chats in Cheney's Pentagon office that Bush didn't appear to have the energy he had displayed in the past. They were right. The president had been diagnosed in the late spring of 1991 with a thyroid condition called Graves' disease, one that at times reduced his energy for the campaign and other activities.

But what concerned them more was that America's attention had turned away from foreign policy to domestic issues, which were never Bush's strong suit. Moreover, enough time had passed since the end of the Gulf War for Americans to see that Saddam Hussein remained in power, demonstrating that the military victory of February 1991 had been incomplete. Similarly, enough time had passed since the fall of the Berlin Wall for Americans to see that new problems were emerging (e.g., Bosnia) that did not fit into the old Cold War narratives. Bush's opponent, Bill Clinton, proved far more adept at capturing the nation's mood, and he emerged victorious on Election Day.

Weeks later, Bush's lame-duck administration initiated one more military operation, dispatching American troops on a mission to deliver food supplies in the midst of a civil war in Somalia. The motivation was humanitarian, but as Bush acknowledged in his diary, there were side benefits: to show that the United States could use its power to assist black Africans and to help Muslims. "There is a feeling in the Muslim world that we don't care about Muslims," Bush told his diary. "A large humanitarian effort backed by force would help us in that category."

Cheney and Powell were unenthusiastic. "I was reluctant," Cheney recalled. "General Powell was even somewhat more conservative than I was." However, they did not directly oppose the mission in Somalia the way they had in Bosnia. It was supposed to be a quick, short-term military operation, without the sort of risks that Bosnia had presented.

There was an unusual, inverse relationship between Bosnia and Somalia: Powell and Cheney were willing to go along with an intervention in Somalia in part because they had already said no to Bosnia. They did not want to be seen as opposing two humanitarian missions in a row, particularly given that Bush was clearly eager to protect the food shipments in Somalia.

* * *

By January, it was time for good-byes, or at least some of them: Cheney was leaving with the rest of the Bush administration, but Powell was not. His four-year term as chairman of the Joint Chiefs had begun on October 1, 1989, and thus would not expire until nine months into the Clinton administration. This led to a series of awkward interactions, above all between Powell and the incoming Clinton team, but also between Powell and Cheney.

In public, the transition went smoothly. On January 12, 1993, in the ceremonial hall at Fort Myer, Virginia, Powell and the other members of the Joint Chiefs of Staff thanked and paid honor to Cheney. Their outpourings of thanks were genuine; Cheney had been popular with military leaders. Their standard for judging defense secretaries was still Robert McNamara, whom they had loathed. Like McNamara, Cheney had regularly interrogated his generals and admirals, pressing them for details, but in his case, this was simply for his own information, not to micromanage what they were doing, as McNamara had done. "When he [Cheney] came to the [National Military] Command Center, he learned and listened," Powell's aide Lawrence Wilkerson observed.

At the Fort Myer ceremony, Powell said of Cheney, "He has led the armed forces through the end of containment, through the end of the Cold War, the end of the Soviet Union, the end of communism, and he has led the armed forces during the period when we saw the triumph of values, the values of freedom and determination." He praised Cheney for making sure "that our military advice was heard throughout the entire political decision process."

Powell then steered from these larger issues to his personal fondness for Cheney. "We spent a lot of time together over the past three and a half years," he told the audience. "We dealt with matters of war and peace. . . . We spent many, many evenings around that little round table in Dick's office. We debated, we discussed, we got annoyed with each other. On occasion, one of us even got chewed out. But it was a remarkable relationship. It was a remarkable experience for me. It was a remarkable friendship."

In turn, Cheney praised Powell, saying that after choosing him to be chairman of the Joint Chiefs, "I have never once during the last four years ever had reason to regret that decision." Powell had "completely mastered one of the most difficult positions and one of the most difficult jobs in the world," he added.

At the end of his speech, Cheney said it was "time to move on. . . . Transitions are never easy, especially for those of us who are leaving." Nevertheless, he concluded, those transitions are "a vital part of the unique and distinguishing feature of our civilization, our system of democratic self-governance."

Those words about the difficulty of transitions set the backdrop for what happened seven days later, an incident that quickly made its way around the Pentagon and into the lore of stories about Cheney. On the day before Bill Clinton's inauguration, as the Bush appointees in the Pentagon were clearing out of their offices, Powell went up to the suite of offices of the secretary of defense to bid Cheney farewell. Cheney's possessions were sitting in boxes on the floor, but when Powell asked Cheney's secretary where he was, she said that he had already left the building hours earlier. He had not stopped to say good-bye to Powell.

Powell was disappointed and hurt. As he explained in his memoir a few years later, he had developed "genuine affection" for Cheney. "He and I, had never, in four years, spent a single social hour together. We were, however, remarkably close in our attitudes," he wrote. "We thought so much alike that, in the Tank [the Joint Chiefs' secure conference room in the Pentagon] or the Oval Office, we could finish each other's sentences."

Perhaps Powell should not have taken it personally. Cheney didn't make the rounds to bid farewell to anyone else in the Pentagon, either. "He didn't see anybody," recalled Dennis Blair, who served under Powell on the Joint Staff. "All of a sudden, he's gone, and we never had a chance to say good-bye to him."

It was vintage Cheney. His relationship with Powell was, first of all, a business relationship, and for him that business was ending. Cheney later told Zalmay Khalilzad that he had been intending to say good-bye to Powell on his way out of the Pentagon, but that he had gotten a call from his wife, Lynne, to say she was waiting for him outside—so he left. There was not much more to it, he suggested.

But that was not the whole story. Cheney was not, to say the least, adept at conveying personal warmth or feelings of any kind. Only years later would he acknowledge his emotions, admitting that his last days at the Pentagon had been bittersweet. "We had a hell of a run," he said. "You know—because I'd been through the process before—that you're not going to see or work with these people again, probably." And so, he explained, "I didn't want to go around and throw my arms around people and say, 'Gee, it's been great.'" In short, it was not that Cheney was unemotional, but that he kept his emotions under rigid control. He would also later acknowledge that throughout his time at the Pentagon, he had had a muscle spasm or knot in his back. "I didn't realize it until I left, and it quit the day I left. It's the tension that you live with all that time."

* * *

In their final weeks at the Pentagon, some of Cheney's civilian advisors observed something curious: Colin Powell was being unusually friendly to them, conveying the idea that they had a natural bond, even though he had sparred with them on a range of issues over the previous few years.

There was a reason: During the transition period between Election Day and Inauguration Day, Powell was starting to deal with the new Clinton team. He was discovering that the internal differences within the Bush administration paled in comparison with their collective differences with the Democrats. All the senior members of the Bush team, from Scowcroft and Baker to Cheney and Quayle, favored a strong national defense, while the Democrats had for years been proposing cuts in the defense budget. From their perspective, Clinton's knowledge of defense issues was deficient; indeed, he was the first president since World War II who hadn't served in the military.

A year earlier, Powell had been so angry with Cheney's aide Eric Edelman that he sought to have him excluded from a meeting. Nevertheless, Edelman remembered years later, "By the end of Bush Forty-One, my relationship with Powell was reasonably good. In fact, I remember having some conversations with him in the transition where he was unburdening himself to me about how hard it was dealing with the Clinton folks."

Just as Powell was uneasy with the members of the incoming Clinton team, they, too, were edgy with him, viewing him as a charter member of the outgoing Republican hierarchy. A few months into the new administration, there was an awards ceremony at the Pentagon. Cheney came back for it, his first visit as a private citizen. At the podium, Powell introduced him to the audience and then quipped, "Welcome back, boss!" President Clinton, Powell's boss now, found out about it and was not pleased.

Nevertheless, Powell made the best of his new situation, putting to good use his charm and sense of humor. One advantage of dealing with the Democrats was that their party was more tolerant and relaxed on questions of race. James Woolsey, the conservative Democrat who served as Clinton's first director of central intelligence, recalled one White House meeting where senior Clinton administration officials were ribbing Powell about a story in the *Washington Post* reporting that he had just bought a new home in Virginia with a four-car garage. Why did he need a four-car garage? one of them teased. Powell reminded them that his hobby was tinkering with old Volvos. "If I couldn't keep them in the garage, if I moved into that neighborhood and they were all outside, folks would say, 'Here come the black folks, and there goes the neighborhood,'" Powell quipped.

But Powell chafed at the Clinton team's slipshod operating style—especially that of the new defense secretary, Les Aspin, who had spent most of his career on Capitol Hill critiquing policy but not making it. Aspin's chronic disorganization made Powell yearn for the Cheney era. "They would go through these interminable meetings, and no decision would be made," said Wilkerson. "Cheney was twenty minutes and a decision. At eighteen minutes, if he did not have the information he needed to make the decision, you got chewed out and you went away to get the information he needed to make the decision. . . . Powell liked an agenda. He liked the agenda to be followed. He liked for time not to be wasted. Aspin's whole modus operandi wasted time."

* * *

The issue that preoccupied Powell at the start of his nine-month tenure in the Clinton administration was gays in the military. During his campaign, Clinton had promised to lift the long-standing prohibition on homosexuals serving in the armed forces. Powell was strenuously opposed.

At a meeting with Clinton during the transition, Powell had appealed for delay, urging the president-elect to put the issue on the back burner for a few months after he took office, perhaps by ordering a study by his new defense secretary. "Don't make the gay issue the first horse out of the gate with the armed forces," Powell said. Clinton rejected the advice. Five days after his inauguration, the new president summoned the Joint Chiefs of Staff to a White House meeting to discuss changing the policy on gays in the military.

All the chiefs were opposed; in that sense, Powell was not unique. But in the debate that followed, he found himself in an awkward position because of his race. Many Democrats, including Clinton, argued that this was a new civil rights issue. The armed forces had been formally segregated until 1948. Some of the arguments made in 1993 in favor of preserving the ban on gays in the military were similar to those that had earlier been used to preserve racial segregation: for example, the claims that integrating gays would undermine the morale of the troops, and that some soldiers felt they should not be forced to live in close proximity with gays.

Powell argued strenuously to Clinton and Vice President Al Gore that they should not view the issue of gays in the military as a civil rights issue on the same order as racial integration. Any comparison between gays and blacks was "off base," he told them, because race is a "benign characteristic" but "sexuality is different." Powell argued that skin color was "non-behavioral," while homosexuality involved behavior and impinged on issues of privacy. He also maintained that ending the ban on gays could bring medical complications, such as an increase in HIV/AIDS among the troops.

The group decided to delay the issue a few months for further study. But during that first meeting, Powell suggested an idea that became the eventual, if temporary, resolution to the issue: the armed forces could simply "stop asking" soldiers or possible recruits if they were gay, he proposed. Months later, the Clinton administration would adapt that idea into its policy of "Don't ask, don't tell." This policy didn't end the formal ban on gays, and in that sense, Powell had won the battle. "Don't ask, don't tell" would endure for nearly two decades until, in 2011, congressional legislation, court rulings, and the Obama administration combined to end the formal ban on gays serving openly in the armed forces.

* * *

The Clinton administration's first months in office were Powell's last ones, and he soon found himself engaging in some of the same debates he had already had under Bush. He found himself making the case, once again, against American military intervention in Bosnia.

He argued that stopping the violence in Bosnia would require tens of thousands of troops, would cost billions of dollars, and would result in many casualties and an open-ended intervention. He analyzed the proposals for a limited use of force and found them all infeasible. "Time and again he led us up the hill of possibilities and dropped us off on the other side with the practical equivalent of 'No can do,'" Madeleine Albright, then Clinton's U.S. ambassador to the United Nations, recalled later on. It was during one of these briefings that Albright asked Powell, "What are you saving this superb military for, Colin, if we can't use it?" Powell later recorded the exchange in his memoir, adding, "I thought I would have an aneurysm. American GIs were not toy soldiers to be moved around on some sort of global game board." For her part, Albright said that Powell's caution showed that "the lessons of Vietnam could be learned too well."

Powell's instinctive restraint about the use of force prevailed once again that spring, in an episode that involved an Iraqi assassination plot against George H. W. Bush. The former president was traveling in Kuwait when authorities discovered a huge car bomb designed to explode near his motorcade. The CIA and FBI soon determined that Iraqi intelligence had been responsible. Furious at this effort to kill an American president, Clinton called in Powell and suggested the idea of a massive military response against Iraq. Powell cooled him down. "You need a response, but not another war," he told him. Taking Powell's advice, Clinton chose a more proportionate response: he approved the firing of Tomahawk missiles on the headquarters building of Iraq's intelligence service.

But by this juncture, Powell was trying to look ahead, speaking out more about how the U.S. military would operate in the future and less about the Vietnam-related issues that had dominated his thinking in the past. At the good-bye ceremony for Cheney in January, Powell had asserted that he and Cheney thought so much alike that they could finish each other's sentences. But in the spring of 1993, Powell began to develop ideas that veered off in strikingly different directions from Cheney's.

That April, the UN Association of the United States, a nonprofit member organization devoted to building support for the United Nations, gave Powell its Global Leadership Award. In his acceptance speech, Powell sketched out a broad, increasingly powerful role for the United Nations in the post–Cold War world. "Without the constraining bonds of the superpower standoff, new UN initiatives have suddenly become possible, initiatives which correspond more closely to the original intent of the signers of the U.N. Charter," he asserted. "We have begun to use the power and influence of the U.N. to make and keep the peace."

Two months later, speaking at Harvard University's commencement, Powell said that under Presidents Bush and Clinton, the Pentagon had been working on "a new strategy," one that would guide America in the post–Cold War world. He did not mention Cheney's DPG, even though it had formally been issued only five months earlier. Powell gave the barest outlines of his own ideas, but to the extent he did, they focused on multilateral approaches to the world. He envisioned that the United States would maintain "a quality, combat-ready force that can go anywhere in the world quickly and fight when it gets there." Such forces, Powell said, would likely act "as part of a great international coalition such as the U.N."

In short, as Cheney and Powell were departing from the Pentagon, Cheney was giving ever-greater emphasis to America's unilateral role as the world's most powerful nation, while Powell was stressing the importance of America acting in concert with other nations.

* * *

By the summer of 1993, Powell was beginning to lay the groundwork for his retirement and a return to civilian life. In August, following a flurry of negotiations with book publishers, he signed a contract with Random House for his autobiography. The value of the deal was estimated at $6.5 million. After living for his entire career on a military salary, he would soon become a wealthy man.

He began to distance himself from daily military operations of the sort that had once taken most of his time. American troops were still on the ground in Somalia—and, in fact, those troops would become embroiled, soon after Powell's retirement, in the "Black Hawk Down" disaster that took the lives of eighteen American soldiers. But Clinton administration officials say that in his final months, Powell tended to avoid high-level meetings on Somalia and left the details to his deputy, Admiral David Jeremiah. "Powell was AWOL on Somalia," asserted Sandy Berger, Clinton's deputy national security advisor. Lawrence Wilkerson acknowledged that in his final months, Powell "couldn't wait to get out the door." Asked what his boss was thinking about Somalia during that period, Wilkerson replied, "I'm retiring—let me out of here."

Powell's departure was as different from Cheney's as it could possibly have been. He wasn't going to slip out the door and avoid saying good-bye. In his final days, he made the rounds in the Pentagon. "When he left, he said, 'Anybody who wants to have a picture taken with me, I'll do it,'" recalled Dennis Blair. "And I think it took him three hours—everybody on his staff who wanted to have a picture taken with him—and he stood there with everyone, and then signed the picture and sent it to him."

Wilkerson was put in charge of Powell's formal retirement ceremony. Planning for the event started in August. "It was an incredible, gargantuan mission to get him out of there," he recalled. Hundreds of people were invited. Powell spent money from his recent book advance to buy engraved silver-framed portraits of himself and give them to about forty of the attendees. Wilkerson arranged for two different receiving lines: one for President Clinton and another for former president George H. W. Bush, who was coming back from Texas for the event.

At 4 p.m. on September 30, 1993, on the parade grounds at Fort Myer, with bands playing and flags flying, Powell said his farewell. The ceremony took on the trappings of a State of the Union address: in addition to Clinton, Gore, Bush, and Quayle, those attending included justices of the Supreme Court, members of the diplomatic corps, various defense ministers visiting from abroad, members of the Joint Chiefs of Staff, and America's military commanders. After greeting them all, Powell went out of his way to give special thanks to "my dear friend" Dick Cheney, who was in the audience that day, and to another defense secretary for whom he had worked, Caspar Weinberger.

Above all, Powell dwelled on his thanks for an institution: the U.S. Army. "The Army has been my home. The Army has been my life," he said. "The Army has been my profession. The Army has been my love for all these many years. . . . The Army took in a young black kid from ROTC in the South Bronx and brought him to this point."

With that, Powell's military career came to a close. He entered his new life as a civilian and a future that virtually everyone believed would be filled with new achievements and new glory. One of the many letters Powell received over the following days was a note from former president Richard Nixon, praising his remarks at the farewell. "This marked, to paraphrase Churchill, not the end or the beginning of the end, but the end of the beginning for your spectacular career," Nixon wrote. Nixon told Powell that whatever Powell did, he would be "crowned with success."

PART THREE

INTERREGNUM

12

ON THE OUTSIDE

When they departed from office in 1993, Colin Powell and Dick Cheney found themselves in fairly similar positions. Both men were still basking in the glow of public admiration following America's military victories in Panama and Iraq, and as a result, both men were mentioned as possible candidates for president. Both men had spent most of their careers on the federal payroll, Cheney as a civilian and Powell in the military. And both men had an interest in making money in the short term, while leaving the door open to a return to public life.

At that point, the two men would have thought of themselves as having comparable views of the world, even though Powell considered Cheney a strong conservative, and Cheney considered Powell too tied to conventional, mainstream thinking. They still agreed on preserving a strong, powerful American military, in the face of repeated calls by the Democratic Congress to slash the defense budget and open the way for a "peace dividend."

During the Clinton years, Cheney and Powell maintained their friendship from a distance. "Are you and Colin still close?" an interviewer asked Cheney in March 2000. "Yes," Cheney replied. Reflecting on his time as defense secretary, he said, "I have fond recollections and memories of all that, and especially the people, and especially guys like Colin Powell—but we still see each other from time to time."

Cheney and Powell engaged in no public disputes over foreign policy issues, and yet, by the end of the 1990s, the two men had grown apart in their thinking and mind-sets, much further than they themselves recognized at the time. Indeed, in an interview conducted in 2011, Powell acknowledged that by the time both men returned to office in the George W. Bush administration, he and Cheney were "not philosophically close enough to each other. The differences were too severe."

How could this be? How could two men who left office in 1993 believing they mostly saw alike on major defense issues, who remained friendly and had no particular disagreements over the following eight years, come to be so profoundly different in outlook by the end of the decade? The answer lies less in anything that either of them did than in the events and circumstances of the 1990s, which drove Dick Cheney and Colin Powell in different directions, politically and philosophically.

* * *

In the years after he left the Pentagon, Dick Cheney made, by his own accounting, "more money than I thought I would ever have." He took positions on the boards of directors of several leading American companies, including Morgan Stanley, Procter and Gamble, and Union Pacific. He also accepted a chair, including a stipend and staff support, at the American Enterprise Institute, the old-line Washington think tank founded to reflect the interests of the oil industry, which had more recently served as an establishment haven for the neoconservative movement.

Much of Cheney's new wealth came from the lecture circuit. In his years immediately after leaving office, he delivered an estimated seventy-five to eighty paid speeches a year. In the summer of 1993, he made an eight-thousand-mile road trip, from Washington, DC, to British Columbia and then to Wyoming, giving speeches along the way. He traveled by car and on his own, once again fitting into the role of the habitual loner; one could never imagine the gregarious Colin Powell choosing to make such a long journey without company.

Along the way, Cheney decided he might want to run for president in 1996. He began to attack the Clinton administration on the grounds that there were still threats to America's security on the horizon and that the country needed a "foreign policy president." In 1994 he formed his own political action committee, with David Addington as one of its two staff members. In that year Cheney traveled around the country once again, doing campaign events, raising money, and seeing whether he really wanted to take on the rigors of a presidential campaign.

The results of the 1994 congressional elections were a stunning triumph for the Republican Party, although also, in one sense, bittersweet for Cheney. The Republicans won control of both the Senate and the House of Representatives—the House for the first time since 1954. In other circumstances, Cheney could have been a leading beneficiary of that victory. He had studied Congress as a student and served there for a decade, so he realized how momentous the changes would be on Capitol Hill, ranging from Republicans gaining control of committee chairmanships and staffs right down to the greater number of offices they would get inside the U.S. Capitol. But what he realized as well was that five years earlier he had been the House Republican whip and that the congressman who had succeeded him in that job, his friend Newt Gingrich, was about to become Speaker of the House.

That Christmas, Cheney gathered with his family and talked about whether to run for president. He decided not to do so. His talk of running had not produced an outpouring of public support on the level necessary for a presidential campaign. He had meanwhile discovered that the qualities that made him popular at the time of the Gulf War, above all his seeming calm in a time of crisis, were not sufficient to make him a good presidential candidate. "That [the experience of running the Gulf War] is not dealing with the abortion issue," he said a few years later. "As soon as you move out of that arena that we were so successful in, over into the political arena, . . . I wasn't comfortable doing that. I wouldn't have been very good at it." He also said he didn't like the idea of "putting my family through the meat-grinder of a national campaign."

At the time, Colin Powell, who was weighing the idea of running for president himself, asked his old friend Cheney why he had decided to drop out. "He just said he didn't want to—the business of raising money had become distasteful," Powell later recalled.

There was another submerged issue Cheney didn't discuss at the time, but which he might have been obliged to deal with in a presidential campaign: his daughter Mary, then twenty-five years old, was gay. Years later, some of his friends and former aides continued to believe that this was one of the reasons he decided not to run for president in 1996. Mary Cheney had told her parents she was a lesbian in the 1980s, when she was a teenager, but the fact had never been made public. In the Republican primaries, it could have posed a problem. (Mary Cheney herself later wrote that she asked her father if she had been a factor in his decision, and he told her she was not; he simply decided he didn't want to raise money, travel so much, or worry whether his positions would be popular.)

After formally announcing in early 1995 that he wouldn't run, Cheney decided that his political career was over. He would never be president of the United States. In what seemed like a joke at the time, he told his friends, "If you can get me the job by appointment, I'll take it. I don't want to run for it."

* * *

In October 1993, Colin Powell became a private citizen for the first time in more than three decades. As chairman of the Joint Chiefs of Staff, he had overseen a staff of ninety people. He took a few of his closest aides from the Pentagon to help him in his new life. One of them was Lawrence Wilkerson, his Pentagon speechwriter. Powell's old friend Prince Bandar bin Sultan, the Saudi ambassador, gave him a new computer to work on.

Standing with Powell on the front steps of Powell's Northern Virginia home one day that fall, Wilkerson asked his boss, "What now?" Would he ever go back into government? Some people were saying he should run for president, Wilkerson continued. "No, I'm not that serious about that," Powell told him. "But a Cabinet position." Wilkerson asked which one, assuming the answer would be secretary of defense. Instead, Powell responded, "Secretary of state. Foreign policy is what interests me."

However, he quickly added, "You have to have a lot of money. You can't be a Cabinet officer unless you have a lot of money. And for a black man, that's especially true, because I have to assure my extended family, and I can't do that without money." In his thinking, a Cabinet officer must not only forego the greater income he or she could earn in the private sector, but may also be obliged to pay money out of pocket on items like entertainment or a spouse's travel expenses.

Like Cheney, Powell was weighing the possibility of returning to government in the future, but he hoped to accumulate some wealth in the meantime. His $6.5 million book advance was a major step toward that goal, and he also traveled around the country making speeches that bolstered his income.

The result was that by the time Henry Louis Gates Jr., the scholar of African American history, interviewed Powell in 1995, Powell was able to tell him proudly, "I'm now a wealthy person. I wasn't wealthy when I retired. I mean, I just figured out what the white guys were doing." He went on to tell Gates that while he was something of a liberal on social issues, he considered himself an old-fashioned Republican on economic issues, because he believed in the importance of lowering taxes and promoting entrepreneurship. "You've got to get the tax burden off business," he declared. "You've got to lower the capital-gains tax. . . . The government's got to get off people's backs."

If those last remarks sounded a bit like a Republican political speech, there was a reason. Powell was thinking seriously about running for president, despite what he had told Wilkerson two years earlier. He had cast aside suggestions or offers of high-level appointments; at the end of 1994, President Clinton tried to persuade him to succeed Warren Christopher as secretary of state, but Powell declined, saying he needed to complete his book.

His memoir, written with Joseph Persico, prompted Powell to make choices about how much he was willing to say about his experiences in government. One of the many questions was what to write about the episode at the end of the Bush administration, when Cheney left the Pentagon without saying good-bye. According to Richard Armitage, Powell's initial draft contained tough, critical language, saying the incident showed that Cheney had little real connection to people. Armitage said he persuaded Powell to soften the tone. "Just think how Liz is going to feel when she reads that," Armitage told Powell, a reminder that Cheney's daughter Liz had gone to work for Armitage. In its final version, Powell's book emphasized how Cheney was a "lone cowboy," but also included the passage saying the two men were so alike in their thinking that they could finish each other's sentences. "I had developed not only professional respect but genuine affection for this quiet man," Powell wrote.

Powell's book, *My American Journey*, came out in the early fall of

1995 and became a publishing sensation. As Powell traveled around the country on a book tour, large crowds turned out to hear him, see him, and have him sign their copies. Over the previous year, his name had come up repeatedly as a possible presidential candidate, and by the time of the book tour, various "Powell for President" committees had formed around the country. For months, Powell flirted with the idea, discussing it regularly with Armitage and with Kenneth Duberstein, a close friend from the Reagan administration. But in early November, Powell concluded that he wasn't going to run, making the announcement at a press conference a few days later.

A number of factors underlay his decision. His wife, Alma, was intensely opposed. She not only worried about the general impact of Powell becoming the center of national attention as the first serious black candidate for president; more specifically, she feared he might be the target of an assassination attempt. "Somebody will try to kill him," she told a family friend.

But Powell had his own reasons for choosing not to run, beyond Alma's opposition. Richard Ben Cramer's 1992 book *What It Takes: The Way to the White House* described the qualities necessary for running for president—above all, an intense desire to be president and, with it, a willingness to withstand the ardors and the rancor of a presidential campaign. Powell concluded that he didn't possess those qualities and, indeed, didn't want them.

This was one of the fundamental differences between him and Cheney. Many years later, Powell would say of Cheney and Donald Rumsfeld, "They're politicians. I'm not." Cheney had won election to Congress six times and had helped run Gerald Ford's 1976 campaign. By contrast, Powell's whole life had been in the military, and he had never been directly involved in politics at all. He had rarely been subjected to the sort of personal attacks a presidential candidate can expect. "For all his very many virtues, [Powell] also has a very thin skin," said Cheney's aide Eric Edelman. "And his thin skin, I think he was self-aware enough to know, would not have survived a presidential campaign. I think he would have had a very tough time dealing with all of that."

Finally, Powell had to confront the obvious political obstacles. To be sure, he was personally popular, but for which party would he run for president in 1996? He obviously couldn't run as a Democrat; Clinton would be running for reelection. But his views on domestic social issues seemed increasingly out of touch with those of the Republican Party. ("I believe in affirmative action. I believe in a woman's right to decide her own fate," Powell said bluntly in an interview a few years later.)

Later in life, he came to conclude that he simply wasn't the sort of person who gravitated to any political party. He thought one of the reasons for this was his long military career. "I have a hard time being partisan because my whole military experience was 'Learn about the other guy, learn about your enemy before you take him on,'" Powell reflected. "So, I always wanted to know both sides of every issue—and not necessarily adopt one side or the other. Because the truth usually lies somewhere in between. So, I could never really be a good politician, at the national level."

In theory, Powell could have run for president as an independent candidate, much as Ross Perot had in 1992, but Powell and his friends considered this approach impractical. History showed that without a party behind him, he would have virtually no chance of winning—and even if he did, he would not be able to govern effectively, because he would have no base in Congress.

Even the process of trying to decide whether to run made Powell unhappy. "It was about as miserable a period as I've ever had in my life," he would later say. "I can usually handle problems, and I can usually handle stress, but I was losing weight."

All in all, Powell recalled, "I looked at it [running for president] in '95, because of the hoopla about the book. It didn't take me long to realize that this is not me, not for me. And not for my family. And I'll just do something else, thank you."

* * *

Through the 1990s, larger trends in America and the world drove Powell and Cheney further apart in their thinking. The first and most important of these was the drift of the Republican Party. The George H. W. Bush administration was, in many ways, a last high point for the tradition of moderate Republicanism dating back to Gerald Ford, Nelson Rockefeller, and, before them, Thomas Dewey. There had long been a separate strain of conservatism within the party, symbolized by Barry Goldwater and Ronald Reagan, and the midterm elections of 1994, in which the Republicans took control of Congress, reflected the renewed strength of this conservatism at the grass roots. Newt Gingrich became Speaker of the House and brought with him a new, scorched-earth confrontational style; the ordinary civil discourse and politesse that Republican leaders had once exhibited became increasingly a rarity. In 1996, Bob Dole, the party's presidential nominee, staked out positions considerably more conservative than those of George H. W. Bush. The Republican platform on which Dole ran that year took strong positions on domestic social issues Bush had sought to downplay: opposition to abortion, support for appointing federal judges who opposed abortion, opposition to same-sex marriage, opposition to affirmative action, and a declaration that "illegal aliens should not receive public benefits other than emergency aid."

These developments served to create greater distance between the centrist Powell and the conservative Cheney. Powell gave a speech for Dole at the 1996 Republican convention in San Diego. He remained enormously popular, still basking in the glow of his military service, the victory in the Gulf War, and his recent book. When he appeared before the delegates, he received a series of ovations. But there was also a smattering of boos when Powell made a plea for diversity, inclusion, and tolerance. "You all know that I believe in a woman's right to choose, and I strongly support affirmative action," he told the convention. "The Hispanic immigrant who becomes a citizen yesterday must be as precious to us as a Mayflower descendant."

Although Cheney proudly called himself a conservative, he, too, was more liberal in his views on social issues than the 1996 party platform or the base of the Republican Party. He had been uncomfortable dealing with the abortion issue as a presidential candidate. He didn't advertise his views on gay rights or gay marriage, but they were considerably more tolerant than the formal Republican positions of that era; he was, after all, the father of a gay daughter. (A few years later, during the 2000 campaign, he would say, "I think we ought to do everything we can to tolerate and accommodate whatever kinds of relationships people want to enter into.")

Nevertheless, Cheney had been a Republican since childhood, and that fact made him fundamentally different from Powell. While Cheney and Gingrich had entered Congress in the same year, 1979, Cheney had gravitated toward the House Republican leadership, while Gingrich became an insurgent who denounced and ran against that leadership. At one point, Cheney had called Gingrich "a pain in the fanny." Still, Cheney had remained on good terms with Gingrich, and his party loyalties were strong. Overall, as the Republicans moved rightward during the 1990s, Cheney went along with them, whereas Powell did not.

Gingrich and the congressional Republicans were focused mostly on domestic policy, not the foreign policy issues that had long preoccupied Powell and Cheney. But there was one provision in the 1996 Republican platform that directly opposed American involvement in the United Nations or other international organizations, such as the International Criminal Court; it condemned the subordination of "American sovereignty to any international authority." That provision ran directly contrary to the spirit of internationalism and multilateralism embodied by the George H. W. Bush administration and its top leaders such as Bush, James Baker, and Brent Scowcroft—and by Colin Powell as well. However, Cheney was more in tune with that Republican "sovereignty" plank. The Defense Planning Guidance document he released in January 1993 had embraced a strikingly unilateralist approach to the world.

Meanwhile, the revival of the neoconservative movement during the mid-1990s also served to pull Cheney to the right, and thus to widen the distance between him and Powell. Many neoconservatives had started out as anticommunist Democrats who then gravitated to the Republican Party during the Reagan administration. They had viewed George H. W. Bush as too weak and too willing to compromise with Mikhail Gorbachev; as a result, in the 1992 election some neoconservatives had supported Clinton over Bush.

For a time, the movement seemed inert, its relevance drawn into question by the collapse of the Soviet Union. But by the mid-1990s, a younger generation of neoconservatives, centered on the writers Robert Kagan and William Kristol in the magazine *The Weekly Standard*, began to denounce Bill Clinton's foreign policies as harshly as they had once condemned those of George H. W. Bush. The neoconservatives attacked Clinton for being unwilling to wield American power around the world

192 | *The Great Rift*

and weak in standing up for the values of freedom and democracy. Above all, they increasingly focused their attention on Iraq, where Saddam Hussein remained in power, defying the predictions at the beginning of the decade that he would not survive his defeat in the Gulf War. Urged on by Iraqi leaders in exile, the neoconservatives began to call for his overthrow.

Cheney was not himself entirely in synch with neoconservative thinking. He rarely emphasized the importance of spreading democracy around the world in the way the neoconservatives did. But the other strands of neoconservative thinking, that the United States should maintain its military might and should take an increasingly assertive stance in dealing with the world, squarely matched Cheney's own views. That was hardly a surprise: while Kagan and Kristol were spearheading the neoconservative revival, aligned with them were several foreign policy officials who had worked directly under Cheney in the Pentagon, including Paul Wolfowitz, Lewis (Scooter) Libby, and Zalmay Khalilzad.

In 1997, the neoconservatives formed an organization called the Project for a New American Century, designed to lobby for a more assertive U.S. foreign policy. Its first "statement of principles" called America to work to "shape a new century favorable to American principles and interests" and challenge "regimes hostile to our interests and values." Among the twenty-five signatories to this founding statement was Dick Cheney.

The document was, by and large, an appeal for a return to what the neoconservatives believed were the policies of the Reagan administration, though they tended to overlook Reagan's conciliatory approach to Gorbachev in his second term. It was not entirely a rejection of the George H. W. Bush administration: the signers of the founding document included the former president's son Jeb Bush as well as Cheney. But in the views it expressed, it was far closer to Reagan's early anticommunism than to Bush's moderate internationalism.

Colin Powell's name was not on the document. Indeed, no one ever asked him if he might be willing to sign. It was the sort of abstract enterprise he had shunned throughout his career.

* * *

Developments abroad during the course of the 1990s also served to accentuate the underlying differences between Cheney and Powell. The most important of these developments occurred in Israel, where the profound changes of the decade can be said to have been propelled forward on a single day, November 4, 1995. That evening, an Israeli ultranationalist named Yigal Amir assassinated Israeli prime minister Yitzhak Rabin as he was leaving a rally on behalf of the Oslo peace accords. Over the previous three years, Rabin had been pressing steadily toward peace with the Palestinians and recognition of a Palestinian state. As the writer Dan Ephron observed, "By deciding Israelis would no longer rule over Palestinians in the West Bank and Gaza, Rabin had struck a blow for the pragmatists over the ideologues. Through the barrel of Amir's Beretta, the ideologues had struck back." The following year, the right-wing Likud Party came to power, and its leader, Benjamin Netanyahu, began serving the first of his three stints as prime minister.

The ascendance of new right-wing governments in Israel would have a considerable if indirect influence on Cheney, reinforcing his own instincts and thinking, not only concerning the Middle East but, more broadly, on how to deal with the world.

Cheney's firsthand experience with Israel had begun with his work on the House Intelligence Committee and his days in the Pentagon; his earliest ties were with leaders of Israeli's intelligence services and the Israel Defense Forces, such as Moshe Arens, the defense minister during the Gulf War. Having ties to Israel's national security apparatus would not by itself have steered Cheney in any particular political direction; Rabin himself, after all, was a former general and army chief of staff, and his partner in the Oslo Accords, Shimon Peres, also had started out in the defense ministry. But Cheney seemed to have a special affinity for those in Israel who favored hard-nosed, defiant stances—those who were opposed to peace accords or concessions to the Palestinians.

William Burns, the Foreign Service officer and Middle East specialist who observed Cheney over the years, said that Cheney became close to right-wing Israelis not as the result of anything secretive but simply because "their views coincided." Cheney could identify with Israel's willingness to stand alone in the world, its profound distrust of multilateral diplomacy, its willingness to use military force whenever it felt necessary, its extensive and adventurous intelligence operations, its regular policy of flouting public opinion as expressed in western Europe or the United Nations. He also identified with Israel's never-ending attention to threats and dangers in the world around it. In all these respects, Cheney might have wanted the United States to be a little more like Israel.

With the Israeli right wing in power, as it was for most of the two decades after Rabin's assassination, Cheney frequently found himself dealing with officials in Israel who would spur him on, come to him with ideas, and buttress his instincts. Cheney prided himself on being a politician willing to stand alone; as a nation, Israel did the same. Israeli officials went to Cheney as the most sympathetic of all American foreign policy leaders.

* * *

The Gulf War, the conflict that made Powell and Cheney household names and solidified their friendship, had been a profoundly multilateral operation. The United States had gone to war with troops from a wide array of countries. It had sought and received authorization for the use of force from the United Nations. And it had obtained at least the acquiescence of the Soviet Union, its geopolitical rival for more than four decades.

But the Gulf War represented a unique moment that would not last. As the 1990s went on, each of the three underpinnings of international support for American policy at the time of the Gulf War began to weaken. At the United Nations, the United States ran up against increasing reluctance to support American initiatives. By the end of the decade, when the United States and its NATO partners went to war against Yugoslavia to stop its abuses in Kosovo, Clinton administration officials decided not to seek UN authorization, because they realized that they would not be able to obtain it.

The new Russia that emerged from the collapse of the Soviet Union began in the early 1990s as a regular partner of the United States. But over the course of the decade, it became increasingly less so. Under the leadership of President Boris Yeltsin, Russia went along, extremely grudgingly, with the expansion of NATO into central and eastern Europe, but that expansion gave rise to grievances that would burst forth under Yeltsin's successor, Vladimir Putin. By the end of the decade, Russia openly opposed American policy in Kosovo.

In 1991, nearly forty nations had joined together in the military coalition supporting the United States in the Gulf War. By the end of the decade, when Clinton launched Operation Desert Fox, a four-day bombing to compel Iraq to go along with inspections of its weapons programs, only a single nation, Britain, joined the United States.

As the decade progressed, the United States increasingly found itself operating on its own on the international stage. Even Bill Clinton, a liberal Democrat and avowed internationalist, found himself casting aside some of the restraints (such as the need for UN authorization) that had limited American policy in the past. This was, to a considerable extent, the inevitable result of the fact that the United States was now the world's sole superpower, operating at peak strength. Its very power made other countries leery of supporting its policies.

To some champions of American power, George H. W. Bush's careful multilateral approach to the world was beginning to seem outdated or unnecessary. The events of the 1990s created an environment in which Dick Cheney's long-held unilateral views could take shape and flourish.

* * *

Colin Powell's ideas concerning the use of force, emphasizing the use of overwhelming military power and clearly defined objectives, had been well suited to the circumstances of the Gulf War, and he continued to propound them in the years that followed. But over the course of the 1990s, the "Powell doctrine" was increasingly called into question. In 1995, the *Wall Street Journal*'s military correspondent Thomas Ricks reported that within the military services and among some senior U.S. officials, there was a growing sense that Powell's ideas were too restrictive; they gave an American president only "all-or-nothing" options for military intervention. Critics called Powell's approach too risk-averse and shaped too much by the army's experience in Vietnam, Ricks reported. "Why is it that whatever the question is—enforcing a peace agreement in Bosnia, evacuating the U.N. from Bosnia, or invading Haiti—the answer is always 25,000 Army troops?" one marine officer asked Ricks.

The question American leaders repeatedly faced in the 1990s was one of humanitarian intervention: whether the United States should use force to help stop ethnic cleansing in Bosnia, Rwanda, or Kosovo; whether to deliver food in Somalia; or whether to force military leaders to honor the results of an election in Haiti.

Both Powell and Cheney had opposed American intervention in the Balkans when they were at the Pentagon, and neither man changed his basic position after leaving office. Powell was particularly impassioned on the subject. "I think you ought to send a clear signal: that we're not going to get involved in this war, and it's not going to end until people are tired of fighting one another," he said in 1995. "If you say that every day, the Muslims will know it and the Serbs will know it and there will be no confusion."

But as the Serbian campaigns of ethnic cleansing went forward, Powell's rules began to lose support on both ends of the political spectrum. Clinton administration officials decided that the abuses in Bosnia had to be stopped, even if this required the use of military force. Meanwhile, leading neoconservatives such as Paul Wolfowitz strongly supported American intervention as well.

There also remained the continuing problem of Iraq. At the end of the Gulf War, Bush administration officials believed that Saddam Hussein would not last long as Iraq's leader. But in an interview in 1996, five years after the war, former British prime minister Margaret Thatcher observed unhappily, "There is the aggressor, Saddam Hussein, still in power." At the time, responding to Thatcher, Powell stuck to the earlier predictions. "In due course, Saddam Hussein will not be there," he said. In 1998, President Clinton signed the Iraq Liberation Act, a law that made it explicit U.S. policy to support a change of regime in Iraq.

* * *

Dick Cheney witnessed the events of the late 1990s from what was, for him, a considerably different perspective: he was a business executive. In mid-1995, a few months after announcing he would not run for president, he accepted a position as the chief executive officer (and eventually chairman) at Halliburton, one of the nation's largest oil services companies. Until that time, he had spent virtually his entire adult life on government payrolls and had little direct experience in business. However, his years as defense secretary made him attractive to Halliburton, which was looking for someone with extensive knowledge of the world and high-level contacts overseas to help bring in new business. Cheney moved his family to Dallas, where Halliburton's headquarters was then located.

During his years at Halliburton, Cheney took on the coloring and viewpoint of a business leader. On foreign policy, he was against trade restrictions and in favor of preserving international stability. Indeed, he staked out positions in those years that seem strikingly at odds with those he espoused later on in his career.

He strongly opposed sanctions against Iran. During an appearance before the World Petroleum Council, Cheney argued that it was time for the United States to put behind it the bitter legacy of Iran's taking of American hostages two decades earlier. "I would hope we could find ways to improve [America's relationship with Iran], and one of the ways I think is to allow American firms to do the same thing that most other firms around the world are able to do now, and that is to be active in Iran," Cheney said at the time. "We're kept out of there primarily by our own government, which has made a decision that U.S. firms should not be allowed to invest significantly in Iran, and I think that's a mistake."

Nor did Cheney take a particularly hard line on Iraq during this period. The neoconservative leaders at the Project for a New American Century quickly began to focus on Iraq as the most important issue for U.S. foreign policy. But when PNAC circulated a letter in early 1998 in which prominent Republicans and conservatives called for the overthrow of Saddam Hussein, Cheney did not sign it. (It seems fair to assume he knew about the letter and was asked to join the other signatories; Donald Rumsfeld and Paul Wolfowitz were among the eighteen who did sign.)

Cheney's caution on Iraq would last through the end of the decade. In 2000 he was asked, in an appearance on NBC's *Meet the Press*, if he favored the use of force to remove Saddam Hussein from office. "I think we want to maintain our current posture vis-à-vis Iraq," he replied.

* * *

Powell took a different path. Where Cheney spent the late 1990s in the corporate world, his old partner at the Pentagon turned to nonprofit organizations and charitable work. After deciding not to run for president, Powell continued to travel around the country, making speeches. But he also joined the boards of directors of the United Negro College Fund, Howard University, the Boys and Girls Clubs of America, and the Children's Health Fund. He also created his own nonprofit, America's Promise Alliance, to raise money and get other help from corporations for programs that benefited children.

In one revealing interview, he said he preferred these activities to working on foreign policy issues. "When somebody said to me, what do you want to do, go into a Boys and Girls Club and talk or do you want to go to AEI and give a speech—hey, I focused on kids, not think tanks," Powell said. "It seems to still surprise people—that they don't understand, that they don't understand who I am and what I've been. It's different for me."

This did not mean that Powell was living a life of sackcloth and ashes. He continued to associate with the wealthy and powerful in American society. In the summers, he went to Bohemian Grove, the exclusive, male-only retreat in the California redwoods where the nation's business and political leaders gather for two weeks of fun, talk, and networking.

He also continued his association with former president George H. W. Bush. As Powell's longtime assistant Peggy Cifrino recalled, "Forty-one [the nickname for the senior Bush] would call here and he'd say, 'Peggy, it's Forty-one. Tell the general to think cruise.'" Eventually, the details would be arranged, and Powell and his wife, Alma, would find themselves sailing in the Aegean with virtually the entire Bush family—everyone but 41's son George W. Bush, who as governor of Texas had to stay home.

"Myself, my wife, and all the Bush kids, grandkids, and Barbara, and George 41. Forty-three [George W. Bush] was governing, so he seldom went with us, but Laura did, and Laura's daughters, and Marvin's kids, and Neil's kids," Powell later recalled. "All of us are on the boat for a week at a time. It wasn't that much of a vacation, because every morning he [President Bush] wanted to go do something. You know, we've got to go walk."

* * *

Colin Powell and Dick Cheney were being tugged in different directions by their different careers, by the drift of Republican Party politics, and by the course of events in the world. Nevertheless, at the end of the 1990s, the two still considered themselves friends, bound together by the triumph in the Gulf War and the bonds of association in the George H. W. Bush administration.

On March 17, 2000, as he neared the end of an oral interview at the Miller Center in Charlottesville, Virginia, Cheney said he was about to leave for Washington to attend a surprise seventy-fifth birthday party in honor of Brent Scowcroft. "The President's going up, and Colin's going to be there," said Cheney happily.

13

THE RETURNS

Dick Cheney's relocation to Dallas proved fortuitous. The year before he moved there to take charge of Halliburton, George W. Bush was elected governor of Texas. The younger Bush hadn't known Cheney well during his father's years in the White House, but he realized that Cheney had been a senior Cabinet member and was now running one of Texas's leading companies. For Cheney, in turn, George W. Bush was not only the son of the president he had served, but also the chief executive in Halliburton's home state. It was natural that the two men would gravitate toward each other, and they did. Cheney began serving on one of the governor's business advisory councils.

Immediately after the 1996 presidential election, George W. Bush began maneuvering for the Republican presidential nomination in 2000. He launched his full-scale campaign two years later and often sought Cheney's help and advice. He twice asked Cheney to become his campaign manager, but Cheney declined, saying he wanted to keep running Halliburton and couldn't possibly do so while overseeing the day-to-day operations of a political campaign. What Cheney did instead was guide the development of ideas and the recruitment of personnel. This was especially true in foreign policy, where the younger Bush had little experience of his own.

On February 24, 1999, Bush met in Austin with his initial collection of foreign policy advisors. Cheney personally phoned Paul Wolfowitz to ask if he could attend, and he helped choose other attendees, including Lewis (Scooter) Libby and Stephen Hadley. The group was not entirely Cheney's, however; another participant was Condoleezza Rice, a young Soviet specialist who had served on Brett Scowcroft's National Security Council staff in George H. W. Bush's administration and had met the younger Bush on a visit to Kennebunkport the previous summer.

After that first session in Austin, Rice and Wolfowitz emerged as Bush's two principal foreign policy advisors for the duration of the campaign, and each traveled from time to time with the candidate.

Bush felt particularly comfortable with Rice. She was charged with putting together an official group of foreign policy advisors, whose names would be released to the press. This group, which met from time to time throughout the campaign, was called the Vulcans, a name Rice coined, almost offhand, because there was a statue of the Roman god Vulcan in her hometown of Birmingham.

Cheney was not formally a member of the Vulcans, but he had helped create the group and, in a sense, stood above it as a guiding spirit. One member, Dov Zakheim, displayed in his office for years afterward a photograph of one of the earliest gatherings. The advisors are standing with Bush. Cheney is in the picture, too, even though, at the time, he was still at Halliburton and held no formal position in the campaign.

* * *

Although Colin Powell was closer to George H. W. Bush than Cheney was, he had never been particularly close to the president's son, and he had no business or other reason to visit Texas during the time the younger Bush was governor. Nevertheless, he was a nationally recognized figure, with a stature that made it certain he would be an asset in a political campaign and also a likely Cabinet member, if he wanted, in the next Republican administration.

When George W. Bush declared his candidacy for the presidency, Powell did not rush to line up behind him. Bush's most serious opponent for the Republican nomination was John McCain, whose service in Vietnam, long military career, and determined support for defense issues as a senator were all obvious attractions for Powell. Powell sent contributions to both the Bush and the McCain campaigns, and he said in one television interview that the Republican Party "has two leading candidates who are very, very strong." Nevertheless, after Bush proceeded to defeat McCain, Powell played two roles that benefited the presidential candidate, one in the realm of foreign policy and the other in domestic politics.

Once the nomination was settled, Powell stood prominently among the veterans of past Republican administrations who gave their blessing to George W. Bush's candidacy and sought to buttress his foreign policy credentials. When Bush held a news conference in the spring of 2000 to call for a reduction in nuclear weapons, he was flanked at the podium by Henry Kissinger, George Shultz, Brent Scowcroft, Donald Rumsfeld, and Colin Powell. Among these party elders, only Powell and Rumsfeld were still young enough to serve in another Bush administration. The fact that Powell was standing next to Rice, who was the campaign's foreign policy coordinator, further underscored that possibility.

At the same time, Powell's presence served a quasi-political function. Unlike the other foreign policy advisors, he enjoyed enough personal popularity that it was assumed he could help deliver votes to Bush. His name repeatedly came up as a possible vice-presidential candidate. The conservative columnist George Will proposed a Bush-Powell ticket. "Powell's experience in defense and foreign policy and the fact that he is pro-choice and favors affirmative action, would help insulate Bush from certain skepticism," Will wrote. "And Powell's appeal to minorities would wonderfully scramble America's political arithmetic." That same month, the *Boston Globe* reported that Powell was "a favorite among Republican kibitzers" for vice president.

The flaw in this line of thinking was that Powell didn't want the vice-presidential nomination or, indeed, the vice presidency. He knew that in order to win the nomination, he would have to overcome intense opposition from Republican conservatives. And if he succeeded, he would then have had to take part in the daily ardors and rough debate of a political campaign. He had already decided, four years earlier, that he wasn't a politician and that he didn't want to do what was necessary to take part in a nationwide political campaign. His mind hadn't changed.

Even if a Bush-Powell ticket were to win, simply being vice president didn't seem attractive. In the two administrations in which Powell had served in senior positions, under Ronald Reagan and George H. W. Bush, the vice presidents (Bush and Dan Quayle) possessed little authority of their own. George H. W. Bush had been belittled as the man whose primary duty was to represent Reagan at the funerals of foreign leaders. Worse, Quayle had turned into something of a national joke. Powell well remembered the crisis in the Philippines in 1989, when Quayle struggled to assert his authority even to run a meeting in the White House Situation Room.

Powell never played a significant role in the internal deliberations of George W. Bush's presidential campaign. He was too senior (and too famous) to take part in the regular, ongoing foreign policy deliberations of the Vulcans, the group run by Condoleezza Rice. They were, in a way, too much like the think-tank discussions he had always shunned.

Even so, he was effectively represented at these meetings because his close friend and former colleague Richard Armitage was a member of the group. Moreover, Powell had worked at one time or another with the Vulcans' neoconservative leaders. He had formed a friendship with Richard Perle when both men were working under Defense Secretary Caspar Weinberger in the Reagan administration; he had even vacationed with Perle at his home in France. Later on, under George H. W. Bush, Powell had teamed up with Paul Wolfowitz to reorganize the military and prevent the Democrats in Congress from cutting the defense budget.

Despite these personal friendships, the Vulcans were generally much closer to Cheney than to Powell, both in their personal relationships and in their outlook on the world. Cheney had been present at the creation of the group, at a time when Powell was still maintaining his impartiality between Bush and McCain. Their differing relationship to the Vulcans underscored the larger point: during the Bush campaign, Powell always remained something of an outsider, while Cheney was on the inside, a central part of its internal deliberations.

* * *

When George W. Bush began his search for a running mate, Cheney was once again involved from the start. In the early spring of 2000, Bush sent his campaign manager, Joseph Allbaugh, to ask Cheney if he was interested in the vice-presidential nomination. Cheney said he wasn't; he wanted to stay at Halliburton. Speaking for Bush, Allbaugh then asked Cheney to take charge of the search for possible candidates and their vetting. He agreed.

Cheney collected a list of names. It was dominated, not surprisingly, by Republican governors and senators, but he added some others. As was invariably the case whenever a top job opened, he put forward the name of his mentor Donald Rumsfeld early on. But it didn't stay on the list for long; the antagonism between Rumsfeld and George H. W. Bush, dating to the 1970s, lingered. By Cheney's own account, George W. Bush "made it pretty clear that as far as the vice presidency was concerned, Rumsfeld wasn't going to be an option." Cheney required the prospective candidates to fill out a detailed questionnaire on their health, finances, and anything else that might be a political liability. Their responses gave him access to detailed personal information that he could draw upon in the future.

According to the official accounts, including the memoirs of Bush and Cheney, in early July, just as this careful vetting process was nearing an end, Bush essentially rendered it meaningless by deciding he wanted Cheney as his running mate. He was attracted by the fact that Cheney had served as White House chief of staff and as defense secretary. "Unlike any of the senators or governors on my list, he had stood next to presidents during the most gut-wrenching decisions that reach the Oval Office, including sending Americans to war," Bush later wrote. Bush had also checked with his father, who told him Cheney would be "a great choice."

What their accounts leave out is that Bush's decision did not come out of the blue, and that in fact he and Cheney had been talking about this possibility during the weeks when Cheney was ostensibly in charge of picking someone else. Mary Cheney later wrote that in talking to her father earlier that spring, Bush made clear "that he wanted a running mate who could help him govern. From time to time, he also made it clear that he still wanted my dad to be on the list of candidates."

At the beginning of July, Bush privately informed Cheney that he had decided to choose him as his running mate, but the decision wasn't final. Over the next two weeks, Bush's aides conducted a private, informal, internal vetting of Cheney and an exploration of what his nomination would mean politically—an examination that was nowhere near as rigorous as Cheney's vetting of the other candidates. Cheney did not have to fill out the written questionnaire he had given to the others. His own physician was permitted to vouch for his health; there was no independent physical exam. Meanwhile, Cheney took Mary on a weeklong father-daughter trip to Latin America and discussed with her the prospect that, if he accepted the nomination, the fact that she was a lesbian would become public. Mary Cheney gave her approval and, in turn, got the assent of her longtime partner.

The biggest obstacle was Karl Rove, Bush's top political advisor, who was opposed to Cheney's selection. Rove viewed Cheney as a political liability in several ways: His health and history of heart attacks could become an issue. He had a conservative voting record in Congress that the Democrats could seize upon. His residency was a problem: Cheney lived in Texas, meaning that there would be two Texans on the ticket, a circumstance that would run afoul of the Twelfth Amendment to the Constitution. Even if he changed his residency to Wyoming, that state possessed only three electoral votes and would be reliably Republican with or without him. All in all, this was not like John Kennedy selecting Lyndon Johnson as a way to win Texas and thus the presidency.

Rove had one more objection: he thought the selection of Cheney would send the wrong message, that George W. Bush represented merely a continuation of his father's administration. If Bush wanted to demonstrate that he represented something new and fresh, then Cheney was not the right choice, Rove argued. In the long run, that notion of continuity from one Bush administration to another turned out to be wrong, and Cheney was one of the main reasons it was wrong.

Rove had failed to grasp what Bush wanted in his vice president. He wanted an experienced hand who could help him run the government. As confident as Bush sounded in public, he was insecure about the prospect of actually serving as president. None of the governors or senators being considered for vice president had executive branch credentials to match Cheney's. Furthermore, Bush was insecure also in a political sense: he didn't want a vice president with his own independent political ambitions, someone who might oppose the president (as Hubert Humphrey did when he belatedly challenged Lyndon Johnson's Vietnam policy in the fall of 1968), or distance himself from the president (as Al Gore would do with Bill Clinton in 2000), or run an independent political operation from the White House (as Quayle had done under Bush's father). Cheney seemed nearly perfect in this regard: he had set aside his own presidential ambitions and seemed to care far more about issues and policy than winning votes.

Bush and Rove met with Cheney in Texas to discuss the vice presidency. Cheney once again brought up the drunk-driving convictions of his youth, just as he had disclosed them more than a quarter century earlier to Donald Rumsfeld and Gerald Ford when they were each preparing to hire him. He also told Bush "he needed to understand how deeply conservative I was." Bush said he already knew that. "No, I mean *really* conservative," Cheney replied. Bush was not to be dissuaded, either by Rove or by Cheney's careful warnings. He formally offered the vice-presidential nomination to Cheney in late July, and Cheney readily accepted.

It is worth pausing here to reflect further on this sequence of events and their consequences for the future Bush administration. Powell would not allow himself to be considered for vice president; he took himself out of the running early and said repeatedly in public that he didn't want the job. Eventually the nomination went to Cheney, who, through his proximity to Bush, came to see new possibilities and scope of action for the role of vice president. Had those decisions gone the other way, the George W. Bush administration would have taken a dramatically different direction.

Powell was hardly written off or forgotten—quite the contrary. By the summer of 2000, his name was regularly mentioned as a possible secretary of state, and the Bush campaign did nothing to deny this speculation. In most administrations, the secretary of state possesses far greater authority than the vice president. But Cheney had ideas about what a vice president could do, and he was willing to accept the nomination that Powell spurned.

Four years earlier, after his failed bid for the presidency, Cheney had quipped that he would like to have the job of chief executive but didn't want to run for it. Now he was going to leave it to George W. Bush to run for president and appoint him to be an extraordinarily powerful second in command. It wasn't a perfect solution, but it was as close to the presidency as Cheney was going to get.

* * *

Colin Powell and Dick Cheney each appeared on the podium before the 2000 Republican National Convention in Philadelphia. They gave strikingly different speeches, ones that could almost have come from the representatives of two different political parties.

Powell's address could easily have been given to the Democratic convention. In it, he urged the Republicans at the convention to reach out to African Americans, "and not just during an election-year campaign." He spoke out in favor of affirmative action. He reminded them that "immigration is part of our life's blood. It's part of the essence of who we are as Americans." He made an appeal for community service. The *New York Times* described Powell's speech the next morning as an example of the Republican Party putting on "its newly moderate and disciplined face." Near the end of his speech, Powell went out of his way to sing the praises of Bush's vice-presidential nominee, "a man I have known and respected for many years and with whom I shared many difficult days and nights during Desert Storm and other crises." He went on: "Dick Cheney is one of the most distinguished and dedicated public servants this nation has ever had."

In contrast to Powell, Cheney gave to the Republican rank and file the hard-line speech they were so eager to hear. Years later, Cheney acknowledged that in doing so, he had defied Bush's political advisors. They had wanted Bush's entire presentation at the convention to convey the soft theme of "compassionate conservatism," a message of moderation that would appeal to independent and undecided voters. Cheney instead drafted a speech that took aim at the Democrats. Its language wasn't in any way new or creative. Instead, he borrowed the words of Al Gore to the Democratic convention of 1992: "It's time for them to go." He repeated this phrase through his speech, and the audience picked up the chant, just as the Democrats had done during Gore's speech eight years earlier.

Bush's campaign aides had asked Cheney to take out the "time for them to go" line. "They believed 'red meat' might play well in the hall, but not in people's living rooms," Cheney wrote years later. "I think they were hoping for a kinder, gentler Dick Cheney, and I listened to what they had to say, and then I ignored their advice." It was the earliest indication that Cheney planned to make his own decisions, even when the president's team objected.

In the weeks before and after the convention, there were clear signs of Republican opposition to Colin Powell playing a major role in a George W. Bush administration. The neoconservative writer Robert Kagan wrote an op-ed column for the *Washington Post* called "The Problem with Powell," pointing out that Powell had been more reluctant than others in the George H. W. Bush administration to intervene with force to oppose Saddam Hussein's invasion of Kuwait. "His [Powell's] judgment during the gulf crisis fit within a broader doctrine of nonintervention derived from his experience in Vietnam," Kagan noted. "Bush's sense of America's role and the use of force is a good deal more expansive than Powell's. . . . What he needs at the State Department is a sober-minded Republican foreign policy heavyweight such as Dick Cheney, Richard Lugar, or Chuck Hagel."

A few days later, after Bush had announced his selection of Cheney, a *Wall Street Journal* editorial accurately foresaw the Cheney-Powell tensions of the future Bush administration, and put itself squarely on Cheney's side. "Mr. Cheney's presence in a Bush White House might be a useful counter-weight to Mr. Powell's more dovish foreign policy views," the editorial said. In retrospect, these articles should have been red flags for Powell, highlighting the resistance he might confront if he were to become secretary of state.

The circumstances surrounding Bush's choice of Cheney belie the myths that would take hold years later: the notion that Cheney had been somehow a "moderate" who then turned into a conservative or a hard-liner after 2001, perhaps (according to one of the myths) because of new cardiac problems. The truth is that Bush, Rove, and Cheney explicitly discussed the political implications of Cheney's long record of conservatism. Cheney gave a hard-line speech to the convention, overriding appeals for moderation from the Bush campaign, and the neoconservatives were lining up behind him.

There is no need to posit a post-2001 conversion to explain Dick Cheney. In the 2000 campaign, he already was what his critics claimed he later became.

* * *

Cheney and Powell campaigned for Bush that fall. Opposing the Democrats was one thing they knew how to do—harking back to their time in the Pentagon, when their task had been to stave off deep cuts in the defense budget. Cheney amplified Bush's appeal to traditional Republicans, conservatives, and the business community. Powell reinforced Bush's message of "compassionate conservatism," aimed at winning votes from independent voters and from centrists of both parties. Powell also helped to deflect accusations that Republican policies were racist. At one point, he sent a public letter to Donna Brazile, the campaign manager for Bush's Democratic opponent, Vice President Al Gore, rebuking her for suggesting that the Republicans had no interest in helping black children. Powell recounted his efforts to help America's children, black and white, and added pointedly, "I do so as a Republican."

Powell's military credentials also provided invaluable aid to the Republican ticket, given that Cheney had not served at all and that Bush had done only a skimpy tour of National Guard duty inside the United States during the Vietnam War. Bush responded to Democratic criticism of his inexperience in diplomacy or foreign policy by pointing to Cheney, Powell, and the other prominent campaign advisors who had served in his father's administration. "I've got one of the finest foreign policy teams ever assembled," he said. But foreign policy was not the central issue in the 2000 campaign. The Republicans attacked Bill Clinton's behavior, tried to link Gore to Clinton, and said it was time for a change; the Democrats, in turn, argued that the economic prosperity of the late 1990s justified a continuation of the Clinton-Gore era.

There was one campaign exchange concerning foreign policy that would attract more attention later on than it did at the time. In the second presidential debate, Bush promised a foreign policy based on humility. "If we're an arrogant nation, they'll resent us. If we're a humble nation but strong, they'll welcome us," he declared. He also warned against "using our troops as nation builders," and asserted, "I don't want to be the world's policeman." Bush was sending signals that he opposed humanitarian interventions of the sort that Clinton had carried out in Bosnia and Kosovo. But years later, after the Bush administration waged long wars in Afghanistan and Iraq, his words in that debate would be called up over and over again as an ironic example of how his views had changed.

The world did not stop for the American elections. On October 12, 2000, seventeen American sailors were killed when a U.S. Navy destroyer, the USS *Cole*, was attacked by two suicide bombers while docked in the port of Aden, Yemen. The terrorist group al-Qaeda claimed responsibility. That incident should have prompted discussion in the campaign, but the candidates said little, other than to call for retaliation against those responsible. For all the foreign policy experience of Cheney, Powell, and the Vulcans, terrorism was not an issue they had confronted in any serious way. Their focus had always been on the conduct of nation-states, not on stateless entities such as al-Qaeda.

The campaign ended in early November, but the election was not decided for another thirty-six days, until the disputes over the votes in Florida made their way through the courts. During that time, it was Cheney who began to put together a future Bush administration, making lists of what he believed needed to be done. When the Supreme Court handed down its decision in *Bush v. Gore* on December 12, 2000, Cheney was ready to get to work.

* * *

After the long election and the partisan passions it had aroused, Bush needed to show quickly that he was taking charge. Two days after the Supreme Court decision that made him president-elect, he announced his first Cabinet appointment: to no one's surprise, he nominated Colin Powell as his secretary of state. There was almost no internal debate or disagreement over the choice. "I was proud of the Powell pick and glad he agreed to join us," Cheney later wrote. "I was looking forward to the chance to work with him again."

Nevertheless, the tensions and divisiveness that would come to plague the Bush administration started immediately afterward. At the press conference to introduce Powell, Bush and Cheney stood at the podium alongside the new secretary of state. But it was Powell who dominated the proceedings, much as he had done when he was chairman of the Joint Chiefs of Staff. He was physically larger and more powerfully built than either Bush or Cheney; he was also more articulate and self-assured. He was becoming America's first black secretary of state. This was a signal event in his career and a historic moment for the country, and he made the most of it, speaking of the special meaning of the day for African Americans.

He also expounded at length on foreign policy issues. He answered reporters' questions not only on matters of diplomacy such as the Middle East, but also on military questions such as the defense budget and missile defense, even though these were subjects that would fall under the purview not of the secretary of state but of Bush's future secretary of defense, a job not yet filled.

Powell did well but perhaps a little too well, in the eyes of his friends and staff. His speechwriter Lawrence Wilkerson thought to himself, "Oh my god, boss, you made a big mistake." Wilkerson worried that Bush's political advisors such as Karl Rove would begin to see Powell as a future political candidate, even a competitor to Bush. Powell's closest friend, Richard Armitage, was even blunter. When Powell called him after the televised press conference to ask how he thought it had gone, Armitage told him, "We're fucked." Armitage had noticed that Cheney, in particular, had seemed uncomfortable and tense during Powell's commanding performance.

That press conference also set off warning bells among conservatives and neoconservatives, who considered the new secretary of state too much of a centrist, and also among Cheney's former civilian advisors in the Pentagon, who recalled their feeling that Powell had been too independent minded and too attuned to public approval during his time as chairman of the Joint Chiefs of Staff. If anyone had failed to grasp the underlying dynamic of the press conference, the news story in the next morning's *New York Times* crystallized the perceptions. "At times, General Powell sounded as if he were speaking not just as the next secretary of state but as the next secretary of defense, too," the *Times* reported. Quickly, the right wing of the Republican Party picked up on this theme, warning of the need to circumscribe Powell's influence. *The Weekly Standard*, the leading outlet of the neoconservatives, ran a story headlined,

"The Long Arm of Colin Powell: Will the New Secretary of State Also Run the Pentagon?"

Within days of the Powell appointment, Cheney and his aides were beginning to hear rumors of what the new secretary of state was telling others in Washington: that Bush was inexperienced in foreign policy, but that he, Powell, would explain foreign policy to him. This was, in fact, a tutoring role that Cheney himself intended to play.

* * *

What followed was the personnel decision that essentially determined the future course of the Bush administration: the choice of a new secretary of defense. Bush's initial instinct had been to appoint someone who was an outsider to defense and foreign policy issues, such as a business executive or political leader, reasoning that the new defense secretary would be preoccupied less with traditional military issues than with transforming the way the Pentagon operated and selling the necessary changes to Congress. Bush at first tried to recruit Fred Smith, the founding chairman of Federal Express, but he declined for health reasons. Bush then turned his attention to politicians such as former senator Dan Coats of Indiana and Governor Tom Ridge of Pennsylvania. He arranged to interview Coats for the job.

This desire to bring in an outsider as defense secretary was linked to another idea: if Bush appointed a politician or business executive as defense secretary, then he might name an insider, someone with hands-on experience in running the Pentagon, as deputy secretary. The name that regularly came up was Richard Armitage, who had been one of the most powerful officials inside the Pentagon during his eight years in the Reagan administration.

While Armitage was a close ally of Powell, he didn't want to work at the State Department. "Rich didn't want to work for me; I'm like his brother," Powell recalled. "He wanted to go back to where he belonged, and that was where he thought he belonged, at the Defense Department." Powell may not have thought that Armitage's appointment as deputy secretary of defense was a way to extend his own influence inside the Pentagon, but certainly the many conservative Republicans who were wary of Powell viewed it that way.

Cheney, however, had his own ideas for who should serve as secretary of defense, and they centered on his former mentor and longtime ally Donald Rumsfeld. Even before Bush interviewed Coats, Cheney called Rumsfeld and arranged a secret meeting. He asked Rumsfeld about his availability for either of two jobs in the new administration: CIA director or defense secretary. Rumsfeld said he was willing and able to do either job.

It was hardly surprising that Cheney put Rumsfeld's name forward; Rumsfeld not only was Cheney's ally but had held the job before. What was more surprising, and unknown at the time, is that, in this two-man mutual-admiration society, Rumsfeld had his own novel idea for who should be secretary of defense: Dick Cheney. Rumsfeld's personal archives and his memoir reveal that, very late in the selection process, Rumsfeld suggested that Cheney, as vice president, could be given the defense portfolio as well. There was some history to this peculiar proposal, though only Cheney and Rumsfeld were aware of it. While both men were serving in the Ford White House, they felt that Vice President Nelson Rockefeller had too much time on his hands and was intruding on everyone else's turf. As a possible solution to the problem, Rumsfeld and Cheney had explored the possibility of giving Rockefeller a Cabinet department to run. In the end, nothing came of this idea; twenty-five years later, the suggestion that Cheney hold the two jobs of vice president and defense secretary didn't go anywhere, either.

The selection of Rumsfeld came over a period of days in late December. Rumsfeld's name leaked to the press, but only for the position of CIA director. An aide to Cheney said in an interview years later that the CIA job was never particularly serious, because Cheney had wanted Rumsfeld as defense secretary all along. Rumsfeld corroborated this in his memoir. But Cheney also knew that he had to move extremely carefully in proposing Rumsfeld. His name was still toxic to the Bush family, as Cheney had discovered when he proposed him for the vice presidency the previous spring. And so, Cheney let others make the suggestion first. Condoleezza Rice, whom Bush had already named as his new national security advisor, had gotten to know Rumsfeld a decade earlier. According to Bush, the first mention of Rumsfeld's name for secretary of defense came from Rice, not Cheney. "Condi threw out an interesting idea: How about Don Rumsfeld?" Bush later wrote.

Word soon spread around Washington that Coats had "flunked his interview" with the president-elect. Critics said he did not have the personal toughness or the experience to serve as a counterweight to Powell, the main qualities conservatives were seeking. Meanwhile, Cheney arranged for Bush to interview Rumsfeld only after the president-elect had talked to Coats, so that he might see how much sharper and more knowledgeable Rumsfeld was.

It was Cheney who called Rumsfeld to ask him to fly to Texas for an interview with George W. Bush, whom Rumsfeld had met only once in his life. Rumsfeld sat down with the president-elect three days before Christmas. Four days later, it was Cheney again who called Rumsfeld with news of Bush's decision. "He told me to tell you he wants you to be secretary of defense," said Cheney.

In most administrations, such offers of a major Cabinet position are made by the president-elect himself. Cheney, however, was already showing well before the inauguration that he would play a more powerful role than any previous vice president.

* * *

The Rumsfeld appointment served as the cornerstone in Cheney's edifice of power and influence within the new administration. It meant that the Department of Defense, the largest Cabinet agency and a central institution in American foreign policy, would be run by a person whom Cheney had known for more than three decades and with whom he had worked extremely closely in two previous administrations. The long-standing bonds between the two men were also social and personal: The two families had vacationed together in the Caribbean. Cheney had taught Rumsfeld's daughter Valerie the skill of parallel parking. On Election Night 2000, the Rumsfelds had been among the few guests invited to the Cheneys' hotel suite in Austin to watch the returns come in.

Once Rumsfeld was appointed, the rest of the administration's top foreign policy jobs began to fall into place. Richard Armitage did not become deputy secretary of defense. He talked about the job with Rumsfeld, who made clear his lack of enthusiasm. Instead, Armitage accepted the job as deputy secretary of state, working directly for Powell, despite his stated desire not to serve under his friend. The conservatives in the administration could now rest easy that the influence of Powell and Armitage would be confined to the State Department, not spread across the government as a whole.

It also became clear that Rumsfeld was merely the most prominent and most important in a series of appointments of Cheney's friends, allies, and former aides throughout the new Bush administration. The job of deputy secretary of defense went to Wolfowitz, who had been Cheney's top civilian advisor when he ran the Pentagon. Earlier, Powell had offered Wolfowitz the job of ambassador to the United Nations, but he had turned it down, explaining to others that Cheney wanted him to be closer to the action in Washington. Stephen Hadley, who had also worked under Cheney in the Pentagon, became deputy national security advisor. Zalmay Khalilzad, yet another of Cheney's Pentagon civilian advisors, became the National Security Council official responsible for Afghanistan and Iraq.

* * *

Of course, each of these individual appointments had its own nuances and complexities. But taken together, they had a profound impact on the George W. Bush administration, both upon the individuals at the top and, more broadly, on the entire operating style of its foreign policy team.

First, the cumulative impact of all these appointments was to constrain Colin Powell and to solidify the influence of Dick Cheney. On December 16, 2000, the day Powell was appointed, the widespread perception was that he would be the dominant influence over the new administration's foreign and national security policies. Within less than two weeks, with the appointment of Rumsfeld, Cheney had laid the groundwork for outweighing Powell in the administration's decision making. The subsequent Bush appointments made this reality ever clearer.

Second, the impact of the new appointments went beyond Cheney and Powell or the ideological cast of the administration. Though no one recognized it at the time, Bush had created a startlingly dysfunctional foreign policy apparatus. One way of looking at the Bush team is that its deliberations were hampered by several pairs of "BFFs" (best friends forever) who had built their careers alongside one another. Rumsfeld was best friends with Cheney, Armitage with Powell. For good measure, there was also the bond between Wolfowitz and Scooter Libby, Cheney's new chief of staff, who had been a student of Wolfowitz's at Yale and then served directly under him in the Reagan and George H. W. Bush administrations.

What all this meant was that in any of the administration's top-level meetings, officials assumed that any individual member of these pairs was probably reflecting the views of the other—or even worse, that the pair had privately discussed the issue at hand and decided how to approach it before the meeting took place. In meetings of the Bush administration's Principals' Committee of top Cabinet-level officials, Cheney and Rumsfeld were often seen as a pair, not just as, separately, the vice president and the secretary of defense. When the Deputies' Committee of second-level officials got together, it was assumed that Wolfowitz, from the Defense Department, and Libby, from the vice president's office, thought alike. Unlike these first two pairs, Powell and Armitage represented the same department, but more than usual for a Cabinet secretary and his deputy, they, too, were thought of as a unit. Finally, the existence of these pairs of BFFs served to amplify the sense of conflict or, indeed, enmity inside the administration. When there were conflicts among members of the Bush team, each best friend could nurse the grievances of the other; in this way, antagonisms were given greater legitimacy and were perpetuated.

During and after George W. Bush's eight years in office, there was always speculation about why its operating style seemed so different from the administration of his father. Why did the first Bush administration seem so harmonious, whereas the second was so full of discord? One explanation, certainly valid, was that the elder Bush made clear that he did not want any infighting within his administration. But it is also worth pointing out that the George H. W. Bush administration was the only one in which Dick Cheney served without Donald Rumsfeld. And it was the only one in which Colin Powell served, in any senior policy position, without Richard Armitage in a nearby office. For whatever reason, Cheney and Powell each seemed to operate more smoothly inside an administration when he didn't have his best friend at his side.

* * *

As the new administration took office, Dick Cheney sent Donald Rumsfeld two photographs. One showed the two of them together in the Nixon administration, three decades earlier. The other had just been taken, with Cheney at Rumsfeld's swearing-in as Bush's secretary of defense. "To Don," the inscription read. "Here we go again."

PART FOUR

FORTY-THREE

14

FROM THE VERY START

Years later, whenever questions arose as to why George W. Bush's administration had been so different from that of his father, Colin Powell would respond that the principal change between the two administrations was the difference between "41 and 43"—that is, the different qualities of the two presidents themselves. This is accurate as far as it goes: George H. W. Bush and George W. Bush differed in experience, style, instincts, and policies. Yet that fact raises the question of why they were different—or, to put it another way, why was each Bush elected president at the time he was?

The underlying reality is that George H. W. Bush could not have won the presidency in the election of 2000. He was a centrist, a moderate political leader in a Republican Party that had turned sharply to the right. He had, in fact, failed to win reelection eight years earlier. The political weaknesses that George H. W. Bush confronted during his presidency and in the 1992 campaign, including his failure to win the enthusiastic support of Republican hawks, evangelicals, or libertarians, were precisely the problems that George W. Bush sought to overcome when he rose as a considerably more conservative politician later in the decade. In this sense, what Powell viewed as a change in the personal qualities of the two Bush presidents was also a change in American politics and in the country itself.

For his own part, Dick Cheney would offer a simple answer to the question of why the two Bush administrations were so different: September 11 changed everything. He maintained that critics who attacked the George W. Bush administration's decisions were reflecting a "pre-9/11 mindset." But, in truth, the views and underlying dynamics of the George W. Bush administration were already established well before September 11. Over the first eight months of the new administration, Cheney and those allied with him began to challenge established thinking about America's role in the world, while Powell put forward more traditional views that represented continuity with the policies of the past. What transpired on September 11 did not transform Dick Cheney, either, as some have suggested; rather, the events of that day brought out and hardened an outlook on the world that he had held for decades.

* * *

At least initially, the disagreements inside the administration were over policy; they were not personal. In fact, at the top levels of the new Bush team, there were striking displays of friendship, starting even during the transition.

In late November 2000, while the election result was still in dispute, Cheney suffered a slight heart attack, his fourth. Doctors performed a cardiac catheterization and inserted a stent, and he returned home a couple of days later; he was soon active again, holding a press conference eight days after the attack. (Before jumping to any conclusion that this heart attack explains his views and behavior afterward, one should consider that Cheney's previous heart attack, a more serious one in 1988, had prompted quadruple bypass surgery; nevertheless, he was appointed defense secretary eight months later, and no one at the time claimed that this earlier heart attack affected his views in running the Pentagon.)

What happened after Cheney's heart attack bears testament to the personal warmth at the top levels of the new Bush team in its formative days. Cheney was stricken two days before Thanksgiving, meaning that he would be in the hospital on the holiday. His family didn't want to rely on hospital food; nor did they have time to prepare a dinner. So, Alma Powell cooked an entire Thanksgiving dinner for the Cheneys. "She had probably been up most of the night to get it all done," Cheney wrote years later, in a memoir that was elsewhere profoundly critical of Powell. "It was one of the kindest gestures we could imagine and one we'll never forget."

This sense of camaraderie lasted into the weeks after the inauguration. Cheney, Powell, Condoleezza Rice, and Donald Rumsfeld began holding regular weekly lunches to discuss foreign policy issues. The other three teased Powell about the luxurious lunches they expected him to host at the State Department, recalling past experiences in attending lunches there for visiting heads of state and other dignitaries. On February 7, Powell welcomed his new colleagues to their first lunch at the State Department. On the table were cloth napkins, silverware, and four silver plates, each under a matching silver cover. Tuxedoed waiters stood by attentively. As Rumsfeld recorded it in a memo at the time, "When we took the silver metal covers off, underneath was a plain paper bag with our sandwich in it. It was a classic ruse."

And yet amid the good humor, the groundwork was being laid for bureaucratic conflict. Cheney made clear early on that, as vice president, he expected to play an unprecedentedly powerful role in the administration's decision making.

He started by enlarging his staff. In past administrations, the vice president usually had a single aide for foreign policy and otherwise relied upon the National Security Council for staff help and expertise. Cheney created an entire foreign policy team, bringing in experts for various regions of the world. They worked under a chief of staff, Lewis (Scooter) Libby, who had been a senior civilian advisor to Cheney during his time as defense secretary. Rice, the new national security advisor, later wrote that the vice president's staff "seemed very much of one ultra-hawkish mind [and] was determined to act as a power center of its own."

Powell thought that Cheney's enlarged staff soon became "his own National Security Council. They had two [the actual NSC and Cheney's]. And it was dysfunctional," Powell said years later. "The reality was that Cheney served as the alternative national security advisor, and as an alternative White House chief of staff. And everything went through Cheney."

The vice president's efforts to augment his power went beyond personnel choices and the size of his staff. He understood from long experience in government how decisions were made and how the top-level meetings helped determine the outcome of those decisions. At the top of the foreign policy apparatus sits the Principals' Committee of the National Security Council, which is composed of the secretaries of State, Defense, and Treasury, the CIA director, and so on. In previous administrations, the national security advisor had presided over these meetings. But Cheney proposed that he, as vice president, should have that role. Rice objected strongly. She appealed directly to Bush, arguing that such an arrangement could undermine his authority as president. Her job as national security adviser, she pointed out, was "to make recommendations to you."

In that particular skirmish, Cheney lost. But he still possessed the bureaucratic skill to exert an influence that was far greater than any of his predecessors. Bill Clinton's vice president, Al Gore, had not even attended the meetings of the Principals' Committee, generally leaving that task to his senior foreign policy advisor, Leon Fuerth. The logic had been plain enough: Gore attended formal meetings of the National Security Council, composed of the Cabinet-level officials plus President Clinton; but given that the president didn't take part in the Principals' Committee meetings, neither did Gore. Cheney didn't accept this logic. He came to the Principals' Committee meetings, too, in order to have a voice in policy recommendations for the president. His presence "made it more difficult for Condi Rice," CIA director George Tenet later observed. "The vice president's presence may also have had an unintended chilling effect on the free flow of views as important policy matters were debated."

While Cheney had good historical reasons to worry about the authority of a vice president and knew he needed to establish his clout, Powell had every reason to feel confident that as secretary of state he would play a leading role in establishing the nation's foreign policy. And so, in the administration's early days, Powell occupied himself with the internal workings of the State Department. He spent his first days on the job seeking to build morale within the Foreign Service. He chose to drive his own PT Cruiser to work, rather than being driven in a staff car; he held a town hall meeting with State Department employees; and he deployed the personal touches and humor for which he was already famous. He disarmed the diplomats with jokes about his military background, apologizing in advance for any lapses "back into my original language, which is Infantry," and telling everyone that "if you perform well, we are going to get along fine. If you don't you are going to give me pushups." It was vintage Powell—and it gave no hint of what was to come, because Powell himself didn't know.

* * *

The hidden disagreements within the administration burst forth for the first time in early March 2001, when Kim Dae-jung, the president of South Korea, came to Washington. Kim had developed what was called a "sunshine policy" toward North Korea, using financial benefits and diplomacy as part of an effort to build trust and forge a relationship with the Communist regime. The Clinton administration had supported and sought to amplify that policy, arranging for Secretary of State Madeleine Albright to visit Pyongyang and holding out the prospect of a trip by President Clinton as well.

Just before Kim was to land in Washington, reporters asked Powell about the new administration's policy toward North Korea. He said the United States would continue to support the sunshine policy, adding, "We do plan to engage with North Korea to pick up where President Clinton and his administration left off. Some promising elements were left on the table." His remarks could have been read to suggest that perhaps Bush would make a presidential visit to Pyongyang, as Clinton had been considering.

It is hard to describe the many ways Powell's comments rubbed raw nerves elsewhere in the administration. The administration hadn't yet settled on a new North Korea policy; in fact, there was a meeting scheduled at the White House for the following day to discuss what the policy should be. To Bush, Powell's remarks were a reminder of the way Powell had dominated the press conference announcing his appointment as secretary of state. To Cheney, and to neoconservative senior officials such as Paul Wolfowitz and Scooter Libby, his comments called to mind their years in the Pentagon when Powell enjoyed close ties with the press and, they believed, used these relationships to help steer how events were covered.

Underneath it all, many other top officials in the new administration simply didn't agree with Powell. Their instinct was to reverse, not perpetuate, Clinton's policies toward North Korea. Among those who thought the new team should take a harder line was Bush himself. He read Powell's comments in the *Washington Post* early the next morning, immediately called up Rice, and ordered her to tell Powell to correct what he had said.

Thus, on Bush's orders, Powell was obliged to come out from a White House meeting to tell the press he had been wrong the previous day. The new administration didn't plan to follow the path of the Clinton administration, he said; rather, the Bush team would develop policies of its own. Specifically, it was not ready to embrace Kim Dae-jung's sunshine policy toward North Korea. Two months later, Powell acknowledged that he had made a mistake in talking so definitively about North Korea before the administration had decided what to do. "Sometimes you get a little too far forward on your skis," he said.

A few days later came another sign of discord that raised questions about Powell's standing. Bush had opposed the Kyoto Protocol (an international agreement limiting greenhouse gas emissions) during the campaign, and so it was not surprising that he would take the same position as president. However, with Cheney taking the leading role, the new administration rejected Kyoto suddenly and secretively, in a way that excluded Powell from the decision making and infuriated the European governments that strongly supported the agreement.

Soon after the inauguration, Cheney had assumed another powerful job title as head of the Bush administration's Energy Task Force, and in early March he told the president that the administration needed to inform the Senate, immediately, of its position on the Kyoto Protocol. At Cheney's prompting, Bush signed a letter that simply and bluntly rejected Kyoto, without including any of the softening words, customary in such documents, that the United States still hoped to work with European leaders to address the problem of climate change in other ways.

No one had told Powell that this letter was in the works, even though, as secretary of state, he was responsible for America's relations with its European allies. At the last minute, he got wind of it and rushed to the White House. With Rice's support, he tried to convince the president to delay the issuance of the letter so that it could be rewritten in more diplomatic language. But it was too late: Cheney had obtained Bush's signature and had already departed for Capitol Hill with the letter in his pocket. Rice told Bush she was "appalled that the vice president had been allowed to take a letter to Capitol Hill on a matter of international importance without my clearance or, more important, that of the secretary of state," she would recall years later.

Rice's complaint was of little avail. Even in those early months, Cheney pursued his own foreign policy initiatives, sometimes leaving Powell in the dark, sometimes launching into ventures of his own that seemed to conflict with official American policy. One State Department expert on North Korea said that in early 2001, a member of the vice president's staff came to him and asked for help in trying to develop a strategy for bringing the North Korean regime to a collapse—all without telling the secretary of state.

* * *

The rejection of the Kyoto treaty was merely one part of a larger pattern in the early months of the new administration. In several other instances, the administration attempted to withdraw or pull back from international treaties or agreements and to throw off commitments that limited America's freedom of action overseas. It rejected an international protocol that sought to enforce a ban on biological weapons. It proposed changes in an agreement on the sale of small arms. The Clinton administration had started to move toward joining the International Criminal Court; the Bush administration made clear it had no intention of joining. Secretary of Defense Donald Rumsfeld served notice that he was eager to withdraw American troops from NATO peacekeeping operations in Bosnia, causing consternation among America's European allies.

Indeed, the administration's highest foreign policy priority during its first eight months involved pulling out of an existing international agreement, the Anti-Ballistic Missile Treaty of 1972, a Cold War arms control agreement negotiated with the Soviet Union, which had limited the ability of the United States to construct missile-defense systems.

The issue engendered several months of skirmishing within the administration, with Cheney and Powell as the leaders of two opposing points of view. Powell argued that it was important to avoid unnecessary frictions with Moscow; he suggested the possibility of trying to amend the existing treaty, rather than withdrawing from it. Cheney maintained that the United States should avoid half measures and simply abrogate the treaty. "As I saw it, the State Department had it backward," he wrote. "Rather than compromising on policies that were in our national interest out of concern that we would offend other nations, we should do what served our security best, while undertaking diplomatic efforts to bring our allies and partners along."

In this case, the result tilted in Cheney's favor, but both men could claim a degree of satisfaction. Powell was given the diplomatic assignment to deal with the Russians and prepare them for the fact that the United States would withdraw from the treaty. At the end of 2001, Russian president Vladimir Putin grudgingly bowed to this reality, taking no countermeasures at the time. Cheney took Putin's seemingly mild reaction as proof that all the fears about what Russia could do had been exaggerated. Powell, meanwhile, viewed the same mild Russian reaction as a testament to his skillful diplomacy with Moscow.

* * *

Underlying the disputes between Cheney and Powell were their contrasting views about the way the United States should deal with the world after the Cold War.

Powell placed a premium on maintaining America's relations with its long-standing friends and allies, even when doing so might require the United States to take actions that in the short term it might not want. He believed that America could maintain its power and leading role in the world only with the support of other nations. By contrast, Cheney put the highest priority on doing whatever he felt to be in America's national interest, and he judged that interest as a matter of traditional military and economic power. He frowned on international agreements, which he viewed as restricting American power and sovereignty. Underlying his views was the assumption that post–Cold War America would often be better off operating on its own than with allies, who might tie America down and turn out to be more trouble than they were worth.

Cheney's views in 2001 were in line with those expressed in the Regional Defense Strategy of 1993, his vision of American primacy in the post–Cold War world. Powell's thinking, while more amorphous, represented traditional American foreign policy during the Cold War—above all, the sense that the United States, while powerful, still needed its allies and should act in concert with them as much as possible. Powell's instincts in 2001 reflected, more than anything else, the approach and thinking of George H. W. Bush and Brent Scowcroft during the late 1980s and early '90s.

In contrast to the George H. W. Bush administration, when Cheney and Powell had gotten along so well, the events of the 1990s had given rise to conflicting points of view between the two men about America's power and its role in the world. No rival had emerged to challenge American power, and there was no such rival on the horizon. That fact served to reinforce Cheney's thinking that America could go it alone in the world, wielding its unrivaled power to reshape the international order. Cheney believed that the United States no longer needed its allies the way it had during the Cold War. Indeed, during the Balkan conflicts, American military commanders had found it a nuisance to coordinate their military actions with various European allies. For Powell, America's preeminence reinforced his thinking that the United States should stick with the same approaches that had worked during the Cold War, placing a premium on its relationships with allies, diplomacy, and international agreements.

In a curious way, each man saw the other's beliefs as old-fashioned, too tied to patterns of thinking that had held sway during the Cold War. Cheney saw Powell as stuck in the *diplomacy* of the Cold War, unable to adjust to the changes and exploit the opportunities in a new unipolar world. Conversely, Powell viewed Cheney's thinking as too tied to the *threats* of the Cold War, unable to adjust to a new order in which there was no comparable threat. Colin Powell once said that in Cheney's mind, "There's always a Soviet Union lurking somewhere. Even if it's going away, it's lurking somewhere."

* * *

During the first nine months of the Bush administration, these philosophical differences burst into the open on a handful of issues such as North Korea, climate change, and the ABM Treaty. But the factional battles within the administration between the Cheney forces and the

Powell forces were also beginning to emerge behind the scenes on the question of what to do about Saddam Hussein in Iraq.

By the time George W. Bush took office, the sense of triumph that followed the end of the Gulf War of 1991 had faded, and even though the Clinton administration had formally adopted a policy of encouraging regime change in Iraq, Saddam was still there. George W. Bush clearly had second thoughts about his father's decision to leave Saddam Hussein in power. Years later, the younger Bush could manage to say carefully only that he "understood" his father's choice to avoid going to Baghdad, not that he agreed with it or that it was the right decision: "I wondered if he would send troops all the way to Baghdad. He had a chance to rid the world of Saddam once and for all. But he stopped at the liberation of Kuwait. That was how he had defined his mission. That was what Congress had voted for and the coalition had signed up for. I fully understood his rationale."

Less than a month after George W. Bush's inauguration, there was a brief, unexpected flare-up in Iraq while the new president was on a trip to Mexico. American and British warplanes enforcing the no-fly zone in Iraq struck targets unusually close to Baghdad, setting off air defenses and prompting Iraq to claim there had been civilian casualties. The incident took the Bush entourage by surprise and attracted intense press coverage; reporters interrupted Bush's press conference with the Mexican president to ask if the United States was going to war.

Powell had accompanied the president on the trip, but his presence was not enough for Bush. That night, Bush called Cheney, seeking advice and reassurance on the meaning and impact of the day's events. Cheney told him that even if the clash with Iraq had been unplanned, the result was a good one, because it demonstrated that the new administration would be tough on Saddam Hussein. Bush's call also underscored his early reliance on Cheney, more than Powell, for guidance on foreign policy.

Over the following months, the Bush team tried to work out its policy toward Iraq, with Cheney and Powell almost immediately finding themselves on opposite sides. Powell favored revising and improving the existing international economic sanctions against Iraq to make them more effective, a policy that was called "smart sanctions." He negotiated a new package of sanctions with other members of the UN Security

Council. Cheney, along with Donald Rumsfeld, opposed "smart sanctions" as ineffective, but in the end the administration accepted them.

Meanwhile, Cheney's and Powell's respective aides and allies inside the administration were engaged in more frequent and more intense battles over Iraq. The forum for these disputes was the Deputies' Committee, the regular meetings of second-ranking officials from the State and Defense Departments and the CIA, who try to resolve (or at least refine) policy disputes before they reach the top. There, in the early months of the administration, Paul Wolfowitz and Scooter Libby argued repeatedly that Saddam Hussein represented a serious threat to American interests and that strong efforts should be made to oust him from power—primarily by supporting Iraqi opposition groups. On the other side, Richard Armitage and Deputy CIA director John McLaughlin tended to downplay the threats and to question the wisdom of various ideas for regime change. Speaking for Powell, Armitage argued that it would be better to seek to contain Saddam Hussein than to overthrow him.

In one top-level discussion of Iraq in those early months, Wolfowitz, sitting in a back row behind Rumsfeld, began to argue for new action against Saddam Hussein. Powell turned around and chided him, "Paul—we won!"—meaning that Saddam was still weakened and limited in his options as a result of his defeat in 1991. In the car ride back to the Pentagon, Wolfowitz said he thought Powell was still fighting the last war. "And so are you!" Rumsfeld told him.

Because of all the internal bickering about Iraq, very little was decided. Powell recalled that military officials were giving Bush contingency briefings for action against Iraq, but that this was "not unreasonable—we have lots of contingency plans." By the beginning of September, the administration had not even settled on the broad outlines of a strategy for dealing with Saddam Hussein, much less the specifics. Zalmay Khalilzad, the National Security Council aide responsible for Iraq policy, observed that the top officials "were not even united on the goals we should be prioritizing. Did we want to contain Saddam or press for regime change?" Khalilzad drafted a series of possible options for the president, short of a full-scale invasion, that Bush might use if he decided to try to overthrow Saddam. However, Khalilzad wrote years later, "In the absence of a clear decision, . . . the option of smart sanctions carried the day by default."

Iraq policy would remain in limbo until events elsewhere tipped the balance of forces inside the administration. Wolfowitz, the leading advocate for regime change during those early months, recalled later that "there was some argument about Iraq, and I don't remember Cheney particularly taking a position at the time, before 9/11."

* * *

Thus, in the earliest months of George W. Bush's presidency, the administration's dynamics and operating style began to take shape. Cheney and Powell found themselves in new roles, ones quite unlike their relatively smooth working relationship in the Pentagon a decade earlier.

As secretary of defense, Cheney had wanted—indeed, desperately needed—Powell's help and cooperation because he was chairman of the Joint Chiefs. If the two men had been at odds, it was Cheney, arguably, who would have been the odd man out. Now, as secretary of state, Powell was the leader of an organization, the State Department, with vastly less public support, leading a bureaucracy that had been portrayed as recalcitrant by one president after another. Cheney didn't need Powell the way he had the last time they were in government together.

Moreover, in the earlier period, Powell had been duty-bound to cooperate with Cheney as secretary of defense. That was the established order, in accordance with the principle of civilian control of the military. But how much authority did the vice president of the United States have over the secretary of state or, indeed, over the foreign policy apparatus in general? The answer was much hazier. Indeed, Cheney and Powell could recall the episode in 1989 when Vice President Dan Quayle had tried to take charge of the U.S. response to a crisis in the Philippines while President George H. W. Bush was on a foreign trip. It was Cheney, then the secretary of defense, who had objected because the vice president had no legal authority.

Cheney's sole constitutional authority was through George W. Bush; as vice president, he wielded power only to the extent that the president chose to rely upon him. In the day-to-day workings of the administration, he was, in formal terms, merely a voice, another seat at the table, not the decision maker. And so, in the early months of Bush's presidency, Cheney increased his power in two ways: first, through his personal relationship with the president, solidifying his role as the leading advisor; and second, by making the Office of the Vice President a weighty, independent force of its own. In the past, foreign policy discussions had tended to be among three entities: the State Department, the Defense Department, and the Central Intelligence Agency. Now there was an additional force that had to be reckoned with: the vice president's office. And as the early discussions on Iraq demonstrated, the lineup often boiled down, in shorthand, to the vice president's office and the Pentagon teaming up against the State Department (which was joined, sometimes, by the CIA). Viewed in terms of the personalities at the top, it was Cheney and Rumsfeld against Powell.

Powell tried to adapt to this new situation, but it was difficult. Inside the State Department, he seemed relaxed and as efficient as ever. He ran large staff meetings, sometimes with thirty or forty department officials, to go over the events of the day or week. At least at the outset, he rarely even mentioned the burgeoning conflicts within the administration. "He would always refer to the Secretary of Defense as 'Mr. Rumsfeld.' Never referred to him as 'Don.' Never said anything critical about anybody. He was very measured in those meetings," recalled Andrew Natsios, who served under Powell as head of the U.S. Agency for International Development. Natsios also noticed that "Powell was very careful" in what he said at staff meetings, "probably because John Bolton was in the room, and other people were in the room, who were not friendly to Powell." Bolton, a prominent conservative, was serving under Powell as an undersecretary of state because Cheney had asked Powell to give him a job.

Although within the walls of the State Department Powell seemed as confident as ever, elsewhere around Washington, officials noticed something surprising: in his dealings with the rest of the administration, he seemed curiously passive. "Powell was not assertive in meetings," Khalilzad recalled. "He articulated his views clearly and logically, but he was not confrontational." At the National Security Council, Khalilzad was responsible for writing summaries of the discussions that had taken place during the meetings of top-level Bush administration officials. Sometimes, after distributing the minutes of the meetings, he would get a call from Armitage, saying that the written minutes didn't properly reflect the position of the State Department and that some point or another should be added or clarified. "That's very interesting, Rich, but that wasn't said by the principal [Powell]," Khalilzad would reply. "I was very surprised [by Powell's reluctance to assert himself], because he had star power, Powell."

In March, soon after Powell was chided for speaking out about North Korea before he checked with the White House, news stories began to report that he was losing clout within the administration. "Powell Losing Policy Battles to Hardliners," said a headline in the *Guardian*. The story reported that "Mr. Powell seems out of step with his Pentagon and White House colleagues on a range of issues."

Those perceptions would not change over the following six months.

In its cover story dated September 10, *Time* magazine put the secretary of state's ever-familiar face on its cover. The cover line read, "Where Have You Gone, Colin Powell? The secretary of state isn't the foreign policy general everyone thought he'd be. What's holding him back?"

On the morning of September 11, 2001, Powell found himself in Lima, Peru, representing the United States at a meeting of the foreign ministers of the Organization of American States. Cheney, meanwhile, was in Washington, inside the White House.

15

SEPTEMBER 11 AND ITS AFTERMATH

Amid their differing views of the world, one opinion that Dick Cheney and Colin Powell had held in common before September 11, 2001, was the relatively low priority they accorded to international terrorism. Throughout their long careers, both men had been fully absorbed by the problems caused by big, powerful nations, above all the Soviet Union. Powell had grown up in the traditions of the U.S. Army, trained to be ready to fight large-scale land wars against an adversary such as Germany or the Soviets. Cheney had no military training, but as a civilian leader he had been, if anything, more preoccupied than Powell with the Soviet threat. In 1990, Powell had been initially hesitant to use American troops against a lesser regional power, Iraq; Cheney, like George H. W. Bush and Brent Scowcroft, had been far more willing to go to war.

In the decade that followed the Gulf War and the Soviet collapse, Powell had bluntly declared that there were few threats to American power on the horizon. Even Cheney, who at other times in his career was prone to exaggerating threats, occasionally acknowledged this reality—although, when he voiced confidence in a threat-free environment, you sometimes had to read his sentences a couple of times to understand what he had just said.

"Now, we've reached the point where it's difficult to articulate a rationale that justifies a need to retain significant forces," Cheney said in a 1996 interview in the Naval Institute proceedings. "I sometimes have the feeling today that the strongest impetus out there [for America] to maintain adequate military forces has less to do with any view of the international situation or our security requirements as much as it's tied to what I would say are small 'p' political considerations: 'Don't close my base. Don't shut down my production line. Don't demobilize my unit.'" Indeed, it was the apparent absence of threats to the United States that had helped give rise to Cheney's vision of an American-dominated world.

Neither Cheney nor Powell had much direct, hands-on experience with terrorist attacks. There had been a spate of such incidents during the Reagan administration, but most of them had occurred before Powell came to Reagan's National Security Council. Terrorism had been at best a minor problem during Cheney's years as defense secretary. Indeed, despite their years of experience in national security, Cheney and Powell arguably had less experience dealing with terrorism than the Clinton administration officials they were replacing, who had lived through the 1993 attack on the World Trade Center and al-Qaeda's attacks in Kenya and Tanzania in 1998 and in Yemen in 2000. President Clinton and his national security advisor, Sandy Berger, had warned the incoming Bush officials that terrorism was one of the most important national security problems they would face.

Still, the Bush team did not react with any alacrity to such warnings, even from the career officials who stayed on after Bush took office, such as Richard Clarke, the National Security Council's counterterrorism specialist, or his counterparts in the Central Intelligence Agency. When these holdover officials reported in the early months of 2001 that al-Qaeda appeared to be preparing some new attack in the United States, Cheney in particular seemed to downplay the danger. "[Osama] Bin Laden planning high-profile attacks," reported the CIA in one of several such reports. According to Michael Morell, the CIA official responsible for providing daily intelligence briefings to Bush and Cheney, "The vice president one morning asked me whether all this threat reporting might not be deception on the part of al Qa'ida—purposely designed to get our attention and to get us to needlessly expend resources in response."

At the top levels of the administration, the responsibility for dealing with terrorism fell primarily to National Security Advisor Condoleezza Rice. Cheney became involved, but only sporadically; when the Bush administration needed help from Jordan or Saudi Arabia on al-Qaeda or wanted to warn them of possible threats, Cheney made the phone calls, drawing on his relationships and knowledge from the time of the Gulf War. But, overall, Cheney was not viewed as the point man; nor did he see himself in that way.

* * *

As soon as the hijacked planes hit the World Trade Center and the Pentagon, Cheney began to take charge. At first, the role he assumed was related to the circumstances of that particular day: President Bush was not in Washington, but in a classroom event in Florida and then, for the remainder of the day, under massive protection at U.S. military bases in Louisiana and Nebraska. Cheney was the man on the spot. And almost immediately, a second factor came into play: Cheney not only happened to be present in Washington, but he also knew the drills and the protocols to prepare American leaders for an attack on the United States, having participated in the continuity-of-government exercises during the 1980s.

Inside the White House, the Secret Service rushed Cheney to the Emergency Operations Center, inside a bunker beneath the White House, where he assumed command. One of his first actions was to call Bush and tell him not to return to Washington. Over the next couple of hours, he concentrated on stopping further attacks by hijacked planes. In the confusion that prevailed that morning, it was reported for a time that another passenger plane was getting close to Washington, and air force officials wanted to know whether to shoot it down. Cheney told them to go ahead. Later on, both Bush and Cheney would claim it was the president who made this decision, after Cheney referred it up to him; but close examinations of the evidence have established that Cheney made the shoot-down decision first, on his own, and then cleared it with Bush afterward. Clearly, Cheney's earlier belief during the Philippine crisis of 1989 that as vice president, Dan Quayle was not in the formal chain of command no longer held true on September 11, when Cheney himself was vice president.

Late that night, after Bush had returned to Washington and met with the National Security Council, Dick and Lynne Cheney flew to what official White House statements called an "undisclosed location"—a phrase that would be repeated so often over the following weeks that it became part of the vernacular and the subject of *Saturday Night Live* skits. Here again, Cheney was following the protocols of the continuity-of-government exercises: that the vice president should generally not be in the same place as the president, to avert the possibility of their both being killed in a single attack. It was a guiding principle that the nation should not be deprived of leadership during a crisis. (Along these lines, Cheney had written out a letter of resignation in March and given it to his aide David Addington, who kept it in his home dresser drawer. It was to be taken out and used if Cheney somehow became incapacitated and unable to perform the job of vice president.)

There was also a third factor at work to explain the powerful role Cheney exerted starting on September 11: he had vastly greater experience than Bush in the workings of the federal government—how policies were made and how they were blocked, how the paper flowed, how Congress could be used or circumvented. Cheney was not alone in having this degree of governmental experience; Colin Powell and Donald Rumsfeld did, too, but Rumsfeld had his hands full running the Pentagon, and Powell was similarly occupied at the State Department. Cheney had no large bureaucracy to manage, and so it was he who had the time, the energy, and above all the intense desire to spearhead the administration's responses to September 11.

* * *

The Bush team's first reaction to the attacks was one of stunned fury. That night, after the immediate threat of further attacks was eliminated and just before Cheney departed for the "undisclosed location," all the top officials (including Bush, Cheney, Powell, Rice, and Rumsfeld) gathered in the White House bunker for their first meeting to decide how to respond. CIA director George Tenet, who was also there, said there was "more raw emotion in one place than I think I've ever experienced in my life: anger that this could have happened, shock that it had, overwhelming sorrow for the dead, a compelling sense of urgency that we had to respond and do so quickly." Robert Gates, who later conversed privately with others on the Bush team, suggested that there was another, unarticulated emotion: guilt for not having stopped al-Qaeda. "I think there was a huge sense among senior members of the administration of having let the country down, of having allowed a devastating attack on America take place on their watch," he said.

Everyone on the Bush team agreed on one intellectual proposition: that the event was of historic importance and that America had entered a new era. But what exactly did a "new era" mean, and how should the United States respond?

For Powell, the fact that America had entered a new era was true simply by definition. The continental United States had not been successfully attacked by a foreign entity since the War of 1812. Now a terrorist organization had done that, and therefore, it was a new era. And yet Powell did not believe that America should change its approach to the world in any fundamental ways, and so did not try to sketch out any new strategy. This was in keeping with his character. As many in the Pentagon had noticed in the early 1990s, Powell was a pragmatist, not a strategist, and his preference for tactics and problem solving had not lessened in the intervening decade.

Instead, Powell's response was to propose new diplomatic initiatives. Inside the bunker that first night, Tenet recalled, Powell told his colleagues, "we had to make it clear to Pakistan as well as to Afghanistan that the time for equivocation is over." The problem for Powell was that his colleagues thought his suggestions did not go far enough.

To be sure, figuring out which countries to talk to and what to tell them was Powell's responsibility as secretary of state. He was no longer the nation's military leader; his current job focused on diplomacy, and so diplomacy was what he emphasized. There was, however, some irony here: In 1990, as chairman of the Joint Chiefs, he had for a time tried to slow down movement toward war with Iraq, and Dick Cheney had warned him at the time, "You're not the Secretary of State. . . . So stick to military matters." Now, eleven years later, Powell was defining his role narrowly and sticking to diplomacy.

It can also be said in defense of Powell that even if he didn't articulate a strategy, he more or less had one: that the United States should form strong alliances, avoid conflict with its allies, assume the role of leader of the free world, and then rely on the inherent power of its alliances to deal with its adversaries. This was the strategy the United States had pursued since the end of World War II. "If we want to go it alone and say we know what's best . . . and lose the support of the world, then I think we will have made a strategic mistake," he observed in a press conference less than two weeks after September 11.

But to some of Powell's colleagues, "new era" had a much broader meaning. Condoleezza Rice had been a Soviet specialist, and so, not surprisingly, after September 11 she thought back to the beginning of the Cold War. The fear of Soviet domination of Europe had prompted the Truman administration not only to develop new concepts (containment, deterrence), but also to establish a series of new government institutions (the National Security Council, the Central Intelligence Agency) to deal with the Soviet threat. Rice was laying the intellectual groundwork for the Bush administration to build new governmental structures after September 11, such as the Department of Homeland Security.

Then there was Cheney. To the vice president, the "new era" thinking after September 11 meant much more than it did to either Powell or Rice. Cheney cared not about creating new institutions, like Rice, but about increasing the overall power of the executive branch of government. He had spent much of his career trying to lift the restraints on presidential authority. For him, the "new era" after September 11 meant this: The restraints were off. The limits that had been placed on the CIA, the National Security Agency, the FBI, and the Justice Department should no longer apply; the Bush administration should go all out in its pursuit of its adversaries.

Cheney rejected Powell's emphasis on diplomacy, alliances, and international organizations. Indeed, at a time when other nations were rushing to express strong support for the United States—"We are all Americans," a headline in *Le Monde* had declared—Cheney cautioned that America's alliances should not limit its freedom of action. He told his colleagues it was important "that we not allow our mission to be determined by others. We had an obligation to do whatever it took to defend America, and we needed coalition partners who would sign on for that. The mission should define the coalition, not the other way around."

This movement toward "coalitions of the willing" was a roundabout way of downgrading the centrality of alliances, and it reflected the strong views of Cheney and, equally, of Donald Rumsfeld. (Rumsfeld said he got this idea from Benjamin Netanyahu, Israel's former and future prime minister, who had told him that "building any permanent alliance . . . would restrict our flexibility in the future.")

* * *

On the weekend after September 11, the top Bush administration officials gathered again, this time at Camp David, to discuss how the United States should respond to the attacks. On Friday night, September 14, Cheney, Powell, Rumsfeld, and Rice had dined at the presidential retreat. Rice found herself almost in awe of her three colleagues. "These men, who collectively had accumulated decades of experience in government, had known one another for years," she wrote. "They'd been through numerous crises separately and together." What followed over the next three years would fall more under the category of "separately" than "together."

At the larger meeting the next day, there were essentially two issues on the table. One involved Afghanistan: should the United States simply attack al-Qaeda or should it seek to overthrow the Taliban regime, and what military means should be used? The second issue was whether the United States should confine its military operations to Afghanistan or broaden them to include other countries or locations.

Underlying these questions was the common belief that the United States had to respond to al-Qaeda more powerfully than it had in the past. The Clinton administration had reacted to the 1998 bombings in Kenya and Tanzania with missile attacks on a factory in Sudan and on an al-Qaeda training camp in Afghanistan. These actions had not deterred al-Qaeda from further attacks, and Bush said later that they had done little more than pound sand. "Dropping expensive weapons on sparsely populated camps would not break the Taliban's hold on the country or destroy al Qaeda's sanctuary," he wrote.

Powell once again emphasized diplomacy. He acknowledged that the United States would have to go to war in Afghanistan, but urged that before any attack, the administration should give an ultimatum to the Taliban regime to turn over bin Laden and also tell Pakistan it was time to decide if it would support the United States. Bush scorned such concerns. Michael Morell, a CIA official at the meeting that day, recalled in his memoir that during a lunch break, a senior State Department official told the president that it was important that America's initial response be a diplomatic one. As the official walked away, Bush turned to Morell and a CIA colleague and said simply, "Fuck diplomacy. We are going to war."

No one at the meeting opposed war in Afghanistan. Much of the discussion concerned various plans to insert Special Forces and CIA paramilitary teams into the country, with orders to dislodge al-Qaeda camps, capture bin Laden, and overthrow the Taliban regime. Bush approved these plans a couple of days later, along with a series of bombing and missile attacks. But Bush and Cheney did accept Powell's recommendation to give an ultimatum to the Taliban first. The analogy in the minds of several officials was there should be no sneak attack like Pearl Harbor. No one expected the Taliban to respond to the ultimatum by turning over bin Laden, even if it had had the power to do so. (As everyone expected, the Taliban spurned the ultimatum.)

The one part of the discussion where disagreement emerged involved Iraq. Within the first twenty-four hours after September 11, several neoconservative leaders, inside and outside the administration, began to argue for military action against Iraq as well as al-Qaeda and the Taliban. This was not by itself surprising; leading neoconservatives had been advocating the overthrow of Saddam Hussein for years. Nevertheless, the speed with which they jumped from September 11 to Iraq was stunning. When CIA director George Tenet arrived at the White House early on the morning of September 12 to brief the president, he encountered the neoconservative former Pentagon official Richard Perle, who had already been inside the White House that morning. "Iraq has to pay a price for what happened yesterday. They bear responsibility," Perle told the CIA director.

In preparation for the weekend gathering at Camp David, the National Security Council staff had drawn up a paper listing possible ways for the United States to respond to those responsible for the September 11 attacks. The first two options were to focus on al-Qaeda alone or on the Taliban regime protecting al-Qaeda in Afghanistan. The third option was "to eliminate Iraq threat." At meetings of the Deputies' Committee that week, Paul Wolfowitz, representing the Defense Department, argued against a narrow focus on Afghanistan and in favor of a much broader campaign.

At Camp David, Rumsfeld turned the floor over to Wolfowitz, who laid out the arguments for moving against Iraq. Wolfowitz argued that Iraq was of vastly greater strategic importance to the United States than Afghanistan, and that if America's aim was not just to punish al-Qaeda but also to prevent future terrorist attacks, then it should move against Iraq.

Powell quickly spoke out against the idea of attacking Iraq. The United States enjoyed strong international support in the aftermath of September 11, he pointed out, and it would lose much of that support if it moved beyond a campaign against al-Qaeda and Afghanistan to attack Iraq as well. Here, Powell was once again emphasizing the importance of the United States' working in concert with other countries, rather than acting alone.

In this instance, Powell carried the day, although not for the reasons he gave. Cheney and others at the table also opposed immediate action against Iraq, on the grounds that the United States needed to concentrate initially on winning the war in Afghanistan and that Iraq would be a distraction. Even Rumsfeld, who had introduced Wolfowitz's presentation on Iraq, maintained his distance and did not embrace it. Afghanistan "should be first," Cheney would write years later. "I believed it was important to deal with the threat Iraq posed, but not until we had an effective plan for taking down the Taliban and denying al Qaeda a safe haven in Afghanistan."

Following the meeting, Bush ordered planning to begin for war in Afghanistan. He rejected Wolfowitz's call to move against Iraq as well. However, his decision was just a deferral, not a final resolution of the issue. Administration officials began calling Afghanistan "phase one" of the war on terror, conveying the message that there would be more phases to come.

* * *

Over the following three months, the Bush administration pursued its military operation in Afghanistan—to completion, or so it seemed at the time. The CIA teams and the Pentagon's Special Forces joined with

Afghan forces opposed to the Taliban, including what was known as the Northern Alliance, to overthrow the Taliban regime. Osama bin Laden fled into the mountains near the border with Pakistan, hiding for a time in the remote caves of Tora Bora. But he was not captured.

Throughout this period, Powell worked in harmony with the other senior members of the Bush team, serving as the administration's point man for the diplomatic efforts necessary to support the war and its immediate aftermath. He traveled to Pakistan to meet with President Pervez Musharraf, shoring up his support for the American-led campaign in Afghanistan.

Powell also supervised the American diplomacy aimed at bringing together various Afghan groups to form a new government, led by Hamid Karzai, to replace the Taliban. Finally, Powell led the successful effort at the UN Security Council to authorize a postwar peacekeeping force for Afghanistan and persuaded British prime minister Tony Blair that the United Kingdom should take a leading role in these efforts to stabilize the country. No one had to ask, "Where have you gone, Colin Powell?" He was on the front pages.

In that period, too, the Bush team's unity of purpose overshadowed its internal differences. In mid-October, Cheney said that Americans had confidence in Bush's team of advisors, ticking off the names of Powell, Rumsfeld, and himself at the top of the list. "There's a lot of tough decisions that are involved here, and some of them are very close calls," he said. "But if I had to go out and design a team of people, . . . this is it."

Near the end of the year, the *New York Times* informed its readers that the September 11 attacks and the war in Afghanistan had brought about a new sense of unity among George W. Bush's top foreign policy advisors. "Once seen as stark competitors, they have been recast by events as loyal aides to a wartime leader," the *Times* reported. One senior official told the newspaper, "The venom is gone." The members of the Bush team "have learned to disagree better," he added.

* * *

On the day after the Camp David meeting, Cheney appeared on NBC's *Meet the Press*, where he said that as part of its response to the September 11 attacks, the United States would have to disrupt terrorist networks and develop intelligence programs aimed at them. We would have to work "sort of the dark side, if you will," he added.

> We're going to spend time in the shadows in the intelligence world. A lot of what needs to be done here will have to be done quietly, without any discussions, using sources and methods that are available to our intelligence agencies. . . . And so it's going to be vital for us to use any means at our disposal, basically, to achieve our objectives.

These words captured the essence of Cheney's view of the world— his preoccupation with intelligence gathering, his love of secrecy, the latent extremism contained in the expression "any means at our disposal." Cheney would complain years later that this statement had been misinterpreted to suggest something sinister, but the phraseology that gave rise to this idea ("dark side," "in the shadows") was entirely his own.

Over the following months, the Bush administration adopted a series of antiterrorist measures without precedent in American history or law. It conducted a pervasive new surveillance program; it established an offshore prison; it opened "black sites" in several countries to interrogate detainees; and, ultimately, by any common definition of the word, it tortured some of those detainees through what it called "enhanced interrogation" techniques. Cheney was not merely a proponent but in most cases the driving force behind these new measures.

Senior administration officials approved these programs in response to events as they unfolded. The surveillance program came before all the others because, immediately after September 11, the Bush team was worried about further terrorist attacks and preoccupied with the task of preventing them. One particular fear was that there might still be al-Qaeda members or teams at large in the United States. U.S. officials had discovered, to their chagrin, that the al-Qaeda operatives who had carried out the attacks had not only slipped into the United States without detection, but had also been communicating with al-Qaeda leaders in Afghanistan.

On September 11 itself, before Bush had even returned to Washington, Cheney summoned his general counsel, David Addington, the former

CIA lawyer who had been for fifteen years his closest aide, and asked him to begin thinking about what new authority the president would need to respond to the terrorist attacks. Addington began consulting with other government lawyers, especially White House counsel Alberto Gonzales, though Addington took charge, much as Cheney did.

Cheney also asked George Tenet, the CIA director, and Michael Hayden, the director of the National Security Agency, about new measures for gathering intelligence on individuals who might be planning further acts of terrorism. The intelligence officials came up with a far-reaching program that was approved by Bush on October 4, only three weeks after September 11. It was given the code name Stellar Wind, although later on, when the administration needed an anodyne name to explain the program to Congress and the public, it became better known as the Terrorist Surveillance Program.

Until then, the NSA had generally been barred from carrying out surveillance inside the United States. It could spy on suspected foreign agents inside the country, but only by obtaining a warrant from a special court; without a warrant, it could conduct its activities only overseas. Stellar Wind gave the NSA legal authority to monitor communications in the United States if one party to the conversation was overseas and if one of the participants was believed to have some connection to al-Qaeda. These loose standards opened the way for the agency to begin collecting massive amounts of data. Previously the NSA had to identify particular individuals to target; with the new data, it could discover individuals it had not previously known and subject them to surveillance. The program operated like a drift net.

The Terrorist Surveillance Program would engender years of intense controversy. The order establishing the program required that it be reauthorized by Bush roughly every forty-five days. At one point in early 2004, Justice Department lawyers, along with FBI director Robert Mueller and Assistant Attorney General James Comey, objected to one part of the secret program and threatened to resign on the grounds that Bush had no constitutional authority to authorize such surveillance without congressional approval. The following year, the *New York Times* revealed the existence of the program, prompting Cheney to say that the newspaper should be prosecuted for publishing classified information.

Nevertheless, the program survived for years in one form or another, largely because of Cheney's dogged support and personal involvement. Nervous intelligence officials insisted that the administration should at least tell a few congressional leaders what it was doing, and the administration agreed to conduct regular briefings at the White House for the leaders of the congressional intelligence committees. At least twelve such briefings were held—in Cheney's office, with Cheney presiding, together with CIA and NSA officials. It was, to say the least, an unusual hands-on role for a vice president of the United States.

The new surveillance program was merely one part of a larger trend: under the rationale that September 11 had "changed everything," Cheney was seeking to reverse what he considered the harmful legacy of the Vietnam War and its aftermath. One of the congressional reforms of the 1970s had been the passage of the Foreign Intelligence Surveillance Act of 1978, the law that restricted NSA operations inside the United States. The new Terrorist Surveillance Program dramatically weakened that law, but Congress was not asked to approve that weakening.

In late September and early October, the sense that the United States was under siege intensified when several Americans, including a staff member in a congressional office, opened letters that contained spores of anthrax. The Bush team tried to figure out how to respond, even briefly exploring the possibility that the entire country would have to be inoculated against the disease. The top-level official assigned to oversee these efforts was, once again, Cheney. By coincidence the vice president and his aide Scooter Libby had earlier taken a special interest in the problem of biological weapons attacks; in the spring of 2001, they had studied the results of a well-known exercise called Dark Winter, about the possible impact of a smallpox attack on the United States.

In short, when it came to the immediate responses to September 11, Cheney seemed to be everywhere. The terrorist attacks and their aftermath brought to the surface a series of issues for which he had had direct personal involvement in the past because of his time as White House chief of staff (presidential succession), or on the House Intelligence Committee (surveillance, covert operations), or as secretary of defense (the war in Afghanistan).

One unnoticed side effect of the anthrax scare was that for a couple of months in the fall of 2001, it pushed aside any discussion of war with Iraq. The Bush team had decided at their Camp David meeting in September to concentrate on military action in Afghanistan, though a number of senior officials still favored an eventual war with Iraq; those officials included Cheney and his top aides. However, the vice president and his team were preoccupied for several weeks that fall with issues stemming from the anthrax attacks. In an interview in 2003, a Bush administration official acknowledged that dealing with anthrax had consumed so much attention that for a time, Iraq stayed on the back burner on which it had been placed after the Camp David meeting.

* * *

By November, as the war in Afghanistan was reaching its peak, the Bush administration faced a new series of questions. U.S. forces had captured a growing number of prisoners, from al-Qaeda and the Taliban. The issue was what to do with them: where should they be held, how should they be treated, should they be put on trial? Here again, Cheney proved to be the driving force, at one point obtaining Bush's approval for a decision even before Powell and Rice (among others) had had a chance to weigh in.

Unlike the earlier controversy over surveillance, several government agencies and Cabinet officials were involved in the detention questions, which fell under the jurisdiction of the Department of Justice (trials), the Defense Department (holding the prisoners), the State Department (dealing with the international community), and the National Security Council, which was supposed to coordinate all these bureaucracies. Still, the vice president, who had no direct constitutional or statutory responsibility for these issues, managed to exert his will.

In the earliest of these disputes, the administration had to decide on the legal process for handling the new detainees. Should al-Qaeda members be considered prisoners of war or international criminals? Should they stand trial in U.S. civilian courts, charged with the deaths and destruction of September 11? Should they instead be tried in some other kind of court? Powell had appointed one of his aides, Pierre Prosper, to oversee an interagency task force addressing this question. But Prosper's group was working extremely slowly, and Cheney decided to bypass it. He assigned Addington to draft an order under which the detainees would have none of the rights or legal protections allowed in civilian courts or regular military courts. Instead, they could be held indefinitely without trial, with their fates to be decided by secret military commissions similar to those established in World War II to try Nazi saboteurs. Some officials, including John Bellinger, a lawyer for the NSC, tried to argue that this precedent no longer applied because it had been invalidated by a series of subsequent laws and treaties. But in bureaucratic warfare, Bellinger "was no match for David Addington," Condoleezza Rice later recalled. Her own staff, she said, "was at times cut out of the process."

On Saturday, November 10, Cheney presided over a small session inside the White House to refine Addington's draft and put it in final form. There were no participants from the State Department or the National Security Council. Three days later, Cheney hand-carried Addington's draft to a private lunch with the president, and Bush signed it. Rice had never seen it beforehand, and Powell first heard about it from CNN. Rice told Bush that if this happened again, she might resign. Among the many unforeseen consequences of the new order was to create intense friction with Britain, America's closest military ally. Eight of the detainees captured in Afghanistan were British citizens; the British government protested for years that these military commissions set up by the United States did not meet the standards of international law. Thus a pattern was set that would be repeated on other occasions: Cheney would initiate new antiterrorism programs, and Powell would find himself trying to defend them when they incurred the wrath and opposition of other countries.

The next question was where to put the hundreds of fighters who had been captured. The military didn't want to keep them in Afghanistan, where any facility in which they were held could become the focus of al-Qaeda attacks. The administration toyed with the idea of holding the detainees on navy ships, but that didn't seem like a long-term solution. There were various secure facilities in the United States, such as Alcatraz, Leavenworth, and military brigs, but these options were rejected, too, for a reason that extended beyond security: the administration's overriding consideration, not always mentioned in public, was the need to get the detainees to talk, particularly about any plans for future attacks, and it was less easy to do that if they were on American soil. As one Bush administration official put it, America's spy satellites, which during the Cold War had been able to monitor Soviet troop deployments for signs of an impending attack, were of far less use against a small and nimble enemy like al-Qaeda. Instead, this official said, "The most promising source of intelligence was the terrorists already captured."

Bush himself said that he didn't want the detainees to be given constitutional protections such as the right to remain silent. For that reason, the administration didn't want to hold the detainees inside the United States, or even in an American territory such as Guam, where they would still enjoy enough constitutional protection to have access to American courts and file writs of habeas corpus. Finally, a solution emerged, and from a familiar source. "The Vice President was, as I remember it, the one who suggested that we find an 'offshore' facility," Rice would recall. In such a place, the detainees would have no access to the courts or other constitutional protections. Cheney maintained later that it was the Defense Department that suggested the U.S. naval base at Guantanamo Bay as the "offshore facility" that would work best. Guantanamo was remote, on the eastern end of the island of Cuba. It was entirely under the control of the U.S. military. And it enjoyed one other advantage over a facility in, say, Thailand or Egypt: "Its use would not further complicate diplomatic relations with a host nation, since our relations with Fidel Castro's Cuba were poor at best," Rumsfeld would later explain. In January 2002, the first prisoners began to arrive at Guantanamo. The Pentagon press office released photographs of prisoners in orange jumpsuits, some with their hands tied behind their backs, with barbed wire and chain link fences in the background. Those photographs were quickly transmitted, published, and broadcast throughout the world.

Colin Powell and the State Department had not been leading players in the decision to put the detainees at Guantanamo. But Powell and America's diplomats found themselves answering questions for years afterward about why the prison existed and what was happening there. Cheney later grumbled that in response to complaints, especially from Europe, the State Department always seemed to be "looking for ways to shut down the facility."

* * *

In many of these early decisions about the new antiterrorist measures, Colin Powell seemed to hold back, avoiding direct involvement. He had a plausible rationale for doing so: he was, after all, in charge of foreign policy, not the home front. But in early 2002 the unfolding series of anti-terrorism programs touched upon an issue that, for a time, galvanized Powell into outright opposition to what the Bush administration and specifically Dick Cheney were trying to do.

The question was whether the detainees were entitled to the protections of the Geneva Conventions, the international treaty that governs the treatment of prisoners of war and sets a series of standards to protect those who are captured in battle—for example, requiring basic food and medical care. More to the point for the Bush administration, Geneva also set out rules that limited the interrogation of prisoners:

> No physical or mental torture, nor any other form of coercion, may be inflicted on prisoners of war to secure from them information of any kind whatever. Prisoners of war who refuse to answer may not be threatened, insulted, or exposed to unpleasant or disadvantageous treatment of any kind.

As was so often the case, Cheney and Addington had been thinking about this problem well before others in the administration. In mid-November, during a question-and-answer session after a speech to the U.S. Chamber of Commerce, the vice president said he thought that a terrorist "is not a lawful combatant. They don't deserve to be treated as a prisoner of war."

By January, as the administration was moving detainees to Guantanamo, the issue came to a head. Justice Department lawyers and White House counsel Alberto Gonzales issued a memo (said to have been drafted by Addington) arguing that the prisoners had no such protection. It maintained that the Geneva Conventions didn't apply to members of al-Qaeda because al-Qaeda wasn't a state and therefore had no rights under international law. The harder issue involved captured fighters who were from Afghanistan's Taliban regime. Afghanistan was a state and thus seemingly covered by the Geneva Conventions, but the Justice Department lawyers and Gonzales argued that it was a "failed state," and therefore the Geneva protections didn't apply to the Taliban captives, either.

The memo went to Bush, who approved it. But when Powell found out, he was infuriated. The issue had been brought to the president when Powell was traveling in Asia, and he hadn't been given any chance to express his views; he hadn't even known Bush was about to make a decision on the Geneva Conventions. From Asia, Powell sent word back that he wanted Bush to reconsider the issue; he also said he wanted to meet with the president to talk about it. Bush, in turn, scheduled a National Security Council meeting, with Powell in attendance, to review the issues he had just decided in Powell's absence.

Underlying Powell's dismay was the fact that he had spent most of his career in the military. He had been trained for decades, and had trained his own troops, in the importance of the Geneva Conventions: after all, they applied not only to those enemy soldiers captured by the United States in wartime, but to captured American soldiers as well.

Powell sent a memo to Gonzales arguing that the Geneva Conventions should apply to the detainees. His points were phrased in dry, matter-of-fact language, which made the memo all the more powerful. A decision not to apply the Geneva Conventions, he said, "will reverse over a century of U.S. policy and practice . . . and undermine the protections of the law of war for our troops, both in this specific conflict and in general." Moreover, such a decision "has a high cost in terms of negative international reaction, with immediate adverse consequences for our conduct of foreign policy. It will undermine public support among critical allies." Worse, "it may provoke some individual foreign prosecutors to investigate and prosecute our officials and troops." On the other hand, a decision that the Geneva Conventions do apply "maintains POW status for U.S. forces."

On the eve of the National Security Council meeting to discuss the Geneva Conventions issue, in a sign that all was not well inside the administration, Powell's memo urging Bush to reconsider his decision was leaked to the conservative *Washington Times*, accompanied by a pronounced anti-Powell spin. "Administration sources last night expressed anger at Mr. Powell, whom they accused of bowing to pressure from the political left," the story said, adding, "Most, if not all, members of the president's national security team are urging him [Bush] not to retreat."

In that last claim, the *Times* story was simply wrong. Powell's view in support of the Geneva Conventions was shared by many others with military experience. Richard Myers, the chairman of the Joint Chiefs of Staff, fervently argued to Donald Rumsfeld in favor of applying the Geneva Conventions, saying that the United States should not try to "weasel out" of its obligations under international law. Indeed, among the Pentagon's civilian leaders, Douglas Feith, a strong neoconservative and one of the most hawkish members of the administration, also argued in favor of applying the Geneva Conventions, saying that they served U.S. interests. The *Washington Times* story did not mention the support for the Geneva Conventions inside the Pentagon.

In the end, Bush issued a final order that made a slight nod toward Powell's objections. He stated that the Geneva Conventions did in principle apply to the Taliban prisoners from Afghanistan—but then rendered the protections meaningless by asserting that the Taliban prisoners were unlawful combatants, not POWs, and therefore did not qualify for the protections. (Four years later, the Supreme Court rejected Bush's position, ruling that the Geneva Conventions applied to all the detainees, whether from the Taliban or from al-Qaeda.)

This public controversy over the Geneva Conventions once again pushed the submerged divisions within the Bush administration into the open, with Powell on one side and anti-Powell conservatives on the other. The dispute also highlighted a related but different division between those who had served in the military in wartime and those who had not.

This second dividing line would also turn into a public issue, and it would become, if anything, a source of even greater rancor than the other divisions within the administration. Both Powell and his deputy, Richard Armitage, had done combat duty in Vietnam, but Cheney had not, and neither had some of his advisors. Bush had served only in the National Guard. As the disputes over Bush's policies became ever more acrimonious, critics outside the administration began to accuse the proponents of war who had not themselves done military service of being "chicken hawks." The charges were incendiary, but the divisions they reflected were genuine and intense, persisting through the rest of Bush's presidency.

* * *

There would be two more policy changes before the administration's Cheney-led journey to "the dark side" was complete.

First, the establishment of Guantanamo was, by itself, insufficient. Run by the Pentagon, it served the purpose of housing hundreds of ordinary, unexceptional fighters. But the CIA required other special locations, even more remote, where it could interrogate the most important detainees, the al-Qaeda members known or suspected of having been involved in the September 11 attacks, who might provide information about al-Qaeda's future plans.

Gonzales set forth one major problem with questioning these "high-value detainees" at Guantanamo. "Historically, our soldiers have long abided by the interrogation methods outlined in the U.S. Army Field Manuals," he explained. The field manuals set limits on what actions could be taken against the person being questioned. "The al-Qaeda training manual, however, taught their recruits how to defeat or resist the well-known U.S. interrogation techniques."

With this in mind, the administration decided to turn over its most important captives to the CIA. Before September 11, the CIA had from time to time dealt with the interrogation of prisoners who refused to talk by employing a technique called rendition: it transferred these prisoners to the intelligence services of countries friendly to the United States, such as Egypt and Jordan, which had the latitude to conduct tough or brutal interrogations with few if any limits. But after September 11, the CIA wanted to do the questioning itself. And so, over the following three years, it set up a series of so-called black sites at secret locations around the world (in eastern Europe and in Thailand, for example), where CIA operatives could interrogate captives in ways that extended beyond the limits of the Army Field Manual.

The stage was now set. Through its decision on military commissions, the Bush administration had made sure that detainees could be held indefinitely without trial. By establishing Guantanamo and the black sites overseas, it had barred detainees from having any recourse in the U.S. court system. Through its decision on the Geneva Conventions, it had stripped the detainees of the protections to humane treatment under international law. By authorizing the CIA rather than the military to question the detainees, the Bush administration had enabled interrogations that would go beyond the limits of the Army Field Manual. The Bush administration was now ready to address one last question: what could the CIA do to the detainees in order to get them to talk?

The question of torture had already begun to be explored in the press. In a prescient *Washington Post* article on October 21, 2001, Walter Pincus, one of the newspaper's most experienced reporters, quoted FBI and Justice Department officials as saying that "traditional civil liberties may have to be cast aside if they are to extract information about the Sept. 11 attacks and terrorist plans." The FBI wasn't contemplating torture on its own, but Pincus's sources suggested that one idea was "extraditing the suspects to allied countries where security services sometimes . . . resort to torture." A couple of weeks later, *Newsweek* published a column by Jonathan Alter that was headlined, simply, "Time to Think About Torture."

For the Bush administration, this issue came to a head at the end of March 2002, when Pakistani forces and the CIA captured Abu Zubaydah, al-Qaeda's third-ranking leader, in a nighttime raid. He was the most senior al-Qaeda operative the United States had ever caught, and the CIA had been searching for him for a long time.

After the capture of Zubaydah, the CIA asked the White House and Justice Department for guidance. At their request, the CIA developed a list of ten specific techniques that went beyond what was allowable under the Army Field Manual. These ranged from slapping the face to sleep deprivation; from putting the detainee in a box with what he is told is a stinging insect to waterboarding him (binding the detainee to a board and pouring water over him so that he feels as if he is drowning). The CIA asked the Justice Department for a written memo affirming that these techniques were legal; it did so because the CIA and some of its individual employees insisted on having legal justification before they began any interrogations. In the past, the United States had treated waterboarding as a war crime; after World War II, several Japanese soldiers were convicted of war crimes for waterboarding American prisoners of war.

It took the Justice Department several months to come up with a written memo authorizing these techniques, while the CIA held Abu Zubaydah. The techniques were refined: the insect-in-a-box ploy was eliminated, but the CIA added a couple of other techniques, such as the use of nudity and the manipulation of diet. Finally, in the summer of 2002, the CIA got what it wanted. The Justice Department declared in writing that these so-called enhanced interrogation techniques did not amount to torture, which would have been prohibited under both international and U.S. law. It narrowly defined torture as anything that causes extreme, excruciating pain, such as pulling out the prisoner's fingernails or applying electric shock to the genitals. Given that the CIA's techniques fell short of this, they didn't amount to torture, the Justice Department maintained.

That August, the CIA interrogated Abu Zubaydah using the newly approved techniques. He broke down and began to give information that led to the capture of other al-Qaeda members. Cheney, in his memoir, makes the claim that the questioning of Abu Zubaydah led directly to the capture of Khalid Sheikh Mohammed, al-Qaeda's operations officer for the September 11 attacks. This may have been an instance of Cheney selectively tailoring facts to fit his argument, because the memoir of CIA director George Tenet makes no such claim. Tenet describes Khalid Sheikh Mohammed's capture in detail but says that human intelligence, including a tipster, led to the capture. Khalid Sheikh Mohammed was then subjected to waterboarding, just as were Abu Zubaydah and a handful of others in the custody of the CIA.

* * *

What role did Dick Cheney play in the CIA's new interrogation techniques? On the one hand, he was not the single driving force for them, as he had been in devising the new rules for warrantless surveillance. Other players were involved, too: the techniques were devised by the CIA and shepherded through the White House by Tenet; the memos approving them were drafted by the Justice Department; and Bush himself was directly involved in giving the go-ahead.

Nevertheless, Cheney was among the principal participants and sup-porters in the decisions that led to the harsh treatment up to and includ-ing waterboarding. Through Addington, the vice president was kept abreast of what was happening, and he was involved in drafting the per-missive new rules. Gonzales later wrote that the decisions on how far the CIA could go with a detainee were drafted in meetings in his own office that included John Yoo from the Justice Department; a CIA lawyer; Gon-zales's assistant; and David Addington.

Of even greater importance, once the CIA's "enhanced" tech-niques had been approved and used, Cheney emerged as their principal defender. He never wavered. He repeatedly proclaimed the value of harsh interrogations before Congress; he was also outspoken in the years after Bush left office. When Senator John McCain, himself a former prisoner of war in Vietnam, sought to introduce legislation in 2005 requiring that all U.S. government officials conduct interrogations under the rules of the Army Field Manual, it was Cheney who tried to dissuade him. In the final years of the Bush administration, when Rice, as secretary of state, led a successful effort to persuade Bush to scale back the CIA's interroga-tion program, Cheney passionately resisted.

In public statements, the Bush administration always held to the formulation that what it was doing was "enhanced interrogation," not torture. "We don't torture," Bush and Cheney both said on a number of occasions. But among themselves, and in their jokes or offhand remarks, administration officials were not always so careful. Robert Gates, who served as secretary of defense during the final two years of the admin-istration, recalled one conversation where he was being urged by other officials to speak out in public forcefully against a ban on cluster muni-tions.

"So, you want me to be the poster boy for cluster munitions?" Gates asked at one meeting.

"Yes," Cheney replied with a smile, "just like I was with torture."

* * *

Colin Powell had emerged as the principal dissenting voice when the Bush administration decided that the Geneva Conventions did not apply to the prisoners it had captured. Over the following years, as the CIA proceeded with its "enhanced interrogation" program, there were occasional signs that it was trying to keep information about it away from Powell. An email from a CIA official, released many years later by the Senate Select Committee on Intelligence, said that at one point Gonzales and others in the White House were "extremely concerned Powell would blow his stack if he were to be briefed on what's been going on."

Yet interviews with Powell's aides and the writings of other administration officials indicate that Powell knew at least the basics of what was taking place. At the key moment after Abu Zubaydah had been captured, when George Tenet recommended to Cheney, Rice, and a handful of other officials the use of "enhanced" techniques including waterboarding, Rice wrote, "I asked that Colin and Don [Rumsfeld] be briefed."

Moreover, a careful reading of the memoirs of senior officials on the Bush team makes clear the broader underlying reality: that Bush's entire National Security Council, including Powell, was informed about a specific, highly secret program of extremely harsh interrogation, conducted by a select unit within the CIA.

George Tenet acknowledged bringing the program before the NSC after the capture of Abu Zubaydah: "We opened discussions within the National Security Council as to how to handle him. . . . Zubaydah and a small number of other extremely highly placed terrorists potentially had information that might save thousands of lives."

Rumsfeld said he was told about the techniques and also confirmed that they were part of a formal CIA program:

> At some point in the months after 9/11, the CIA established an interrogation program for high-level al Qaeda operatives captured around the world. . . . As a member of the National Security Council, I was made aware of the Agency's interrogation program—but, as I now understand it, it was not until well after it had been initiated.

Powell also served on the National Security Council. There is no record of his having dissented from what was taking place. "Yeah, it [the program] was briefed to the NSC—not everything, but there was an understanding that they were going to use enhanced interrogation techniques," he acknowledged in 2018. "Nobody [on the NSC] was asked to approve it. . . . I was present, but they never asked anybody to raise their hands on this. And frankly, it didn't sound all that bad. It wasn't until later, after we had Abu Ghraib, that we really started hearing what they were doing. That said to me, 'This is nutty.'"

He did not discuss the issue with even his closest aides. Looking back years later, they had the sense that he knew much more than he ever told them. Information about "enhanced interrogation" was provided only to those who needed to know, and Powell's subordinates didn't need to know. Moreover, in not telling them, he was protecting them. Lawrence Wilkerson, who had become Powell's chief of staff, said that Powell never told him about the NSC meetings where "the principals were engaged in conversations about ongoing torture."

As it happened, the only senior official in the Bush administration with direct, personal experience with waterboarding was Richard Armitage. In his military service, Armitage had taken part in covert operations in Vietnam; by several accounts, he had some undefined connection to the Phoenix Program, aimed at neutralizing the Vietcong by eradicating its political apparatus in the countryside. As preparation for his Vietnam assignment, Armitage had been subjected to the navy's SERE (Survival, Evasion, Resistance and Escape) training, aimed at instructing American soldiers and operatives how to resist interrogation. In that training, Armitage was himself waterboarded.

In 2002, more than three decades later, Armitage was kept ignorant of the CIA's "enhanced interrogation" program. As a matter of bureaucratic routine, most of the foreign policy issues under debate were discussed at the regular meetings of the Deputies' Committee before they went to the top. But the use of the "enhanced interrogation" techniques was discussed only by the principals, not their deputies.

Powell did not tell Armitage what the top levels had decided. "There was only one thing that Powell didn't share with me at the time, and that was the treatment [of detainees]," Armitage said. "At some point, he was told there was some sort of treatment. He never told me. We shared everything, but he never told me." Later on, after the harsh techniques became public, Powell told Armitage, "I was afraid you'd quit."

Even a decade later, Armitage said he was appalled that the "treatment," as he called it, had been the result of an official program, formally cleared at the most senior levels of the administration. "It never occurred to me that we were going to mistreat [prisoners]," he said. "I know in war we fuck things up. I was there [in Vietnam]. I fucked things up. You sometimes do things you wish you didn't do. But as a deliberate program? No, I couldn't imagine it. It never occurred to me."

16

THE TWO TRIBES

After one year in office, the George W. Bush administration was beginning to divide into two competing factions, each possessed of its own view of how America should deal with the rest of the world after the end of the Cold War—one faction stressed the importance of American military power whereas the other emphasized the alliances that had prevailed against the Soviet Union. Dick Cheney stood at the apex of the first grouping, Colin Powell at the top of the second.

The two principals remained cordial and polite toward each other. (Trying to describe his strained relationship with Cheney during the George W. Bush administration, Powell chose a double negative: "We were never *not* friends.") Each of their sets of followers and associates, however, took a profoundly disparaging view of the opposing faction. One political scientist later described what developed inside the administration as a poisonous form of "bureaucratic tribalism." The members of each tribe were loyal to fellow members and intensely mistrustful of the other tribe. Each tribe strove regularly for advantage over the other.

* * *

The nucleus of the Cheney tribe was the small, close group of officials who had worked for him at the Department of Defense during the

George H. W. Bush administration. These included David Addington, Scooter Libby, Paul Wolfowitz, and Zalmay Khalilzad. The Cheney group also encompassed lower-ranking officials working in the Office of the Vice President and at the Pentagon.

Beyond this core network, the Cheney tribe featured one other prominent official who outranked all the others: Donald Rumsfeld. Rumsfeld was too strong and too prickly a personality to view himself as belonging to any mere network or grouping, or even to see himself as subordinate to Cheney, but the two men were personally close, and on most of the foreign policy issues that would emerge during the following years, Rumsfeld stood with Cheney.

Some members of the Cheney tribe, such as Wolfowitz and Libby, were adherents of the neoconservative movement—and so the entire group became known in popular jargon as the "neocons," even though, in fact, some of them weren't. The neoconservatives favored spreading democracy around the world; many members of Cheney's tribe (including Cheney himself) cared far less about making other countries democratic than about extending American power and making other nations friendly to and compliant with American interests.

The Cheney tribe's core beliefs were epitomized by a joke that made the rounds in the early months of 2002, when Cheney and those around him were beginning to lobby for American military action against Iraq. Richard Perle told the joke to a Washington audience. It went like this: A French diplomat, a UN official, and an American were all captured in a remote location in Africa and were sentenced to death. Each one was given a last wish. The French official spoke first and asked to have "La Marseillaise," the French national anthem, played before his execution. Next, the UN official asked to be allowed to give a speech on the importance of globalism and the United Nations. When it was the American's turn, he asked to be shot second, so that he didn't have to listen to the speech on globalism. When Perle finished telling this joke, he observed, "What other people call 'unilateralism,' I call leadership. What is sometimes called 'multilateralism,' I call acquiescence."

This was a fair representation of the Cheney tribe's view of the world: a deep-seated mistrust of multilateralism coupled to a strategy of combating any challenges to American power. Before becoming vice president, Cheney said that the United States "had to be prepared to defeat anyone who tried to dominate a region of the world that was close to us." This was also a fair summation of the Defense Policy Guidance he had sponsored and embraced near the end of the George H. W. Bush administration.

To say the least, Cheney was not a charismatic leader for the tribe. He preferred to operate behind the scenes and in the shadows, as he had during his earlier days in government. "I'm not a traditional, backslapping, glad-handing politician," he said, in a classic understatement. His style was as laconic as ever. In meetings, he would hold back for long periods, before posing a query or two. "He was always a presence in the National Security Council meetings," said Andrew Natsios, one of Powell's State Department aides. "He never lost his temper or raised his voice. And I have to say, he asked some of the best, most pointed questions: 'How is this actually going to work in practice?' 'What are the second- and third order consequences of our action?'" Then the vice president would lapse into silence again, without committing himself to any specific position. While Cheney could be frosty in dealing with opponents, he was not openly confrontational. He tended to wage his battles in private, out of the presence of his adversaries. Other senior officials believed that he sometimes let his staff play the role of the "bad guy" in interagency discussions so that he didn't have to play that role himself. He was so aloof that even Rumsfeld, who knew Cheney better (and longer) than anyone else in the administration, was to say many years later, "The combination of keeping his opinions to himself, and yet being influential, gave Cheney an air of mystery."

Cheney was not much more outgoing in other contexts—not during public events and not in private sessions with his aides, either. "You never quite knew with Cheney whether he was agreeing or disagreeing with you," said one staff aide who briefed him regularly. Still, he was profoundly loyal to the members of his own team, as they were to him.

The core of Cheney's power lay in his relationship with Bush, and he kept the details of that relationship even more obscure than his other activities. Whenever Bush was present at large meetings, such as those of the National Security Council, Cheney spoke less than usual and avoided taking any positions at all. "Whatever he did, he talked to the president about it privately," said Franklin Miller, an NSC staff expert on arms control. Cheney did not talk about those one-on-one sessions with anyone else, not even his closest friends and allies. "Dick did not share with me his private conversations with the President," Rumsfeld recalled. It was quite a change from the spirit of comity that had prevailed during the George H. W. Bush administration, when Cheney, as defense secretary, had disagreed with Powell, the chairman of the Joint Chiefs, but had allowed Powell to make his case directly to the president anyway.

At the State Department, Powell and Richard Armitage came up with a phrase for how they thought Cheney operated with Bush. Cheney was "building coral" with the president: feeding him information favorable to Cheney's own point of view that would then gradually form the underpinning for Bush's decisions. Eventually, Powell sought to counter Cheney's influence by trying to talk privately with the president on his own—approaching Bush on Air Force One, for example, to try to get a pending decision reversed. Powell occasionally succeeded, but far less often than Cheney. Not only did the president often agree with Cheney and defer to him, but beyond that, Cheney's vice-presidential office was within a minute or so from the Oval Office, while Powell was off the premises entirely, at the State Department. Cheney could see Bush at the beginning, middle, or end of a day; Powell tended to see Bush in formal meetings like those of the National Security Council. "I could get the president to care [about an issue] if I got there early enough and in time, and if I could make the case," Powell said years later. "But when you have a crowded room, it's a little hard—and you know, in this town, proximity is almost everything."

Members of the Cheney tribe as a whole devoted extraordinary attention to the intelligence coming in from abroad, but they tended to look for morsels of intelligence that supported their own point of view. They were convinced that the intelligence community was glossing over information about threats to America's security, particularly concerning weapons of mass destruction in places such as Iraq, Iran, and North Korea. The Cheney tribe sought to overcome what they viewed as the CIA's biases or deficiencies by reviewing the raw intelligence directly as it came in—notably, they set up a new intelligence unit inside the

Pentagon—and by visiting the CIA's headquarters to ask further questions about the agency's reporting and its conclusions.

Cheney himself took the lead in these efforts. He always preferred to see the raw intelligence (the National Security Agency's transcripts of intercepted conversations, satellite images of an arms shipment) rather than the CIA analysts' efforts to digest this information and put it into perspective. During his earliest days in government, Cheney's aides had noticed how he preferred to take in information through written material. Each morning he would rise early to read not only the President's Daily Brief, prepared by the CIA for Bush, but also a special addendum to the PDB—"behind the tab," Cheney called it, as the PDB was in a ring binder—containing further intelligence that Cheney had asked the CIA to prepare especially for him.

If Cheney noticed a piece of intelligence helpful to his arguments, he would remember it and use it, sometimes for more than it was worth. After the September 11 attacks, an early intelligence report said that Mohamed Atta, the lead hijacker, had met with an Iraqi intelligence official in Prague. Cheney was the first administration official to disclose this intelligence report to the public. The CIA and FBI then investigated further and concluded that the original report was untrue. Nevertheless, as the former CIA deputy director Michael Morell lamented, "Despite our efforts to un-ring the bell on the Iraqi–al Qaeda connection, a few in the administration—Vice President Cheney, in particular—repeatedly raised it in public comments."

Cheney's style was to convey an air of certainty about his convictions and to predict a terrible impact, even doom, for the United States if his opponent's ideas or policies were put into effect. When James Comey joined the Bush administration as deputy attorney general and argued that the secret, warrantless electronic surveillance program was illegal, Cheney told him gravely, "Thousands of people are going to die because of what you are doing."

Above all, Cheney was preoccupied with avoiding perceptions of weakness, a theme that, as we have seen, stemmed from his experience in the Ford administration, when he felt that America had been weakened in dealing with the rest of the world and that the executive branch had been weakened in dealing with Congress. His speeches and writings

were peppered with the words *weak* and *weakness*, reflecting his preoccupation with this subject. To Cheney, power was not simply important;
it was necessary. He once dismissed concerns about America's role in the
Middle East by saying, "The only legitimacy we need comes on the back
of an A-1 tank."

It was not that Cheney believed the United States should stand alone
and friendless in the world, but that he had his own distinct definition
of which nations should be the United States' close friends and allies. He
was profoundly skeptical of trying to work in tandem with America's
traditional European allies, such as France and Germany. Rather, he put
the highest premium on ties with those countries that possessed close,
if clandestine, intelligence and security relationships with the United
States: Saudi Arabia, Egypt, Jordan, and above all, Israel.

Israel, and the unending conflict between Israel and the Palestinians,
lay close to the heart of the tension between the Cheney and Powell tribes.
Cheney deepened the close ties to Israel's defense and intelligence establishment that he had forged during the Gulf War a decade earlier. And in
general, the Cheney team felt that Powell and the State Department were
too willing to take actions that might compromise Israel's security. Con-
trarily, the Powell tribe thought that Cheney and his team were trying to
rearrange the larger Middle East in a way that would further Israel's interests. Powell himself believed this. From his earliest days as secretary of
state, he said, he encountered "the views of some of the guys in the administration that, 'Oh boy, if we could only do something in Iraq, all of the
Middle East will be changed forever, and Israel will be safe forever.'" Powell added that in the debates and bureaucratic skirmishing leading up to
the war in Iraq, "Israel was always sort of lurking in the shadow of this."

In policy battles, the strength of the Cheney tribe lay in its knowledge
of how to work within the U.S. government to get the desired results.
Cheney knew all the bureaucratic ploys. He decided to give each member of his staff two formal job titles, one as an aide to the vice president
and a second as "assistant to the president." As presidential aides, they
had a right to attend all the White House meetings and find out what
was going on there. And yet, whenever a time came that senior White
House officials opposed what Cheney's aides were doing, the aides could
say that they worked for the vice president, not for the White House chief

of staff. David Addington once worked this two-hat routine to perfection by putting Cheney's name onto a Supreme Court brief opposing gun control, to the dismay of White House Chief of Staff Josh Bolten.

Most important, Cheney and his aides knew how to accomplish things smoothly, quickly, and quietly. The early decision to withdraw from the Kyoto environmental accord was a classic example: Bush signed the decision and handed it to Cheney before Powell even knew about it. At the same time, the Cheney tribe knew how to block things from happening, too. One of Cheney's aides explained how it worked. When you wanted to get an issue stalemated, he said, you referred it to the National Security Council, because the NSC was dysfunctional: it tried to come up with a consensus position, but there often could be no consensus between the Cheney tribe and the Powell tribe, only endless argument. As a result, nothing would happen.

If the Cheney tribe's advantage lay in its ability to work the internal government processes, its disadvantage lay in the more public aspects of policy. This was Cheney's chronic weakness, one that had cropped up throughout his career: he didn't care if the press coverage was negative. His press aides tried, sometimes desperately, to get the vice president to do interviews, and they had to twist his arm even to appear on Fox, the network that could be counted on to be sympathetic.

Nor did Cheney keep an eye on public opinion polls, since he believed they had no binding or immediate effect on policy. Donald Rumsfeld was struck by the fact that Cheney felt no need at all to improve his public standing. Indeed, at times Cheney seemed almost to revel in his unpopularity. His former aide Eric Edelman observed that while Powell could sometimes be thin-skinned and sensitive to criticism, Cheney "has got a hide like a rhinoceros. He just doesn't care what people think of him—to a fault, by the way."

One result of not paying attention to public perceptions was that Cheney and his tribe could preserve their sense of certainty and purpose through the ups and downs of daily events. But the defect of this approach was that they were unwilling and unable to modify their views or policies when major problems arose. Another drawback was that the Cheney tribe usually couldn't control the way events and issues were framed and cast, whether in Congress or in the media.

The public sphere was one where Powell and his tribe held the upper hand over Cheney.

* * *

Depending on how you looked at it, the Powell tribe was either smaller than Cheney's or much larger. It was smaller in the sense that Powell did not possess a tight network of loyal officials from his time in the George H. W. Bush administration, as Cheney did. Powell had served in the Pentagon at the same time as Cheney, but his aides were in the military; by the nature of their jobs, they tended to move around the country and the world from assignment to assignment, while Cheney's aides had stayed close to one another, often at Washington think tanks. Throughout his career, Powell had tended to attract mentors and patrons, but not disciples, as Cheney had. Instead, Powell operated in tandem with his closest friend, Richard Armitage, who was, if anything, even more passionately loyal to him than Cheney's aides were to Cheney.

In a different sense, the Powell tribe was huge. It included, more broadly, most of the career officials in the foreign policy agencies: the Foreign Service officers at the State Department, the intelligence professionals at the CIA, the uniformed military leaders at the Pentagon. The career officials reflected and embraced the collective experience, gathered over past decades, about what worked and what didn't, what was feasible and what wasn't. The Powell tribe also included many foreign policy luminaries from past administrations, such as former national security advisors Brent Scowcroft and Zbigniew Brzezinski and former secretary of state Lawrence Eagleburger.

It would be unfair to say that the members of the Powell tribe stood simply for the status quo, because many of them had their own ideas for changing the way America operated. But the Cheney tribe was challenging long-held policies, practices, and assumptions about America's role in the world—and in reaction to what the Cheney team was seeking, the Powell tribe did often seek to uphold the status quo. The early disputes over the responses to September 11 serve as good examples: The Cheney tribe wanted to say that the Geneva Conventions were no longer applicable; Powell and the career military resisted. The Cheney team sought to link the September 11 hijackers to Iraq; the CIA objected. The Cheney tribe sought to downplay the idea of working in concert with America's traditional allies; the State Department argued that the alliances formed after World War II remained as important as ever.

At the most fundamental level, the two tribes disagreed profoundly in their views of America's recent history, notably how the Cold War had come to an end. The Powell tribe believed that the United States had triumphed over the Soviet Union not on its own but together with its NATO allies, operating through the policies of containment and deterrence. The Cheney tribe believed the decisive factors were America's military power and its values; they believed that Ronald Reagan's defense buildup and his public denunciations of communism had won the Cold War.

Unlike the Cheney tribe, the Powell tribe had no need to find circuitous ways around the bureaucracy or the normal processes of government. Powell's tribe *was* the bureaucracy, operating the normal processes of government, and its strength lay in that fact. Powell and Armitage themselves were extremely talented and knowledgeable Washington operators. They had, together, virtually run the Pentagon during the Reagan years. Nevertheless, they were not quite as skillful as Cheney, who, with the help of his network, could set up a new intelligence unit at the Pentagon or get a final decision made about the treatment of detainees while a task force on the subject led by the State Department was still in the middle of its work.

Still, Powell and Armitage knew how to shape press coverage, and they did so far more adroitly than anyone on Cheney's team. They regularly briefed the reporters covering them. They supplied additional details to investigative journalists, notably Bob Woodward of the *Washington Post*, whom Powell had known for years. What came through in the stories was the Powell tribe's point of view, including, often, its dim view of whatever the Cheney tribe was trying to do.

Above all, the Powell tribe held a key asset: Powell himself, with all his personal popularity and charisma. Neither Cheney nor anyone on his team had anything like Powell's skill in dealing with the public. A Gallup poll taken in 2002 found that Powell was considerably more popular than Bush, Cheney, or Rumsfeld. He was more than that: he was "the most popular political figure in America," Gallup found. An astonishing

88 percent of Americans had a favorable view of Powell, "one of the highest such ratings in Gallup Poll history."

And yet it was already becoming clear after the Bush administration's first year in office that Powell's high standing outside the administration did not help him win the internal policy battles. In Cabinet-level meetings, Powell was obliged to deal regularly with both Cheney and Rumsfeld, and thus was often outnumbered. More important, during the previous administrations in which Powell had served, under Ronald Reagan and George H. W. Bush, he had enjoyed the strong personal backing of the president himself. That fact seemed to have given him extra confidence, and so Powell had been assertive, sometimes astonishingly so: as chairman of the Joint Chiefs of Staff, he had not shrunk from arguing, in public and in private, whether America's civilian leaders should go to war or not.

But Powell did not possess the same level of support from George W. Bush, who from the start seemed skeptical of him, wary of his popularity, and often more sympathetic to Cheney's arguments. Powell, realizing this, became less assertive in meetings. Some senior State Department officials also believed that Cheney had worked assiduously to undercut Powell's relationship with Bush. William Burns said that the vice president, along with Rumsfeld, actively encouraged Bush to believe that the secretary of state wasn't on the team and that he didn't support the administration's positions.

In meetings, Powell presented his views and the position of the State Department, but his colleagues felt he was not as forceful as he might have been. He would complain sometimes, particularly about Rumsfeld, but he would air his grievances to Condoleezza Rice, not to the president. "[T]ruthfully, I wondered why he [Powell] did not take greater advantage of his extraordinary stature," Rice later recalled. She would occasionally suggest to Bush that he have a quiet dinner with Powell. "I often told the President before one of those sessions that Colin was very unhappy and would tell him so. He didn't, and the President sometimes had difficulty gauging the extent of Colin's dissatisfaction. I hate pop psychoanalysis, but I did sometimes wonder what held Colin back; perhaps the 'soldier' felt constrained, and, of course, he had to be aware that he probably would have been President had he chosen to run."

In theory, Powell might also have tried to influence the Bush administration's policies through public opinion, by laying out in speeches and other public appearances his views and his arguments against what the Cheney tribe was doing. He was known, after all, as one of the country's most talented speakers, a skill he had honed first in the military and then in touring for his book in the 1990s.

However, Powell liked to give certain kinds of speeches and not others. He preferred to deliver folksy speeches full of anecdotes and humor, and he had an almost effortless knack for doing so. Lawrence Wilkerson, who started as Powell's speechwriter in the army, said that when Powell first interviewed him, he asked, "Can you write a speech for a black Baptist church?" As Wilkerson was stammering an answer, Powell stopped him, saying, "Never mind, I can write those myself." Powell's own files show that he drafted in his own hand many of his speeches for events such as swearings-in and departure ceremonies—including the graceful, appreciative speech he had given on the occasion of Dick Cheney's departure from the Pentagon in January 1993.

What Powell did not enjoy, and so did not often deliver, were speeches about policy, strategy, or other abstract ideas. He left those to his subordinates, who inevitably had less influence. "Speeches by a secretary of state can make policy and resonate around the world," wrote Richard Haass, Powell's director of policy and planning at the State Department. "Over time, I devoted less and less time to this last function, largely because Colin Powell wasn't inclined to give policy-laden speeches. He much preferred more personal and less formal talks along the lines of those he honed during his years on the speaking circuit. I ended up giving a number of policy-filled speeches, which was a distant second-best given my lower rank and the inevitable questions that would arise about whom I was speaking for."

* * *

The bottom line was that, in their seemingly unending battles with one another, the members of the Cheney and Powell tribes were each convinced that their side was right and their opponents wrong.

The bitter antagonisms started with rancorous disputes over everything from the Middle East to North Korea, from NATO to climate change to Iran, and from China to Iraq. But the animosities became intensely personal, too. The Powell tribe thought Cheney and the people around him were zealots and that they were deceptive, adept at maneuvering Bush into making decisions before he had heard all sides of the argument. Conversely, the Cheney tribe thought Powell and those around him were too wedded to mainstream thinking. Many years later, Cheney would write that Powell was "attuned to public approval." Coming from Cheney, ever disdainful of public opinion, this was the ultimate insult.

17

THE NONDECISION

The conflicts within the Bush administration over Iraq were the culmination of the struggle between the Cheney tribe and the Powell tribe. It was a bureaucratic battle with enormous consequences: in the end, the United States would engage in a war that cost more than four thousand American lives and two trillion dollars, made the United States an object of opprobrium even among its close allies, and sapped the nation of the desire and energy to continue to play the sort of global leadership role that it had played since World War II. Iraq would tarnish the reputations of both Cheney and Powell, the opposite outcome to the Gulf War victory parades.

The deliberations over invading Iraq also marked the peak in acrimony in the running philosophical debate about America's post–Cold War role. Without the Soviet Union, the United States had found itself without any serious rival; it was unclear what that new, overwhelming power would mean and how it would be executed. For more than a decade, the questions had loomed: Was American power sufficient to upend the existing order and to reshape various regions of the world, such as the Middle East, in its own interest? Was the United States so strong that it could operate without the support of its Cold War allies? Would America be able, on its own and through sheer military strength, to replace dictators who were cruel to their own people or regimes that were inimical to American interests? Did the American people have the desire and stamina to take on such a role? The Iraq War provided answers to these questions, and in all cases, the answer was a resounding no.

* * *

On the weekend after September 11, 2001, in their meeting at Camp David, President Bush and his top aides had rejected the idea of an immediate war against Iraq in order to concentrate on defeating the Taliban regime that had provided sanctuary for al-Qaeda in Afghanistan. Powell had argued firmly against attacking Iraq, a position supported by Cheney, who viewed it as a distraction from the coming operation in Afghanistan. Afghanistan was to be "phase one" in what was coming to be called the "war on terror."

But by the late fall, after the Taliban fled Kabul, the administration began to consider again the idea of military action against Saddam Hussein's regime. Bush asked the Pentagon to update its military planning for an invasion of Iraq, and before the end of the year General Tommy Franks, the American military commander for the Middle East, submitted initial plans for an attack. On January 29, 2002, as part of his State of the Union address, Bush condemned three specific countries—Iran, Iraq, and North Korea—for seeking to acquire weapons of mass destruction that might be provided to terrorists. In singling out the three countries and labeling them an "axis of evil," Bush was echoing the concerns of Dick Cheney and his fellow hawks in the administration.

America's European allies strongly criticized Bush's "axis of evil" speech, viewing the phrase as dangerous rhetoric that could serve as a pretext for war, even though there was no indication that Iran, Iraq, and North Korea were collaborating with one another in the fashion of the Axis powers of World War II. But Powell, the allies' greatest champion in the administration, had known beforehand that the president would single out the three countries and use the "axis of evil" language, having read advance drafts of the speech. "The secretary and I had read it time and again," Richard Armitage confirmed. "Never did we look at [changing the phrase] 'axis of evil.' That just didn't strike us as out of the ordinary."

It was in these months in early 2002 that the administration's infighting over Iraq burst forth, not yet on the question of going to war, but over the role of the Iraqi exiles who had fled Iraq under Saddam Hussein. The United States in 1998 had formally committed itself to supporting regime change in Iraq, yet nothing in the Iraq Liberation Act had specified either how Saddam was to be removed from power or who should replace him. As the Bush administration began to focus on Iraq, it sought to address these two questions.

On how to get rid of Saddam, the choices boiled down to either a coup d'état or a military invasion. The CIA tended to favor an internal coup that would put some other strongman, probably a military leader, in charge of the country. That way, CIA officials argued, the new authoritarian leader could impose order and keep Iraq from falling apart.

It was far from certain, however, that a military coup could succeed. Saddam had frustrated several such plots against him in the years following the Gulf War. Moreover, members of the Cheney tribe didn't like the idea of a coup. They wanted to see a new, more democratic leadership, headed by the Iraqi exile leaders they supported. "It would be a tragedy if Saddam is removed only to be replaced by another tyrant," Richard Perle said in one public appearance. Thus, administration officials decided in early 2002 that the best option for ousting Saddam Hussein from power would be an invasion, not a coup.

It was the question about a future, post-Saddam Iraqi leadership that brought forth the acrimony. The issue was sometimes formulated in abstract terms as whether the United States should support the "externals" or "internals." The "externals" were the exile groups and leaders living outside Iraq; the "internals" were those Iraqis opposed to Saddam who continued to live inside the country. The Defense Department and Cheney's office believed that the exile leaders would win wide public support and legitimacy inside Iraq after Saddam was no longer in power; Powell's State Department contended that the exile groups were widely mistrusted inside Iraq and that only "internals" could garner enough public support to hold the country together.

Underlying these abstract formulations was a dispute over a single person: Ahmed Chalabi, the leader of the Iraqi National Congress, who had been seeking to organize opposition to Saddam and his regime from outside Iraq for more than a decade. Chalabi was a friend of Perle, and he enjoyed the support of many of Cheney's longtime associates, including Wolfowitz and Libby. Chalabi was supplying them with reports from inside Iraq of Saddam Hussein's brutality and of Iraq's supposed weapons of mass destruction; the latter reports would turn out to be mostly wrong. From the outset, the State Department and the CIA were strongly opposed to Chalabi, arguing that he had little support inside Iraq and citing his history of financial irregularities, including an embezzlement conviction and his mishandling of funds his organization had received from the CIA.

These internal battles broke out in early 2002, after Libby proposed that the United States sponsor a conference of all the Iraqi exile leaders and groups, who would then jointly condemn Saddam Hussein. The hope was that such a group might play a role similar to that of the "Free French" who operated in London during World War II. The State Department opposed the idea on the grounds that such a conference would become a vehicle for Chalabi and the Iraqi National Congress to be anointed as the core of a future Iraqi leadership. And even though Powell and Armitage eventually agreed that the State Department would sponsor such a conference, they delayed for many months the date when it would be held.

The bickering over Chalabi was intense. Those in the Powell tribe were convinced that the officials around Cheney were conspiring on behalf of Chalabi. Those in the Cheney tribe believed that Powell and the State Department were conspiring *against* him. "The fight was vicious," Khalilzad observed. Chalabi would continue to be the subject of deep divisions within the Bush administration, up to and during the war in Iraq. President Bush himself seemed to share some of the skepticism voiced by the CIA and the State Department. When a Defense Department official spoke during a White House meeting of a future Iraqi leadership under Chalabi, Bush slammed his hand on a table and exclaimed, "We are not putting Chalabi in charge! The Iraqi people will decide who their leader is going to be—not us, and not Chalabi."

Years later, Cheney's associates and allies insisted they had not been wedded to Chalabi as the future Iraqi leader, despite their persistent championing of him. "If the people who didn't like Chalabi had come forward and said, 'We would support a different Iraqi government, but we don't like the idea of one led by Chalabi,' . . . I don't think we would have argued with them, frankly," said Wolfowitz. "I mean, I didn't have a particular stake in Chalabi—I had some reservations about him myself, and Rumsfeld did, too." This was said in hindsight, however; at the time, the members of the Cheney tribe did nothing to dispel the perception that they strongly supported Chalabi and were working closely with him.

In the memoir he published eight years after the invasion of Iraq, Cheney continued to espouse the general principle that the Iraqi exiles were deserving of American support. "The idea that we shouldn't work closely with opponents of Saddam who were living in exile slowed us down," he wrote. However, in the memoir's lengthy account of the Iraq War and the events leading up to it, Cheney did not once mention Chalabi's name.

* * *

Iraq was not the only issue that divided Cheney and Powell in the early months of 2002. The two men and their tribes were engaged in two policy skirmishes at once—one over Iraq and the other over Israel and the Palestinians. Each of these disputes aroused fierce animosity inside the administration.

The two issues were interrelated, but even the question of *how* they were interrelated was the subject of controversy. Powell, Armitage, and their colleagues at the State Department argued that the Bush administration needed to address the dispute between Israel and the Palestinians *before* taking any action to dislodge Saddam Hussein from Iraq. Otherwise, they argued, the United States would risk losing the support of other Arab governments for any campaign against Iraq. As usual, the Powell tribe stressed the importance of maintaining alliances.

Cheney and his team, for their part, placed far greater stress on U.S. military power. They contended that the way to deal with the conflict between Israel and the Palestinians was *first* to get rid of Saddam Hussein. Once Saddam was dislodged from power, they argued, the Palestinian leader Yasser Arafat would be more isolated and thus more willing to make concessions. They cited the aftermath of Saddam Hussein's defeat in the Gulf War, when Arafat had found himself marginalized and in a weak position, a period that led to the Oslo Accords in 1993. In the view of Cheney's team, Saddam Hussein and the Palestinian leadership each gave intangible sustenance to the other; if one was weakened, so was the other. They argued that it would be easier to deal with Iraq than to resolve the protracted, complicated dispute over the Palestinians.

Dennis Ross, the longtime Middle East specialist, said that Powell and Cheney were "completely at odds" during this period. "Powell sees the Palestinian issue as being at the heart of this conflict," Ross explained. "Cheney's not denying it has importance, but he says you can't hold up everything else you're going to do in the region while we have to deal with that. And Powell's basically saying back to him, 'You're dreaming if you think you can deal with Iraq if you haven't dealt with the Palestinians.'"

Powell himself believed that dealing with the Palestinians was precisely what Bush did not want to do. "He hated the whole Middle East issue, as did Cheney," Powell asserted years later. "They didn't want anything to do with the Palestinians."

During this time, Cheney and Powell each made a trip to the Middle East, Cheney in March and Powell in April. The end result of the two trips was to solidify the Bush team's opposition to Arafat's leadership of the Palestinians and to underscore in dramatic fashion Cheney's strength and Powell's isolation within the administration.

Cheney's trip was his first venture overseas as vice president. Its purpose was related more to Iraq than to making peace between Israel and the Palestinians: he was seeking to line up support from other Arab governments for an American effort to drive Saddam Hussein from power. But at virtually every stop, Arab leaders gave Cheney a version of the same argument that Powell had been making in Washington: you need to deal with the Palestinian issue first.

No top-level Bush administration official had yet met with Arafat. The Palestinian leader was living in the West Bank but was forbidden by the Israeli government from traveling even to Beirut to attend a summit meeting of Arab leaders. For a time, Cheney worked on persuading Israel to let Arafat travel and, at one point, announced that he would be willing to meet with Arafat. But Arafat delayed such talk about a meeting, and Cheney returned to Washington holding out the possibility that he might yet meet with Arafat. Then a Palestinian suicide bomber killed thirty Israelis attending a Passover Seder at a hotel in Netanya, and the idea of a Cheney-Arafat meeting came to an end.

In response to the suicide bombing, Israeli forces carried out a sweeping military offensive in the West Bank and put Arafat's headquarters under siege, confining the Palestinian leader inside. The Israeli actions, in turn, brought forth expressions of outrage by the Palestinians and by other Arab governments. Bush responded to the turmoil by dispatching Powell to the region to try to ease the crisis.

Powell's trip to the Middle East epitomized his lack of support inside the administration. "Cheney didn't want me to go," Powell later reflected. "As soon as I took off from Andrews Air Force Base, they started to throw knives in my back, to make sure I didn't get anything."

Powell made a series of stops to try to bring an end to the violence, including meetings with Arafat in the West Bank. He also began to float the idea of some sort of international or regional peace conference. Back in Washington, Cheney adamantly opposed the idea, arguing that it would give legitimacy to Arafat, and Bush agreed with him.

The issue came to a head on the final night of Powell's trip, as the secretary of state was drafting a departure statement in which he would once more hold out the prospect of an international conference. Condoleezza Rice called Powell from Washington to tell him that the president did not support the idea. She advised him to leave the region without reviving the conference proposal.

Powell felt that the rug had been pulled out from under him. "He was royally pissed," recalled the State Department's William Burns, who had accompanied both Cheney and Powell on their trips. "And embarrassed in a way, too, because he had gone out on a limb. And what all of his counterparts, in Israel, the Palestinians, the Arab world were going to see was, he couldn't deliver. And he knew what people would conclude." On the following morning, as Powell was about to depart for Washington, Burns went to the airport to say good-bye to him. (Burns was staying on to visit other capitals in the Middle East.) "Good luck," Powell told Burns sadly. "I've just burned up my heat shield on this issue."

This brief flurry of Middle East diplomacy ended in failure. During his trip, Powell told Arafat that if nothing changed and the Palestinian violence continued, it would be the last time Arafat ever saw him. That prediction turned out to be true: the Bush administration soon decided to stop dealing with Arafat. In June, Bush delivered a speech in which he called upon the Palestinians to elect new leaders who were "not compromised by terror." Once they did, he said, the United States would be ready to support the idea of a Palestinian state.

These skirmishes over Middle East policy marked a turning point for Powell's relations with Cheney. It was clear that the two men, close collaborators under the first President Bush, were becoming open adversaries in the second Bush administration. It was also clear that Cheney enjoyed the president's support while Powell could not count on it. Cheney himself wrote years later that Powell's trip to the Middle East had been "a watershed moment in relations between the State Department and the White House," a phrasing in which "State Department" was clearly intended to mean "Powell." Cheney acknowledged that Powell and Armitage had looked upon the White House's rejection of Powell's proposal for a peace conference "as a personal affront." It was, Cheney observed, "as though a tie had been cut."

* * *

Somewhat later that spring, the Bush administration began to focus more intensively on the idea of war with Iraq. In a series of National Security Council meetings, the top members of the administration explored the implications of such a war: what it would cost and how much foreign support the United States would have. On May 13, Powell warned his colleagues that a war with Iraq would be a "long-term proposition . . . it will require a lot of money, and we need to understand this is probably a long-term commitment of our troops."

At that same meeting, Cheney raised a critical question, the one for which neither he nor others in the administration would ever have a satisfactory answer. "What is the case?" Cheney asked. "What is the *casus belli*? Is the case strong enough to justify our military actions? Is the case strong enough for our allies to join us?" Those words by Cheney underscore the fundamental point that he (and increasingly Bush) had already decided to go to war, at least tentatively, and were merely struggling to find the right words to explain why. The proponents of war wanted above all to alter the strategic map of the Middle East, giving an edge to America and its supporters and weakening the countries that opposed the United States. They had sought for years to force Saddam Hussein from power, and they believed they now had the capacity to do so. They also believed that the September 11 attacks had somehow provided a reason for attacking Iraq. But none of these were proper legal justifications for war, and so they kept returning again and again to various formulations of what their case for war would be.

These early NSC discussions about Iraq established patterns that would set the course for the many debates to follow. While Powell and Cheney usually found themselves on opposite sides, the arguments inside the administration usually weren't about the fundamental issue of whether to go to war, but about secondary questions such as when to go to war, whether there was enough international support for war, or whether to get formal approval from the UN Security Council.

Powell seemed to hold back from opposing the war itself. He knew that if he came out against the war and his opposition became known, all American efforts to win the support of allies would collapse. Moreover, Powell wanted to preserve his influence within the administration and his relationship with Bush. If he had opposed the war directly, he almost certainly would have had to resign. Of course, resignation may sometimes be the right choice for a senior official who thinks the president is making a mistake; one of Powell's predecessors as secretary of state, Cyrus Vance, had resigned when President Jimmy Carter pursued military action in Iran that Vance thought was unwise. But Powell was not the sort of person who resigns; he had been an inside player for most of his career.

Over the summer, the debate over Iraq came to a head. Cheney was impatient for military action, while Powell continued to balk and to raise tactical questions. At an NSC meeting on July 24, Donald Rumsfeld reported that U.S. military commanders preferred to go to war in the winter. Cheney attacked the idea of delay; the longer we wait, he said, the more likely that Saddam Hussein can hurt us.

Powell raised different objections concerning timing. "We're not there yet internationally," he told his colleagues. Some of America's European allies "feel that Saddam has been contained somewhat," he added. Cheney in turn rejected any suggestion that the United States should adopt a strategy of containment, arguing that the situation had changed after September 11. He raised the prospect that Saddam Hussein could use weapons of mass destruction. "We have to do it, the sooner the better," he asserted.

"Yes, we need allies," he told Powell. "But we do not let them set the pace or tell us what to do."

Powell replied that America's allies in Europe and the Middle East didn't accept Cheney's argument that Iraq was a threat. "They do not view this as a real danger or a crisis," he said. "Our allies know this devil [meaning Saddam Hussein]; they do not know the devil that may come. . . . You have to have a strong case before taking action. Can we make the case? Yes, but it will be expensive in terms of international opinion. Some allies will join us, but perhaps tepidly." As it turned out, Powell was understating the extent to which many of America's allies would oppose the Iraq War. It is also worth noting here that, in the process of registering his objections, Powell was making small concessions to Cheney's argument. ("Can we make the case? Yes, but . . .") Meanwhile, Cheney's assertions about Saddam Hussein's weapons of mass destruction went unchallenged.

The Cheney and Powell tribes also skirmished inside the foreign policy bureaucracies. The Powell tribe felt that Cheney's team was trying to pressure the CIA and other intelligence agencies to reach stronger conclusions about the existence of weapons of mass destruction in Iraq. Conversely, the Cheney tribe was nervous about Powell's continuing influence with the military as a former chairman of the Joint Chiefs of Staff. They feared that Powell would somehow sway the views of uniformed military leaders about going to war. This was a particularly sore subject because Rumsfeld was urging military leaders to discard Powell's ideas concerning the use of overwhelming force and to come up with an invasion plan that used fewer troops than Powell's old rules would have suggested.

Out of a sense of propriety, Powell tried to avoid or limit his contacts with the military, yet he was just active enough to spur concerns that he was interfering. After General Tommy Franks presented an updated war plan to the NSC that summer, Powell called him to voice criticism. "I've got problems with force size and support of that force, given such long lines of communications," Powell said. Franks, noting that Powell "no longer wore army green," reported what he had said to Rumsfeld, who instructed Franks to be polite and answer Powell's criticisms point by point. Summarizing these conversations years later, Powell said he had tried to tell Franks he didn't think that the Iraq War plan was very good, but "he thought I was just an old geezer with the Powell doctrine."

Cheney and his aides suspected that Powell's phone call was merely the tip of the iceberg. "Powell was reaching in [to the Pentagon], talking to a lot of his former colleagues about what Rumsfeld was trying to do with the war plan and everything else," Cheney's aide Eric Edelman later recalled. Asked whether Powell was in fact contacting old Pentagon friends during this period, Richard Armitage smiled and pointed to himself. "Me, not him!" he replied. Then he added: "That's bullshit, Powell didn't call. Now, I would also be misleading you if I didn't say that some of those [military officers] in the Pentagon were calling *him*."

Still, the impact of these contacts is open to question. Armitage pointed out that Powell had already been out of the military for nine years, and that the four-star generals of the 2002–3 period had likely been merely colonels when Powell was chairman of the Joint Chiefs of Staff. Lawrence Wilkerson said that Powell was so reluctant to call military leaders that Wilkerson had to beg him to do so. "I'm not in the military anymore. I'm secretary of state," Powell told Wilkerson. In fact, one administration official who was not generally an admirer of Powell gave him credit for, on the whole, not trying to impose his views on military issues during the National Security Council deliberations on Iraq.

The extraordinary sensitivity within the Cheney tribe over conversations between Powell and military leaders was comparable to the wariness in the Powell tribe over the Cheney team's visits to CIA headquarters. In both instances, it underscored the intense level of mistrust and suspicion inside the administration.

* * *

That summer, the internal bickering over Iraq was accompanied by an ever-sharper public debate, sometimes involving former high government officials. In August, Brent Scowcroft, George H. W. Bush's national security advisor during the Gulf War, published an op-ed piece in the

Wall Street Journal that was bluntly headlined "Don't Attack Saddam." In it, Scowcroft laid out some of the same points that Powell had been making, along with additional, tougher arguments.

Scowcroft argued that the Bush administration needed to make progress toward peace between Israel and the Palestinians before initiating a war with Iraq. He also contended, as Powell had, that the United States needed to get UN support for any military action. Scowcroft held out the prospect of "an Armageddon in the Middle East," suggesting that if there were a war, Saddam might use weapons of mass destruction against Israel.

In Scowcroft's own mind, he was merely putting into writing ideas he had already laid out on television earlier that summer. However, the *Wall Street Journal* piece came as a shock to the White House: Scowcroft was, after all, a close friend of the president's father and a mentor to Condoleezza Rice.

One of the people not taken by surprise was Colin Powell, who had been talking to Scowcroft that summer. "I knew that Brent was having these thoughts," Powell said. "He didn't show it [the op-ed] to me, but I don't think I was surprised when he wrote it. I don't know if he told me he was going to put it [the op-ed] in or not." In the days after Scowcroft's piece was published, James Baker and Lawrence Eagleburger, former secretaries of state under George H. W. Bush, also said they were opposed to any immediate war with Iraq and argued that the United States should take its case to the United Nations.

Cheney brushed off this chorus of warnings from his onetime colleagues with a simple explanation: they were stuck in the past, he said, because none of them had been responsible for protecting the United States after September 11. "The world had changed," Cheney later wrote, commenting on Scowcroft's article. "We were at war against terrorist enemies who could not be negotiated with, deterred, or contained, and who would never surrender." Of course, this explanation did not answer whether Iraq had anything to do with those terrorist enemies, or whether an American military intervention there would stop future terrorist attacks.

At this point, Cheney did something unusual: he sought to lead the public debate on his own, abandoning his customary role as someone who operated behind the scenes. In a speech to the annual convention of the Veterans of Foreign Wars, he made a public case for quick military action against Iraq. He rejected the arguments that the United States should ask the United Nations to put UN weapons inspectors back in Iraq. That would be useless, Cheney said, because "Saddam has perfected the art of cheat and retreat." He also sought to rebut Scowcroft's suggestion that war could lead to turmoil in the Middle East. He argued instead that the overthrow of Saddam Hussein would undercut extremists and give heart to moderate Arabs throughout the region. Here, it can be argued that it was Cheney who was stuck in the world of the 1990s. The fact that the Gulf War had isolated extremists and buttressed moderate leaders in the Middle East did not mean that a new, different war in Iraq, a decade later and without broad international support, would have the same result.

To those who opposed going to war, Scowcroft had made the public case that Powell should have been making. A *New York Times* editorial earlier that summer had urged Powell to "stand his ground" and to "throw a tantrum or two." At the same time, the proponents of war argued that Cheney, in speaking out, was assuming the role that Powell should have been playing. Powell was the Bush administration's most effective spokesman and one of the most popular leaders in the nation; and so, the hawks argued, he should have been putting his considerable talents to use on behalf of whatever the president was seeking to do. William Kristol, the leading neoconservative journalist, argued that Powell should figure out "how best to execute the president's policy—or he could step aside and let someone else do the job."

If Powell was underplaying his role, Cheney was overplaying his. As vice president, he was to speak in public for the administration as a whole, not on behalf of himself or a faction within the government. After Cheney delivered his pro-war speech to the VFW, President Bush was not pleased. He instructed Rice to call the vice president and say that he had gotten far out in front of the administration's position in arguing that there wasn't time to get new UN weapons inspections. The vice president quickly retreated; he asked Rice to dictate softer language for him, laying out the administration's more cautious position. A few days later, Cheney delivered the new language word for word.

* * *

On the night of August 5, following a National Security Council meeting on Iraq, Colin Powell had dinner with President Bush at the White House. The two men had what would be their longest conversation since taking office. It was, in retrospect, a fateful meeting, one that helped shape the course the administration would take in going to war with Iraq.

Powell warned Bush about the consequences of military action with Iraq, laying out what any president would need to do and to think about if he were to go to war. A war would cost a lot, Powell said. It could destabilize the Middle East. Bush would consume the administration's attention and its energy for a very long time. In order to prosecute the war successfully, he would need allies and friends overseas. After the war was won, the United States would need to find a way to govern Iraq and to prevent chaos from breaking out. Iraq was like "a crystal glass," Powell told Bush. "It's going to shatter." He concluded with a line he had worked out beforehand: "If you break it, you own it." Those words later came to be known as the "Pottery Barn rule."

However, when Bush asked directly for Powell's recommendation, the answer was cautious, qualified, and focused on the short term. "We should take the problem to the United Nations," Powell replied, adding that the United States should explore whether there could be a diplomatic solution. Then, having taken the case to the United Nations, "If war becomes necessary, you will be in a better position to solicit the help of other nations to form a coalition."

What is most significant here is what Powell did not say. He did not directly challenge the idea of going to war. While he gently touched on the question of possible long-term, harmful consequences, he spoke of these merely as problems to be addressed. He did not say that war with Iraq would be a disaster, one that could harm the United States for years or, indeed, decades to come. "I didn't say to him, 'I oppose this war,'" Powell later acknowledged. "What I said to him was 'The United Nations is the offended party. So, if we can avoid a war, we should avoid this war. I'm all for trying to avoid this war.'" Asked directly why, in his conversations with Bush, he had not taken a stronger position against the war, he replied, "Because it wouldn't have worked."

Nor did Powell threaten to leave the administration. To suggest that he might have done so may seem far-fetched, but to take one counterexample, at the height of the controversy over the Terrorist Surveillance Program that Cheney had championed, FBI director Robert Mueller did threaten to resign—and to do so immediately. Bush changed his mind and altered course on the policy.

Powell's circumspect approach in dealing with Bush was in keeping with his own history and personality. Throughout his long career, he had focused on tactical questions, often with great success, rather than dwelling on larger, more fundamental issues. Lawrence Wilkerson saw underlying similarities between Powell's behavior in 2002–3 and his actions in 1990. On the earlier occasion, as chairman of the Joint Chiefs of Staff, Powell had discreetly sought to question other members of the George H. W. Bush administration about the wisdom of going to war to reverse the Iraqi invasion of Kuwait; in the end, Powell led the military into war. At the time, Powell's high-level maneuvering had brought forth comparisons to military leaders like Eisenhower and George Marshall. In 2002, as secretary of state, Powell was once again carefully raising warnings about an invasion of Iraq, while at the same time seeming to keep his options open to support the war in the future and stand among the victors if it succeeded.

Despite his attempts to keep all options open, there are ample accounts of Powell's private views during this time, and they make clear that he was far more acerbic about Cheney and about the prospect of war than he let on in public, at White House meetings, or in his conversations with the president. British foreign minister Jack Straw recalled as much from a meeting with Powell in August 2002. "Not for the first time, and certainly not for the last, Colin opened up to me about his intense frustration, with parts of the Administration, in particularly Dick Cheney and Don Rumsfeld," he said.

To the extent that Powell hoped to turn Bush around on the fundamental decision to go to war, he failed. He did not summon forth the intensity of the feelings he expressed to others. The most succinct description of the dynamic between Powell and the president was given years later by Rice: "The president sometimes had difficulty gauging the extent of Colin's dissatisfaction." Powell was known throughout his career for his extraordinary effectiveness in getting things done, but he was spectacularly ineffective at registering dissent.

Even so, he did succeed in persuading Bush to go to the United Nations, despite Cheney's repeated argument that this would mean long delays and that, in any event, the United States didn't need the broad coalition of nations against Saddam Hussein that it had assembled for the Gulf War. "Hopefully, we will have others, but the UK, Australia and Turkey are about all we need," Cheney said at one NSC meeting. The vice president argued if the United States did take the Iraq issue to the United Nations, it should merely ask for a quick declaration that Iraq was already in violation of existing Security Council resolutions; Bush should not go through the time-consuming process of seeking a new resolution.

Powell countered that the United States did in fact need allies for a war against Iraq. Throughout the debates, he was as impassioned on this subject as he was aloof on the ultimate decision of whether it was right or wise to use force in Iraq. "If we had tried to go to war without going to the UN, giving that one opportunity for Saddam Hussein to comply, we would have been there alone—and guess what, we wouldn't have been there," he later explained. "We wouldn't have had access, we wouldn't have had friends, we wouldn't have had our overflights."

The question of how much the United States needed allies lay at the core of the disagreements between Cheney and Powell. This issue hadn't mattered so much during the Cold War, when the United States' European allies needed American protection against the Soviet Union and the United States correspondingly needed them. But after the Soviet collapse, a new strain of thinking had emerged: that alliances tied America down and that the United States should serve as the dominant power in the world, on its own. Among top-level officials, Cheney was the leading proponent of this viewpoint.

* * *

Bush was scheduled to address the UN General Assembly in mid-September. American presidents regularly speak there, but he had a particular task: to explain his future course on Iraq. At a National Security Council meeting on September 10, 2002, in what amounted to the end of the administration's summer-long series of discussions about Iraq, Cheney inveighed against getting bogged down at the United Nations. "Saddam is a threat to the United States," he said. "We have to eliminate the threat, and if we adopt a strategy to put the decision out of our hands, that is a mistake." Powell again held firm on the need to get UN approval for American policy. "There is no support internationally for giving cover to the United States for regime change in Iraq," he responded. "If we go alone, we may have trouble getting access from other countries." Bush made his decision shortly afterward: the United States would ask for a new UN resolution, one that would require new inspections of Saddam Hussein's weapons programs, as Powell had proposed.

Looking back, the impact of Powell's actions in the summer of 2002 was to shift a broader debate about whether to invade Iraq into a narrower question of tactics: whether to go to the United Nations. As a result, there was never a single, focused discussion at the highest levels of the Bush administration on the merits of going to war at all. In September 2001, the question of war with Iraq had been set aside to concentrate on Afghanistan. Then, in the summer of 2002, the question was turned into a debate over whether to seek support at the United Nations.

Afterward, even some of the war's strongest proponents would remark on the striking absence of extended debate on the basic issue of whether to go to war. Paul Wolfowitz, the lone member of the administration to call for military action against Saddam Hussein immediately after September 11, observed many years later, "There was never an open argument about whether to confront Iraq." On this point, Powell concurred. "It's true, there was no meeting, there was no NSC meeting" to debate the decision to go to war, he said. Even fifteen years later, he could not pinpoint exactly when Bush decided on the course of war. "I cannot tell you when he crossed the Rubicon," he admitted.

Rice, as national security advisor, was the official responsible for making sure all the president's decisions were thoroughly discussed. Years later, she sought to rebut the argument that there had been no full-scale administration debate about going to war with Iraq. She claimed that at the same NSC meeting in early September 2002 in which Cheney and Powell had argued the wisdom of going to the United Nations, Bush had ended the discussion by saying, "Either he [Saddam Hussein] will come clean about his weapons, or there will be war." Rice then commented: "There was no disagreement. The way ahead could not have been clearer." If this amounted to a full-scale discussion of the merits of going to war, it was an unusual, extremely cursory one.

18

THE ROAD TO BAGHDAD

It was now Colin Powell's turn at center stage. As secretary of state, he was the one responsible for mounting a diplomatic campaign to win a new UN resolution, one that would require Iraq to accept new inspections of its weapons program, to disclose its alleged programs for weapons of mass destruction (WMD), and, finally, to give them up. Powell at first confronted considerable resistance within the UN Security Council, particularly from France and Russia, which did not want a resolution that would specifically authorize military action if Iraq did not comply. At the same time, Powell also faced pressure from Dick Cheney and the Pentagon to win support for a UN resolution that would, in fact, specifically authorize the use of force.

Powell negotiated his way through these obstacles. On November 8, 2002, after two months and 150 phone calls, he won approval of Resolution 1441, which gave Iraq a "final opportunity" to disclose its WMD programs and to give them up. If Iraq did not comply, the resolution said, it would be in "material breach" of previous resolutions. That wording fell short of the tougher language the United States had sought, an authorization to use "all necessary means" to compel Iraq's compliance. Nevertheless, the United States considered the softer wording enough to support military action.

The vote on the Security Council was 15 to 0 in favor of the resolution. This was hailed as a great victory for Powell. Newspapers offered detailed reconstructions, helped along by Powell, of how he had won the day. There were also suggestions that he now had the upper hand within the administration. The *Washington Post* carried a long front-page story by Bob Woodward with the headline "A Struggle for the President's Heart and Mind: Powell Journeyed from Isolation to Winning the Argument on Iraq." Bush himself praised Powell for his "leadership, his good work and his determination."

Not surprisingly, the hawks inside the administration were far less pleased. Many thought the resolution gave Saddam Hussein too much room to maneuver. Some argued that it put far too much focus on the single issue of weapons of mass destruction when, in fact, there were many other reasons to force Saddam Hussein from power. Douglas Feith, the undersecretary of defense, remarked that the resolution "ignored the logic of the rationale for regime change—that Saddam's record of aggression was so long and so bloody as to be irredeemable."

Outside the administration, some of those who opposed the invasion of Iraq also viewed Powell's success at the United Nations as less than a triumph. "Colin Powell won the battle but lost the war," observed Jean-David Levitte, the French ambassador to the United Nations, who pointed out that during the time that Resolution 1441 was debated, passed, and implemented, American troops were pouring into the Middle East. By the time the Bush administration decided whether to go to war, the decision would seem as though it had already been made.

* * *

That fall, the Bush administration scored two other victories that were prerequisites for military action against Iraq. In early October, Bush won congressional approval for an authorization for the use of military force against Iraq. A month later, the Republican Party did unusually well in the 2002 midterm elections, taking control of the Senate and gaining eight seats in the House. It marked the first time since 1934 that any president had picked up seats in the midterm elections of his first term. Bush now could claim to have public and congressional support for military action.

Resolution 1441 had set a one-month deadline for Iraq to issue a report providing full details of all its programs for weapons of mass destruction. Iraq delivered a semblance of a report on time, but it was deemed woefully inadequate; all factions inside the Bush administration criticized it, and Hans Blix, the leader of the UN inspection team, deemed it "rich in volume but poor in new information."

Within weeks, the Bush administration began the task of trying to put together a public case to justify military action against Iraq. That would require, among other things, declassifying intelligence. Bush asked the CIA to distill what it had collected into a single presentation. The idea, in the phrase that was used inside the administration at the time, was to prepare an "Adlai Stevenson" moment: In 1962, in a speech to the UN Security Council during the Cuban Missile Crisis, U.S. ambassador Adlai Stevenson displayed aerial photographs of Cuba that proved the presence of Soviet missiles there. A similar visual presentation would be needed now, but Bush had not yet decided which official would be assigned the Stevenson role to present the case at the United Nations.

CIA officials came to the White House just before Christmas to respond to Bush's request. With CIA director George Tenet alongside him, the agency's deputy director, John McLaughlin, laid out in a dry manner the evidence concerning Iraq. The presentation went over poorly; Bush was openly displeased. "Nice try," he told McLaughlin, before saying to Tenet, "Surely we can do a better job." (It was at this juncture that Tenet famously sought to overcome Bush's misgivings by saying the case was a "slam dunk.") Afterward, two administration officials, Scooter Libby, Cheney's top aide, and Steve Hadley, Rice's deputy, were assigned to pull together a new draft of the administration's case against Saddam. The two men were both lawyers; the idea was that they might produce something more convincing than what the CIA had given the president.

By this point, it had been more than six months since Cheney had asked the question, "What is the *casus belli*?" The administration was still struggling to answer that question. It might have dawned on the president or his advisors that if the administration had to keep asking what was the reason for going to war, and if it didn't like the answers it was getting, it should think again about the wisdom of an invasion. But the war preparations not only continued; they picked up speed.

* * *

Over the months leading up to the American invasion, the Cheney and Powell tribes were at loggerheads over three fundamental issues, in gradually increasing degrees of animosity. The first skirmish was over military strategy—in particular, the size of the invasion force—and the leading protagonists, although from a distance, were Colin Powell and Donald Rumsfeld. Rumsfeld questioned how applicable the Powell doctrine was to the planned invasion of Iraq. "I appreciated the merits of overwhelming force, but complex operations in the real world often don't adhere to hard and fast rules," he later wrote.

In the months following Powell's call to General Franks, in which he voiced skepticism about the invasion plan, the secretary of state had made additional phone calls to Franks and others, questioning the small size of the force and the long communications lines. Rumsfeld would later insist that Powell had never made clear to him that he felt more troops were needed. This was a careful evasion, because Powell had told Franks, who in turn told Rumsfeld; and Powell also told Bush, who reviewed the invasion plans carefully with Rumsfeld and Franks. "No one can legitimately argue that those who made the decision to go in relatively light [in Iraq] were not warned," said the State Department's Richard Haass.

As it turned out, the invasion force of approximately 178,000 troops (including 45,000 from the United Kingdom) was less than one-third the number of troops that had been deployed by the United States and its allies in 1991. The relatively small deployment would prove to be adequate for conquering Iraq, but disastrously small for occupying the country and maintaining stability. The mistake was not just a flaw in military planning, but was linked to a broader strategic error: U.S. officials, particularly those aligned with Cheney, had miscalculated how the Iraqi people would respond to an American invasion. They had assumed that American troops would be greeted as liberators, and that therefore, a relatively smaller number could handle problems such as civil disorder and ethnic tensions.

Cheney remained mostly aloof from the question of troop levels, leaving it to Rumsfeld and the military to deal with Powell's questions.

Cheney did get directly involved in other planning matters. Franks had initially called for tens of thousands of American troops to enter Iraq from the north, through Turkish territory. However, the Turkish government balked at giving its approval. It was the State Department's job to win Turkey over, and the Cheney team complained that Powell and the diplomats weren't working hard enough. An aide to Cheney at one point called State Department officials and dictated an ultimatum to Turkey, but after it was delivered, it was ignored. In the end, the Turkish legislature refused to approve the use of its soil for the invasion, and the whole idea of a "northern front" collapsed.

Cheney's allies blamed Powell for the failure to bring Turkey on board. "He had made some phone calls on the matter but had not taken the time to visit Turkey," Douglas Feith later asserted. "Given that the problem involved winning over a large group of parliamentarians, Powell's prestige and charm might have made the difference." It was a classic example of how the Cheney tribe admired Powell for his personal strengths, but disparaged him when they could not use those strengths for the purposes they sought in the ways they wanted.

* * *

The second issue dividing the two tribes involved the planning for how to govern Iraq after the ouster of Saddam Hussein. The Cheney forces continued to push for a government led by the Iraqi exiles, and Ahmad Chalabi in particular. Powell, the State Department, and the CIA resisted this approach.

The State Department had conducted what was called the "Future of Iraq Project," in which it examined the tasks that would have to be carried out by a new Iraqi government. Working groups were set up to address issues such as public health, water, agriculture, and the judicial system. The project would eventually produce a twelve-hundred-page, thirteen-volume report about governing Iraq.

But this effort was largely ignored, because by the fall of 2002, the Defense Department was making clear that it wanted to control everything related to running Iraq after the invasion. Ryan Crocker, a leading Middle East specialist at the State Department, said that the Pentagon displayed "disdain, utter disdain" for State's work on Iraq and simply refused to participate in it. Late that fall, Feith, the undersecretary of defense, called the NSC to say that Rumsfeld wanted a specific presidential directive giving control of postwar Iraq to the Pentagon, rather than the State Department.

The conference of Iraqi leaders that had first been discussed at the beginning of 2002 was finally held in London that December. Bush appointed Zalmay Khalilzad as the U.S. representative to the conference—a choice that reflected, once again, the intense bickering inside the administration. "The principals could not agree on anyone else," Khalilzad explained. He spoke Arabic and was knowledgeable enough to pass muster with Powell and the State Department, yet he was also a former aide to Cheney and thus acceptable to the vice president's supporters as well. Powell told Khalilzad that if he succeeded in uniting the various Iraqi groups and leaders, Powell would nominate him for a Nobel Peace Prize. At the conference, Khalilzad managed to produce some uneasy, temporary accommodations among the exiles, but he could do nothing about the greater source of disunity inside the Bush administration itself. "Among the opposition leaders, the Pentagon and vice president's office were closest to Chalabi," he wrote.

On January 20, 2003, President Bush signed National Security Presidential Directive 24, handing over to the Defense Department the full responsibility for Iraq during the postwar period and giving Donald Rumsfeld the authority he had been seeking. Bush's order dismayed the State Department, particularly those officials who had been working for months on the Future of Iraq Project. "The lower echelons [of the State Department] did not want that to happen, but Powell conceded," Khalilzad recalled. "He didn't fight." Even so, the president balked at suggestions from Pentagon officials that Chalabi should be put in charge of the country.

* * *

That January, as he laid the groundwork for the invasion, Bush finally decided who should make the public case at the United Nations for war against Iraq. He might have given the job to the U.S. ambassador to the United Nations, John Negroponte, but he wanted to reach higher. He chose Colin Powell, the administration official with by far the greatest stature, popularity, and public standing.

It is difficult to argue that Powell was being somehow used or deceived into giving this speech, because he knew where things stood. The administration was by this time clearly laying the groundwork for a military invasion of Iraq, and Powell supported Bush on this. "I knew that if we went to the U.N. and the problem was not solved [that is, if Iraq did not change course], then we were on a path to war," Powell said. "I'm not going to tell the president to go to the UN, and if it fails, I'm quitting." Powell said he had acknowledged to Bush in January that the approach of taking the issue to the U.N. had failed, and he told the president, "if you feel you have to go to war, I'll be with you."

The process of deciding precisely what Powell should say to the United Nations marked the culmination of the third major dispute between the Cheney and Powell tribes.

Looking back years later, many people understandably assume that this must have been an argument over what to say about Iraq's supposed possession of weapons of mass destruction. But that is not correct; it was a much broader dispute. Cheney was directly involved, both personally and through Scooter Libby, his senior aide and chief of staff.

During the fall of 2002, Cheney had made a few visits to CIA headquarters, with Libby at his side, to question intelligence officials about the evidence they were gathering on the links between al-Qaeda and Iraq. George Tenet recalled that the first visit was a disaster because "Libby and the vice president arrived with such detailed knowledge on people, sources and timelines that the senior CIA analytic manager doing the briefing that day couldn't compete." For the next visit, CIA officials prepared intensively, even holding practice sessions to get ready for the possible questions.

Did this amount to an effort by Cheney to pressure the CIA? Tenet and other senior CIA officials insisted they didn't think so. "The vice president was thorough and came armed with a lot of questions, but he did not push a particular line of argument," recalled Michael Morell, who attended two of the briefings. To Franklin Miller, an NSC staffer, Cheney's visits were reminiscent of the time when, as defense secretary, he had asked to meet with working-level officials involved in nuclear planning. "What he wanted to know was the facts and figures, not as it was filtered by high-level command. He wanted to know what was going on," Miller said. Still, as Tenet later acknowledged, some of the lower-level intelligence officials working on Iraq definitely perceived the Cheney visits as a kind of pressure.

In the weeks after Bush declared himself unsatisfied with Tenet and McLaughlin's presentation of the CIA's evidence concerning Iraq, Libby took the lead in drafting the public case for war. He put together three separate papers of twenty to forty pages each, covering different policy areas. The first described Iraq's supposed weapons of mass destruction, the second discussed Iraq's links to terrorism, and the third described Saddam Hussein's human rights violations and brutality toward the people of Iraq.

There matters stood at the end of January, when Bush informed Colin Powell that he would deliver the U.S. evidence concerning Iraq to the United Nations the following week, a decision that led to renewed tension between Powell and Cheney. When Powell first reviewed Libby's draft documents, with the idea that these should serve as the factual predicate for his speech to the United Nations, he immediately balked. Libby's papers included passages seeking to tie Iraq not just to terrorism in general, but to al-Qaeda and the September 11 attacks in particular. Cheney and Libby had been pursuing this line of argument for more than a year—even though the CIA had concluded that the reports of secret meetings in Prague between Iraq and al-Qaeda were untrue, and even though Libby had earlier tried but failed to persuade the president himself to embrace these claims of an Iraq–al-Qaeda linkage.

Cheney telephoned Powell directly to praise Libby's work and urged him to "take a good look" at it. Powell ignored the vice president's appeal. Instead, he decided to take his aides to CIA headquarters, where they could examine the intelligence on their own, and then draft a speech based on their review of the CIA's material. Tenet had been scheduled to travel to the Middle East, but Powell asked him to postpone the trip. "You're not going to the Middle East. You gotta stay here and work with me on this presentation," he told the CIA director.

When Powell and his team began reviewing the material, they soon discovered that time was too short to do a thorough job on their own. As the basis for their claims about Iraq's weapons of mass destruction, they instead decided to rely on the National Intelligence Estimate about Iraq that had been produced in the fall of 2002—a report that was later found to be defective. "George [Tenet] brought in the NIE," recalled Lawrence Wilkerson, who was supervising the drafting of Powell's speech. "And—stupid me—the NIE was just as flawed as that 48-page script [from Libby]. But it had the imprimatur of the DCI [director of central intelligence]."

Those words pointed to the broader error made by Powell and his team. They were suspicious of the validity of claims made by Cheney and Libby yet they were not suspicious enough of the CIA's own material. Even so, there were frictions between Powell and the CIA leadership, particularly when the CIA argued that some of the intelligence that Powell's staff had cut from the presentation should be restored. "By the time we got to the dress rehearsal in the cafeteria of the U.S. Mission to the United Nations in New York, the day before the presentation, you could have cut the tension between McLaughlin and Powell with a knife," Wilkerson later said. "I thought Powell was going to hurl him out of the top floor of the building."

But these tensions were smoothed over. After the speech was in its final form, Powell insisted that Tenet sit directly behind him as he delivered his presentation. "It wasn't enough for the secretary of state to be up there reading someone else's work," Powell later explained. "I needed George there, so everybody could see it wasn't just a policy presentation. The director of central intelligence was right there, behind me, nodding and smiling—and trying not to fall asleep, because he'd heard it about sixteen times by then."

* * *

Some members of the Bush administration had proposed that Powell give two or three speeches to the United Nations over a period of days: one concentrating on weapons of mass destruction and one or two more on connections to terrorism and on human rights abuses. That idea was dropped after Powell pointed out that it would be hard enough to get the delegates to pay attention to one speech, much less three.

As a basis for military action, the material on Iraq's human rights abuses was inherently problematic because it couldn't answer the obvious question: why now? Saddam Hussein had been brutal to his own people for decades. What had changed in such a way as to justify a military invasion?

Meanwhile, in their drafting sessions at the CIA, Powell's team had removed much of the material on Iraq and terrorism as lacking sufficient evidence. The issue of Iraq's possession of weapons of mass destruction was what remained. As a result, it became the heart of Powell's speech, and the portion that listeners would remember.

On February 5, 2003, speaking before a packed chamber at the UN Security Council, with Tenet sitting behind him, Powell told the delegates, "My colleagues, every statement I make today is backed up by sources, solid sources. These are not assertions. What we're giving you are facts and conclusions based on solid intelligence." He went on to list several examples supposedly pointing to Iraq's possession of weapons of mass destruction, including what he described as a chemical weapons site, underground bunkers for chemical weapons, and mobile labs for biological weapons.

Though few remembered it afterward, Powell also included in his speech a lengthy passage on terrorism, trying to link Iraq to al-Qaeda. He called attention to a "sinister nexus between Iraq and the Al Qaeda network, a nexus that combines classic terrorist organizations and modern methods of murder. . . . Iraqi officials deny accusations of ties with Al Qaeda. These denials are simply not credible."

What this passage indicates is that Powell did not succeed in removing all the Libby material on terrorism from his speech, as his aides subsequently suggested he had, though he did eliminate any references to a specific meeting in Prague before September 11 to plan the World Trade Center attacks. As a result, some of Cheney's aides were able to claim, years later, that Powell's speech was closer to the one drafted by Libby than was commonly assumed. Eric Edelman maintained that Powell "just sort of rearranged" what Libby had originally written. To that, Richard Armitage reacted scornfully, saying that what the vice president's office had provided to Powell had been "total bullshit." It had included the Prague meeting that never took place and "every bullshit thing," he said.

This dispute underscored once again the antagonism between the Powell and Cheney forces. However, it did not address the larger problem with Powell's speech. His UN address turned out to be significantly inaccurate, because the CIA's intelligence was faulty. Just how inaccurate became clear when no weapons of mass destruction were found after the invasion of Iraq.

Even Cheney would acknowledge years later that "much of what Powell said about weapons of mass destruction was wrong." Some of the CIA's sources had been fabricators, while other information was otherwise flawed. Indeed, in one or two cases, the CIA had been warned that the information the sources provided was dubious, but the agency didn't change its reporting to reflect these warnings.

Powell was "pretty happy" in the days immediately after the speech, Wilkerson later recalled. "It was probably one of the toughest things he ever did—just mastering it, technically and logistically." It was only over the following years, as no weapons of mass destruction were found and the intelligence fell apart, that Powell recognized the enormity of what had happened. The United States had given the American public and the international community false information and had used it to justify a war, and Powell had served as the spokesman for the fictions. He was angry with the CIA for its errors and, especially, with the CIA officials who later said they had known that one or another piece of information given to him was wrong or shaky. "Thanks a lot," Powell said.

More than two years later, after he had left the Bush administration, Powell gave voice to his regrets. Asked in a television interview whether the speech would tarnish his reputation, he replied, "Of course it will. It's a blot. . . . [It] will always be a part of my record. It was painful. It's painful now."

* * *

In the months before the invasion of Iraq, there were at least two serious attempts by senior State Department officials to persuade Powell to oppose the invasion. In both cases, he simply took the memos and chose not to respond.

Powell had asked officials in the Bureau of Near East Affairs to examine what might happen in Iraq after an invasion. In response, they put together a memo titled, "The Perfect Storm." It laid out all the things that could go wrong: tensions and score settling among the Shia, Sunnis, and Kurds; political fights between returning exiles and those who had stayed under Saddam; proxy battles involving outside powers such as Iran and Saudi Arabia. Ryan Crocker, who had worked on the memo, was informed, in his recollection, "that the secretary found it fascinating and will figure out a way to deploy it to maximum effect. And we never heard another word."

Separately, Richard Haass, the director of policy planning, also wrote a long memo to Powell, arguing that it was not too late for the administration to reverse course. Even though the American and British troops were already deployed in the Middle East and preparing for war, he said, there were still alternatives to war, such as further weapons inspections and a tightening of sanctions. Haass urged Powell to give the memo to the president. He was soon disappointed. "Powell read it and put it in his pocket—literally," he later wrote.

Such episodes left State Department officials deeply frustrated with Powell's caution and his seeming passivity about the war. "From my perch, way down the food chain, he and Armitage just never took a position," said Crocker. They seemed to oppose the war, and they insisted they were engaged in tactical stratagems against the Cheney team. "Armitage used to talk about jiujitsu, about turning the [hawks'] own strategies against them—whatever that meant," Crocker added.

The record shows that in early 2003, Powell did speak with Bush about the problems with invading Iraq. However, he did so privately, registering an insider's quiet reservations, and at the end of the conversation he gave the president his support. In his memoir, summarizing the views of his top advisors about the war, Bush wrote that "Colin had the deepest reservations. In a one-on-one meeting in early 2003, he had told me he believed we could manage the threat of Iraq diplomatically. He also told me he was not fully comfortable with the war plans. . . . I asked if he would support military action as a last resort. 'If this is what you have to do,' he said, 'I'm with you, Mr. President.'"

That was vintage Powell: reservations but no strong dissent. This time, his careful politicking as an insider would prove costly to his reputation.

* * *

In late February and early March, Powell launched another round of diplomacy at the United Nations. British prime minister Tony Blair had urged the Bush administration to seek a second UN resolution, one that would specifically authorize the use of force against Iraq for having failed to meet the terms of the previous resolution. Blair said that he needed a new UN resolution in order to win support for the war (and to avoid losing a no-confidence vote) in the British Parliament.

Powell was far less successful the second time. Beforehand, he told the White House he thought there was a good chance of getting nine or ten votes on the fifteen-member UN Security Council and that two Latin American nations, Mexico and Chile, could be persuaded to support the resolution. Those hopes proved far too optimistic. France, Russia, and Germany delivered a crushing blow when they announced their opposition. Mexico and Chile were unwilling to support the American position, either. Within weeks, the Bush administration decided to shelve the resolution without bringing it to a vote. Powell would later insist that this defeat didn't matter because the earlier UN resolutions provided sufficient authorization for military action. "The second resolution was not something that we needed," he said. "The fact of the matter is, the only purpose of the second resolution was to give Tony Blair what he needed to get a successful parliamentary vote. . . . The effort to get a second resolution satisfied his needs."

Yet Powell was glossing over the negative consequences of this failed diplomacy. One result was that the war in Iraq would lack the international and multilateral support that the Gulf War had enjoyed in 1991. The new war would become, overwhelmingly, an American endeavor with British support. The war would increase the willingness of old allies such as Germany and France to distance themselves from the United States. Indeed, the war would eventually strain America's ties even with Britain. A decade later, in 2013, the British Parliament would refuse to join the United States in its proposed military action against Syria.

* * *

With its diplomacy coming to an end, the Bush administration moved quickly toward war. American troops were already deployed and mobilized in the countries around Iraq, and administration officials believed there would be logistical problems with having them sit there for an extended period of time.

At this juncture, in March 2003, there was no discussion inside the administration over the wisdom, strategy, morality, or practicality of going to war. Bush and his team acted as though that debate had already taken place and been resolved. This was the crowning irony of Bush's decision the previous September to take the issue to the United Nations, an idea that Powell had so strongly recommended and Cheney had opposed: the decision to go to the United Nations had delayed and, in the end, substituted for the debate that should have taken place about going to war itself. In theory, there was no reason that the Bush administration could not have had this broader debate six months later. But by that point, the troops were in place and Bush had already decided to go to war. In this way, ironically, going to the United Nations had ultimately proved helpful to Cheney and undercut Powell.

Many years later, Powell reflected on this problem. Saddam Hussein hadn't complied with the UN resolution that Powell had proposed and sponsored; and the large and growing American troop deployments in the region hadn't intimidated the Iraqi leader or forced him to change course. "After a while, you're stuck," Powell acknowledged. "You have to go to war."

On March 16, 2003, just after the effort to obtain a second UN resolution collapsed, Powell and Cheney appeared on Sunday television shows to talk about what would happen next. Both men made clear that war might come very soon. "There is no question but that we are very close to the end," Powell said. "We're getting close to the point where the president's going to have to make an important decision," said Cheney.

Cheney went further, offering predictions that would be remembered for their false optimism. As usual, his deep voice conveyed a sense of assurance and certainty. "I'm confident that our troops will be successful and that it will go very quickly," he said. An American-led invasion of Iraq would result in victory within "weeks, rather than months."

"My belief is we will, in fact, be greeted as liberators," Cheney told Tim Russert, the host of NBC's *Meet the Press*. Russert pressed him on that claim. "If your analysis is not correct, and we're not treated as liberators, but as conquerors, and the Iraqis begin to resist, particularly in Baghdad, do you think the American people are prepared for a long, costly, and bloody battle with significant American casualties?" he asked.

"Well, I don't think it's likely to unfold that way, Tim, because I really do believe that we will be greeted as liberators," Cheney replied. It is hard to be more wrong than that on a war-and-peace, life-and-death question. Years later, Cheney would try to argue that he had meant *some* Iraqis would treat the Americans as liberators, and that in fact some did. But that was not what he told the American people on the eve of war. It was the quintessence of Cheney, dropping all nuance and claiming more certainty than he actually possessed.

* * *

The invasion of Iraq began four days later, and for a time it appeared that Cheney's optimistic forecasts might come to pass. The Iraqi forces melted away. In the second week of April, American and British forces entered Baghdad. Saddam Hussein went into hiding. An American M88 tow truck pulled down a massive statue of Saddam Hussein in Baghdad, while a small crowd of Iraqis cheered.

However, the initial sense of triumph did little to ease the divisions inside the Bush administration. Condoleezza Rice was surprised to discover that a few days after the fall of Baghdad, Dick Cheney had hosted a party at his home to celebrate the liberation of Iraq. Members of Cheney's tribe, including Paul Wolfowitz and Scooter Libby, were invited to the party. However, "Colin and I were not," Rice said.

When Cheney was asked about the need for cooperation within the U.S. government in running Iraq after the end of the war, he quickly retorted, "The Pentagon just liberated Iraq. What has the State Department done?"

19

CHAOS

In March 2000, only a few months before he became George W. Bush's running mate, Dick Cheney sat for a long oral history that covered the Gulf War and his service as secretary of defense from 1989 to 1993. In it, he reflected on the many things that had gone well during Operation Desert Storm and then admitted, in retrospect, that there had been some defects, too. "If I had a checklist to go back over with [*sic*], I'd probably allocate more time to some kind of effort that would have focused on the end of the war and how you end the war," Cheney said. At another point, he said, "If there was a weakness there, we hadn't done a lot of planning for what happens after the war."

Cheney's thoughts about the Gulf War seem ironic in light of the disaster that took place after the invasion of Iraq in 2003. The George W. Bush administration had no single, well-thought-out plan for what should take place after the collapse of Saddam Hussein's regime. It was instead forced into a series of hasty, ad hoc improvisations that didn't solve the problems and sometimes made them worse. The military plans for the invasion had been drafted, refined, and readjusted for well over a year, but there was nothing remotely comparable in the administration's planning for postwar Iraq.

Before the invasion, the State Department, the Defense Department, and the CIA devoted considerable time and thought to postwar issues, but no consensus emerged. The State Department and the Pentagon fought bitterly with one another, not only over Ahmad Chalabi but also about which bureaucracy would have ultimate control over who ran postwar Iraq.

Zalmay Khalilzad told a story that illustrates well what this bickering in Washington meant to American officials on the ground in Baghdad. Khalilzad and Ryan Crocker, the State Department's Middle East specialist, had rushed to Baghdad after the invasion to begin working with Iraqi leaders who could be part of an interim government. Crocker asked Khalilzad, who had seniority over him as President Bush's personal representative in Iraq, to cable the State Department a request for resources such as staff help, communications gear, and secure cars. Khalilzad soon got an angry call from Paul Wolfowitz at the Pentagon. "He suspected that State was seeking to undermine the Pentagon's authority by establishing an embassy," Khalilzad recalled. "Paul, don't we work for the same government?" Khalilzad asked.

There were similar, continuing struggles over personnel, as the Pentagon sought to exclude State Department officials from the teams assigned to manage postwar Iraq. At one point, Jay Garner, the retired general who was the first official assigned by the Pentagon to take charge of postwar Iraq, hired Thomas Warrick and Meghan O'Sullivan, State Department officials who were knowledgeable on Iraq. Soon afterward, Garner was ordered to get rid of his new hires. When he tried to find out why, he was told that "the word had come from Cheney." Powell called Rumsfeld to seek an explanation, and was told that the postwar planning should be carried out by people who strongly supported Bush's policies.

In formal terms, it was the responsibility of President Bush and Condoleezza Rice to overcome this bureaucratic wrangling, but Bush was still relying heavily on advice from Cheney, especially on foreign policy and even more so on questions of waging war. For Rice's part, although she was national security advisor and thus in charge of coordinating policy across the government, she had far less experience than Powell and Rumsfeld, and she seemed reluctant to confront them about having their departments work in tandem.

As a result, it seems fair to conclude that it is Cheney who should bear much of the blame for the persistence of the intense divisions within the Bush administration over postwar Iraq. He was vice president and senior advisor to Bush, in theory standing above these bureaucratic battles. Because of Cheney's past service as White House chief of staff and as defense secretary, he had the experience to bring together the warring advisors and agencies. But instead, Cheney either took a hands-off approach to the sniping inside the government or, more often, behaved like a tribal leader on behalf of his faction of aides and former aides. Cheney did not object when virtually everyone inside and outside the Bush administration began to use the phrase "the vice president's office and the Pentagon" as though they were a single collective noun.

More than a decade later, Scooter Libby, Cheney's top aide, sought to rebut the frequent criticism that the Bush administration had had no plan for what would happen after the war. To the contrary, he said that there had been two basic plans for the governance of Iraq, and these plans were in conflict—one from the Pentagon, which wanted to hand governance over to Iraqi leaders quickly, and another from the State Department, which wanted the United States to govern Iraq for a two-year period before handing over control. But if there were conflicting plans, Cheney bore a good share of the responsibility for this flaw. He often liked to convey the aura of a calm, prudent business executive, but no CEO would launch any major new venture with the incoherence and the factionalism of the Bush administration's plans for postwar Iraq.

* * *

The problems began within days of the fall of Baghdad. As American troops and their British allies and other partners took control of the city, and as Saddam Hussein went into hiding, Iraqi officials vanished from their offices and ministries. Almost immediately, there was a wave of vandalism and looting. Trucks pulled up to government offices, and Iraqis rushed in to take away TV sets, computers, furniture, paintings—anything that could be carried and even things that couldn't.

The looting spread to other buildings, including the National Museum, where thieves made off with roughly fifteen thousand artifacts. When asked by Pentagon reporters about the looting, Rumsfeld issued a dismissive reply: "Stuff happens." He went on: "It's untidy and freedom's untidy and free people are free to make mistakes and commit crimes and do bad things. They're also free to live their lives and do wonderful things." Rumsfeld's "stuff happens" marked the first example of a phenomenon that would recur repeatedly over the next two years: as the situation on the ground in Iraq worsened, members of the Cheney tribe sought to dismiss or minimize the significance of that deterioration.

In the following months, the looting and chaos in Iraq gave way to violent attacks and then bombings. In August, Sergio Vieira de Mello, the senior UN representative in Iraq, was killed, along with at least fifteen other people, in a suicide bombing. In October, while Paul Wolfowitz was visiting Baghdad, his hotel was struck by eight rocket-propelled grenades. Wolfowitz dismissed the incident as "desperate acts of a dying regime of criminals" who, he said, "refuse to accept the reality of a free Iraq."

Wolfowitz's words were of a piece with Rumsfeld's earlier comments that the lawlessness represented merely random acts by the dwindling numbers of Saddam Hussein's supporters. Where Wolfowitz called them "criminals," Rumsfeld called them "dead-enders." Such descriptions made the violence sound as if it would be merely a temporary phenomenon. Rumsfeld explained that those in Iraq who opposed the American forces were a motley, disorganized collection of five separate groups: looters, criminals, remnants of Saddam Hussein's regime, foreign terrorists, and Iranian-backed Shiites. "All are slightly different in why they are there and what they are doing," he said. "That doesn't make it anything like a guerrilla war or an organized resistance."

Cheney voiced many of these same themes. The situation in Iraq was under control, he kept insisting; there was nothing taking place on the ground that the Bush administration hadn't anticipated. "There's no question but what we've encountered resistance," he said in the fall of 2003. "But I don't think anybody expected the time we were there to be absolutely trouble-free." Cheney was obliged to begin qualifying and explaining away his prewar prediction that the American forces would be greeted as liberators.

Inside the Bush administration, Cheney and his aides sought to squelch the notion that what was taking place inside Iraq represented anything like guerrilla warfare or an organized insurgency. "I once wrote something—this would have been the summer of '03—saying, basically, this looked like an insurgency, so shouldn't we [respond with] counterinsurgency?" recalled Aaron Friedberg, who worked in Cheney's office. "And I was told to tear it up—we don't want it, stay out of this, it's none of your business. It was the only time I felt like someone was telling me just to shut up and go back to my office."

The inability of the U.S. military to contain the spreading violence in Iraq brought to the surface once again, in a more pointed way, questions about the relatively small size of the invasion force. In addition to the erroneous assumption that the Iraqi population would overwhelmingly welcome the Americans, the invasion plan had also assumed that some American troops would enter northern Iraq from Turkey. When Turkey had refused to give permission, that meant there were no U.S. troops in northern Iraq in the early stages of the war—which, in turn, meant that the Sunni areas there became a refuge for Sunnis fleeing Baghdad and, later, a breeding ground for Sunni resistance to the American occupation.

Years later, Condoleezza Rice observed that the invasion plan had "worked well for the defeat of Saddam's army and his overthrow," but that "We had too few troops to stabilize the postwar environment. As I watched the chaos unfold, I kept harkening back to all those briefings where the President had been told that the plan was 'adequately resourced,' meaning there were enough troops."

Of course, hovering over all these questions about the size of the invasion force was the figure of Colin Powell. Before the invasion, he had made it known, first to Franks and later to the president, that he was worried that there were not enough troops. In the early days of the invasion, Powell was asked whether the war plan and the size of the invasion force violated the principles of the Powell doctrine on overwhelming force. He was evasive. He said he was sure the Pentagon would, in time, "bring decisive force to bear." Then he switched the subject.

* * *

The efforts to stabilize postwar Iraq also quickly brought to the surface the deep, long-standing differences between Powell and Cheney over the role of the international community—or, to put it another way, over Powell's multilateral approach to the world and Cheney's penchant for unilateralism.

In a speech just a few weeks after the invasion, Cheney emphasized that he saw no value in giving the United Nations or major European powers such as France and Germany any significant role in rebuilding Iraq, given that they had been involved in efforts to stop the American drive toward war. "The French and the Germans, in particular, did everything they could to prevent us from going forward and enforcing the U.N. Security Council resolutions," he said. He noted pointedly that the French, Germans, and Russians all seemed to be interested in oil deals and in contracts to help rebuild Iraq. "Perhaps time will help in terms of improving their outlook," he said.

When the Bush administration sought a United Nations resolution formally authorizing the United States to take charge of rebuilding Iraq, Cheney's office and the Pentagon tried several times to insert language that would limit the scope of the United Nations and the role of other countries in the American effort. This ran directly contrary to Powell's thinking. "One day, we're going to be trying to give this tar baby to the U.N.," he told Condoleezza Rice.

Indeed, as the war dragged on, Cheney began to soften his tone to acknowledge the need for help from other countries. In January 2004, he declared, "Cooperation among our governments, and effective international institutions, are even more important today than they have been in the past."

Yet some of the hawkish officials allied with Cheney continued to believe that the United States should deal with Iraq alone and rely on outside help as little as possible. Years later, when asked what the United States should have done differently in Iraq, Wolfowitz replied, "One of the big mistakes was the push to internationalize the mission, to bring in other countries." The result, he said, was that "we turned over the whole Shia part of the country to incompetent foreign forces. We had a whole division under Polish command with no rules of engagement that would work. . . . With the right group of capable forces, it probably would have had to be mostly American, we could have kept stability in the south." Exactly where those additional American forces would have come from was left unanswered; it was Wolfowitz who, before the war, had repudiated the idea that there should have been more troops.

* * *

Oddly enough, the one major decision on which the Cheney and Powell tribes found common ground was the appointment that blew up on the entire administration: the selection of L. Paul "Jerry" Bremer to take charge of American operations in Iraq.

Within weeks of the invasion, administration officials concluded that the original plan to install a retired general, Jay Garner, as the senior U.S. civilian official in Iraq was not working out and that they needed a new presidential envoy in Baghdad to take charge. At the time, Bremer, formerly a senior State Department official, was working for Kissinger Associates, the private consulting firm of the former secretary of state.

According to Franklin Miller, who was working under Rice at the NSC, it was Kissinger who first suggested Bremer for the job. "I think Cheney helped bring him in," Miller recalled. By Bremer's own recollection, he was first contacted about going to Iraq by Scooter Libby and Paul Wolfowitz. Rumsfeld also met with Bremer, and he, too, was enthusiastic. "I like him. I think he is the man," Rumsfeld wrote in a memo to White House chief of staff Andrew Card. "My impression is that you and Condi and the Vice President all agree that he is the preferred person."

Bremer was so well connected in Washington that the Powell forces didn't object to his appointment, either. Bremer had known the secretary of state for decades, dating back to when he was ambassador to the Netherlands during Powell's time as commander of the Army's V Corps in Germany. Powell later said that when Rumsfeld had called to sound him out about appointing Bremer, Powell intentionally tried to display a lack of enthusiasm—knowing that, given the antipathy between the State and Defense Departments, his sounding negative about Bremer might actually help him get the job. "I tried to keep my voice lukewarm on the phone. But when I hung up, I flat-out whooped with joy. The people in my outer office thought I'd just won the lottery," Powell said.

Bremer persuaded Bush to give him a broad mandate, insisting that Khalilzad be dismissed from his job as the presidential envoy to Iraq, where he had been trying to form an interim government. That decision effectively changed the nature of the American presence in postwar Iraq, switching the emphasis away from trying to transfer sovereignty to Iraqis and toward an American occupation of the country. Khalilzad recalled that Powell was blindsided by the decision and "agitated" by it.

After moving to Baghdad, Bremer quickly issued the orders that would come to haunt the American presence in Iraq for years. He required that all senior members of Saddam Hussein's Baath Party be removed from their jobs and barred from future government employment, an order that disqualified tens of thousands of Iraqis who could have helped run the country. The program for de-Baathification was run by Ahmad Chalabi, the former exile leader. Next, Bremer ordered the dissolution of the Iraqi army, which effectively left hundreds of thousands of Iraqi soldiers on the streets.

Bremer's orders caught many senior American officials by surprise. "I read about it [in] the newspaper the next morning," Powell recalled. "[The Joint Chiefs of Staff] were surprised. CIA surprised. Condi and President surprised." But not everyone in Washington was in the dark. Undersecretary of Defense Douglas Feith, an aide to Rumsfeld, had drafted the broad order for de-Baathification and given it to Bremer before he left for Iraq; in fact, Bremer had asked Feith to delay the order so that he could announce it upon his arrival in Baghdad. The order to disband the Iraqi army was also cleared with Feith and Rumsfeld. The fact that other senior officials didn't know about these orders was a classic example of the lack of coordination and intense mistrust within the Bush administration.

Years later, Bush himself ruefully gave a concise, retrospective description of the impact of these orders to disband the army and exclude Baath Party members. "The orders had a psychological impact I did not foresee. Many Sunnis took them as a signal they would have no place in Iraq's future. . . ." he wrote in his memoir. "Thousands of armed men had just been told they were not wanted. Instead of signing up for the new military, many joined the insurgency."

Franklin Miller at the NSC later observed that disbanding the army served the interests of Chalabi, who was still seeking to emerge as Iraq's next leader and wanted a new army loyal to him. Before the invasion, Miller said, NSC officials had prepared recommendations for the postwar period that specifically included the warning not to disband the army. When Bremer's order was sent to Washington, Powell and other State Department officials sought to delay it, pointing out that dissolving the army had not been the administration's policy.

"When we found out about it," Richard Armitage recalled, "Powell called Condi right up. He said, 'Condi, what the hell? These decisions are not the ones the president made.' She said, 'Yes, I know, Colin.' Powell said,

'The president's gotta change this. This is terrible.' She said, 'I've taken it up with the president, and he now thinks we've got to support our commander in the field.'"

Bremer was working in Iraq for barely a few months before he began to lose some of his support in Washington. Rumsfeld began to complain that Bremer was talking to the president and Rice without going through him first. In October, after Rice set up a new group inside the White House to keep track of developments in Iraq, Rumsfeld washed his hands of all responsibility for Bremer, despite having earlier insisted repeatedly that the Pentagon was in charge of Bremer's work. "I recommend that Jerry Bremer's reporting relationship be moved from DoD to the President, Condi Rice or Colin Powell, as you may determine," he wrote in a memo to Bush. It was another illustration of the administration's internal bickering over Iraq.

Rumsfeld was Cheney's old friend and ally. If anyone could have urged Rumsfeld to stop battling with others in the administration and to show more respect for his colleagues, it would have been Cheney. This never happened. Rumsfeld's wrangling with Powell and Rice, with the State Department and the NSC, never subsided. It was a case where Cheney's inaction and passivity mattered more than anything he said or did.

* * *

It is easy to fall into thinking of Colin Powell as a dissenting voice inside the Bush administration, but day in and day out, he wasn't. He had sought to slow down the movement toward war in Iraq, without directly opposing the war itself. He had quietly questioned the military plan for the invasion, but he also often joined in what others in the administration were saying. He sometimes chided opponents of the war for being too negative about Iraq or too strident in their criticisms. On a visit to Iraq that September, Powell said he found "a sense of hope here even in this time of difficulty. Those who are so critical of the administration might want to hold their fire a bit." He echoed Cheney's description of the American role in Iraq. "We are not occupiers," Powell told a news conference in Iraq. "We are liberators."

Still, there were occasional public reminders of the enduring bitterness that lay beneath the surface. In August 2003 the *Washington Post* carried a front-page story, based on unnamed sources, that Powell and Armitage had told the White House they would be leaving the administration at the end of a single term, even if Bush were to be reelected.

The story, though brief, touched several sensitive nerves: it implied that Powell and Armitage operated in tandem, as one faction within an often-divided administration; and it suggested that, amid the growing upheaval in Iraq and Washington, some in the administration were thinking about domestic politics, while other were beginning to contemplate their own futures. Powell quickly dismissed the report as "gossip."

* * *

In the months after the invasion, Cheney appeared to be at the peak of his power and influence. He had led the way into the war. His views remained rock-hard, even as others in the administration adjusted theirs to take account of developments or changing circumstances.

Cheney's focus remained intensely on what he always described as a worldwide terrorist network—a "determined, organized, ruthless enemy," as he described it in a speech in October 2003. He continued to make the claim that Saddam Hussein had had "an established relationship with al Qaeda," training the terrorist network in how to make poisons, gases, and bombs—even though this claim had been refuted or called into question by the CIA.

He viewed Iraq as the main battleground in a worldwide struggle against terrorism, and he saw terrorism as the single preoccupying national security challenge of his time—to such an extent that he pushed other important issues to the sidelines. Aaron Friedberg recalled that when there were early signs of China's growing assertiveness, Cheney said, "We've got too much on our plate," and put off any broad reexamination of American policy toward China. "He was not oblivious to the problem," Friedberg said. "I think he just made a conscious decision that this was going to be lower priority."

Nevertheless, the violence in Iraq did not subside. Cheney's prediction that American troops would be greeted as liberators was beginning to wear thin. Far worse from the standpoint of his credibility, no one could find the weapons of mass destruction that Iraq was supposed to possess and that had served as the primary justification for the war. After early searches turned up nothing, Ryan Crocker of the State Department asked one of Cheney's allies why the administration didn't just admit the WMD weren't there, give up, and move on. But this official and others were convinced that "they had to be there, and we would find them," Crocker said.

During a speech in the fall of 2003, Cheney placed great stock in the ongoing efforts of the Iraq Survey Group, a team of American, British, and Australian officials dispatched to Iraq to find Saddam Hussein's weapons of mass destruction. Cheney noted in his speech that the group was headed by David Kay, "a respected weapons scientist and former U.N. inspector" in Iraq. However, less than four months after Cheney's speech, Kay resigned, saying he did not believe there were any weapons of mass destruction in Iraq. He concluded that in the years following the Gulf War, Saddam Hussein had pretended to possess WMD in order to bluff other countries, notably Iran, that he was still powerful and that they should not attack him. Kay's resignation represented a profound embarrassment for the Bush administration as a whole and for Cheney in particular. The Iraq Survey Group's final report later that year later confirmed Kay's findings.

* * *

The failure to find weapons of mass destruction in Iraq served to deepen the considerable antipathy between Powell and Cheney individually and between the Powell and Cheney tribes. Previously, the members of the two groups had displayed an icy, clenched-teeth sufferance toward one another, even as they tried to suppress these differences and work together to make the invasion of Iraq a success. By late 2003, however, after the invasion bogged down and it became clear that no WMD would be found, the sense of sufferance curdled into open bitterness and hostility. By this point, the Powell team and the Cheney team (and, indeed, each of the two leaders) nursed grievances, and their brooding over the recent past took the nasty form of recalling who had done what to whom.

Powell's grievance against the Cheney group was fairly straightforward: When no WMD turned up, he suffered a deep and lasting blow to his reputation because of his speech to the United Nations making the case for war against Iraq. He was now obliged to confront unending questions about why he had been so wrong.

Some of Powell's ire was directed at the CIA, which had provided him with the intelligence that was now shown to have been faulty. Yet, from Powell's perspective, Cheney and his aides had been pushing the CIA to build a stronger case against Iraq and had been more willing even than the CIA to make use of questionable intelligence, some of it from Chalabi and his allies. Cheney's chief of staff, Scooter Libby, had written an early draft of the UN speech, and it was more strongly worded than the one Powell actually gave.

It was hardly comforting to Powell that, after the WMD did not turn up, members of Cheney's team responded with a series of after-the-fact rationalizations. They hadn't wanted to base the case for war in Iraq just on the WMD, they said; they had wanted to emphasize Iraq's ties to terrorism and Saddam Hussein's brutality. Furthermore, they suggested, Powell had erred in his UN speech by referring to Iraq's "stockpiles" of WMD when what Iraq still possessed weren't actual stockpiles, but the programs to be able to produce the WMD. Yet even Cheney admitted on occasion that he had wrongly thought there were stockpiles. ("We still had not found the stockpiles of chemical or biological weapons we had believed Saddam possessed," he wrote in his memoir.) Complaining about Powell's choice of words amounted to a classic case of blaming the victim.

Cheney's sense of grievance toward Powell was also deep, and it, too, grew indirectly from the failure to find WMD. It stemmed from the federal investigation and eventual prosecution of Scooter Libby, who had been the Cheney aide most closely involved in building the case for war against Saddam Hussein.

In July 2003, a former U.S. ambassador named Joseph Wilson had written an op-ed for the *New York Times* describing how the Bush administration had turned inaccurate intelligence about Iraq's efforts to buy uranium in Niger into a justification for war. A few days later, the conservative columnist Robert Novak revealed that Wilson's wife was a CIA agent named Valerie Plame. Because it is illegal to identify a CIA agent by name, the FBI opened an investigation of the leaked information, and attention soon began to focus on Libby as a possible culprit.

The controversy over the investigation and eventual prosecution of Libby would drag on for several years. Cheney was fiercely loyal to Libby and enraged by the investigation, and one of the targets of his fury was Powell. The secretary of state was not directly responsible for the investigation of Libby, of course, but Cheney suggested that Powell could have intervened in a way that might have exculpated Libby. It turned out that Richard Armitage had also been talking with Novak, and that Armitage had been the initial and primary source for the column identifying Plame. While the probe of Libby went forward, Cheney wrote years later, "Over at the State Department, Armitage sat silent. And, it pains me to note, so did his boss Colin Powell."

The investigation of Libby began in late 2003. He would remain on the job as Cheney's chief of staff for another two years, until he resigned when he was formally indicted for perjury and obstruction of justice. Nevertheless, the mere opening of the investigation sapped energy from Cheney's office. Paul Wolfowitz, who had been Libby's earliest mentor and his boss during Cheney's years in the Pentagon, said that he didn't realize at first "how much he [Libby] was handicapped in arguing for [various policy issues] and how preoccupied he was with all of his testimony and going through records.

"I thought of him [Libby] as my best ally, and he *was* my best, all in all, but I think he was somewhat handicapped in putting positions to Cheney that would be difficult to pursue," Wolfowitz said. For example, "It was not easy to go to Cheney with criticisms of Rumsfeld. I tried it once or twice, very diffidently," in a case where Wolfowitz thought the Pentagon was not giving Cheney the full picture of the worsening problems in Iraq. What Wolfowitz was saying here was that Libby had served not just as the vice president's most influential advisor, but also as a channel for messages to him from other members of the Cheney network throughout the administration. The launch of the federal investigation of Libby marked the beginning of Cheney's own decline in influence.

* * *

On December 13, 2003, the Bush administration received one bit of good news when American troops captured Saddam Hussein near Tikrit, in the area northwest of Baghdad where he had been born. However, over the coming months the violence in Iraq not only continued but increased, with a growing number of car bombings, suicide bombings, and mortar attacks. In April 2004, 137 Americans were killed in Iraq, the largest number in any single month since the invasion. That same month, American news organizations unearthed a story that would profoundly alter the larger dynamics of the war in Iraq and in Washington.

CBS's *60 Minutes II* and the *New Yorker* published accounts with graphic pictures of the abuse of Iraqi detainees inside Abu Ghraib prison, west of Baghdad. The pictures showed Iraqi prisoners being subjected to a variety of abuses. They were stripped of their clothes and put in degrading poses while their American guards smiled, smirked, and gave the thumbs-up. In one case, a female prison guard posed holding the end of a dog leash attached to a naked detainee.

Abu Ghraib destroyed whatever slim hope the Bush administration still harbored for winning support for the war, not only in the Middle East but also in Europe or indeed anywhere else overseas. "We never really recovered from Abu Ghraib," Condoleezza Rice later admitted. The guards who had posed for these pictures while humiliating the prisoners "became, for some, the public face of U.S. military forces." Even Douglas Feith, the most obdurate of all the hawks inside the administration, realized that the release of the Abu Ghraib photos "seems to have been a watershed in the Iraq War."

Abu Ghraib marked a watershed at the top levels of the Bush administration, too, though this fact wasn't recognized at first. The pictures reopened many of the sensitive issues that had produced divisions among Bush's senior advisors, in particular between Powell and Cheney. The most obvious one concerned the treatment of prisoners. Less than two years earlier, Powell had argued, over Cheney's opposition, that prisoners detained by American forces should be treated under the terms of the Geneva Conventions. Bush had put that issue aside with the bland assurance that prisoners would in any event be treated humanely—but Abu Ghraib provided clear evidence that this was far from the case. So, too, Abu Ghraib served as a reminder of the Guantanamo Bay detention camp and all the controversy surrounding it. The scandal drew attention to the broader issues surrounding the detention and interrogation of prisoners. At this point, the public and the press did not know about the secret CIA programs to employ harsh interrogation or torture techniques at secret locations around the world, but Cheney certainly did. The Abu Ghraib scandal had nothing to do with those programs, but it brought inquiries into matters he wanted to keep hidden.

In the early days after the story broke, Bush administration officials argued that the pictures from Abu Ghraib showed merely a small number of soldiers who were acting on their own and not carrying out instructions or official American policy. Cheney was among those who sought to separate the Abu Ghraib prison guards from larger judgments about the war. "The recent misconduct of a few does not diminish the honor and the decency that our servicemen and women have shown in Iraq," he asserted. He also sought to limit the release of photographs from Abu Ghraib, saying there were more important considerations than "just satisfying the desires of the press that want to have more pictures to print."

Abu Ghraib raised broader questions about the American invasion of Iraq. If a handful of U.S. troops were acting on their own, why were they so undisciplined and out of control? The U.S. military officials in charge of the facility explained that they had been swamped by a sudden, unanticipated influx of prisoners. But this explanation led eventually into the controversy over the Powell doctrine: had the United States sent enough troops to Iraq? So, it was, too, for Donald Rumsfeld's assertion that one of the causes of Abu Ghraib had been a lack of training. One reason for the lack of training for dealing with large numbers of prisoners was that there weren't supposed to be many prisoners in the first place; after all, Cheney had predicted that Iraqis would welcome the American troops as liberators.

* * *

Abu Ghraib also reopened the personal feuding and backbiting among the senior members of the Bush administration. Powell said the photos had "stunned every American." His aides let it be known that he had repeatedly urged the Bush White House and Rumsfeld to deal with the growing number of detainees in Iraq. "It's something Powell has raised repeatedly—to release as many detainees as possible—and second, to ensure that those in custody are properly cared for and treated," an unnamed senior State Department official told the *Washington Post*.

Powell then went further. A week after the scandal broke, he compared Abu Ghraib to the My Lai scandal during the Vietnam War, in which American troops shot hundreds of unarmed Vietnamese. Speaking as a soldier and Vietnam veteran, Powell observed, "In war, these sorts of horrible things happen every now and again, but they're still to be deplored."

With this comparison, Powell's train of thought seemed clear enough: Both Abu Ghraib and My Lai concerned abuses by American troops. Both had seriously damaged, if not destroyed, American efforts to shore up public opinion for ongoing wars. Both scandals had come to light through investigative reporting in the United States (in both cases, led by journalist Seymour Hersh). Powell was not alone in drawing the analogy to Vietnam; Senator John McCain, a former prisoner of war in Vietnam, did so, too. Nevertheless, Powell's remarks outraged Rumsfeld, who rejected the comparisons by pointing out that My Lai had involved the outright murder of civilians.

Abu Ghraib brought a wave of calls for the president to fire his secretary of defense. Indeed, Rumsfeld offered Bush his resignation, and the president considered accepting it. Bush and other White House officials had been blindsided by the scandal, and they thought that Rumsfeld should have done more to warn them, particularly about the horrifying pictures.

Rumsfeld would write years later that he wished he had stepped down at that point, rather than staying at the Pentagon for another two and a half years. However, Bush and Cheney both had strong reasons to keep him on the job. Bush didn't want to change his defense secretary while the war was raging, and he didn't have an obvious candidate to replace him. Moreover, 2004 was a presidential election year, and replacing Rumsfeld might have been taken as an acknowledgment that things in Iraq weren't going well, which could have hurt Bush politically.

Cheney had his own additional reasons for keeping the defense secretary on the job. One of them, of course, was their long-standing relationship. But Cheney's rationale went far beyond sentiment: keeping Rumsfeld as secretary of defense meant that the vice president could continue to wield powerful influence at the Pentagon and over all defense-related issues. Moreover, Rumsfeld served as, by far, Cheney's most powerful ally on the National Security Council.

After Rumsfeld submitted his resignation, Bush asked Cheney to persuade his old friend to stay. Cheney went to the Pentagon, sat down in Rumsfeld's office, and told him that his resignation would harm the ongoing military campaigns. He also made a personal appeal, recalling their history since 1969. "Don, thirty-five years ago this week, I went to work for you," Cheney said, "and on this one you're wrong." Rumsfeld stayed on.

* * *

It was at this point, in the aftermath of Abu Ghraib, that Bush concluded he had had enough of the feuds and bickering within his own administration. He decided he needed to make some far-reaching changes—not immediately, but after Election Day. "The spring of 2004 marked the end of my tolerance for the squabbling within the national security team," he would later write.

By this point, the infighting at the top echelons of his administration had reached a level of intensity that now seems almost absurd. Members of Cheney's tribe frequently complained that Powell and Armitage were leaking information to the press. Members of Powell's tribe charged that Cheney was using his one-on-one meetings with the president to get Bush to make decisions that should have been debated in larger meetings with Powell present. For good measure, both sides brought their grievances to Rice, whose job as national security advisor was to resolve differences inside the administration; it was almost like two basketball teams trying to work the referee. Rumsfeld grumbled that Rice was slanting decisions toward Powell and the State Department, while Powell told her that Cheney and Rumsfeld were undermining him and that she should be supporting him and the State Department more than she did. He also told Rice that he was afraid to travel overseas because Cheney and his allies were trying to get decisions made while he was out of the country. Dennis Ross, the veteran Middle East specialist who had friends on both the Powell and Cheney teams and was talking to them regularly during this period, said he could not believe the level of rancor. "There was at times a kind of venom about it, kind of 'us versus them,'" he recalled.

It was not surprising, then, that Bush decided he needed to shake up his administration.

* * *

Rumsfeld was not the only senior official to tell Bush he was willing to step aside. During the run-up to the 2004 presidential election, Cheney and Powell did so, too.

Cheney told Bush he should feel free to choose someone else as his running mate. Cheney made the offer three times; the first two times, Bush didn't seem to take it seriously, but the third time, he said he wanted to think about it for a few days. He then conferred with his political advisor Karl Rove and White House chief of staff Andrew Card about the possibility of replacing Cheney with Bill Frist, then the Senate majority leader.

Cheney "was seen as dark and heartless—the Darth Vader of the administration," Bush acknowledged in his memoir. Moreover, Bush admitted, because Cheney was widely portrayed as the de facto president running the administration with a hidden hand, "accepting Dick's offer would be one way to demonstrate that I was in charge."

Nevertheless, Bush decided that he wanted Cheney for the second term. The reasons he had chosen Cheney in the first place remained unchanged. He didn't want a vice president with presidential ambitions of his own, who would spend his time getting ready to run in the next presidential election. Bush still felt he wanted and needed Cheney to help run the White House in the second term. Cheney was, among other things, the administration's most senior official and leading expert for a wave of secret counterterrorism programs (surveillance, interrogation, black sites) that were still unknown to the public in 2004. Finally, there was another factor: If Cheney were pushed off the ticket, he could conceivably cause all sorts of difficulties for Bush. It was possible to envision Cheney on the outside, criticizing some of the initiatives Bush launched during his second term, such as an attempt at diplomacy with North Korea. From Bush's point of view, it was far better to have him on the inside.

* * *

Colin Powell had offered his resignation earlier than the others. He informed Bush in the first months of 2004 that he was ready to leave as secretary of state. In fact, he went further: he told the president that he needed to shake up his entire foreign policy and national security team after he won the November election.

Bush didn't seem disturbed; he told Powell there had been similar frictions in past administrations, such as the long-running battles between the State and Defense Departments in the Reagan years. Powell, who had been a witness to those earlier battles, said that the situation in this administration wasn't the same; it was far worse. "We're too much apart," he told Bush. "And we hide things, kind of go around each other. It's not the way it should be. You really need to change this all, after the election. And it begins with me, because I'm the one that's so different from the others."

Bush asked Powell to stay on the job until after the November election to make for an orderly transition. But when the time came, Powell's departure turned out to be anything but smooth. It turned into a tawdry affair, a series of humiliations to a proud man with a long and distinguished record of public service.

Having let it be known earlier he didn't want to serve in the second term, Powell decided belatedly that in fact he might want to remain as secretary of state, at least for a time. Wilkerson, his chief of staff, recalled running into Richard Armitage on the morning after Bush's reelection. Armitage told him bluntly, "I want out of here," but then added that Powell wanted to serve as secretary of state for a while longer. "He wanted to stay on through the Iraqi elections, which were in late January," Wilkerson explained.

Meanwhile, Cheney was working to push Powell out. "I felt strongly that major change was needed in the national security team," the vice president would recall. "Getting a new secretary of state was a top priority." By this time, Cheney's animus was unconcealed. "The vice president's perspective was that Powell was leaking," said Zalmay Khalilzad, pointing to the secretary of state's practice of providing (or having his aides provide) accounts "on background" that were favorable to his own point of view. Cheney grumbled that Powell had been "superb" as chairman of the Joint Chiefs of Staff but not as secretary of state. He complained that Powell registered his opposition to the war in Iraq to the press and to others outside government, but not in meetings inside the administration.

In any event, Bush needed little last-minute convincing. He had begun to think about choosing a new secretary of state well before the election, after Powell had told him he didn't want to serve a second term. Within hours after it was clear that Bush had won reelection, he sounded out Condoleezza Rice about becoming the next secretary of state.

* * *

The final days were downright ugly. After Election Day, Colin Powell returned to his office at the State Department believing he could decide, on his own terms and in his own time, when to leave. The Iraqi elections that he had set as a possible point of departure were still more than two months away.

A White House official made what seemed like a routine call to Wilkerson, giving him the instructions that would apply to all Cabinet members: please inform the White House if you're planning to leave or not. A few minutes later, another White House official called Wilkerson to ask what he thought Powell would do. Then the White House called Powell's office to ask him to submit his resignation. According to Wilkerson's account, Powell promptly sat down, typed a resignation letter, and submitted it. The White House called again to say that there was a typo that needed to be corrected. Powell had to type his resignation letter a second time.

"You kind of half expect the president might call and say, 'Colin, you're a great guy, I love you to death. Go,'" Powell said of this episode. "But that isn't what happened. Nobody in the Cabinet got called by the president. It was [White House chief of staff] Andy Card who called me and said the president wanted my resignation letter, along with others." Powell asked Card if he could "wait a couple of months," citing the importance of an upcoming conference of democracies and the Iraqi elections. Card called back quickly and told him no; he should resign immediately.

In a final humiliation for Powell, it turned out that he was the only senior member of the national security team to be replaced after the 2004 election. Bush did not heed Powell's advice to shake up or replace the entire team. Rumsfeld stayed on at the Pentagon. Bush elevated Rice to secretary of state and promoted her deputy, Stephen Hadley, to be national security advisor. When the time for change came, Powell said ruefully, "I thought that when he began with me, it wasn't going to end with me."

It turns out that Bush did consider replacing Rumsfeld along with Powell, but Cheney persuaded him, once again, to keep Rumsfeld on the job. "I made the case that Rumsfeld was doing a tremendous job, that he was carrying out administration policy, and that replacing him would signal dissatisfaction with the strategy the president himself had set," Cheney acknowledged years later.

* * *

Eleven years earlier, when Powell had stepped down as chairman of the Joint Chiefs of Staff, most of Washington had turned out for the elaborate ceremonies honoring him: the president and vice president and their immediate predecessors, members of the Supreme Court, military commanders, ambassadors, and other foreign dignitaries.

Powell's departure from the State Department could not have been more different. He was obliged to stay on as secretary of state until the Senate approved Rice as his successor, and various delays in her confirmation meant that she wasn't ready to be sworn in until the end of January—ironically, after the Iraqi elections. There was a farewell ceremony for him at the State Department a few days before Rice arrived, but it was primarily for those diplomats and other employees working in the department; it had none of the pomp or flourish of his earlier leave-taking.

In 1993, when he stepped down as chairman of the Joint Chiefs of Staff, Powell interrupted his remarks to give special thanks to the man he called "my dear friend Dick Cheney." This time, Cheney did not attend, and Powell did not mention him.

PART FIVE

DISPENSABLE

20

ISOLATION

In theory, the departure of Colin Powell should have ushered in a new era in which Dick Cheney dominated the Bush administration. Powell had served as a counterweight to Cheney during the first term. Whereas Cheney maintained that the September 11 attacks justified throwing out all the old rules and principles, Powell often argued for their continuing validity. He was a link to the ideas and the leading personnel of past Republican administrations—to Ronald Reagan and George H. W. Bush, to George Shultz, James A. Baker, and Lawrence Eagleburger.

Yet, during Bush's second term, Cheney's influence declined, at first slowly and then dramatically, until, by the final year of the administration, he was often left isolated in its internal deliberations. Several factors contributed to his marginalization. One was that events themselves undercut him. A second was that the arrival of Condoleezza Rice as secretary of state and, later, the appointment of Robert Gates to replace Rumsfeld at the Pentagon weakened Cheney's clout. The third factor was Bush himself: after four years on the job, he had both less need to rely on Cheney's experience and greater confidence in his own judgments, which came to differ more often from Cheney's.

Cheney's office operated in Bush's second term much as it had during the previous four years. But scars from the first term's battles were evident. Aaron Friedberg recalled that whenever CIA analysts came to brief Cheney and his team, "It was like a dysfunctional family Thanksgiving. Everybody was really uncomfortable. There was a lot of tension." Cheney's office and the CIA had each blamed the other for the erroneous intelligence reports about Iraq's weapons of mass destruction. CIA officials blamed Cheney's team for the leak that exposed its agent Valerie Plame. As a result, when the CIA came to Cheney's office, "You wouldn't get one person, you'd get a team," said Friedberg. "It was like Soviet diplomats in the Cold War: they didn't travel alone. And there was always somebody in the back writing down everything you said and everything that they said in response."

* * *

As national security advisor, Condoleezza Rice had not been a driving force in setting policy. She had often tried to mediate between the Cheney and Powell factions, rarely challenging Cheney on her own. As secretary of state, however, she was considerably more forceful and influential: she clashed repeatedly with Rumsfeld and on occasion with Cheney. Rice, it turned out, brought to the State Department assets that Powell lacked, despite the general's longer experience in government. Above all, she had a strong relationship with Bush and with the new national security advisor, Stephen Hadley, who had been her deputy.

Meanwhile, Cheney's network was beginning to weaken. Paul Wolfowitz left his job as deputy secretary of defense to run the World Bank. Scooter Libby was seeking to fend off a federal investigation. Even Rumsfeld had become a bit less brash in the wake of Abu Ghraib and carried a premonition that he would be replaced during Bush's second term. In October 2006, Cheney tried to cheer up Rumsfeld by saying, "There are only 794 days left until the end of the term." Rumsfeld replied, "Dick, there are 794 days left for you. Not for me."

As a result of these changes, decision making within the Bush team became progressively less acrimonious and less tribal in nature. Even the meetings seemed different. William Burns, a senior American diplomat, observed that during Bush's first term, "If you were sitting in the State Department, you always had the sense that the deal was cooked." The suspicion was that close friends such as Cheney and Rumsfeld (or Libby and Wolfowitz) had already worked out a common position and, thus, any session to hear the State Department's views was merely a formality. By contrast, Robert Kimmitt, a former aide to Secretary of State James A. Baker who was appointed deputy secretary of the treasury in 2005, said that the top-level deliberations during George W. Bush's second term seemed similar to those in the relatively harmonious George H. W. Bush administration. "I never felt that the table was tilted in the second term," Kimmitt said. "That was in the first term."

* * *

Bush suffered two serious political setbacks in the first year of his second term. Soon after his second inaugural, he pressed Congress to approve legislation for a partial privatization of Social Security. But he had greatly overestimated domestic support for such an initiative, and by the fall of 2005, in the face of growing resistance in Congress, he was forced to withdraw his proposal before it ever came to a vote. Then, in late August, Hurricane Katrina struck the Gulf Coast and hit New Orleans with full force, breaking the levees and flooding the city. The Federal Emergency Management Agency failed to respond quickly or adequately to the growing crisis, thus fostering a perception of incompetent governance from which Bush would never really recover.

The defeat on Social Security and the mishandling of Hurricane Katrina affected the entire Bush administration. In addition, a handful of other events in late 2005 and early 2006 damaged Cheney in particular, more than any of his colleagues. On October 28, 2005, Scooter Libby was indicted on charges of making false statements and lying to the grand jury during the investigation into the Valerie Plame case. Libby resigned the same day. Cheney released a terse statement in which he called Libby "one of the most capable and talented individuals I have ever known." Sixteen months later, Libby would be convicted on four of the five counts against him.

The impact on Cheney was considerable. First, Libby had served as Cheney's chief of staff since the start of the Bush administration, and his departure immediately affected the entire operation of the Office of the Vice President. Second, Cheney needed to watch closely the ongoing investigation and trial. He had been involved personally in the events that had led to the charges against Libby, and there was speculation that the federal prosecutors were looking at whether Cheney, as Libby's boss, was ultimately responsible for the leak. At Libby's trial, the lead prosecutor, Patrick Fitzgerald, told the jury that Libby's lies had prevented him from ascertaining Cheney's actions surrounding the disclosure of Plame's identity.

Finally, in ways that would not be recognized at first, Libby's prosecution came to alter the relationship between Cheney and Bush. Before the fall of 2005, Cheney's efforts to help Libby had been directed at preventing an indictment. After the verdict, Cheney's efforts came to be focused on the one person who could help Libby by pardoning him: George W. Bush. The Libby case thus created a tension between the president and the vice president that would last and intensify through the end of the administration.

* * *

Cheney had spearheaded the secretive programs through which the Bush administration responded to the September 11 attacks. In the late months of 2005, these programs began to come to light and, in some instances, to unravel. For the remainder of the term, the Bush administration as a whole and Cheney in particular would find themselves on the defensive, trying to justify and protect the programs they had set up a few years earlier.

On November 2, 2005, just five days after Libby's indictment, the *Washington Post* broke the story of the CIA's "black sites," the secret prisons at eight locations around the world where the agency had been holding and interrogating al-Qaeda prisoners, often using "enhanced interrogations techniques." The door was opened for years of diplomatic disputes over the black sites and congressional investigations into the interrogation methods, many of which, like waterboarding, seemed to violate international agreements such as the UN Convention Against Torture.

Even before the existence of the black sites was brought to light, Cheney had been quietly maneuvering to protect the CIA agents who worked at the sites from legal consequences. In the wake of Abu Ghraib, Congress was considering new legislation to prohibit torture or any other cruel and degrading treatment of any prisoners in U.S. custody, an effort led by two Republican senators, John McCain of Arizona and Lindsey Graham of South Carolina.

At the time the legislation was being considered and before the *Washington Post* revelations, only a few members of the congressional leadership and the intelligence committees knew about the black sites. Unlike Abu Ghraib, where low-level soldiers abused low-level Iraqi prisoners without authorization, more for their own entertainment than for purposes of interrogation, the black sites were part of a formal program approved by the president under which the CIA interrogated high-level detainees.

Nevertheless, Cheney recognized that the wording of McCain's Abu Ghraib bill could also apply to the CIA's activities at the black sites. In the fall of 2005, Cheney and the new CIA director, Porter Goss, went to Capitol Hill and began quietly urging Congress to add language exempting the CIA and its employees from the legislation. As he so often did, Cheney made dire predictions about the possible impact, contending that the provisions of the bill could hamper the president's ability to protect the United States against terrorist attacks. This was the first in what became many years of efforts by Cheney to win public support for protecting CIA employees from legal consequences stemming from the interrogation program.

While Cheney sought to block the bill banning torture, a familiar figure lined up to support McCain and his legislation: Colin Powell, the former secretary of state. He reprised some of the arguments he had made while in office, when he had objected forcefully to the decision not to follow the Geneva Conventions in dealing with the prisoners captured in Afghanistan. Once again, Powell focused primarily on the impact for the U.S. military: if our troops did not treat prisoners humanely, he argued, then America would have a hard time insisting on humane treatment when U.S. troops were captured. Powell joined with nearly thirty other retired generals and admirals to endorse a provision in McCain's bill that would require all interrogations to be conducted under the rules of the Army Field Manual. McCain's legislation "will help deal with the terrible public diplomacy crisis created by Abu Ghraib," Powell said.

Despite Cheney's pleas, Congress approved McCain's bill, formally known as the Detainee Treatment Act, though some vague language was included that gave CIA interrogators some leeway to defend themselves in court. The bill banned cruelty to prisoners and then defined cruelty under the standards of U.S. constitutional law, which in turn defined it as anything that "shocks the conscience."

What followed was a classic example of the ways in which Cheney worked to undercut legislation and redefine policy in the directions he favored. His aide David Addington came up with the argument that when viewed against the risk of another terrorist attack, enhanced interrogation or even waterboarding might not really "shock the conscience." Then Cheney went on television, in an interview with ABC's *Nightline*, to amplify the point, carefully tucking waterboarding and the other harsh techniques into the bland phrase "effective interrogation":

> *Now, you can get into a debate about what shocks the conscience and what is cruel and inhuman. And to some extent, I suppose, that's in the eye of the beholder* [italics added]. But I believe, and we think it's important to remember, that we are in a war against a group of individuals and terrorist organizations that did, in fact, slaughter 3,000 innocent Americans on 9/11, that it's important for us to be able to have effective interrogation of these people when we capture them.

Nevertheless, McCain's bill put pressure on the CIA to rein in its detention and interrogation programs. Despite Cheney's efforts to limit the scope of the new legislation, CIA officials worried about being charged with illegality if the agency continued to use its "enhanced interrogation" techniques without interruption. Goss temporarily halted the program while the agency tried to decide what to do.

In mid-December 2005, only six weeks after the *Washington Post* revealed the existence of the black sites, the *New York Times* pulled back the curtain on another central element in the Bush administration's responses to September 11. This was the program for which Cheney had served as the primary supporter and patron since its inception: the "Stellar Wind" program, which allowed the National Security Agency to collect massive amounts of information on individuals inside the United States without a court order. The Bush administration had sought to prevent publication of the story, but failed. From that point forward, the administration as a whole and Cheney in particular would spend considerable time and effort trying to defend this once-secret surveillance program.

Once again, Powell was asked for comment, but this time he offered no objection to the program. "In the aftermath of 9/11, the American people had one concern that was 'Protect us,'" he said. "I see nothing wrong with the president authorizing these kinds of actions." In condemning the interrogation techniques but not the surveillance, Powell was reflecting his own background in the military: he knew and cared intensely about the treatment of prisoners; he had far less experience with or interest in the NSA and its surveillance techniques.

The next blow to the counterterrorism programs Cheney had championed was struck six months later. This time, the blow came from an institution more powerful than any newspaper: the Supreme Court of the United States. On June 29, 2006, in the case of *Hamdan v. Rumsfeld*, the Court issued a sweeping ruling that struck down the military commissions set up to try detainees. Cheney and his aide David Addington had drafted the executive order to create those commissions and had won Bush's approval for it in late 2001, bypassing Powell's State Department in the process. The Court also ruled that prisoners at Guantanamo Bay were entitled to the protections of the Geneva Conventions. That was, of course, what Colin Powell had argued without success four years earlier.

The Supreme Court decision, coming on the heels of McCain's Detainee Treatment Act, forced the Bush administration to review its programs, including the black sites and "enhanced interrogation." In the debates that followed, Rice played a central role. As secretary of state, she, like Powell before her, found herself besieged by questions from other governments about the treatment of prisoners; even Britain, America's ally in the Iraq War, pressed for details about British detainees.

In the year before the court decision, Rice had begun to urge changes in the administration's policies in the war on terror, though without much success. Her aides had drafted a secret memo proposing that all prisoners in the black sites be transferred into Guantanamo and accorded the protections of the Geneva Conventions. The memo made the argument that considerable time had passed since the terrorism of 2001 and that even if the extraordinary measures adopted after the September 11 attacks had been necessary at the time, they no longer were. Cheney's office and the Pentagon had objected to the memo, and its recommendations were shelved.

Cheney recommended that Bush make as few changes as possible in response to the Supreme Court decision. He suggested that Bush simply ask Congress to overturn the Supreme Court decision by passing a law that said the president possessed full legal authority to take all necessary measures in the war on terror, without seeking congressional authorization.

Rice strongly disagreed. At a National Security Council meeting in August 2006, she recommended that Bush acknowledge the existence of U.S. detention and interrogation programs, close the black sites, and move the detainees to Guantanamo. Cheney countered that the CIA should maintain control of all the detainees and reserve the right to interrogate them. "For several minutes, the Vice President and I went back and forth; no one else spoke," Rice later recalled. "It was the most intense confrontation of my time in Washington, but it was civil, not personal."

Inside the administration, Rice largely won this debate with the vice president, where Powell had not. In September, Bush announced that he was moving all the prisoners out of the CIA's secret sites to the prison at Guantanamo. The president also acknowledged in public the existence of the CIA's "enhanced interrogation" techniques. Meanwhile, Goss's successor as CIA director, Michael Hayden, banned seven of the thirteen "enhanced" techniques the CIA had employed, including waterboarding.

Even though the administration later persuaded Congress to pass a law setting up military commissions in a way that would satisfy the Supreme Court, and even though the CIA carefully retained the option to bring prisoners to black sites in the future, the new limitations on detention and interrogation nevertheless amounted to a stinging defeat for Cheney. Where he had once operated largely without oversight or restrictions, now his programs were subject to limitations set by the courts and Congress. A new dynamic was taking hold: Cheney was on the defensive, Rice was gaining in influence, and Bush was no longer so willing to heed the advice of his vice president.

* * *

In the months following the invasion of Iraq, Cheney, Rumsfeld, and other administration officials had been slow to acknowledge that the violence against American forces there was attributable to an organized insurgency. By 2004 it was no longer possible to deny its existence. And in the spring of 2005, Cheney came up with a new formulation to minimize the impact of what was happening on the ground in Iraq: the insurgency was in its "last throes," he said. In June 2006, more than a year later, when there was no sign of improvement in the war, he was asked if he still believed the insurgency was in its last throes. Cheney said he did.

His "last throes" predictions served as a bookend to Cheney's claim before the war that U.S. forces would be greeted as liberators. In both instances, he was seeking to win support for the war, but in doing so, he gave the American public a false picture of the calamitous reality inside Iraq, which was now moving toward civil war.

Years later, Cheney admitted to a degree of miscalculation, though he blamed it in part on the nature of Iraqi society. "It is fair to say that we underestimated the difficulty of rebuilding a traumatized and shattered society," he would write in his memoir. He also acknowledged that the administration had misjudged the strength of the insurgency. "I don't think anybody anticipated the level of violence that we've encountered," he said. "We didn't anticipate . . . the devastation that 30 years of Saddam's rule had wrought, if you will, on the psychology of the Iraqi people." In saying that no one had anticipated what happened, Cheney was inaccurate again: the Middle East specialists in the State Department and the CIA had warned before the war of the chaos and the sectarian strife that could follow an American invasion. Those warnings had been ignored.

By the fall of 2006, some Bush administration officials were coming to far more pessimistic views of the war than those of the vice president. "Mr. President, what we are doing is not working—really not working. It's failing," Rice told Bush after one visit to Baghdad that fall. Cheney was sitting alongside as Rice gave the president her report, but he said nothing.

Outside the administration, support for the war had long since faded—and the critics of the war now included Colin Powell. Nearly two years out of office, Powell was traveling frequently around the country, giving speeches. He talked about many different subjects, but he was always asked about the war. He was in an awkward position because it was his own speech to the United Nations that had laid out the administration's justifications for military action. Powell tried to find ways around the problem. He told one audience that the initial invasion had gone well, but then "the insurgency started, and we pretended it wasn't happening." It was now becoming a civil war, he said, "even if some of my colleagues, including the White House, don't want to call it that." In December, in a television interview, he said simply, "The United States is losing in Iraq."

* * *

Dick Cheney's standing had begun to diminish after the 2004 election, but in the last two months of 2006, he took another blow, one from which he never really recovered.

Earlier that fall, Senator Mitch McConnell, the second-ranking Republican in the chamber, told Bush in a private meeting that the president had become so unpopular that the Republicans could lose control of Congress in the upcoming midterm elections. McConnell urged Bush to begin withdrawing troops from Iraq. Bush refused; he decided he wasn't going to let domestic politics influence what he did in Iraq.

The results in November bore out McConnell's forecast. The Democrats took control of the House of Representatives for the first time since 1994, and they gained six seats in the Senate to become the majority there. As Bush colorfully described the results the next day, he and the Republicans had taken "a thumping." None of this, by itself, had any direct bearing on Cheney. However, Bush had been considering further changes in his administration, changes he had held in abeyance until after Election Day.

In late October, Bush called in Cheney and told him, "I've decided to make a change at Defense." He was going to fire Rumsfeld. Cheney had fought to get Rumsfeld the job, he had twice gone to great lengths to persuade Bush not to fire Rumsfeld (after Abu Ghraib and after the 2004 election), and he had worked to keep Rumsfeld himself from quitting. As Cheney drily recounted, "This time, the president didn't wait around after he told me he had made up his mind. He turned around and was out the door fast. He knew I'd be opposed, and I suspect he didn't want to hear the arguments he knew I'd make."

In one quick move, Bush had dismissed Cheney's closest ally at the top level of the Bush administration and in the process made clear that he was confident and firm in his own judgments. He didn't want to hear disagreements or even receive further advice from the vice president.

There was more to come. Bush had also selected Rumsfeld's replacement without consulting Cheney. The new secretary of defense would be Robert Gates. He was a close friend of Rice; during the administration of the president's father, Gates had been deputy national security advisor while Rice worked under Gates as the NSC's leading specialist on the Soviet Union. When Bush told her that he intended to appoint Gates, Rice was enthusiastic. "I could barely contain my joy," she said. Cheney, of course, was not so pleased.

If there were any doubt that Bush was aiming to limit Cheney's influence, the president's job interview with Gates made the point clear. Gates met secretly with the president at his ranch in Crawford, Texas, where the two men talked for an hour, mostly about Iraq. Near the end of the conversation, Bush asked if Gates had any questions. Gates said no. Bush smiled and asked, simply, "Cheney?" Gates smiled and let the president answer his own question. "He is a voice, an important voice, but only one voice," Bush told him. That was, to say the least, an extraordinary message for this president to deliver.

In preparing to take charge, Gates sought out advice from a few people who understood the Pentagon and how it worked. One of them was Colin Powell, whom Gates described as an old friend. "Colin not only knew the Pentagon well, but retained many good contacts (and sources) in uniform," Gates later explained. That was, of course, one reason that Cheney and Rumsfeld had been so wary and mistrustful of Powell during Bush's first term.

* * *

In the final two years of the Bush administration, Dick Cheney was a diminished figure. The president no longer heeded his advice in the way he once had. Gates saw eye to eye with Rice on most issues, including the need for diplomacy even with adversaries and the importance of limiting further American military involvements overseas.

It did not take long for the overall pattern to emerge. "By early 2007, Vice President Cheney was the outlier on the team," Gates recalled. In top-level meetings, he said, Cheney "got to the point where he would often open his remarks with 'I know I'm going to lose this argument' or 'I know I'm alone on this.'"

Cheney's problem went far beyond the amity between Rice and Gates. He was also at odds with other senior officials in the White House, including the president. After a *Washington Post* columnist reported in the spring of 2007 that some administration officials were thinking of changing policy in a way that would appeal more to the Democratic majority in Congress, Cheney told Bush that he needed to do something about the leaks, which he said were harming the president. Afterward, Steve Hadley, the national security advisor, came to see Cheney, closed the door, and told him that he, Hadley, had been the source of the leaks and that he had spoken to the columnist at the instruction of the president.

For years, European diplomats and Washington columnists had sought out Cheney, attracted by his grave demeanor, his deep voice, and the way he took their questions seriously and offered answers that focused on dire consequences, if not doom. They had viewed him as above the day-to-day concerns of other politicians. But there had always been a hidden dimension to their respect for him: consciously or not, they recognized the power he wielded.

By 2007, that power was eroding fast. "What Has Happened to Dick Cheney?" ran the title of one influential newspaper column. Speculation began to creep into the press that perhaps Cheney's heart problems had caused the change. Yet Cheney had had heart problems for a quarter century, and no one had resorted to cardiological explanations before. What had changed was that the president and the secretary of defense no longer heeded Cheney's views. And this new reality was in turn a reflection of the fact that his views and policy recommendations no longer commanded much public support. Over the previous six years, his predictions—that Iraq possessed weapons of mass destruction, that the Iraqi people would greet American troops as liberators, that the insurgency in Iraq was in its last throes—had simply not been borne out. Cheney had been too wrong too often.

* * *

Bush followed up his appointment of Robert Gates with a series of changes in his Iraq policy. The president ordered a surge in American forces there and named a new military commander, David Petraeus, to carry out a new counterinsurgency strategy.

The changes were among the few in Bush's final two years that found Cheney largely in agreement. The vice president became a strong supporter of the surge. Gates and Hadley had also agreed on the need for more troops, whereas Rice had been skeptical of the idea. However, there was an important change in the underlying dynamic: Bush himself was the driving force behind the surge. Cheney was more a follower than a leader.

From outside the administration, Colin Powell voiced the sort of open dissent from which he had refrained while in office. As Bush was nearing a decision about whether to increase troops, Powell appeared on CBS's *Face the Nation* to warn in unqualified terms against it. "I am not persuaded that another surge of troops into Baghdad for the purposes of suppression of this communitarian violence, this civil war, will work," he declared.

Powell was now clearly speaking in the role of a former chairman of the Joint Chiefs of Staff, harking back to the rules for the use of force he had helped develop under Caspar Weinberger in the Reagan administration: "If somebody proposes that additional troops be sent, if I were still chairman of the Joint Chiefs of Staff, my first question to whoever is proposing [a surge]: what mission is it that these troops are to accomplish?"

Powell was, moreover, concerned about the impact of the Iraq War on the institution in which he had spent most of his adult life. Amid the ongoing wars in Afghanistan and Iraq, he asserted, the U.S. Army was "about broken."

* * *

Cheney's loss of influence in the final two years of the Bush presidency was most noticeable when it came to the administration's policies toward two other countries: North Korea and Iran, the other two members of the "axis of evil" Bush had singled out in 2002. Whereas Bush had chosen to use military force against Iraq, he now explored the opposite approach, diplomacy, to persuade North Korea and Iran to abandon their nuclear programs. A general pattern soon emerged at the top levels of the administration: Rice pressed for greater scope for the State Department to negotiate with Iran and North Korea, and Gates generally supported these efforts, believing strongly that the United States should avoid new military involvements while the wars in Iraq and Afghanistan were still being waged. Bush gave Rice the backing and leeway to go forward.

Cheney became the principal opponent of these efforts, arguing that the administration was making useless concessions, and sometimes suggesting (in the case of Iran) that the administration solve the problem once and for all through the use of military force. Indeed, in dealing with both countries, Cheney contended that the United States should at least threaten war, even if it didn't actually go to war. "I believed that our diplomacy would have a far greater chance of being effective if the North Koreans and Iranians understood that they faced the possibility of military action if the diplomacy failed," Cheney later explained.

Cheney had been dealing with the North Korea issue for a long time, dating back to his tenure as secretary of defense under George H. W. Bush, and he had always taken a hard line. One Pentagon official recalled how, at the beginning of the 1990s, he and several of his associates, including Paul Wolfowitz, tried to persuade Cheney that the United States might try to experiment with a slightly different approach. Cheney said, "I want to hear how you argue this," and then sat smiling through their presentation. He was polite and friendly, but he made it clear that this was just a game. There was no way he was going to relax the policy.

A decade later, during George W. Bush's first term, the State Department occasionally tried to explore possibilities for diplomacy with North Korea, but the White House restricted them, with Cheney leading the way. In one instance, the White House rewrote the State Department's instructions for a trip by Assistant Secretary of State James Kelly, to make clear that he could have no side conversations with the North Koreans, no dinner or socializing with them, and should not even sit in the center of the negotiating table opposite them. Powell was furious.

In 2006, North Korea fired a series of missiles into the Sea of Japan and then conducted its first nuclear test. In response, the Bush administration persuaded the United Nations to impose a tough new series of economic sanctions. But it also launched a diplomatic initiative, led by

Rice and Christopher Hill, the assistant secretary of state for East Asian and Pacific affairs. Over the next two years, Hill negotiated some concessions: the North Koreans temporarily shut down their nuclear reactor at Yongbyon and blew up the reactor's cooling tower there in a staged television spectacular. But North Korea balked at any serious steps to abandon its nuclear weapons program; it made promises to provide an accounting of its nuclear activities and then repeatedly put off doing so while continuing to demand a series of rewards from the United States and other countries.

As Hill went forward with his diplomacy, Cheney opposed him, step by step. The vice president's approach reflected his broader view that it made no sense to negotiate with a rogue regime like North Korea, because the leaders in Pyongyang could not be trusted to carry out any agreement. It was better, he argued, to apply economic pressure, play for time, and see if the regime might eventually collapse.

"Hill and Rice made concession after concession to the North Koreans," Cheney complained. "I concluded that our diplomats had become so seized with cutting a deal, any deal with the North Koreans, that they had lost sight of the real objective, which was forcing the North to give up its weapons." In this case, Cheney's predictions about the North Koreans proved accurate. Even though in October 2008 the Bush administration removed North Korea from its list of state sponsors of terrorism, Pyongyang never provided verification that it had stopped its nuclear program.

A similar dynamic played out with Iran: Rice sought negotiations, which she conducted through her undersecretary of state, William Burns. The president supported her efforts while Cheney resisted.

Burns recalled the scene when Rice went to the White House in 2008 to suggest it was time to talk to the Iranians. "I marched over with her. She had gotten a meeting with the president and the vice president, and she made the pitch, and the president right away agreed. I'm sure she had talked to him ahead of time, and had talked to Hadley. Cheney was not happy, and he argued against it in there."

Unlike with North Korea, Cheney was willing to consider a military attack on Iran—and indeed, suggested the idea more than once. At one point, Gates, on a trip to the Middle East, told the king of Saudi Arabia that Bush wouldn't use force against Iran because he would be impeached if he did. When Cheney heard about this, he got the administration to send word to the king that Gates was speaking only for himself, not reflecting U.S. policy.

One of Cheney's regular arguments was that the Bush administration needed to "take care of" Iran's nuclear program before it left office. As Bush's time in the White House was running out, with Burns's negotiations in deadlock, Cheney argued that the future of Iran's nuclear program should not be left up to the next president, who might be less inclined to use force.

Cheney also suggested that if the Bush administration didn't want to bomb Iran's nuclear facilities, it should encourage or allow Israel to do so. This was the other important difference between Iran and North Korea: Iran's location in the Middle East; it was not far from Israel. Indeed, Burns observed, Cheney tended to support "not just any Israeli point of view, but usually the most right-wing one." In particular, Cheney seemed to sympathize with Israel's willingness to use military force or covert intelligence operations to achieve its objectives overseas—and to defy international opinion or European opposition in the process.

Israeli officials and pro-Israeli groups felt, with good reason, that the vice president was their special friend and that, through Cheney, they had "a direct line into the White House," as Rice later put it. She later complained that during a crisis in Lebanon, Cheney was having his own private conversations with the Israelis, meeting them on his own, without the presence of other Bush administration officials—thereby undercutting Rice's own negotiations and, she feared, leading Israel to believe the United States might support Israeli military action.

* * *

In the early spring of 2007, the director of the Mossad, Israel's foreign intelligence service, came to Washington with satellite pictures showing the construction of a nuclear reactor in Syria. The reactor was strikingly similar to a North Korean nuclear facility, and further intelligence from the CIA showed that North Korean nuclear specialists were working with the Syrians to build the plant.

Israel's prime minister, Ehud Olmert, specifically requested that the United States destroy the Syrian plant. Cheney recommended strongly that Bush agree to Israel's request, arguing (as he had often done) that the use of force would "send an important message," both to the North Koreans and to the Syrians. It would "demonstrate our seriousness" concerning proliferation of weapons and would "enhance our credibility" in the Middle East, where other countries' leaders would recognize that the United States was willing to use force.

Those phrases capture an essential difference between Cheney and Powell. For Cheney, military action was not merely a means to overcome a specific adversary. It was also a message, a demonstration, a show of strength to other countries. Conversely, an unwillingness to use force was, for him, a sign of weakness—and thus to be avoided at all costs. For Powell, however, the use of military force wasn't a signal or a message to be delivered, but rather, a problem to be addressed: you had to know how to do it, and you had to make sure you were successful—and even if you were, there were invariably unforeseen consequences.

On the question of an American attack on Syria, as with Iran, Gates and Rice teamed up in opposition to Cheney. "I was convinced Americans were tired of war, and I knew firsthand how overstretched and stressed our troops were," Gates wrote. Thus, whereas in Bush's first six years Cheney had the regular support of the secretary of defense, in the final two years he did not. When it came time for Bush and his top aides to make a decision on an American strike to destroy the Syrian reactor, Cheney argued in favor. Bush then asked, "Does anyone here agree with the vice president?" As Cheney later recalled ruefully, "Not a single hand went up around the room."

Nothing could have better demonstrated Cheney's loss of influence. Nevertheless, he did achieve a partial victory of sorts. Olmert told Bush that if the United States didn't destroy the Syrian nuclear reactor, Israel would do so on its own. Gates and Rice wanted Bush to deliver a strong warning to Israel not to act. But Bush believed Israel was confronting what it considered an existential threat, and he was unwilling to confront Olmert over the issue. On September 6, 2007, Israel used its own warplanes to destroy the reactor.

* * *

By Cheney's final year as vice president, there were occasions when he operated more on his own than as a member of the Bush administration.

In 2007, the U.S. Court of Appeals for the District of Columbia

Circuit struck down a ban on handguns in Washington, DC, on the grounds that it violated the Second Amendment. The Bush administration appealed the ruling to the Supreme Court, arguing that the lower-court ruling was too broad and that it should be overturned. In February 2008, a large group of senators and members of the House filed a friend-of-the-court brief on the opposite side, urging the Supreme Court to rule that the Second Amendment did in fact apply to a ban on handguns. Viewed from a distance, none of this was particularly unusual. The Justice Department regularly appeals lower-court decisions, and from time to time members of Congress join together to file a brief that lays out their own views.

But there was something unusual, indeed startling, about the final signature added at the last minute to the congressional brief in this case: "President of the United States Senate Richard B. Cheney." In other words, in his often forgotten role as president of the Senate, Cheney was taking a position before the Supreme Court at variance with the administration in which he served as vice president.

Cheney had become involved after a congressional staff member telephoned David Addington to tell him about the preparation of the legal brief. Addington alerted Cheney, who decided to join in with the members of Congress. (Later, when White House chief of staff Josh Bolten tried to rebuke Addington for his role in these events, Addington told Bolten that he worked only for the vice president, not for the White House chief of staff.)

In many other respects, however, Cheney operated in the final year of the Bush administration just as he had in the earlier years. He exhibited the same attributes, the same attitudes and beliefs. In March, on the fifth anniversary of the invasion of Iraq, the ABC correspondent Martha Raddatz interviewed Cheney about the war.

"Two thirds of Americans say it's not worth fighting," Raddatz told the vice president. Cheney responded with a single word: "So?"

There was a long pause. "So?" Raddatz persisted. "You don't care what the American people think?"

"No," Cheney answered. "I think you cannot be blown off course by the fluctuations in the public opinion polls."

Not surprisingly, Cheney's "So?" attracted plenty of attention. It reflected hardheartedness toward public sentiment in the midst of an ongoing war. Yet it was also vintage Cheney, a reflection of the dim, narrow view he had always held toward public opinion. Cheney's way of thinking was almost formalistic: The only measurement of public opinion that counted at all was the one taken at the polls on Election Day. In between, elected leaders were supposed to make decisions on their own, without regard to whether those decisions were popular. Indeed, in line with Cheney's obsession with the general themes of strength and weakness, defying public opinion was "strong" and doing what seemed popular was "weak."

This was, of course, the outlook of someone who had never run for office on his own outside Wyoming and who had obtained his high-level positions through appointment. "He really didn't give a damn if people didn't like him or didn't agree with him. He really couldn't have cared less. He was really an un-politician politician," said Aaron Friedberg.

Cheney also never second-guessed his decisions. He acknowledged error only when he could scarcely avoid doing so; and when he did, he tended to redirect blame elsewhere. When the insurgency in Iraq turned out not to be in its "death throes," as he had claimed in 2005 and 2006, he could admit several years later that he had been wrong, but he went on to say that he had underestimated what Saddam Hussein had done to Iraq.

In the end, Cheney's way of operating in Washington turned out to be simply counterproductive even for his own goals. He did not develop the skill necessary for building a consensus. He did not learn to accept the checks and balances that are inherent in America's constitutional system. With his extensive experience both in the executive branch and in Congress, he could theoretically have emerged as a leader in forging agreements and compromises between these two branches of government. In practice, though, his mistrust of Congress combined with his personal qualities (his innate secretiveness, his reserve, his reluctance to engage in give-and-take) in a way that caused him to refrain from seeking to reach solutions with those who disagreed with him. In both Bush administrations, Cheney strongly opposed asking Congress for approval to launch military action, but in both cases, the president rejected his advice.

Above all, Cheney was not given to agonized self-reflection in the fashion of Robert McNamara in the later stages of the Vietnam War. And so, five years after the invasion of Iraq, at a point when nearly four thousand Americans had been killed, it was not out of character for Cheney to answer a question about American sentiment against the war with a simple "So?"

* * *

The presidential election of 2008 was the first in more than half a century in which neither the incumbent president nor the incumbent vice president ran for his party's nomination. Eight years earlier, Bush had said that one of the reasons he chose Cheney as his running mate was that Cheney harbored no presidential ambitions of his own, unlike Al Gore, Dan Quayle, or, for that matter, Bush's own father.

Nothing had changed in those calculations. Bush was prohibited from running for a third term, and Cheney sat on the sidelines, watching the 2008 election unfold just as Bush did. Senator John McCain, Bush's principal rival for the nomination eight years earlier, emerged as the Republican nominee.

Cheney's inactive role in 2008 extended well beyond merely not running. Other Republican candidates kept as far away from him as they could. Cheney didn't campaign for them because he wasn't asked. At the Republican National Convention in St. Paul, he was scheduled to speak early on the opening night, a time when few people would be watching. However, a powerful hurricane caused the first night's program to be cancelled, and Cheney didn't come to the convention at all. Thus, he was not present for the introduction of McCain's running mate, Governor Sarah Palin of Alaska, a vice-presidential candidate who was the opposite of Cheney in everything from personal style to governmental experience.

Shortly after McCain's nomination, the Bush administration was confronted with the financial crisis that would consume the remainder of its time in office. Cheney's conduct during that crisis was emblematic of where he stood within the Republican Party at the end of his many years in government. Faced with the potential collapse of some of the nation's biggest financial institutions, Bush drew up a $700 billion rescue package, the Troubled Asset Relief Program (TARP). Conservative Republicans in Congress balked at approving it, calling it a bailout and arguing that it represented the sort of expensive big-government solution they had always opposed.

Throughout his career, Cheney had always identified himself as a conservative. In theory one might have envisioned him aligning himself with the congressional Republicans in opposing the TARP legislation, much as he had joined with Congress in opposing gun control earlier that year.

But that didn't happen. Cheney worked hard to line up Republican votes for the passage of TARP. Saving the economy was vastly more important to him than positioning himself with fellow conservatives. Financial collapse would have diminished America's power and its standing in the world, which had been Cheney's core interest since his earliest days in government. Moreover, throughout his career he had enjoyed close ties to the American business community, which was lobbying hard for the rescue package. In opposing the TARP legislation, Republicans in Congress were starting down the road toward a new form of economic populism that would later emerge in the Tea Party movement. Cheney was not joining in.

* * *

For Colin Powell, the 2008 election brought a new problem he hadn't faced before: which candidate should he endorse? He was a registered Republican; he had served three consecutive Republican presidents as national security advisor, chairman of the Joint Chiefs of Staff, and secretary of state. He had endorsed Republican candidates and had spoken at Republican conventions. He also got along well with John McCain, the party's nominee. Over the years, the two men had often found themselves in agreement, sharing the same pro-military perspective on issues ranging from opposing torture to maintaining the defense budget.

Still, Powell found much to admire in the Democratic nominee, Barack Obama: not only the historic nature of Obama's candidacy as the first African American major-party nominee, but also his personality, cool demeanor, and sense of balance. And so, Powell temporized through most of 2008 without saying whom he would support. He didn't attend the Republican National Convention.

He waited until mid-October and then endorsed Obama. In the end, the decisive factor for Powell was the way the Republican Party was changing. "I have some concerns about the direction the Republican Party has taken in recent years," he said on NBC's *Meet the Press.* "It has moved more to the right than I would like to see it." In particular, he pointed to rising anti-Muslim sentiment among Republicans. He denounced those Republicans who claimed Obama was a Muslim, when he had been a Christian all his life. "But what if he is?" Powell added. "Is there something wrong with being a Muslim in this country? The answer is no."

Powell was speaking a few years before Donald Trump began his rise to the top of the Republican Party. But he had accurately gauged where the Republicans were heading, and he wanted no part of it.

* * *

During the transition to the next administration, Cheney had one remaining important piece of business: he wanted Bush to pardon Scooter Libby, his former chief of staff. After Libby's conviction in 2007, he had been sentenced to thirty months in prison and was stripped of his license to practice law. A few weeks later, the president had commuted his sentence, so that he served no jail time. Yet the question of a pardon was left open until the final weeks of the administration.

Cheney pushed insistently. He pointed out that Powell's deputy, Richard Armitage, was the official who had first leaked the name of CIA agent Valerie Plame—the action that had given rise to the investigation of Libby. He also pressed for Bush to meet in person with Libby. Bush and his chief of staff, Josh Bolten, refused to allow such a meeting; instead, Libby met with two lawyers assigned by the president to review the case.

In the White House, Bush agonized over the case until the final weekend of his term, before deciding against granting a pardon. Cheney's reaction was revealing: "You are leaving a good man wounded on the field of battle," he told Bush. In Cheney's mind-set, he and his team had been fighting a war, in Washington as well as overseas, and his aides were soldiers in combat.

Bush later acknowledged that Cheney's words had stung. He consoled himself that his friendship with Cheney survived because Cheney had said a few days later that he was honored to have served with Bush. Nevertheless, in Cheney's memoir three years later, he included a sentence about the Libby pardon that was devastatingly critical of the president. "George Bush made courageous decisions as president," he wrote, "and I wish that pardoning Scooter Libby had been one of them."

* * *

On Inauguration Day, January 20, 2009, the nation witnessed the swearing in of Barack Obama and Joe Biden, with their predecessors Bush and Cheney looking on. There was one noteworthy surprise at the ceremony: Cheney was in a wheelchair. He had been packing boxes in the vice-presidential mansion over the previous weekend and had injured his back. The injury wasn't particularly serious or lasting, but the result was that after eight years of seeking to project strength, whether in the Middle East or at home, Dick Cheney, on the final day of the Bush administration, was a frail, elderly-looking figure.

Cheney had come to Washington four decades earlier seeking to land a staff job in the Congress he later came to disdain. Since then, he had run the White House staff, had led the Pentagon through a successful war, had ridden alongside Colin Powell through cheering crowds in a victory parade, and had served as vice president during an especially turbulent period when America was attacked and then during a war of choice that went terribly awry. Now, at the very end of his career, he was leaving government as a diminished figure. Dick Cheney's last days in the George W. Bush administration were, in their own way, just as humbling as Colin Powell's had been four years earlier.

EPILOGUE

On September 8, 2015, a small group of demonstrators gathered outside the Washington headquarters of the American Enterprise Institute to protest an appearance by former vice president Dick Cheney. It was a late summer day, already getting warm by mid-morning, but the heat did nothing to dissipate the anger of the protesters. They hoisted signs reading, "He Misled Us Once, Don't Let Him Do It Again!" and "Cheney Wrong on Iraq, Wrong on Iran!"

It had been six and a half years since the end of the Bush administration, but in retirement, Cheney was still speaking out on many of the same issues that had preoccupied him while in office: the importance of American power, especially military power; the need for extensive surveillance and what he still called "enhanced interrogation" to combat terrorism; and, overall, the need for the United States to avoid any appearance of weakness, compromise, or conciliation in its dealings with the rest of the world.

The occasion that had brought out the protesters on this day was a speech by Cheney about an agreement that President Obama had just concluded with Iran to restrict its nuclear weapons program. Under it, Iran had agreed to limit its production of nuclear fuel over a fifteen-year period in exchange for a lifting of economic sanctions. Earlier in his presidency, Obama had won unprecedented international support for those economic sanctions; now, through multilateral diplomacy, he was proposing to ease them.

Inside the building, the audience for Cheney's speech included former aides such as Scooter Libby, Paul Wolfowitz, and Eric Edelman. There were also officials who represented a younger generation of Cheney-ites: Senator Tom Cotton of Arkansas, who was emerging as a leading hawk in the Senate, and Cheney's daughter Liz Cheney Perry, who was preparing to run the following year for her father's old congressional seat from Wyoming.

Dick Cheney was seventy-four years old; his shoulders stooped and his back hunched considerably more than when he was in the White House. But his voice seemed undiminished. And on that day, as he spent forty minutes excoriating President Obama's Iran deal, he summoned forth virtually all the time-tested Cheney motifs, the themes and patterns of thought that he had used throughout his career.

There were the usual predictions of doom. The results of the Iran deal "could well be catastrophic," Cheney warned. He invoked history to show that he was more far-sighted than his opponents. "I know of no nation in history that has agreed to guarantee that the means of its own destruction will be in the hands of another nation, particularly one that is hostile," he declared, apparently overlooking the series of arms control agreements the United States had negotiated with the Soviet Union during the Cold War. "Now, as at other fateful turns in our history, the alternative to nightmarish scenarios that we all wish to avoid is not to make concession after concession." Cheney also stressed Iran's ties to terrorism—just as, more than a decade earlier, he had repeatedly made claims about Iraq's ties to terrorism. "Iran's ties to terrorist groups are extensive," he said. As evidence, he cited a claim by General Michael Flynn, a former director of the Defense Intelligence Agency, who said that Iran was allowing al-Qaeda operatives to pass through its territory.

Above all, Cheney emphasized the effectiveness of military power. He boasted that the Libyan leader Muammar Gaddafi had given up his nuclear weapons program after seeing how the United States had captured Saddam Hussein in Iraq. Cheney also pointed to how Israel had succeeded in destroying the nuclear reactor that Syria had been building. "In each of these cases, it was either military action or the credible threat of military action that persuaded these rogue regimes to abandon their weapons program," Cheney maintained. He did not call directly for the United States to take military action against Iran, but the idea hung in the air as a possibility—much as Cheney intended it to. His audience reacted to his speech with warm, hearty applause.

Colin Powell, not surprisingly, took an entirely different view on Iran. Powell threw his support to the agreement Cheney so vehemently opposed. "I think it is a good deal," he said on *Meet the Press* that same week. Powell said the opponents of the deal—he did not name Cheney— "are forgetting the reality that they [the Iranians] have been on a super-highway for the last ten years to create a nuclear weapon or a nuclear program, with no speed limit." Iran would get nothing until it began to comply with the deal, he pointed out. Finally, as he had so often argued as secretary of state, Powell said that the United States did not want to be isolated from its European allies. "All of these other countries that were in it with us are going to move forward, the U.N. is going to move forward," he said. America did not want to be left "standing on the sidelines."

* * *

Thus, back in private life, Cheney and Powell continued to see the world differently, resuming the old disagreements of the past. Where Cheney spoke of the efficacy of military power, Powell emphasized the importance of America's alliances, seeing them as the principal source of U.S. strength. Cheney tended to denigrate diplomacy; Powell saw it as a necessity for the United States to maintain unity with its allies. Cheney was willing to topple regimes of countries that stood in America's way. Powell, by contrast, always emphasized the importance of stability; he was reluctant to overturn the status quo. During that same *Meet the Press* appearance in which Powell endorsed the Iran nuclear deal, he also criticized some of Obama's policies during the Arab Spring. "Once you pull out the top of a government, you can expect a mess," he said that day. "We saw that totally in Libya [after the fall of Gaddafi]. Perfect example. We got rid of [Hosni] Mubarak [in Egypt], and now we have another general in charge of the country after a detour with the Muslim Brotherhood. So be very, very careful when you try to impose your system or your thinking on a society that's been around for thousands of years."

These last words were a fair summation of Powell's views throughout his career. Under the political shorthand that we commonly use, Cheney is called a conservative, and that description is accurate. But in a handful of specific ways—that is, when it came to going to war or seeking to overthrow a regime—it was Cheney who sought to change the status quo and Powell who was profoundly conservative, a general who was reluctant to disturb existing arrangements.

Looking back at his long career, Powell reflected mordantly on some of the ironies inherent in the public debates. "People asked me for ten years, 'Why didn't you go to Baghdad?'" he said, referring to the aftermath of the Gulf War. "And then we went to Baghdad, and no one has asked me since." He still believed in his old doctrine calling for the use of overwhelming or decisive force, the idea cast aside by Donald Rumsfeld and Tommy Franks before the 2003 invasion of Iraq. They favored a much smaller force, Powell said, "and we're still there [in Iraq]. We're still there in Afghanistan, seventeen years later."

Asked fifteen years after the invasion of Iraq how he now felt about that war, Powell replied, "My view is that it would have been great if we could have avoided a war. We didn't need a war at that time. Iraq was not threatening anything or anybody." Yet this was tragic hindsight: Powell had not opposed going to war, but had, in fact, made the case to the United Nations that Iraq's weapons of mass destruction were threatening the world.

* * *

In retirement, Cheney and Powell even seemed to disagree about retirement itself. Cheney continued to speak out on the issues of the day, setting forth his views in occasional op-ed pieces for the *Wall Street Journal*, which he wrote with his daughter Liz. In contrast, Powell mostly stepped back, although he still did television interviews from time to time. Once, he walked by mistake into a room in a Washington think tank where about fifty or sixty foreign policy specialists had gathered to hear a presentation by someone else. Virtually everyone in the room had either worked with Powell or covered him at the Pentagon or State Department.

Powell didn't stop; he hurried out of the room as fast as he could. "I'm just passing through," he murmured.

In private, Powell joked with former colleagues about Cheney's continuing efforts to speak out in retirement. In one email exchange with Condoleezza Rice, she said Cheney should "concentrate on quality time with his grandkids and let it go." Powell shot back, "Hee, hee, he won't."

* * *

It took only a few months after George W. Bush left the White House for Cheney to emerge as the leading spokesman for the policies of the Bush administration's eight years in office. Bush elected not to play that role, and he followed the practice of many earlier presidents in holding back on criticism of his successor. Cheney felt no such restraint.

Soon after he was sworn in, Barack Obama began to reverse some of Bush's antiterrorism measures. He signed an executive order requiring the CIA to conduct all interrogations according to the rules in the Army Field Manual. He announced plans (never realized) to close the prison at Guantanamo Bay. Furthermore, the new Obama team began to move toward public release of some of the memos about interrogation that had been produced in the Bush years.

Cheney was watching closely, and after a few months he had had enough of the silence of retirement. On May 21, 2009, he delivered a speech that amounted to an elaborate attempt to defend the Bush administration's antiterrorism policies, probably the most comprehensive such speech he ever gave. The entire context of the speech was the continuing importance of the September 11 attacks. Cheney portrayed his responses in personal terms, recalling his own experience on that day. "I'll freely admit that watching a coordinated, devastating attack on our country from an underground bunker at the White House can affect how you view your responsibilities," he said.

In a few passages of his speech, Cheney sought merely to delineate issues without offering judgments. "We're left to draw one of two conclusions," he asserted. "You can look at the facts and conclude that the comprehensive strategy [of the Bush administration] has worked, and therefore needs to be continued as vigilantly as ever. Or you can look at the same set of facts and conclude that 9/11 was a one-off event—

coordinated, devastating, but also unique and not sufficient to justify a sustained wartime effort."

However, most of Cheney's remarks amounted to a blistering critique of the changes Obama was trying to make and a determined defense of the intelligence agents who had been involved in interrogating prisoners during the Bush administration. "No moral value held dear by the American people obliges public servants ever to sacrifice innocent lives to spare a captured terrorist from unpleasant things," he said.

Cheney kept up his criticisms throughout Obama's two terms in office. He regularly boasted that the Bush administration's responses to September 11 had succeeded in preventing any similar terrorist attacks inside the United States. In judging Cheney's argument, it is worth noting that Obama prohibited torture and "enhanced interrogation" in his earliest days in office, and yet it turned out that there were no terrorist attacks on the order of September 11 during the eight years of the Obama administration, either. Still, Cheney continued to speak out in public in defense of "enhanced interrogation," even as he continued to insist that it wasn't torture. "It worked," he said in 2018. "If it was my call, I'd do it again."

* * *

Most of the officials who served under George W. Bush wrote books about their time in office, including Cheney, whose memoir, *In My Time*, spans his entire career. One of the only exceptions was Colin Powell, who published no account of his years as secretary of state. Powell's earlier autobiography, *My American Journey*, covers his upbringing, his military career, and his service as national security advisor and chairman of the Joint Chiefs of Staff, and was one of the best-selling nonfiction books of the 1990s. He did not want to do a second memoir.

In 2016, Powell briefly gave vent to how unhappy his experience had been during the George W. Bush years. "That's why I didn't write a memoir of that period," he said. "I have better things to do in life than grind my molars down over those years. I have no passion or desire to go through the ups and downs again."

Powell did write a book of a different kind. *It Worked for Me: In Life and Leadership*, published in 2012, was designed as a series of tips for successful adults, from business executives to army officers. The book touches in passing on a few of Powell's experiences in the Bush years, such as his speech to the United Nations. But discussions of political issues and international affairs were secondary to sections titled "Know Yourself, Be Yourself" and "Trust Your People," or advice such as "I insist on punctuality."

Characteristically, Cheney as author became ever more heavily political as Powell became less so. After writing his memoir, the next book he wrote (together with his daughter Liz) was a foreign policy tract called *Exceptional: Why the World Needs a Powerful America*, a title that sums up his approach to the world. "The damage that Barack Obama has done to our ability to defend ourselves is appalling," the Cheneys conclude. The book, published in 2015, voices the hope that Obama's successor, whoever that person might be, would "recognize that the realistic and credible threat of military force gives substance and meaning to our diplomacy."

After Cheney's book came out, Powell joked about it privately in emails with an old friend, Kenneth Duberstein, who had served with him in the Reagan White House. Speaking of Dick and Liz Cheney, Powell said, "They are idiots and spent force peddling a book that ain't going nowhere."

Powell's disparaging email accurately reflected how the ties between the two men had hardened into outright hostility. Sometimes, after old political adversaries return to private life, they forge new bonds with one another: Bill Clinton and George H. W. Bush come to mind. That was not the case for Powell and Cheney; if anything, they grew still further apart.

During their years at the Pentagon, their relationship had been warm and their views converged. "We thought so much alike that, in the Tank or the Oval Office, we could finish each other's sentences," Powell had written in the mid-1990s. Even during the first year of the George W. Bush administration, as they began to disagree regularly, their personal relations had remained relatively amicable. But the prolonged disagreements over Iraq and the bureaucratic battles that accompanied them had taken their toll. By the time of Powell's last couple of years at the State Department, and even more so afterward, their relationship had deteriorated in a way that became obvious to those who knew and dealt with both men.

The year 2011 marked the twentieth anniversary of the Gulf War. Texas A&M University, which houses the George H. W. Bush Presidential Library and Museum and the Bush School of Government and Public Service, sought to mark the occasion by inviting the leading American officials involved in Operation Desert Storm to an event in College Station, Texas.

In planning this event, Ryan Crocker, the dean of the Bush School, discovered he had a problem: Cheney and Powell didn't want to participate alongside each other. "That was a murderously hard negotiation, one of the toughest negotiations I ever had," said Crocker, who had previously served as U.S. ambassador to Iraq. The crux of the difficulty, he said, was "to get them together on the same stage." In fact, he added, "They never would have done it had it not been for Forty-one"—a reference to President George H. W. Bush.

The organizers arranged for a private plane to fly Cheney, Powell, and Brent Scowcroft from Washington to Texas for the event. Twenty years earlier, the three men had served together as secretary of defense, chairman of the Joint Chiefs of Staff, and national security advisor. Since then, Cheney had fallen out with Powell, and Scowcroft had been at odds with Cheney after criticizing the invasion of Iraq.

At the start of the flight, the atmosphere on board was palpably cold. "They were all hiding behind their newspapers—not even a hello," said Crocker. But during the ride, they began to converse with one another, and to the relief of organizers, there was no overt sign of the earlier tension at the event itself. Indeed, a *New York Times* reporter covering the gathering observed that Powell and Cheney had displayed "an almost chummy rapport." Yet those with a view behind the scenes saw clearly the antipathy between the two men. "For Cheney and Powell, that's when I realized how much they loathed each other," said Crocker.

* * *

The rise of Donald Trump in the 2016 presidential campaign represented something of a dilemma for Dick Cheney. For Powell, on the other hand, Trump represented the realization of a gloomy prophecy.

Some of what Trump said on the campaign trail amounted to a blunt rejection of George W. Bush's presidency. During the Republican primaries, Trump repeatedly disparaged the thinking that had led to the Iraq War. He claimed that he had always been against it, even though the record shows this isn't true: he had at first supported the war. Trump also said that Bush and Cheney had lied about weapons of mass destruction in Iraq—not a novel claim, but a startling one for a Republican candidate to make about the most recent Republican president. Moreover, Trump accused the Bush team of failing to prevent the September 11 attacks. Early in 2016, Cheney appeared on Fox News and denounced Trump. "He sounds like a liberal Democrat to me," the former vice president said. "If he operates the way he's operating, sounding like a liberal Democrat, I don't think he'll get the nomination."

Nevertheless, some things that Trump said appealed to Cheney. Trump was unique among the candidates in his explicit, open support for torture. "Don't tell me it doesn't work—torture works," Trump said in one campaign appearance. "Okay, folks? Torture—you know, half these guys [say]: 'Torture doesn't work.' Believe me, it works. Okay?" Here, the difference between Trump and the former vice president was that Cheney had always maintained that what the United States did after September 11 was "enhanced interrogation," not torture. Trump skipped the nuance and just talked about torture.

To be sure, Cheney might have been more comfortable with one of the other Republican candidates in 2016, such as Marco Rubio or Jeb Bush, based strictly on their more traditionally hawkish views of foreign policy. Indeed, the two presidents under whom Cheney had served, George H. W. Bush and George W. Bush, announced that they would not support Trump and would therefore refrain from any endorsements in 2016. However, Cheney viewed himself as a Republican, indeed a fairly partisan one, and he had fewer qualms about Trump than did the Bushes. In May, he announced that he would support Trump as the Republican nominee.

During the election, as Trump's campaign was gaining strength, Colin Powell's email account was hacked, and his emails were made public on a website called DCLeaks. Powell's office soon confirmed that the emails were genuine, merely one part of the much larger series of hacks that year that included emails from the Democratic National Committee, the Clinton campaign headquarters, and the office of Senator John McCain.

News reports at the time indicated that DCLeaks had Russian connections, and three years later, Robert Mueller's formal report on Russian activities in the 2016 election found that Russia's military intelligence agency, the GRU, had created DCLeaks as a vehicle for releasing information it obtained through its hacking operations.

Powell's emails to his friends and associates showed that he was unflattering to both major-party candidates. He called Trump "a national disgrace and an international pariah." He said of Hillary Clinton, the Democratic nominee, "I would rather not have to vote for her, although she is a friend I respect. A 70-year-old person with a long track record, unbridled ambition, greedy, not transformational."

The emails also demonstrated that, in retirement, Powell was becoming, if anything, ever more skeptical of the value of American military interventions overseas. During 2015–16, as the Islamic State was gaining strength in the Middle East, he wrote that "these are movements, not fixed enemies, and we'd be nuts to send in the American army again in strength." He was against any extended American military role in Syria, and he was opposed to sending U.S. forces back to Iraq. This put Powell in the position of being more dovish concerning the use of American troops than President Obama, who sent a small contingent of troops back to Iraq.

Still, in the end, whatever Powell's misgivings about Hillary Clinton, the 2016 presidential election did not pose a difficult choice for him. Eight years earlier, in explaining why he had supported Obama over his friend and fellow Vietnam veteran John McCain, Powell said he was concerned about the direction of the Republican Party and, in particular, the rising anti-Muslim sentiments within it. By the 2016 election, Trump demonstrated that the party was heading in precisely the direction Powell had feared. In October, Powell formally announced that he was supporting Clinton. His explanation was brief. Trump, he said, "insults us every day" and had sold Americans a "bill of goods" he couldn't deliver.

Powell's private emails give a more detailed explanation of how he felt. General Eric Shinseki, who served as secretary of veterans' affairs in the Obama administration, had emailed Powell in March 2016, urging him to enter the presidential campaign as an alternative to Trump. Powell responded by saying, "C'mon, Rick. I would be 80 upon my first months in office."

He continued: "Yes, every day someone kindly mentions that I should have [run for president]. I didn't want to and nothing has changed." Then he added the broader judgment: "I can't carry the burden of the GOP. They left me years ago."

* * *

As president, Donald Trump presented Cheney with, once again, a complicated calculus. He withdrew from Obama's nuclear agreement with Iran. He pursued policies in the Middle East that were more pro-Israel than even Cheney had been. In 2018, Trump appointed John Bolton, who was close to Cheney, as his national security advisor. And above all, he took the action that Cheney had sought so intensively a decade earlier: he granted a full pardon to Scooter Libby. Cheney issued a quick statement praising the move. "I am grateful that President Trump righted this wrong," he said. On this issue, at least, Trump proved to be more in line with Cheney than George W. Bush had been.

Nevertheless, in other ways, Trump's presidency represented a wholesale rejection of policies and ideas that Cheney had embraced throughout his long career. This was true even on domestic issues such as free trade and fiscal austerity, causes that Cheney had espoused (at least rhetorically) for many years. But it was especially true when it came to foreign policy and national security. Most noteworthy was Trump's courtship of Vladimir Putin. Cheney had throughout his career stood out from among other officials in Washington for his tough, hawkish stance toward Moscow. He had been skeptical that even Mikhail Gorbachev could be an agent of change. During his years in national office, Cheney would have heaped criticism on Trump's eagerness for an accommodation with Putin. Even in retirement, Cheney couldn't entirely hold back. In 2017, he said that Russia's attempts to interfere with the 2016 presidential election in the United States could be considered an "act of war" against the United States. "There's no question there was a very serious effort made by Mr. Putin and his government, his organization, to interfere in major ways with our basic fundamental democratic processes," he added.

So, too, Trump's eagerness for summit meetings with North Korea's leader, Kim Jong-un, ran counter to Cheney's long opposition to any attempts at conciliation with North Korea. During Bush's second term, Cheney had repeatedly scorned Christopher Hill, an assistant secretary of state, for seeking a deal with North Korea, and Condoleezza Rice for supporting the idea. When it came to North Korea, Trump was going much further than the former Bush administration officials Cheney had so determinedly opposed.

Cheney generally tried to keep his disagreements with Trump hidden, but occasionally his unhappiness slipped out. In March 2019, at a private retreat sponsored by the American Enterprise Institute, Cheney repeatedly pressed Vice President Mike Pence to explain and defend Trump's foreign policy. Cheney questioned Trump's concessions to North Korea, his disregard for the intelligence community, and especially Trump's recurrent hostility to American alliances. Trump's treatment of America's allies, Cheney said, "feeds this notion on the part of our allies overseas, especially in NATO, that we're not long for that continued relationship."

Donald Trump, it seemed, was turning the aging Dick Cheney into something of a traditionalist.

* * *

What the Trump administration demonstrated was that the post–Cold War era, in which Powell and Cheney had played such prominent roles, had come to a close. Throughout that era, America remained the nation's leading, unchallenged military and economic power. It used that power on behalf of its worldwide alliance system and a liberal international order.

Cheney and Powell were prominent figures in the era not just because of the positions they held, but also because they frequently represented opposing sides in the recurrent debates of the period. How should the United States use its uncontested military power? Should it use (or threaten) military force to defeat potential rivals, as Cheney maintained, or should it avoid military action and seek where possible to maintain the status quo, as Powell advocated? Should it work in tandem with its allies and the United Nations, as Powell favored, or would the allies and the United Nations get in the way of U.S. objectives, as Cheney often believed? Did international terrorism justify an American response that disregarded all the rules, including the treaties and agreements banning torture, as Cheney argued? Or should the United States treat captured terrorists under the same rules as prisoners of war, as Powell maintained?

These arguments continued well after Cheney and Powell retired from public life. Yet, with the arrival of Donald Trump, the United States was clearly in a new era. Trump frequently belittled the international order that the United States had constructed over the previous seven decades. America began to demean its allies and question the value of alliances. The allies, in turn, began to plan for a world in which they were not tied to the United States. Meanwhile, it was no longer as clear as it had been in the 1990s or the early 2000s that the United States would remain indefinitely the most powerful nation on earth.

Powell and Cheney had begun their careers in the shadow of the Vietnam War. They had risen to prominence in an era when walls were coming down and America was assuming the leadership of a new, globalized world. Early on, at the time of the Gulf War, the two men were able to work closely together because the Cold War was just ending and the underlying disagreements between them didn't seem to matter so much. A decade later, during the George W. Bush administration, at a time when the United States faced no rival power, their differences came to a head.

The world had been transformed once again, and America itself had changed. By 2017, leaders across the world were seeking to put up walls again. Cheney and Powell walled each other off, too. Their era and their debates had become simply history.

Notes

Preface

2 "*Remember the old saw, 'What will all the preachers do'*" Remarks by Gen. Colin L. Powell, commander in chief, Forces Command, to the Association of the United States Army Symposium, Carlisle Barracks, PA, May 16, 1989.

3 "*Our commitment to the exercise*" Italics added. "Remarks by Secretary Cheney at the Center for Strategic and International Studies," May 10, 1989, in Folder 91117-003, USSR Collapse Files, Brent Scowcroft Collection, George H. W. Bush Presidential Records, George H. W. Bush Presidential Library, College Station, Texas. The memo concerning Baker's diplomacy is in this file.

3 "*They said, 'What are you doing?'*" Author interview with Lawrence Wilkerson, December 14, 2015 (hereafter "Wilkerson interview").

5 "*Everywhere Powell would go, he was a rock star*" Author interview with Paul Wolfowitz, December 18, 2015 (hereafter "Wolfowitz interview").

5 "*Colin Powell wasn't inclined to give policy-laden speeches*" Richard N. Haass, *War of Necessity, War of Choice: A Memory of Two Iraq Wars* (New York: Simon and Schuster, 2009), p. 177.

6 "*Lynne Cheney is a lot of the eminence grise here*" Jon Meacham, *Destiny and Power: The American Odyssey of George Herbert Walker Bush* (New York: Random House, 2015), p. 589.

7 *Scowcroft had "a pre-9/11 mindset"* Dick Cheney, *In My Time: A Personal and Political Memoir* (New York: Threshold Editions, 2011), p. 388.

7 "*it was not 9/11. It was the anthrax attacks*" Author interview with Andrew Natsios, December 2, 2016.

1. Useful Young Men

11 "*I would spend nearly twenty years*" Colin L. Powell, *My American Journey* (New York: Ballantine Books, 1995), p. 79.

11 "*I was of the opinion*" Interview with Dick Cheney, March 16, 2000, George H. W. Bush Oral History Project, Miller Center, University of Virginia, Charlottesville, VA (hereafter "Cheney, Miller Center interview").

12 *dance with Princess Diana* Colin Powell, *It Worked for Me* (New York: Harper Perennial, 2012), pp. 237–41.

12   "'*cone in space*'" David Roth, *Sacred Honor: Colin Powell—The Inside Account of His Life and Triumphs* (Grand Rapids, MI: Zondervan Publishing House, 1993), p. 37.

12   *cadet colonel* Powell, *My American Journey*, pp. 27, 34.

13   *had to look on a map* Ken Adelman interview with Colin Powell, *The Washingtonian*, May 1990, p. 67 (hereafter "Adelman interview with Powell").

13   *a month without bathing* Powell, *My American Journey*, p. 94.

14   "*slide-rule prodigies*," "*Deep thinkers*," "*Experts often produce*" Ibid., pp. 98–100.

14   "*willing to pay the price*" Ibid., p. 125.

15   "*half-hearted half-war*," "*politics of last resort*" Ibid., p. 143.

15   "*He was very popular*" Author interview with Dave Gribben, July 18, 2002.

16   "*beer was one of the essentials*" Cheney, *In My Time*, p. 27.

16   *roadside motels . . . bourbon . . . jail* Ibid., pp. 28–30.

16   *Cheney disclosed the arrests* Donald Rumsfeld, *Known and Unknown: A Memoir* (New York: Sentinel, 2011), p. 178.

16   *confess, to Bush and his political adviser* Cheney, *In My Time*, p. 263.

17   "*I didn't spend a lot of time thinking about it*" Cheney, Miller Center interview.

17   "*I had other priorities*" George Wilson, "Cheney Believes Gorbachev Sincere," *Washington Post*, April 5, 1989, p. A-12.

17   *his family urged him to get out* Powell, *It Worked for Me*, p. 192.

18   "*I was more interested*" Roth, *Sacred Honor*, p. 91.

18   *FBI . . . Romney* Author interview with Colin Powell, September 13, 2018 (hereafter "Powell 2018 interview").

18   "*He had the diplomatic finesse*" Author interview with Frank Carlucci, January 11, 2002.

19   *Carlucci "created Colin Powell"* Author interview with Jim Webb, February 21, 2002.

19   '*This isn't going to work*" Cheney, *In My Time*, p. 41.

19   "*I flunked the interview*" Richard Cheney, "Government Must Help Business Flourish," *American Business and the Quest for Freedom* (Washington, DC: Ethics and Public Policy Center, 1986), p. 13.

19   *spent a weekend writing a memo* Author interview with Dave Gribben, December 17, 2001.

20   *the two drunk-driving arrests turned up* Cheney, *In My Time*, p. 51.

20   "*When you gave something to Dick*" Author interview with Frank Carlucci, January 11, 2002.

20   *flipping charts* Cheney, *In My Time*, p. 61.

21   "*Cheney was focused more*" Rumsfeld, *Known and Unknown*, p. 79.

21   "*I watched*," "*we didn't leave a lot of paper*" Cheney, Miller Center interview.

22   *Clausewitz's principles . . . Vietnam* Powell, *My American Journey*, p. 200.

23   *The percentage . . . 7 percent* Bureau of Labor Statistics figures cited in Office of the Under Secretary of Defense, "Population Representation in the Military Services, Fiscal Year 2002," Table D-27, Black Active Component Officers by Service with Civilian Comparison Group, FYs 1973–2002, https://www.rand.org/content/dam/rand/pubs/monographs/MG265/images/webG1209.pdf.

23   *Alexander tripled the number of black generals* Henry Louis Gates Jr., *Thirteen Ways of Looking at a Black Man* (New York: Random House, 1997), p. 78.

24   "*Finally!*" Author interview with Colin Powell, June 30, 2003 (hereafter "Powell 2003 interview").

24   "*I ain't that black*" Gates, *Thirteen Ways*, pp. 83–84.

24   *Blacks in Jamaica* Adelman interview with Powell.

24   "*This work you're describing*" Powell, *My American Journey*, p. 220.

25   "'*that kind of analytical work*'" Author interview with William Odom, March 28, 2002.

25   *army chief of staff sent word* Powell, *My American Journey*, pp. 226–27.

26   "*a friggin' mess officer*" Letter from Richard Danzig to John Kester, in General Colin J. Powell Papers, National Defense University Library, Fort Lesley J. McNair, Washington, DC.

2. The Quiet Conservative

27 *Rumsfeld was on vacation* Donald Rumsfeld, "Memorandum—Rumsfeld Personal file, August, 1974," Rumsfeld Archive, http://library.rumsfeld.com/doclib/sp/72/08-1974.pdf.

28 *Harlow . . . a list of three possible candidates* Rumsfeld, *Known and Unknown*, p. 168.

28 *future of the Republican Party* Cheney, *In My Time*, p. 68.

28 *"all I've got is you"* Cheney, Miller Center interview.

29 *"No assignment was too small"* Rumsfeld, *Known and Unknown*, pp. 178–79.

29 *a locked safe . . . It was empty* Dick Cheney, "1974-09-29 From Dick Cheney re Safe with Attached Receipt (II-115-4)," September 29, 1974, Rumsfeld Archive, http://library .rumsfeld.com/doclib/sp/146/1974-09-29%20From%20Dick%20Cheney%20re%20 Safe%20with%20Attached%20Receipt%20(II-115-4).pdf.

29 *"Backseat" . . . saltshakers . . . plumbing* See James Mann, *Rise of the Vulcans* (New York: Viking, 2004), pp. 59–60, with files from Gerald R. Ford Presidential Library, Grand Rapids, MI.

30 *"stay out of the national security area"* Author interview with Dick Cheney, December 6, 1996.

30 *"Today, America can regain" . . . Kissinger was irate* Henry Kissinger, *Years of Renewal* (New York: Simon and Schuster, 1999), pp. 534–35.

31 *Rumsfeld and Cheney sent Ford a biting memo* "Memorandum for the President from Donald Rumsfeld and Richard Cheney," Rumsfeld files.

32 *desire to get rid of Secretary of Defense James Schlesinger* Gerald R. Ford, *A Time to Heal* (New York: Harper and Row, 1979), pp. 320–27.

32 *Scowcroft then voluntarily gave up* Bartholomew Sparrow, *The Strategist* (New York: Public Affairs, 2015), pp. 179–80.

32 *"I leaned pretty hard on Don"* Cheney, *In My Time*, p. 92.

33 *"Really, they lived very modestly"* Author interview with Jeanne Kirkpatrick, April 24, 2002.

33 *Ford visited China . . . "Henry didn't like"* Author interview with Dick Cheney, December 6, 1996.

34 *"Dick is great!"* Rumsfeld, *Known and Unknown*, p. 179.

34 *"My method was direct"* Cheney, *In My Time*, p. 94.

34 *"Dick Cheney I don't know anymore"* Jeffrey Goldberg, "Breaking Ranks," *The New Yorker*, Vol. 81, Issue 34, October 31, 2005, p. 54.

35 *"making sure the trains ran on time"* Author interview with Cheney, December 6, 1996.

35 *"I was careful"* Cheney, Miller Center interview.

36 *"more conservative" . . . "on most issues"* Ibid.; Craig Shirley, *Reagan's Revolution: The Untold Story of the Campaign That Started It All* (Nashville, TN: Nelson Current, 2005), p. 52.

36 *"to the right of Ford, Rumsfeld, or, for that matter, Genghis Khan"* Robert T. Hartmann, *Palace Politics* (New York: McGraw-Hill, 1980), p. 283.

36 *"My own strong feeling . . . conservative wing of the Republican Party* Memorandum, Dick Cheney to Don Rumsfeld, July 8, 1975, Box 10, Richard Cheney Files, Rumsfeld Archives, Gerald R. Ford Presidential Library, Grand Rapids, MI.

37 *"I hadn't agreed"* Cheney, *In My Time*, p. 116.

38 *Congress asserted a new, more powerful role* Kissinger, *Years of Renewal*, pp. 832, 846.

39 *hypothetical . . . executive privilege* Richard Cheney, handwritten notes re strategy to cope with Church Committee, March 24, 1975, Office of the Deputy Assistant to the President, White House, Gerald R. Ford Presidential Library, Grand Rapids, MI.

39 *Cheney edited it* "Gerald R. Ford White House Altered Rockefeller Commission Report: Removed Section on CIA Assassination Plots," February 29, 2016, National Security Archive, http://nsarchive.gwu.edu/NSAEBB/NSAEBB543-Ford-White-House-Altered -Rockefeller-Commission-Report.

39 *bringing criminal charges . . . search Hersh's apartment* Box 6, Folder "Intelligence— New York Times articles by Seymour Hersh (1)," Richard B. Cheney Files, Gerald R. Ford Presidential Library, Grand Rapids, MI.

40   *"pulled me out of obscurity"* Transcript of interview with James A. Baker III, March 17, 2011, George H. W. Bush Oral History Project, Miller Center, University of Virginia (hereafter "Baker, Miller Center interview").

40   *Reagan as his running mate* Shirley, *Reagan's Revolution*, p. 328.

41   *Morality in Foreign Policy plank* See Mann, *Rise of the Vulcans*, pp. 72–73.

41   *"We took a dive"* Cheney, Miller Center interview.

42   *"My job was"* Ibid.

42   *it fell to Cheney to persuade Ford to issue a retraction* Cheney, *In My Time*, p. 106.

42   *"After the ordeal of Watergate"* Powell, *My American Journey*, p. 219.

42   *vacation in Eleuthera* Rumsfeld, *Known and Unknown*, p. 240.

42   *putting Ford on the ticket as the vice-presidential nominee* Author interview with Richard Allen, July 16, 2002; Richard Allen, "George Herbert Walker Bush: The Accidental Vice President," *New York Times Magazine*, July 30, 2000, p. 36; see also Meacham, *Destiny and Power*, p. 248.

43   *"slide-rule commandos," "flabby thinking"* Powell, *My American Journey*, p. 100.

3. Climbing the Ladder

45   *played racquetball regularly* Powell, *My American Journey*, pp. 233–34.

46   *"You staked out . . . The only ones who spoke"* Ibid., p. 276.

47   *escorting Weinberger* Ibid., p. 244.

47   *"I knew Carlucci a little better"* Powell 2018 interview.

47   *"Just call me Frank"* Powell, *My American Journey*, pp. 246–47.

47   *"depend on the military aide"* Author interview with Frank Carlucci, January 11, 2002.

48   *"runaway dad"* J. Edward Lee and Toby Haynsworth, *White Christmas in April* (New York: Peter Lang Publishing, 1995), p. 85.

48   *"We were both Vietnam vets"* Author interview with Richard Armitage, March 9, 2017.

49   *"hired gun"* T. R. Reid, "White House Staff Chief, in Love with Governing, Now Runs for Congress," *Washington Post*, August 28, 1978. See also Martin Tolchin, "House G.O.P. Looks to Young Stars," *New York Times*, April 6, 1982.

49   *"Cheney's second choice"* Lou Cannon, "From the White House to the Hustings: Richard Cheney Wants to Work on Capitol Hill," *Washington Post*, October 16, 1978.

49   *"pain in the fanny"* Steven V. Roberts, "One Conservative Faults Two Parties," *New York Times*, August 11, 1983, p. A-18.

50   *conservative on the issues* See Matthew Vita and Dan Morgan, "A Hard-Liner with a Soft Touch," *Washington Post*, August 5, 2000.

50   *MX nuclear missiles* James Coates, "How the MX Found a Home in Wyoming," *Chicago Tribune*, November 23, 1982.

50   *"tell them I'm a conservative"* Author interview with Dave Gribben, December 17, 2001.

50   *"Our relationship was useful"* Cheney, *In My Time*, p. 132.

51   *Cheney laid out these views . . . "tools at his command"* Richard Cheney, "U.S. Foreign Policy: Who's in Charge," *SAIS Review* 4, no. 1 (Winter 1984): 107–13.

52   *"We haven't had"* Powell, *My American Journey*, p. 270.

52   *"When you talked to Weinberger"* Author interview with Lawrence Korb, February 12, 2003.

52   *"Colin even then was a guy who could just get things done"* Author interview with Robert Kimmitt, March 8, 2016 (hereafter "Kimmitt interview").

53   *Armitage . . . mornings at the Pentagon* Author interview with Torkel Patterson, August 1, 2002.

53   *"Rich always checked the traps"* Author interview with Karl Jackson, October 29, 2015.

53   *Carlucci's advice on dealing with Weinberger* Miller Center Interview with Frank Carlucci for Ronald Reagan Oral History Project, August 28, 2001, page 23. http://web1.millercenter.org/poh/transcripts/ohp_2001_0828_carlucci.pdf.

53 *"He was as good with people . . . They know how to play"* Author interview with Jim Webb, February 21, 2002.
54 *above his pay grade* Ibid.
54 *small group of senior officers* Powell, *My American Journey*, p. 269.
55 *"I was developing . . . not good enough"* Ibid., pp. 280–81.
56 *America should not* Caspar Weinberger, *Fighting for Peace* (New York: Warner Books, 1990), pp. 280–81.
56 *In his memoir* Powell, *My American Journey*, p. 292.
56 *"similarities"* Powell, *It Worked for Me*, pp. 202–4.
57 *"The Army guy on the beach"* Cheney, Miller Center interview.
58 *intelligence reports . . . Stealth fighter* These details are taken from Cheney, *In My Time*, pp. 140–43.
58 *"He was the only member"* Robert M. Gates, *Duty* (New York: Alfred A. Knopf, 2014), p. 97.
58 *"He had a voracious"* Author interview with Aaron Friedberg, November 18, 2015 (hereafter "Friedberg interview").
58 *"given to personally sifting"* Condoleezza Rice, *No Higher Honor* (New York: Crown, 2011), p. 170.
59 *"continuity of government" exercises* For a fuller description of this program, see Mann, *Rise of the Vulcans*, pp. 138–45.
60 *suspended in the early 1990s . . . some core functions were preserved* William M. Arkin, "Back to the Bunker," *Washington Post*, June 4, 2006.
60 *left the United States for the first time . . . passport* Cheney, *In My Time*, p. 54.
61 *Cheney was introduced to . . . Powell* Cheney, Miller Center interview, p. 39; Cheney, *In My Time*, p. 161; Powell, *My American Journey*, p. 316.

4. "Your Buddy, Colin"

63 *"I had no choice"* Powell, *My American Journey*, pp. 317–19.
64 *"a certain degree of familiarity"* Transcript of Colin Powell interview for George H. W. Bush Oral History Project, Miller Center, University of Virginia, December 16, 2011.
64 *"If it hadn't been for Iran-Contra"* Gates, *Thirteen Ways*, p. 78.
64 *"Can He Recover?" Time*, March 9, 1987, cover story.
64 *"The government damn near collapsed"* Author interview with Colin Powell, November 2, 2006 (hereafter "Powell 2006 interview").
64 *Powell called him from Germany* Kimmitt interview.
65 *"He [Powell] ran as orderly a meeting"* Author interview with Bill Burns, August 24, 2016.
65 *"to satisfy ourselves that each one of them . . . made sense"* Powell, Miller Center interview.
65 *"Frank didn't have a great passion"* Powell 2006 interview.
66 *"Those were the most fun meetings"* Ibid.
66 *"The Joint Chiefs didn't fight"* Ibid.
67 *Dolan countered with a diatribe* Powell, *My American Journey*, pp. 321–22.
67 *"It's time for the Wall to come down"* "NSC Comments on Berlin Speech (5/21/87—12:00 noon draft)," WHORM files SP1140, 501964, Ronald Reagan Presidential Library, Simi Valley, CA.
67 *Powell raised objections* Author interview with Peter Robinson, November 1, 2006; author interview with Thomas Griscom, June 30, 2006.
67 *"Roz— . . . At this point"* Memo, "26 May to Amb. Ridgway," Box 92476 (5), White House Staff and Office Files of Colin Powell, Ronald Reagan Presidential Library, Simi Valley, CA.
68 *"Cheney's natural habitat is behind the scenes"* Janet Hook, "House GOP Elects Three Mid-Level Leaders," *Congressional Quarterly*, June 6, 1987, pp. 1185–86.
69 *"I'm worried"* David S. Broder, "Protect the President's Notes," *Washington Post*, February 8, 1987, p. C-7.

69   *interviewed Powell about Iran-Contra* Iran Arms Transaction: Congressional Interview of Gen. Colin Powell (04/17/1987), Box CFOA 1130, Arthur B. Culvahouse Files, Ronald Reagan Presidential Library, Simi Valley, CA.

69   *Powell gave another round . . . a pardon* For the most concise summary of Powell and the Iran-Contra investigation, see Karen DeYoung, *Soldier: The Life of Colin Powell* (New York: Alfred A. Knopf, 2006), pp. 147–54.

70   *"secrecy, deception and disdain"* Report of the Congressional Committees Investigating the Iran-Contra Affair, 100th Congress [hereafter "Iran-Contra Report"], S-Report 100–216, November 17, 1987, p. 11.

70   *minority report* The minority report was written not by Addington but by Michael Malbin, another aide working for Cheney on the committee staff.

70   *"aggrandizing theory," "Unconstitutional statues," "political guerrilla warfare"* Iran-Contra Report, pp. 437–38.

70   *"The boundless view"* Ibid., p. 457.

71   *Reagan was turning against the hawks* For a fuller account, see James Mann, *The Rebellion of Ronald Reagan* (New York: Viking, 2009).

72   *"As deputy [national security advisor], Powell had proved"* George P. Shultz, *Turmoil and Triumph* (New York: Charles Scribner's Sons, 1993), p. 991.

72   *Powell had defended the idea* Richard Halloran, "National Security Council: Case of the Reluctant General," *New York Times*, October 5, 1987.

73   *"The President should be free"* White House transcript released by Office of the Press Secretary, "Interview of General Colin Powell by Knight Ritter Editors, November 16, 1987."

73   *"I just took the best excuse"* Ivo H. Daalder, interview with General Colin L. Powell, November 23, 1999, in Ivo H. Daalder and I. M. Destler, "The Role of the National Security Advisor," Oral History Roundtables, 11, http://www.cissm.umd.edu/publications/role-national-security-adviser-0 (hereafter "Daalder interview with Powell, November 23, 1999").

74   *"it was an unwritten rule that . . . blacks could serve only"* Carl T. Rowan, "A Reagan Breakthrough for Blacks," *Chicago Sun-Times*, November 8, 1987.

74   *no note takers . . . no substitutions* For the best account of these meetings, see Daalder interview with Powell, November 23, 1999.

74   *"If the three of us agreed, that was it"* Author interview with Frank Carlucci, January 19, 2005.

74   *"I would never, ever characterize"* Powell 2006 interview.

75   *invoking the Twenty-Fifth Amendment* Jane Mayer, "Worrying About Reagan," *The New Yorker*, February 24, 2011, citing Jane Mayer and Doyle McManus, *Landslide: The Making and Unmaking of a President, 1984–1988* (Boston: Houghton Mifflin, 1988).

75   *"He slowed down," "he was starting to have some trouble"* Author interviews with Frank Carlucci (January 19, 2005) and Colin Powell (November 2, 2006).

75   *"Right, go ahead and do it"* Mann, *The Rebellion of Ronald Reagan*, p. 281.

75   *"I'd go and see the president"* Powell 2006 interview.

76   *"Didn't get to it"* "Your Meeting with Dick Cheney," Note from Alison B. Fortier, Colin L. Powell files, Ronald Reagan Presidential Library, Simi Valley, CA.

77   *"Dave Addington says . . . spoken to Colin about this"* Memo, Box 92477, Chron. Official 1988 II, Colin L. Powell files, Ronald Reagan Presidential Library, Simi Valley, CA.

77   *"Dear Dick," "Your thoughtfulness"* Correspondence files of Colin L. Powell, Ronald Reagan Presidential Library, Simi Valley, CA.

78   *"She's already bought the groceries"* Shultz, *Turmoil and Triumph*, p. 983.

78   *"When do you think I ought to give him the cufflinks?"* Powell 2006 interview.

78   *a small dinner for him with Kryuchkov* Robert M. Gates, *From the Shadows* (New York: Simon and Schuster, 1995), pp. 424–25.

79   *"I came away from the evening"* Cheney, *In My Time*, p. 167.

79   *"He's not ready to get down on his knees for you"* Powell 2006 interview.

79   *Reagan ... talk to Gorbachev about a belief in God* Memorandum of Conversation, The President's First One-on-One Meeting with General Secretary Gorbachev, May 29, 1988, Fritz Ermarth, Boxes 992084-5, White House Staff and Office Files, Ronald Reagan Presidential Library, Simi Valley, CA.

80   *"wants to talk about a better relationship"* The President, Box 92477, Colin Powell files, Ronald Reagan Presidential Library, Simi Valley, CA.

80   *"The President was musing"* Powell 2018 interview.

80   *"the Iranians claim that four of the hostages"* Memorandum for the Record, Box 92477, Colin Powell Files, Ronald Reagan Presidential Library, Simi Valley, CA.

81   *"I did not wish to be involved"* Ibid.

82   *"He counseled me against leaving"* Author interview with Dennis Ross, March 1, 2016.

82   *"bright as a new nickel"* George F. Will column, quoted in DeYoung, *Soldier*, pp. 174–75.

83   *"They offered me a job at CIA"* Powell, Miller Center interview, December 16, 2011.

83   *"one of the happiest days of my life"* Powell, *It Worked for Me*, p. 193.

83   *"America's celebrity culture"* "Not Selling Out," *The Economist*, Issue 7581, December 17, 1988, p. 38.

84   *"would have the opportunity to work together"* Cheney, *In My Time*, p. 161.

84   *Powell scrawled a handwritten note* Powell note to Cheney, December 21, 1988, correspondence file, Ronald Reagan Presidential Library, Simi Valley, CA.

5. Appointments

88   *"we needed somebody fast"* Author interview with Brent Scowcroft, January 3, 2002.

88   *"He had a reputation for integrity"* George H. W. Bush and Brent Scowcroft, *A World Transformed* (New York. Alfred A. Knopf, 1998), p. 22.

89   *"I worry about his game playing"* Meacham, *Destiny and Power*, p. 364.

89   *"What about you?" "a promising career in the House," "it wasn't a close call"* Dick Cheney, Miller Center interview, p. 32.

90   *reminded Bush ... driving under the influence* Cheney, *In My Time*, p. 157.

90   *"I got married and stopped hanging out in bars"* Ibid., p. 158.

91   *Wolfowitz ... offer from Tower* Wolfowitz interview.

91   *"I'd met Paul socially"* Cheney, Miller Center interview, p. 78.

92   *"I made the decision"* Ibid., p. 38.

93   *Powell received his fourth star ... "Love, Barbara"* Record of Powell correspondence in papers of General Colin L. Powell, USA (Ret.), National Defense University Library, Fort Lesley J. McNair, Washington, DC.

94   *"they had this kind of plan"* Wilkerson interview.

94   *"I don't know"* Author interviews with Richard Armitage, August 21, 2002, and October 15, 2015 (hereafter "Armitage 2015 interview"). Armitage went on to serve in special assignments under George H. W. Bush, most notably as the chief negotiator in talks over the future of U.S. bases in the Philippines.

95   *when the devil is dead* Colin Powell, "National Security Challenges in the 1990s: The Future Ain't What It Used To Be," speech given at the Army War College, Carlisle Barracks, PA, May 16, 1989, later published in *Army*, July, 1989, pp. 12–14.

95   *"'I'm not your everyday general'"* Wilkerson interview.

95   *"We hear that world politics"* Remarks by Secretary Cheney at the Center for Strategic and International Studies," May 10, 1989, in Folder 91117-003, USSR Collapse Files, Brent Scowcroft Collection, George H. W. Bush Presidential Library, College Station, Texas.

96   *part of the reason Cheney decided* Cheney, Miller Center interview, p. 33.

96   *"almost a kind of sociology"* Author interview with Dennis Ross, March 1, 2016.

96   *"he hated the open bureaucratic warfare," "if you expose differences, you're out"* Ibid.

97   *"kept his distance"* Rumsfeld, *Known and Unknown*, p. 266.

97   *"Someday, I think it should be Colin Powell"* Meacham, *Destiny and Power*, pp. 376–77.

97   *Alexander Haig* Cheney, Miller Center interview, p. 39.

97   *"To jump him"* Miller Center, George H. W. Bush Oral History Project, "Interview with Brent Scowcroft," November 12–13, 1999, p. 35, https://millercenter.org/the-presidency/presidential-oral-histories/brent-scowcroft-oral-history-national-security-advisor.

97   *Cheney believed* Cheney, *In My Time*, p. 171.

98   *Wolfowitz told Cheney directly* Wolfowitz interview.

98   *Cheney wanted Colin Powell very hard* Scowcroft, Miller Center interview, p. 35.

98   *"I didn't ask him about the job"* Cheney, Miller Center interview, p. 39.

98   *I was fairly sure* Powell, *My American Journey*, p. 393.

98   *"this was a guy who loved the U.S. Army"* Cheney, Miller Center interview, p. 39.

99   *as did Barry Goldwater* FOIA 2008-1193-5, Ronald Reagan Presidential Library files.

6. The First Invasion

101   *"He keeps arguing"* Powell 2006 interview.

101   *ordered an increase in preparations* Ronald H. Cole, *Operation Just Cause: Panama* (Washington, DC: Pentagon Joint History Office, Office of the Chairman of the Joint Chiefs of Staff, 1995), p. 12.

101   *"a severe case of 'clientitis'"* James Baker, *The Politics of Diplomacy* (New York: Putnam, 1995), p. 111.

101   *"Fred, the President has decided to make a change"* Cole, *Operation Just Cause*, p. 13.

102   *"debacle," "I did not find"* Powell, *My American Journey*, p. 406.

102   *Sunday front page* Andrew Rosenthal and Michael R. Gordon, "A Failed Coup: The Bush Team and Noriega," *New York Times*, October 7, 1989.

102   *"sort of Keystone Kops"* Sparrow, *Brent Scowcroft: The Strategist*, pp. 330–32.

102   *"We've got to keep her in power"* Author interview with Karl Jackson, October 29, 2015.

103   *"The State Department," "anxious young pilots," former colonial power* Powell, *My American Journey*, p. 429.

103   *"You fly, you die"* Author interview with Jackson.

103   *Cheney refused to come* Bush and Scowcroft, *A World Transformed*, p. 161.

104   *"Some of us remember"* Powell, *My American Journey*, p. 427.

104   *the most conservative of all, "I find this disturbing"* Meacham, *Destiny and Power*, pp. 385–87.

105   *"All of us vowed"* Baker, *The Politics of Diplomacy*, p. 187.

105   *"There will be a few dozen casualties"* Ibid., p. 189.

106   *massive military intervention* Cole, *Operation Just Cause*, p. 29.

106   *"He put in another division"* Author interview with Richard Armitage, October 15, 2015.

106   *Wolfowitz . . . wasn't convinced* Powell, *My American Journey*, p. 409.

106   *mocked him for being too timid* Wolfowitz interview.

106   *Operation Blue Spoon . . . Operation Just Because* Cole, *Operation Just Cause*, p. 32; Wolfowitz interview.

108   *marine amphibious units* Powell, *My American Journey*, pp. 409–10.

108   *"No one [of the military commanders] would dare"* Powell 2018 interview.

108   *"I was empowered . . . by Dick Cheney"* Ivo Daalder, interview with Powell, in Ivo Daalder and I. M. Destler, "The Role of the National Security Adviser," October 25, 1999, Center for International and Security Studies, University of Maryland School of Public Policy, College Park, MD (hereafter "Daalder interview with Powell, October 25, 1999").

109   *"gave me enormous influence"* Powell 2018 interview.

110   *"Scowcroft was making me crazy"* Powell, Miller Center interview, p. 25.

110   *"The only way to learn it is to do it"* Cheney, Miller Center interview, p. 127.

111   *"Panama established an emotional predicate"* Baker, *The Politics of Diplomacy*, p. 194.

111   *"do not apologize for going in big"* Powell, *My American Journey*, pp. 420–21.

111   *"he had to know it was doable"* Wilkerson interview.

7. A Much Bigger War

113 *"Getting Ahead of Gorbachev"* Folder 91117-001, USSR Collapse Files, Brent Scowcroft Collection, George H. W. Bush Presidential Library, College Station, TX.

113 *Sasser . . . McNamara* David E. Rosenbaum, "Spending Can Be Cut in Half, Former Defense Officials Say," *New York Times*, December 13, 1989.

114 *from 760,000 to 525,000; "These levels would be tough to sell"* Powell, *My American Journey*, p. 423.

115 *"If we don't do it," "'peace dividend, peace dividend'"* Cheney, Miller Center interview, pp. 89–91.

115 *"Cheney was worried"* Author interview with Eric Edelman, October 8, 2015 (hereafter "Edelman interview").

115 *"Let's not go through a demobilization"* Hearing Before the Committee on the Budget, 101st Cong. 14 (1990), (statement of Gen. Colin L. Powell, U.S. Army, Chairman, Joint Chiefs of Staff), "Administration's Defense Budget," February 7, 1990, p. 14.

115 *"Save the army"* Wilkerson interview.

115 *"We just knew each other so well"* Powell 2018 interview.

116 *"The cold war," "not a fire sale"* George H. W. Bush, "Remarks at the Aspen Institute Symposium," Aspen, Colorado, August 2, 1990.

117 *"Do you defend" . . . revised what Crowe had written* Cheney, Miller Center interview, p. 90; Cheney, *In My Time*, p. 181.

117 *Moshe Arens . . . warned Cheney* Yossi Melman and Dan Raviv, *Friends in Deed: Inside the U.S.-Israeli Alliance* (New York: Hyperion, 1994), pp. 381–82.

117 *"Arens is saying, 'I told you so'"* Folder CF01618-019, Files of Richard N. Haass, National Security Council Collection, George H. W. Bush Presidential Library, College Station, TX.

117 *more than $23 billion* Elaine Sciolino, *The Outlaw State* (New York: John Wiley, 1991), pp. 144–47.

118 *"the day the Cold War ended," "essentially passive reactions"* Baker, *The Politics of Diplomacy*, pp. 1–2.

118 *one of the primary reasons for America's failure* This point of view was eventually laid out in full in the 1997 book, *Dereliction of Duty*, by Gen. H. R. McMaster. That book reflected the collective thinking of military leaders over the quarter century since American troops departed from Vietnam.

118 *"I had been appalled"* Powell, *My American Journey*, p. 451.

119 *"His formative years were in Vietnam"* Haass, *War of Necessity, War of Choice*, p. 96.

119 *"our reluctant generals"* Cheney, Miller Center interview, p. 55.

119 *"our strategic interests in Saudi Arabia and oil"* Bush and Scowcroft, *A World Transformed*, p. 322.

120 *"Saudi Arabia will cut and run"* Transcript of National Security Council meeting re Iraqi Invasion of Kuwait, August 2, 1990, CF01618, Presidential Meeting File, Richard N. Haass files, George H. W. Bush Presidential Library, College Station, TX.

120 *"Iraqi threats to use CW"* Letter dated August 1990, Box 36, Desert Shield Files, Brent Scowcroft collection, George H. W. Bush Presidential Library, College Station, TX.

120 *oil and weapons of mass destruction were intertwined* On the issue of weapons of mass destruction, see Cheney, *In My Time*, p. 184.

120 *"Does anybody really care about Kuwait?"* Cheney, Miller Center interview, p. 134.

120 *"Should we put out a strong redline?"* Transcript of August 2, 1990, NSC meeting, CF01618, Presidential Meeting File, Richard N. Haass files, George H. W. Bush Presidential Library, College Station, TX.

120 *"Had the President just committed"* Powell, *My American Journey*, p. 453.

120 *"This would be the NFL"* Bush and Scowcroft, *A World Transformed*, p. 324.

121 *"You're not Secretary of State"* Powell, *My American Journey*, pp. 451–52.

121 *Cheney argued against including Powell* Cheney, *In My Time*, p. 188.

121 *"Can you arrange a private meeting . . . ?" "Why do we want to go to war with Iraq?"* Author interview with Dennis Ross, March 1, 2016.

122 *"containment was: . . ."* Author interview with Zalmay Khalilzad, April 14, 2016 (hereafter "Khalilzad 2016 interview").

122 *"No non-military action"* Cheney, *In My Time*, p. 186.

123 *"I really don't think we have time"* Powell, *My American Journey*, 467.

123 *"Guilty"* Ibid.

123 *"I didn't want Powell to be able to say"* Cheney, *In My Time*, p. 198.

123 *"We are at a fork in the road"* Bush and Scowcroft, *A World Transformed*, p. 394.

124 *"It was a terrible plan"* Interview with Brent Scowcroft, January 3, 2002.

124 *"I better not go out of town"* Norman Schwarzkopf, *It Doesn't Take a Hero* (New York: Bantam Books, 1992), p. 368.

124 *"It looked like a dry version of Vietnam"* Author interview with Henry Rowen, February 11, 2002.

125 *"Colin Powell never wanted the Gulf War"* Miller Center, George H. W. Bush Oral History Project, "Interview with John H. Sununu," June 8, 2000, p. 42, http://web1.millercenter .org/poh/transcripts/ohp_2000_0608_sununu.pdf.

125 *"My experience with the military"* Miller Center, George H. W. Bush Oral History Project, "Interview with Robert M. Gates," Robert M. Gates interview, Miller Center Oral History Project, July 23, 2000, p. 50 (hereafter "Gates, Miller Center interview"), http:// web1.millercenter.org/poh/transcripts/ohp_2000_0723_gates.pdf.

126 *"we spent a lot of time together"* Cheney, Miller Center interview, p. 141.

126 *"To the day I die," "Cheney's jaw dropped"* Gates, Miller Center interview.

126 *"The price for winning Powell's support"* Haass, *War of Necessity, War of Choice*, pp. 96–97.

127 *"Once you had 500,000 troops"* Cheney, Miller Center interview, p. 87.

127 *"They'd cover their fannies"* Ibid.

127 *"If it had anything to do with Congress"* Powell 2018 interview.

128 he only served two terms Cheney, Miller Center interview, p. 87.

128 *"I was wrong"* Cheney, *In My Time*, p. 88.

128 *"catastrophic"* See James Mann, *The Obamians* (New York: Viking, 2012), p. 29.

128 *"We thought the numbers would be in the thousands"* Powell, Miller Center interview, p. 19.

129 *"what happens when you screw it up"* Cheney, Miller Center interview, p. 87.

129 *"the resources to prevail"* Cheney, *In My Time*, p. 210.

129 *"It was a rough transition"* Wilkerson interview.

130 one reason that General David Petraeus never became chairman Kimmitt interview.

130 *"What time in the morning"* See Powell, *It Worked for Me*, p. 130.

130 *"I'ma kick yo' ass"* Gates, *Thirteen Ways*, p. 92.

131 *"We spent quite a bit of time worrying about bugs and gas"* Cheney, Miller Center interview, p. 58.

131 *"The threat clearly was that we'd use, or threaten to use, nuclear weapons"* Ibid.

131 *"how many tactical nuclear weapons"* Ibid.

131 *"oh my god, weapons of mass destruction"* Powell, Miller Center interview, December 16, 2011, p. 26.

132 *"how many tactical nuclear weapons" . . . seventeen . . . "Colin really didn't want"* Cheney, Miller Center interview, pp. 59–62.

132 *"Cheney wants to let them go"* Meacham, *Destiny and Power*, p. 460.

133 *"I wish Powell and Cheney were ready to go right now"* Bush and Scowcroft, *A World Transformed*, p. 472.

8. Deciding Not to Go to Baghdad

135 *"there was a kind of groupthink"* Author interview with Dennis Ross, April 18, 2002.

135 *"I honored the warrior's code"* Powell, *My American Journey*, p. 506.

135 *"We're killing literally thousands of people"* Baker, *The Politics of Diplomacy*, p. 410.

135 *"It really bothered Powell"* Gates, Miller Center interview, July 23, 2000, p. 58.

136 *"General Powell and the president"* Cheney, *In My Time*, p. 223.

136 *"Our stated mission"* George Bush and Brent Scowcroft, *A World Transformed*, p. 464.

137 *"we'd done what we set out to do."* Cheney, Miller Center interview, p. 64.

137 *"There was something called Iran"* Powell, Miller Center interview, p. 22.

137 *"enough power to survive as a threat to an Iran"* Powell, *My American Journey*, p. 516.

137 *"Militarily, we can go on . . ." "the President got everything right"* Author interview with Karl D. Jackson, October 29, 2015, and memo written to author by Jackson.

138 *"It is a legitimate criticism"* Powell, Miller Center interview, p. 22.

138 *calling a halt before the escape routes," "arguably some misjudgments"* Cheney, *In My Time*, pp. 223–26.

139 *"Vietnam will soon be behind us"* Bush and Scowcroft, *A World Transformed*, p. 484.

139 *"It's great to win one"* Author interview with Dennis Ross, March 1, 2016.

139 *"There was a palpable sense"* Cheney, *In My Time*, p. 226.

140 *"They didn't want to hear because it was time to celebrate"* Khalilzad 2016 interview.

140 *"me to Baker and him [Wolfowitz] to Cheney"* Author interview with Dennis Ross, March 1, 2016.

141 *ticker tape parade* Memorandum for the Chairman, "New York City Ticker Tape Parade," in files of Colin Powell, National Defense University Library.

141 *"It's a great day"* Robert D. McFadden, "In a Ticker-Tape Blizzard, New York Honors the Troops," *New York Times*, June 11, 1991.

142 *"The Gulf War was a limited-objective war"* Colin L. Powell, "U.S. Forces: Challenges Ahead," *Foreign Affairs* 71, no. 5 (Winter 1992): 32–45.

142 *quick . . . minimal casualties* Stephen Sestanovich, *Maximalist* (New York: Vintage Books, 2014), p. 289; see also Statement of Dick Cheney Before House Armed Services Committee, February 6, 1992, https://apps.dtic.mil/dtic/tr/fulltext/u2/a246700.pdf. *"there's nothing else for them to do but train," "we got somebody else to pay for it"* Cheney, Miller Center interview, p. 158.

142 *"we hadn't done a lot of planning"* Cheney, Miller Center interview, p. 65.

142 *"Without Israel's courageous action"* Cheney, *In My Time*, p. 227.

143 *Khalilzad received a call from Bernard Lewis . . . meet with Chalabi* Zalmay Khalilzad, *The Envoy* (New York: St. Martin's Press, 2016), pp. 73–74.

9. The Soviet Collapse

144 *"Colin Powell and I worked hard"* Cheney, Miller Center interview, p. 105.

144 *"Let's wrap this up"* Author interview with Dave Gribben, December 17, 2001.

145 *Cheney described their relationship as "very close"* Cheney, Miller Center interview, p. 42.

145 *"Cheney was my boss, but we were very close personal friends"* Daalder interview with Powell, November 23, 1999.

145 *"Dick and I were friends"* Powell 2018 interview.

145 *"we would talk late at night"* Powell, Miller Center interview, December 16, 2011, p. 6.

145 *"It's ugly, it's dirty"* Powell, *My American Journey*, p. 26.

146 *"Why doesn't he [Cheney] write it up himself?"* Khalilzad 2016 interview.

146 *interim report* "Conduct of the Persian Gulf War: An Interim Report to Congress," Department of Defense, July 1991, https://apps.dtic.mil/dtic/tr/fulltext/u2/a249445.pdf. *"We were fortunate"* Department of Defense, "Conduct of the Persian Gulf War: Final Report to Congress," April 1992, page XIX.

147 *"We called him 'Weird David'"* Wilkerson interview.

148 *"Not one of my civilian advisors," "right-wing nuts like you"* Powell, *My American Journey*, pp. 525–26.

148 *"Powell, for all his many considerable virtues"* Edelman interview.

149 *"his one Achilles' heel"* Ibid.

149 *"Not much of a strategist"* Wilkerson interview.

149 *"I don't like think tanks"* Powell 2003 interview.

149 *informal seminar on events in the Soviet Union* The Soviet experts attending included Peter Reddaway, Stephen Sestanovich, Rose Gottemoeller, and Paul Goble.

150 *"Let's round up"* Wolfowitz interview.

150 *Powell . . . wouldn't stay long* Author interview with Fritz Ermarth, March 14, 2002.

150 *"it was my responsibility"* Cheney, Miller Center interview, p. 103.

151 *"could reverse"* Patrick Tyler, "Webster Sees No Revival of Soviet Threat," *Washington Post*, March 2, 1990, p. A1.

151 *"There was always some suspicion"* Author interview with William Burns, August 24, 2016 (hereafter "Burns interview").

151 *the CIA was reporting* Kirsten Lundberg, "CIA and the Fall of the Soviet Empire," Case Study C16-94-1251.0, 1994, p. 44, Intelligence and Policy Project, John F. Kennedy School of Government, Harvard University, Cambridge, MA.

151 *"the next thing you know"* Khalilzad 2016 interview.

152 *"Cheney treated him like royalty," "devoutly to be wished"* Wolfowitz interview.

152 *"I'm getting good deals from Gorbachev"* James Baker, conversation with the author and other reporters on plane ride from Mongolia to Moscow, July 29, 1991.

153 *didn't include the word "condemn"* Gates, *From the Shadows*, p. 523.

153 *"Cheney against the field"* Ibid., pp. 529–30.

154 *"He had looked into Gorbachev's eyes"* Lawrence Wilkerson interview for the Guantanamo Bay Oral History Project, p. 30, http://www.columbia.edu/cu/libraries/inside/ccoh_assets/ccoh_8960747_transcript.pdf.

154 *"somewhere in the middle of the debate"* Gates, *From the Shadows*, p. 530.

155 *"Powell was really much closer"* Edelman interview.

155 *"you really pissed off the chairman," "throw me under the bus"* Ibid.

10. Cheney's Blueprint

157 *"I'm running out of demons"* Jim Wolffe, "Powell, 'I'm Running Out of Demons,'" *Army Times*, April 5, 1991.

157 *"The threats have become remote"* Dick Cheney testimony to House Armed Services Committee, February 6, 1992, https://apps.dtic.mil/dtic/tr/fulltext/u2/a246700.pdf.

158 *"Our planning assumptions"* Author interview with Dick Cheney, December 6, 1996.

158 *Perle . . . Wohlstetter* Author interview with Zalmay Khalilzad, May 28, 2003.

158 *draft leaked* Patrick E. Tyler, "U.S. Strategy Plan Calls for Insuring No Rivals Develop," *New York Times*, March 8, 1992.

159 *"prevent the reemergence of a new rival," "any hostile power," "advanced industrial nations"* "Defense Planning Guidance FY 1994–1999," National Security Archive, "The Nuclear Vault: The Making of the Cheney Regional Defense Strategy, 1991–1992," Document 3, https://nsarchive2.gwu.edu/nukevault/ebb245/index.htm.

159 *"threat-based thinking"* Zalmay Khalilzad, "The 1992 DPG and the 2003 Iraq Invasion," paper published in adapted form in *The National Interest*, April 18, 2016.

159 *led to future wars* By "future wars," they meant World War II and the Korean War, respectively.

159 *"Pearl Harbor showed us"* Text of Dick Cheney speech at Pearl Harbor, December 5, 1991.

160 *"renationalization of defense"* in Germany and Japan Edelman interview.

160 *"the document can be faulted"* Eric Edelman, "The Strange Career of the Defense Planning Guidance," in Melvyn P. Leffler and Jeffrey W. Legro, *In Uncertain Times: American Foreign Policy After the Berlin Wall and 9/11* (Ithaca, NY: Cornell University Press, 2011), p. 75.

160 *"That was just nutty"* Scowcroft interview in Derek Chollet and James Goldgeier, *America Between the Wars, 11/9 to 9/11* (New York: Public Affairs Press, 2008), p. 25.

161 *"one more attempt"* Doyle McManus, "U.S. Role Abroad Splits Presidential Candidates," *Los Angeles Times*, March 13, 1992, p. A-4.

161 *"to keep Europe down"* Khalilzad, "The 1992 DPG and the 2003 Iraq Invasion."

161 *"He didn't want to be associated with it"* Author interview with Zalmay Khalilzad, May 28, 2003.

161 *"You've discovered a new rationale"* Khalilzad, *The Envoy*, p. 81.

161 *"shape the security environment," "strategic depth"* This account of the Defense Planning Guidance relies largely on my earlier book, Mann, *Rise of the Vulcans*, pp. 210–13.

161 *turned around the press coverage* See Patrick E. Tyler, "Pentagon Drops Goal of Blocking New Superpowers," *New York Times*, May 24, 1992.

161 *were not even willing to schedule a meeting* Khalilzad, "The 1992 DPG and the 2003 Iraq Invasion."

162 *1992 campaign . . . "the vision thing"* See Edelman, "The Strange Career of the Defense Planning Guidance," p. 76.

162 *"reflected the consensus thinking"* Paul Wolfowitz, "Shaping the Future," in Leffler and Legro, *In Uncertain Times*, p. 59.

162 *"unexceptional principles"* Edelman interview.

163 *Eagleburger . . . put together a memo* Chollet and Goldgeier, *America Between the Wars*, pp. 47–52.

163 *"new policy directions"* "The Nuclear Vault: The Making of the Cheney Regional Defense Strategy, 1991–1992," Document 8, National Security Archive, https://nsarchive2.gwu.edu/nukevault/ebb245/doc08.pdf.

164 *"should be carried out in the public domain"* Tyler, "U.S. Strategy Plan Calls for Insuring No Rivals Develop."

164 *"the Joint Staff, which reported to Powell"* Khalilzad, *The Envoy*, p. 79.

164 *believed the leaker was Powell* Author interview with Khalilzad, April 14, 2016.

164 *Wolfowitz or someone else on his staff* Powell 2018 interview.

11. Departures

166 *"the most effective . . . Babe Ruth and Lou Gehrig"* Maureen Dowd, "Stars of War Room Are Auditioning for the Presidential Battles to Come," *New York Times*, February 11, 1991.

166 *replace John Sununu* Cheney, Miller Center interview, pp. 161–62; Cheney, *In My Time*, pp. 237–38.

167 *Ross . . . suggested putting Powell on the ticket* Author interview with Dennis Ross, April 18, 2002.

167 *Vernon Jordan approached Powell* See Powell, *My American Journey*, p. 539.

167 *"Dad said no"* George W. Bush, *Decision Points* (New York: Crown Publishers, 2010), p. 49.

167 *"what's the encore?"* Cheney, Miller Center interview, p. 151.

168 *"one of the most spirited"* Baker, *The Politics of Diplomacy*, pp. 649–50.

168 *"cannot be the policeman of the world"* Reuter News Agency, "Cheney: U.S. Is Not World's Policeman," July 17, 1992.

169 *"As soon as they tell me it is limited"* Michael A. Gordon, "Powell Delivers a Resounding No on Using Limited Force in Bosnia," *New York Times*, September 28, 1992.

169 *"more for their money"* Unsigned editorial, "At Least: Slow the Slaughter," *New York Times*, October 4, 1992.

169 *"military force is not always the right answer"* Colin L. Powell, "Why Generals Get Nervous," *New York Times*, October 8, 1992.

169 *weekend warriors* Samantha Power, *"A Problem from Hell": America and the Age of Genocide* (New York: HarperCollins, 2003), p. 285.

170 *"We were in total agreement"* Cheney, Miller Center interview, p. 152.

170 *"We're constrained to some extent"* Barton Gellman, "Cheney Warns Arms Cuts Won't Be Easy to Realize," *Washington Post*, January 5, 1993.

170 *Graves' disease* Meacham, *Destiny and Power*, pp. 470, 475.

171 *"There is a feeling in the Muslim world"* Ibid., p. 529.

171 *"I was reluctant"* Cheney, Miller Center interview, p. 98.

171 *"learned and listened"* Wilkerson interview.

172 *"We spent a lot of time together"* Pentagon transcript of farewell ceremony for the secretary and deputy secretary of defense, January 12, 1993.

172 *"I have never once," "Transitions are never easy"* Ibid.

172 *had not stopped to say good-bye, "we could finish each other's sentences"* Powell, *My American Journey*, p. 554.
173 *"All of a sudden, he's gone"* Author interview with Dennis Blair, December 21, 2015.
173 *call from his wife, Lynne* Khalilzad 2016 interview.
173 *"hell of a run" . . . muscle spasm* Cheney, Miller Center, March 17, 2000, pp. 170–71.
174 *"how hard it was dealing with the Clinton folks"* Edelman interview.
174 *"Welcome back, boss!"* Ibid.
174 *"'Here come the black folks and there goes the neighborhood'"* Author interview with James Woolsey, March 29, 2002.
175 *"these interminable meetings"* Lawrence Wilkerson interview, "The Guantánamo Bay Oral History Project: The Reminiscences of Lawrence B. Wilkerson," Columbia Center for Oral History, Columbia University, New York, pp. 35–36, http://www.columbia.edu /cu/libraries/inside/ccoh_assets/ccoh_8960747_transcript.pdf (hereafter "Wilkerson, "Guantánamo Bay Oral History Project").
175 *"Don't make the gay issue"* Powell, *My American Journey*, p. 550.
175 *White House meeting . . . gays in the military* The minutes of this White House session were declassified and released in 2014. See Josh Gerstein, "Clinton, Powell Talked Gays in Military," *Politico*, October 10, 2014.
176 *"What are you saving this superb military for?" "lessons of Vietnam could be learned too well"* In Madeleine Albright, *Madam Secretary* (New York: Miramax Books, 2003), pp. 181–82. *"aneurysm," "global game board"* In Powell, *My American Journey*, p. 561.
177 *"a response, but not another war"* Meacham, *Destiny and Power*, pp. 541–42.
177 *"to use the power and influence of the U.N."* Remarks by Gen. Colin Powell to the United Nations Association of the United States of America, in Department of Defense: Defense Issues: Vol. 8, No. 21 (April 21, 1993), included in personal papers of Colin Powell, Special Collections, National Defense University Library, Washington, D.C.
178 *"a great international coalition such as the U.N."* Remarks by Gen. Colin Powell at the Harvard University Commencement, June 10, 1993, https://www.harvardmag.com /media/1993_Powell.pdf.
178 *$6.5 million* Sarah Lyall, "General Powell to Trade the Sword for the Pen," *New York Times*, August 18, 1993.
178 *"Powell was AWOL on Somalia"* Author interview with Sandy Berger, February 20, 2003.
178 *"couldn't wait to get out the door"* Wilkerson interview.
178 *"Anybody who wants to have a picture"* Author interview with Dennis Blair, December 21, 2015.
179 *"The Army has been my home"* Gen. Colin Powell remarks at farewell ceremony, September 30, 1993, transcript published in Defense Department Early Bird news summary, October 1, 1993.
179 *letters Powell received . . . Richard Nixon* Powell materials, National Defense University.

12. On the Outside

183 *"especially guys like Colin Powell"* Cheney, Miller Center interview, pp. 169–71.
184 *"The differences were too severe"* Powell, Miller Center interview, December 16, 2011, p. 18.
184 *"more money than I thought I would ever have"* Cheney, Miller Center interview, p. 168.
184 *lecture circuit . . . road trip* Cheney, *In My Time*, p. 241; Cheney, Miller Center interview, p. 168.
185 *a "foreign policy president"* Dick Cheney, "Getting Our Priorities Right," speech to American Enterprise Institute, December 8, 1993.
185 *1994 congressional elections . . . bittersweet* Cheney, *In My Time*, p. 245.
185 *"That is not dealing with the abortion issue"* Cheney, Miller Center interview, p. 169.
185 *"the meat-grinder of a national campaign"* Cheney, *In My Time*, p. 246.
185 *"had become distasteful"* Powell 2003 interview.

186 *told her parents . . . he didn't want to raise money* Mary Cheney, *Now It's My Turn* (New York: Threshold Editions, 2006), pp. 33–36.
186 *"If you can get me the job by appointment, I'll take it"* Cheney, Miller Center interview, p. 169.
186 *"What now?"* Wilkerson interview.
186 *"You have to have a lot of money"* Ibid.
187 *"I'm now a wealthy person," "You've got to get the tax burden off business"* Gates, *Thirteen Ways*, pp. 73, 98.
187 *"Just think how Liz is going to feel"* Armitage 2015 interview. See also DeYoung, *Soldier*, p. 243. It is worth noting that these accounts by Armitage and Powell about what was taken out of the book came only in interviews given after the Cheney-Powell frictions of the George W. Bush administration.
187 *"genuine affection for this quiet man"* Powell, *My American Journey*, p. 554.
188 *"Somebody will try to kill him"* DeYoung, *Soldier*, p. 259.
188 *"They're politicians. I'm not"* Powell 2003 interview.
188 *"[Powell] also has a very thin skin"* Edelman interview.
189 *"I believe in affirmative action"* Powell 2003 interview.
189 *"I have a hard time being partisan"* Powell 2018 interview.
189 *"as miserable a period"* Powell, Miller Center interview, p. 7.
189 *"this is not me, not for me"* Ibid.
190 *smattering of boos . . . "You all know"* Kevin Merida, "Powell Makes Plea for Diverse Party," *Washington Post*, August 13, 1996.
190 *"everything we can to tolerate"* Mary Cheney, *Now It's My Turn*, p. 87.
193 *"had struck back"* Dan Ephron, *Killing a King: The Assassination of Yitzhak Rabin and the Remaking of Israel* (New York: W. W. Norton and Company, 2015), p. 243.
193 *"their views coincided"* Burns interview.
195 *"Why is it"* Thomas E. Ricks, "Colin Powell's Doctrine on Use of Military Force Is Now Being Questioned by Senior U.S. Officials," *Wall Street Journal*, August 30, 1995.
196 *"I think you ought to send a clear signal"* Gates, *Thirteen Ways*, p. 91.
196 *"There is the aggressor," "In due course"* Both quotes taken from "The Gulf War: Oral History," *Frontline*, PBS.org, January 9–10, 1996.
197 *"I would hope . . . mistake"* Jeffrey Jones, "Cheney Urges End to Iran Sanctions," Reuters News Agency, (Calgary) *Herald*, June 15, 2000, p. D-4.
197 *"we want to maintain our current posture"* Dick Cheney appearance on *Meet the Press*, NBC, August 27, 2000.
198 *joined the boards of directors* See DeYoung, *Soldier*, p. 283.
198 *"I focused on kids, not think tanks"* Powell 2003 interview.
198 *"Myself, my wife, and all the Bush kids"* Powell, Miller Center interview, December 16, 2011.
199 *"Colin's going to be there"* Cheney, Miller Center interview, pp. 169–71.

13. The Returns

200 *twice asked Cheney . . . couldn't possibly do so* See Cheney, *In My Time*, pp. 252–54.
201 *personally phoned Paul Wolfowitz* Wolfowitz interview.
202 *contributions to both . . . campaigns, "two . . . candidates who are very, very strong"* DeYoung, *Soldier*, p. 288.
202 *call for a reduction in nuclear weapons* Alison Mitchell, "Bush Says U.S. Should Reduce Nuclear Arms," *New York Times*, May 24, 2000.
202 *"scramble America's political arithmetic"* George F. Will, "Bush-Powell in 2000," *Washington Post*, March 19, 2000.
202 *"a favorite among Republican kibitzers" for vice president* Michael Kranish, "Now, the Veepstakes," *Boston Globe*, March 12, 2000, p. A-1.
204 *"Rumsfeld wasn't going to be an option"* Cheney, *In My Time*, p. 258.
204 *access to detailed personal information* For an excellent account of Cheney's operations as head of the vice-presidential search committee, see Barton Gellman, *Angler: The Cheney Vice Presidency* (New York: Penguin Press, 2008), pp. 1–30.

204 *"Unlike any of the senators," "a great choice"* Bush, *Decision Points*, p. 68.

204 *"a running mate who could help him govern"* Mary Cheney, *My Turn*, p. 2.

205 *father-daughter trip to Latin America* Ibid., pp. 1–4.

205 *Rove was opposed to Cheney in several ways* Karl Rove, *Courage and Consequence* (New York: Threshold Editions, 2010), pp. 169–70.

206 *"No, I mean really conservative"* Cheney, *In My Time*, p. 264.

206 *he would like to have the job . . . but didn't want to run* Cheney, Miller Center interview, p. 169.

207 *"newly moderate and disciplined face"* Richard Berke, "Republicans Open Convention, Emphasizing Unity," *New York Times*, August 1, 2000.

207 *"Dick Cheney is one of the most distinguished and dedicated public servants"* Transcript of Colin Powell speech to Republican National Convention, as reported by the Associated Press, August 1, 2000.

208 *"I think they were hoping for a kinder, gentler Dick Cheney"* Cheney, *In My Time*, pp. 269–70.

208 *"[Powell's] judgment during the gulf crisis," "a good deal more expansive than Powell's"* Robert Kagan, "The Problem with Powell," *Washington Post*, July 23, 2000.

208 *"a useful counter-weight"* "His Way," *Wall Street Journal* editorial, July 26, 2000.

209 *"I do so as a Republican"* Melinda Henneberger, "Gore Aide's Words Draw a Rebuke from Powell," *New York Times*, January 7, 2000.

209 *"one of the finest foreign policy teams ever assembled"* Frank Bruni, "Bush Question's Gore's Fitness for Commander in Chief," *New York Times*, May 31, 2000.

209 *"a humble nation," "the world's policeman"* Transcript, "The 2000 Campaign; 2nd Presidential Debate Between Gov. Bush and Vice President Gore," *New York Times*, October 12, 2000.

210 *"I was proud of the Powell pick"* Cheney, *In My Time*, p. 298.

211 *"you made a big mistake"* Wilkerson interview.

211 *"but as the next secretary of defense, too"* Alison Mitchell, "Powell to Head State Dept. as Bush's First Cabinet Pick," *New York Times*, December 17, 2000.

212 *"The Long Arm"* Matthew Rees, "The Long Arm of Colin Powell," *Weekly Standard*, December 25, 2000, p. 17.

212 *Cheney and his aides* Author interview with a former aide to Cheney.

212 *"Rich didn't want to work for me"* Powell 2003 interview.

213 *Cheney, as vice president* Donald Rumsfeld personal memo, "2000-12-28 re Getting the Secdef Offer," December 28, 2000, Rumsfeld Archive, http://library.rumsfeld.com/doclib/sp/116/2000-12-28%20re%20Getting%20the%20Secdef%20Offer.pdf; Rumsfeld, *Known and Unknown*, p. 285.

213 *Cheney had wanted Rumsfeld as defense secretary* Rumsfeld, *Known and Unknown*, p. 275.

213 *"Condi threw out an interesting idea"* Bush, *Decision Points*, p. 84.

214 *fly to Texas . . . "He told me to tell you"* Rumsfeld, *Known and Unknown*, pp. 275–85.

214 *the skill of parallel parking* Ibid., p. 148.

214 *Election Night 2000* Cheney, *In My Time*, p. 288.

215 *ambassador to the United Nations* Kimmitt interview.

217 *Cheney sent Donald Rumsfeld two photographs* Rumsfeld, *Known and Unknown*, p. 289.

14. From the Very Start

222 *"a pre-9/11 mindset"* Cheney, *In My Time*, p. 388.

222 *a slight heart attack, his fourth* The previous ones were in 1978, 1984, and 1988.

222 *"She had probably been up most of the night"* Cheney, *In My Time*, pp. 292–94.

223 *"When we took the silver metal covers off"* Secretary of Defense memorandum, "Snowflake 1 02-08-2001," February 8, 2001, Rumsfeld Archive, http://library.rumsfeld.com/doclib/sp/240/Snowflake%201%2002-08-2001.pdf; See also Rumsfeld, *Known and Unknown*, p. 321.

223 *"one ultra-hawkish mind"* Rice, *No Higher Honor*, p. 17.

223 *"his own National Security Council"* Powell 2018 interview.

224 *"to make recommendations to you"* Rice, *No Higher Honor*, p. 17.

224 *"an unintended chilling effect"* George Tenet, *At the Center of the Storm: My Years at the CIA* (New York: HarperCollins, 2007), p. 138.

224 *"my original language," "give me pushups"* Quoted in DeYoung, *Soldier*, p. 307.

225 *"We do plan to engage with North Korea"* State Department transcript of Powell press conference, March 6, 2001, https://2001-2009.state.gov/secretary/former/powell/remarks /2001/1116.htm.

226 *"a little too far forward on your skis"* William Douglas, "Powell Acknowledges Some Miscues," *Newsday*, May 5, 2001, p. A-7.

227 *"appalled that the vice president"* Rice, *No Higher Honor*, p. 42.

227 *a strategy for bringing the North Korean regime to a collapse* Author conversation with a former State Department official.

227 *withdraw or pull back from international treaties* See James Mann, *George W. Bush* (New York: Times Books, 2015), pp. 55–56.

228 *"As I saw it"* Cheney, *In My Time*, p. 325.

229 *"There's always a Soviet Union lurking somewhere"* Powell, Miller Center interview, pp. 8–9.

229 *"we were a band of brothers . . . The differences were too severe* Ibid., p. 18.

230 *"I wondered if he would send troops all the way to Baghdad"* Bush, *Decision Points*, p. 226.

230 *tough on Saddam Hussein* Rice, *No Higher Honor*, pp. 27–28.

231 *regime change . . . contain Saddam* Douglas J. Feith, *War and Decision* (New York: Harper, 2008), pp. 203–5.

231 *Paul—we won!"* Wolfowitz interview.

231 *"contingency plans"* Powell 2018 interview.

231 *"were not even united on the goals," "carried the day by default"* Khalilzad, *The Envoy*, pp. 98–99.

232 *"I don't remember Cheney particularly taking a position"* Wolfowitz interview.

233 *"probably because John Bolton was in the room,"* Author interview with Andrew Natsios, December 2, 2016.

233 *"not assertive in meetings"* Khalilzad, *The Envoy*, p. 96.

234 *"That's very interesting, Rich"* Khalilzad 2016 interview.

234 *"Powell Losing Policy Battles"* Martin Kettle, "Powell Losing Policy Battle to Hardliners: From Korea to Kosovo, the Pragmatic Secretary of State Is Being Forced into Increasing Isolation," *Guardian*, March 12, 2001, p. 13.

15. September 11 and Its Aftermath

236 *"Now, we've reached the point"* "Interview with Dick Cheney," *Proceedings, U.S. Naval Institute* 122/5/1,119 (May 1996): 34.

236 *"The vice president one morning asked me"* Michael Morell, *The Great War of Our Time* (New York: Twelve, 2015), p. 41.

237 *Cheney made the phone calls* Rice, *No Higher Honor*, p. 67.

237 *continuity-of-government exercises* Mann, *Rise of the Vulcans*, pp. 138–45.

237 *Cheney made the decision first* See Gellman, *Angler*, pp. 118–28.

238 *letter of resignation* Cheney, *In My Time*, pp. 320–22.

238 *"raw emotion"* Tenet, *At the Center of the Storm*, p. 170.

239 *"having allowed a devastating attack"* Gates, *Duty*, p. 93.

239 *"we had to make it clear"* Tenet, *At the Center of the Storm*, p. 171.

240 *"If we want to go it alone"* Colin Powell interview on *Meet the Press*, NBC, September 23, 2001.

240 *"The mission should define the coalition"* Cheney, *In My Time*, p. 331.

241 *got this idea from Benjamin Netanyahu* Rumsfeld, *Known and Unknown*, p. 354.

241 *"decades of experience in government"* Rice, *No Higher Honor*, p. 82.

241 *"expensive weapons on sparsely populated camps"* Bush, *Decision Points*, p. 191.

241 *tell Pakistan it was time to decide* Rice, *No Higher Honor*, pp. 86–87.

242 *"Fuck diplomacy"* Morell, *The Great War of Our Time*, p. 63.

242 *"Iraq has to pay a price"* Tenet, *At the Center of the Storm*, p. xix.

242 *"to eliminate Iraq threat,"* Wolfowitz argued Feith, *War and Decision*, pp. 48–49.

243 *"not until we had an effective plan"* Cheney, *In My Time*, p. 334.

244 *"If I had to go out and design a team of people"* Bob Woodward, "CIA Told to Do 'Whatever Necessary' to Kill Bin Laden," *Washington Post*, October 21, 2001.

244 *"The venom is gone"* David E. Sanger and Patrick E. Tyler, "Foreign Policy Team: Wartime Forges a United Front for Bush Aides," *New York Times*, December 23, 2001.

245 *"the dark side, if you will . . . any means at our disposal"* Cheney interview, *Meet the Press*, September 16, 2001, transcript at http://www.washingtonpost.com/wp-srv/nation/specials/attacked/transcripts/cheney091601.html.

246 *new measures* For an excellent summary of the significance of the new program, see Gellman, *Angler*, pp. 140–49.

246 *New York Times story* James Risen and Eric Lichtblau, "Bush Lets U.S. Spy on Callers Without Courts," *New York Times*, December 16, 2005.

247 *in Cheney's office* Tenet, *At the Center of the Storm*, p. 238.

248 *Iraq on the back burner* Author interview with a senior administration official, 2003.

249 *Addington to draft an order* Gellman, *Angler*, pp. 162–63.

249 *"no match for David Addington . . . cut out of the process"* Rice, *No Higher Honor*, pp. 104–5.

249 *Cheney presided* Tim Golden, "After Terror, a Secret Rewriting of Military Law," *New York Times*, October 24, 2004.

249 *she might resign* Rice, *No Higher Honor*, p. 106.

249 *friction with Britain* Alberto R. Gonzales, *True Faith and Allegiance* (Nashville, TN: Thomas Nelson, 2016), p. 173.

250 *"The most promising source of intelligence"* Feith, *War and Decision*, p. 159; Bush, *Decision Points*, p. 166.

250 *"The Vice President . . . 'offshore' facility"* Rice, *No Higher Honor*, p. 106.

250 *Its use would not further complicate"* Rumsfeld, *Known and Unknown*, p. 566.

250 *Powell and America's diplomats* DeYoung, *Soldier*, p. 366.

250 *"looking for ways to shut down the facility"* Cheney, *In My Time*, p. 355.

251 *"No physical or mental torture"* Language of Geneva Convention, taken from Congressional Research Report, "Lawfulness of Interrogation Techniques Under the Geneva Conventions," September 8. 2004, https://www.everycrsreport.com/files/20040908_RL32567_462880f1947fa49df83968234dd375d2523f1e3d.pdf.

251 *"is not a lawful combatant"* Remarks by Vice President Dick Cheney to the U.S. Chamber of Commerce, November 14, 2001, https://georgewbush-whitehouse.archives.gov/vicepresident/news-speeches/speeches/vp20011114-1.html.

251 *drafted by Addington,* see Gellman, *Angler*, p. 170.

252 "will reverse over a century of U.S. policy" Memorandum to Counsel to the President from Colin L. Powell, January 26, 2002, document obtained from National Security Archive, https://nsarchive2.gwu.edu/torturingdemocracy/documents/20020126.pdf.

252 *"Administration sources last night expressed anger at Mr. Powell"* Rowan Scarborough, "Powell Urges POW Status," *Washington Times*, January 26, 2002.

253 *"weasel out,"* Myers and Feith support for Geneva Conventions Feith, *War and Decision*, pp. 160–61.

254 *"Historically, our soldiers have long abided"* Gonzales, *True Faith and Allegiance*, p. 198.

254 *black sites* See Dana Priest, "CIA Holds Terror Suspects in Secret Prisons," *Washington Post*, November 2, 2005.

255 *torture . . . explored in the press* Walter Pincus, "Silence of 4 Terror Probe Suspects Poses Dilemma for FBI," *Washington Post*, October 21, 2001; Jonathan Alter, "Time to Think About Torture," *Newsweek* Special Issue, November 5, 2001.

255 *CIA developed a list of ten specific techniques* Gonzales, *True Faith and Allegiance*, pp. 195–96. Gonzales is quoting from a declassified Justice Department memo written for Acting CIA General Counsel John Rizzo, August 1, 2002, which can be found at https://www.hsdl.org/?view&did=37518.

255 *waterboarding as a war crime* See Evan Wallach, "Waterboarding Used to Be a Crime," *Washington Post*, November 4, 2007.

256 *Justice Department declared . . . did not amount to torture* Gonzales, *True Faith and Allegiance*, pp. 185–86.

256 *capture of Khalid Sheikh Mohammed* Cheney, *In My Time*, p. 358.

256 *human intelligence . . . led to the capture* Tenet, *At the Center of the Storm*, pp. 250–54.

257 *Gonzales's office* Gonzales, *True Faith and Allegiance*, p. 189.

257 *Cheney passionately resisted* Rice, *No Higher Honor*, p. 502.

257 *"Yes, . . . just like I was with torture"* Robert M. Gates, *Duty*, p. 253.

258 *"Powell would blow his stack"* Report of the Senate Select Committee on Intelligence, Committee Study of the CIA's Detention and Interrogation Program, December 9, 2014, pp. 118–19, https://www.intelligence.senate.gov/sites/default/files/publications/CRPT-113srpt288.pdf.

258 *"I asked that Colin and Don [Rumsfeld] be briefed"* Rice, *No Higher Honor*, p. 117.

258 *We opened discussions within the National Security Council"* Tenet, *At the Center of the Storm*, p. 241.

258 *"At some point in the months after 9/11"* Rumsfeld, *Known and Unknown*, p. 583.

259 *"they never asked anybody to raise their hands"* Author interview with Powell, September 13, 2018.

259 *Powell never told him* Wilkerson interview.

259 *Armitage had taken part in covert operations* See Mann, *Rise of the Vulcans*, p. 45.

259 *Armitage was himself waterboarded* Armitage 2015 interview.

259 *"He never told me," "I know in war we fuck things up"* Ibid.

16. The Two Tribes

261 *"We were never not friends"* Powell 2018 interview.

261 *"bureaucratic tribalism"* Francis Fukuyama, *America at the Crossroads* (New Haven, CT: Yale University Press, 2006), p. 61.

262 *joke that made the rounds . . . "What other people call 'unilateralism'"* Richard Perle speech at Madison Hotel, April 17, 2002, from author's notes.

263 *"had to be prepared"* Cheney, Miller Center interview, March 16, 2000.

263 *"I'm not a traditional, backslapping"* Cheney, *In My Time*, p. 276.

263 *"He was always a presence"* Author interview with Andrew Natsios, December 2, 2016.

263 *let his staff play the role of the "bad guy"* Gates, *Duty*, p. 98.

263 *"an air of mystery"* Rumsfeld, *Known and Unknown*, p. 320.

263 *"Whatever he did"* Author interview with Franklin Miller, June 7, 2016.

264 *"Dick did not share with me"* Rumsfeld, *Known and Unknown*, p. 320.

264 *"building coral"* Armitage 2015 interview.

264 *Powell sought to counter* Wilkerson interview.

264 *"in this town, proximity is almost everything"* Powell 2018 interview.

265 *"behind the tab"* Cheney, *In My Time*, p. 314.

265 *"Despite our efforts to un-ring the bell"* Morell, *The Great War of Our Time*, p. 81. Cheney himself insisted that in his later public comments he added qualifying words of uncertainty about the Prague report. See Cheney, *In My Time*, p. 414.

265 *"Thousands of people are going to die"* James Comey, *A Higher Loyalty* (New York: Flatiron Books, 2018), p. 86.

266 *"The only legitimacy we need"* Burns interview.

266 *"Middle East will be changed . . . lurking in the shadow"* Powell 2018 interview.

266 *worked for the vice president, not for the White House chief of staff* See Cheney, *In My Time*, pp. 306, 495.

267 *Cheney felt no need at all* Rumsfeld, *Known and Unknown*, p. 320.
267 *"a hide like a rhinoceros"* Edelman interview.
269 *"the most popular political figure in America"* David W. Moore, "Powell Remains Most Popular Figure in America," Gallup, September 30, 2002.
270 *encouraged Bush to believe* Burns interview.
270 *"[T]ruthfully, I wondered"* Rice, *No Higher Honor*, pp. 21–22.
271 *one of the country's most talented speakers* Powell would one day devote an entire book chapter to tips for public speeches; the chapter was called "Speaking Is My Business." Powell, *It Worked for Me*, p. 243.
271 *"Can you write a speech for a black Baptist church?"* Wilkerson interview.
271 *"Colin Powell wasn't inclined to give policy-laden speeches"* Haass, *War of Necessity, War of Choice*, p. 177.
272 *"attuned to public approval"* Cheney, *In My Time*, p. 185.

17. The Nondecision

274 *"The secretary and I had read it time and again"* Author interview with Richard Armitage, August 21, 2002.
275 *"It would be a tragedy if Saddam"* Debate between Richard Perle and Leon Fuerth sponsored by the University of Maryland School of Public Affairs and the Hudson Institute, April 17, 2002; Todd S. Purdum, "After Saddam, What?" *New York Times*, February 17, 2002.
276 *"The fight was vicious"* Khalilzad 2016 interview.
276 *"We are not putting Chalabi in charge"* Author interview with Frank Miller, June 7, 2016.
276 *"If the people who didn't like Chalabi"* Wolfowitz interview.
277 *"The idea that we shouldn't work closely with"* Cheney, *In My Time*, p. 387.
278 *"completely at odds"* Author interview with Dennis Ross, March 1, 2016.
278 *"He hated the whole Middle East issue, as did Cheney"* Powell 2018 interview.
279 *"knives in my back"* Powell 2018 interview.
279 *"He was royally pissed," "burned up my heat shield"* Burns interview.
279 *Powell told Arafat* See DeYoung, *Soldier*, p. 383.
280 *"watershed moment," "as though a tie had been cut"* Cheney, *In My Time*, pp. 381–82.
280 *"It will require a lot of money," "What is the case?"* Bush's White House counsel Alberto R. Gonzales gave these verbatim accounts of portions of the NSC debates on Iraq in his book *True Faith and Allegiance*, p. 232. The quotes appear to have been taken from NSC memoranda of conversations, although it's possible they're from Gonzales's own notes.
281 *"We're not there yet internationally"* This and the following quotes from the debate of July 24, 2002, are in Gonzales, *True Faith and Allegiance*, pp. 234–36.
282 *"They do not view this as a real danger"* Ibid.
282 *"I've got problems with force size"* Gen. Tommy Franks, *American Soldier* (New York: Regan Books, 2004), p. 394.
283 *"he thought I was just an old geezer"* Powell 2018 interview.
283 *"Powell was reaching in"* Edelman interview.
283 *"Me, not him!"* Armitage 2015 interview.
283 *gave him credit for* Author interview with a senior Bush administration official.
284 *"an Armageddon in the Middle East"* Brent Scowcroft, "Don't Attack Saddam," *Wall Street Journal*, August 15, 2002.
284 *"I knew that Brent was having these thoughts"* Powell 2003 interview.
284 *Baker and Lawrence Eagleburger . . . said they were opposed* James A. Baker III, "The Right Way to Change a Regime," *New York Times*, August 25, 2002; transcript of Lawrence Eagleburger on *Crossfire*, CNN, August 19, 2002.
284 *"The world had changed"* Cheney, *In My Time*, p. 388.
285 *"Saddam has perfected"* Dick Cheney speech to Veterans of Foreign Wars' 103rd annual convention, August 26, 2002.

285 *"stand his ground," "throw a tantrum or two"* Unsigned editorial, "D-Day for Colin Powell," *New York Times*, July 28, 2002.

285 *"step aside and let someone else do the job"* William Kristol, "The Axis of Appeasement," *The Weekly Standard*, Vol. 7, No. 42, August 26, 2002, p. 7.

285 *He instructed Rice to call the vice president* Rice, *No Higher Honor*, p. 180.

286 *consequences of military action . . . "You break it, you own it"* DeYoung, *Soldier*, pp. 401–2.

286 *"We should take the problem to the United Nations"* This and the following quotes are taken from Powell's own account in Powell, *It Worked for Me*, pp. 210–11.

286 *"I didn't say to him, 'I oppose this war'"* Powell 2018 interview.

287 *"Not for the first time"* Report of the Iraq Inquiry (Chilcot Report), 2016, "Mr. Straw's Meeting with Secretary Powell, August 20, 2002," also quoting from memoir of Jack Straw, *Last Man Standing* (New York: Macmillan, 2012).

287 *"The president sometimes had difficulty"* Rice, *No Higher Honor*, p. 21.

288 *"The UK, Australia and Turkey are about all we need"* Gonzales notes of NSC discussions, *True Faith and Allegiance*, p. 239.

288 *"If we had tried to go to war without going to the UN"* Powell 2003 interview.

289 *"Saddam is a threat," "There is no support internationally"* Gonzales, *True Faith and Allegiance*, p. 246.

289 *"There was never an open argument"* Wolfowitz interview.

289 *"I cannot tell you when he crossed the Rubicon"* Powell 2018 interview.

290 *"Either he [Saddam Hussein] will come clean"* Rice, *No Higher Honor*, p. 181.

18. The Road to Baghdad

291 *150 phone calls* Steven R. Weisman, "How Powell Lined Up Votes, Starting with His President's," *New York Times*, November 9, 2002.

292 *front-page story* Bob Woodward, "A Struggle for the President's Heart and Mind: Powell Journeyed from Isolation to Winning the Argument on Iraq," *Washington Post*, November 17, 2002.

292 *"ignored the logic"* Feith, *War and Decision*, pp. 336–37.

292 *"Colin Powell won the battle but lost the war"* Author interview with Jean-David Levitte, June 5, 2003.

293 *"rich in volume but poor in new information,"* Statement of Dr. Hans Blix to UN Security Council, January 9, 2003, https://www.un.org/Depts/unmovic/bx9jan.htm.

294 *"I appreciated the merits"* Rumsfeld, *Known and Unknown*, p. 438.

294 *Powell's call* DeYoung, *Soldier*, p. 426.

294 *Rumsfeld would later insist*, Ibid., p. 234.

294 *"No one can legitimately argue"* Haass, *War of Necessity, War of Choice*, p. 254.

295 *"had not taken the time to visit Turkey"* Feith, *War and Decision*, p. 395.

295 *"Future of Iraq Project"* See "New State Department Releases on the 'Future of Iraq' Project," National Security Archive Electronic Briefing Book No. 198, https://nsarchive2.gwu.edu/NSAEBB/NSAEBB198/.

295 *"disdain, utter disdain"* Author interview with Ryan Crocker, May 29, 2018 (hereafter "Crocker interview").

296 *control of postwar Iraq to the Pentagon* Author interview with Frank Miller, June 7, 2016.

296 *"The principals could not agree on anyone else"* Khalilzad, *The Envoy*, p. 152.

296 *"Among the opposition leaders"* Ibid., p. 151.

296 *"He didn't fight"* Khalilzad 2016 interview.

296 *Chalabi should be put in charge* Author interview with Frank Miller, June 7, 2016.

297 *"we were on a path to war . . . I'll be with you"* Author interview with Powell, September 13, 2018.

297 *a few visits to CIA headquarters* Tenet, *At the Center of the Storm*, p. 343.

297 *"he did not push a particular line of argument"* Morell, *The Great War of Our Time*, p. 85.

297 *"What he wanted to know"* Author interview with Frank Miller, June 7, 2016.

298 *Cheney telephoned Powell directly* Cheney, *In My Time*, p. 396.

298 *"You're not going to the Middle East"* Powell 2003 interview.

299 *"George [Tenet] brought in the NIE"* Author interview with Lawrence Wilkerson, December 14, 2005.

299 *"By the time we got to the dress rehearsal"* Ibid.

299 *"I needed George there"* Author interview with Powell, June 30, 2003.

299 *two or three speeches* Rice, *No Higher Honor*, p. 200; DeYoung, *Soldier*, p. 439.

300 *"based on solid intelligence"* Colin Powell speech to the United Nations on Iraq, February 5, 2003, https://2001-2009.state.gov/secretary/former/powell/remarks/2003/17300.htm.

300 *"sinister nexus"* Ibid.

301 *"much of what Powell said about weapons of mass destruction was wrong"* Cheney, *In My Time*, p. 396. In his memoir, Cheney would continue to insist that the evidence about Saddam Hussein's support for terrorism had been valid—though he significantly dropped the linkage to al-Qaeda and instead spoke only of "ties to terror."

301 *He was angry . . . "Thanks a lot"* Powell 2018 interview.

301 *"It's a blot"* Barbara Walters interview, see "Colin Powell on Iraq, Race, and Hurricane Relief," ABC News, September 8, 2005, https://abcnews.go.com/2020/print?id=1105979.

301 *"The Perfect Storm"* The title "The Perfect Storm" appears to have been a popular one among the Middle East specialists in the U.S. government in the year before the invasion. The CIA, too, put together a memo on the harmful consequences of an invasion, including possible anarchy in Iraq and instability in the wider Middle East—and it, too, was called "The Perfect Storm."

301 *It laid out all the things* Crocker interview.

301 *CIA memo* Tenet, *At the Center of the Storm*, pp. 317–18.

302 *"we never heard another word"* Crocker interview.

302 *"Powell read it and put it in his pocket"* Haass, *War of Necessity, War of Choice*, pp. 233–34.

302 *"he and Armitage just never took a position," "turning the [hawks'] own strategies against them"* Crocker interview.

302 *"Colin had the deepest reservations"* Bush, *Decision Points*, p. 251.

303 *a good chance of getting nine or ten votes* Rice, *No Higher Honor*, pp. 201–2.

303 *"the second resolution was not something that we needed"* Powell 2003 interview.

303 *there would be logistical problems* Rice, *No Higher Honor*, p. 201.

304 *"you're stuck. . . . You have to go to war"* Powell 2018 interview.

304 *"we are very close to the end"* Colin Powell interview, *This Week with George Stephanopoulos*, ABC, March 16, 2003.

304 *"greeted as liberators"* Author interview with Dick Cheney, *Meet the Press*, NBC, March 16, 2003.

305 *Cheney had hosted a party* Rice, *No Higher Honor*, p. 208.

305 *"What has the State Department done?"* Ibid.

19. Chaos

306 *"we hadn't done a lot of planning"* Cheney, Miller Center interview.

307 *"Paul, don't we work for the same government?"* Khalilzad, *The Envoy*, p. 173.

307 *"the word had come from Cheney,"* Powell's call to Rumsfeld Thomas E. Ricks, *Fiasco: The American Military Adventure in Iraq* (New York: Penguin Press, 2006), pp. 103–4.

308 *Iraq . . . plans were in conflict* Author interview with Scooter Libby, October 5, 2018.

308 *National Museum . . . fifteen thousand artifacts* Robert M. Poole, "Looting Iraq," *Smithsonian*, February 2008, https://www.smithsonianmag.com/arts-culture/looting-iraq-16813540/.

309 *"stuff happens"* Transcript of Donald Rumsfeld briefing at the Pentagon, April 11, 2003, http://archive.defense.gov/Transcripts/Transcript.aspx?TranscriptID=2367.

309 *"desperate acts"* Donna Miles, "Wolfowitz Unhurt, Says Hotel Terrorist Attack Won't Deter Mission," American Forces Press Service, October 26, 2003.

309 *"That doesn't make it anything like a guerrilla war"* Vernon Loeb, "No Iraq 'Quagmire,' Rumsfeld Asserts," *Washington Post*, July 1, 2003.

309 *"There's no question"* Transcript of Dick Cheney interview, *Meet the Press*, NBC, September 14, 2003.

310 *"tear it up"* Friedberg interview.

310 *"We had too few troops"* Rice, *No Higher Honor*, p. 210.

310 *"bring decisive force to bear"* David Sanger, "As a Quick Victory Grows Less Likely, Doubts Are Quietly Voiced in Washington," *New York Times*, March 30, 2003.

311 *"The French and the Germans, in particular"* Richard W. Stevenson and Eric Schmitt, "After Weeks of Criticism, Cheney Claims Vindication as Iraqis Hail Outcome of War," *New York Times*, April 10, 2003.

311 *"One day, we're going to be trying to give this tar baby to the U.N."* Rice, *No Higher Honor*, p. 215.

311 *"Cooperation among our governments"* Mike Allen, "Cheney Reaches Out to Iraq War Critics," *Washington Post*, January 25, 2004.

311 *"One of the big mistakes . . . internationalize the mission"* Wolfowitz interview.

312 *"Cheney helped bring him in"* Author interview with Franklin Miller, June 7, 2016.

312 *"I think he is the man"* Donald Rumsfeld to Andrew J. Card Jr., " To Andrew H. Card Jr. re Ambassador Paul Bremer 04-24-2003," Rumsfeld Archive, http://library.rumsfeld .com/doclib/sp/330/To%20Andrew%20H.%20Card%20Jr.%20re%20Ambassador%20 Paul%20Bremer%2004-24-2003.pdf.

312 *"I tried to keep my voice lukewarm"* L. Paul Bremer III, *My Year in Iraq* (New York: Simon and Schuster, 2006), p. 76.

312 *"agitated"* Khalilzad, *The Envoy*, p. 174.

313 *"I read about it [in] the newspaper"* Powell emails, quoted in Andrew Kaczynski, "Personal Emails Show Colin Powell's Pessimism on ISIS Policy and a Trump Presidency," BuzzFeed, https://www.buzzfeednews.com/article/andrewkaczynski/personal-emails show colin powells pessimism on isis policy.

313 *Feith had drafted the broad order* Bremer, *My Year in Iraq*, p. 39; Feith, *War and Decision*, pp. 427–28.

313 *cleared with Feith and Rumsfeld* See Rumsfeld, *Known and Unknown*, pp. 516–17.

313 *"a psychological impact I did not foresee"* Bush, *Decision Points*, p. 259.

314 *"The president's gotta change this"* Armitage 2015 interview.

314 *"I recommend that Jerry Bremer's reporting relationship be moved"* Donald Rumsfeld to George W. Bush, "2003-10-06 to President George W Bush re Iraq Reporting Relationships," October 6, 2003, Rumsfeld Archive, http://library.rumsfeld.com/doclib/sp/355 /2003-10-06%20to%20President%20George%20W%20Bush%20re%20Iraq%20Reporting %20Relationships.pdf.

314 *"hold their fire a bit," "We are liberators"* Rajiv Chandrasekaran, "Powell, in Baghdad, Suggests That Critics Hold Their Fire," *Washington Post*, September 15, 2003.

315 *leaving the administration at the end of a single term* Glenn Kessler, "State Department Changes Seen If Bush Reelected: Powell and Armitage Intend to Step Down," *Washington Post*, August 4, 2003.

315 *"gossip"* Mike Allen, "Powell Calls Resignation Report 'Gossip,'" *Washington Post*, August 5, 2003.

315 *"ruthless enemy," "established relationship with al Qaeda"* Vice President Cheney remarks to the Heritage Foundation, October 10, 2003, https://georgewbush-whitehouse.archives .gov/news/releases/2003/10/text/20031010-1.html.

315 *"too much on our plate," "made a conscious decision"* Friedberg interview.

316 *"they had to be there"* Crocker interview.

316 *"a respected weapons scientist,"* Vice President Cheney remarks to the Heritage Foundation, October 10, 2003, https://georgewbush-whitehouse.archives.gov/news/releases /2003/10/text/20031010-1.html.

317 *"We still had not found the stockpiles"* Cheney, *In My Time*, p. 411.

318 *Armitage had been the initial and primary source* Neil A. Lewis, "First Source of CIA Leak Said to Admit Role, Lawyer Says," *New York Times,* August 30, 2006.

318 *"Over at the State Department"* Cheney, *In My Time,* p. 407.

318 *"how much he [Libby] was handicapped"* Wolfowitz interview.

319 *"We never really recovered from Abu Ghraib"* Rice, *No Higher Honor,* p. 274.

319 *"seems to have been a watershed"* Feith, *War and Decision,* p. 485.

320 *"The recent misconduct of a few"* Mike Allen, "Bush Speaks Out on Iraq Abuse," *Washington Post,* May 15, 2004.

320 *"just satisfying the desires of the press"* Demetri Sevastopulo, "Senators See New Photographs," *Financial Times,* May 13, 2004.

320 *lack of training,* Rumsfeld, *Known and Unknown,* p. 551.

320 *"It's something Powell has raised repeatedly"* Robin Wright and Bradley Graham, "Bush Privately Chides Rumsfeld," *Washington Post,* May 6, 2004.

321 *"In war, these sorts of horrible things happen"* Elisabeth Bumiller and Richard W. Stevenson, "Rumsfeld Chastised by President," *New York Times,* May 6, 2004.

321 *wished he had stepped down* Rumsfeld, *Known and Unknown,* p. 551.

321 *Bush didn't want to change his defense secretary* Bush, *Decision Points,* p. 89.

322 *"on this one you're wrong"* Rumsfeld, *Known and Unknown,* p. 551.

322 *"the end of my tolerance"* Bush, *Decision Points,* p. 89.

322 *brought their grievances to Rice* Rice, *No Higher Honor,* pp. 17–22, 291.

322 *"a kind of venom"* Author interview with Dennis Ross, March 1, 2016.

323 *"dark and heartless"* Bush, *Decision Points,* pp. 86–87.

324 *"We're too much apart"* Powell 2018 interview.

324 *"He wanted to stay on"* Wilkerson interview.

324 *"Getting a new secretary of state was a top priority"* Cheney, *In My Time,* pp. 425–26.

324 *"The vice president's perspective"* Khalilzad 2016 interview.

325 *he sounded out Condoleezza Rice* Rice, *No Higher Honor,* p. 289.

325 *called Powell's office to ask him to submit his resignation* Wilkerson interview. See also Wilkerson, "Guantánamo Bay Oral History Project," pp. 93–95.

325 *"You kind of half expect"* Powell 2018 interview.

326 *"I thought that when he began with me"* Ibid.

326 *"I made the case that Rumsfeld was doing a tremendous job"* Cheney, *In My Time,* p. 442.

20. Isolation

330 *"It was like a dysfunctional family Thanksgiving," "like Soviet diplomats"* Friedberg interview.

330 *"There are only 794 days left"* Rumsfeld, *Known and Unknown,* p. 706.

330 *"the deal was cooked"* Burns interview.

331 *"I never felt that the table was tilted"* Kimmitt interview.

331 *"one of the most capable"* David Johnston and Richard W. Stevenson, "Cheney Aide Charged with Lying in Leak Case," *New York Times,* October 29, 2005.

332 *prevented him from ascertaining Cheney's actions* R. Jeffrey Smith, "Cheney's Suspected Role in Security Breach Drove Fitzgerald," *Washington Post,* March 7, 2007.

332 *"black sites"* Dana Priest, "CIA Holds Terror Suspects in Secret Prisons," *Washington Post,* November 2, 2005.

333 *Cheney made dire predictions* Josh White, "President Relents, Backs Torture Ban," *Washington Post,* December 16, 2005.

333 *"will help deal with the terrible public diplomacy crisis"* Joseph Galloway and James Kuhnhenn, "Senate Votes to Ban Torture," *San Jose Mercury News,* October 6, 2005.

334 *Addington came up with the argument* The details of these efforts to undercut McCain's legislation are from the excellent account in Gellman, *Angler,* p. 353.

334 *"Now, you can get into a debate"* Transcript of interview with Dick Cheney, *Nightline,* ABC, December 18, 2005.

334 *Goss temporarily halted* Cheney, *In My Time,* p. 360.

334 *"Stellar Wind" program* James Risen and Eric Lichtblau, "Bush Lets U.S. Spy on Callers Without Courts," *New York Times*, December 16, 2005.

335 *"I see nothing wrong"* Colin Powell, "Powell: Warrants Would Have Prevented Spying Uproar," interview on *Morning Edition*, National Public Radio, December 26, 2005, https://www.npr.org/templates/story/story.php?storyId=5069681.

336 *reserve the right to interrogate them* CIA officials had a shorthand way of referring to these secret programs: RDI, which stood for "rendition, detention, and interrogation."

336 *"It was the most intense confrontation"* Rice, *No Higher Honor*, p. 502.

336 *The CIA carefully retained the option*, Author interview with Michael Hayden, May 27, 2010.

337 *"last throes"* Thomas E. Ricks, "Cheney Stands By His 'Last Throes' Remark," *Washington Post*, June 20, 2006.

337 *"we underestimated," "we didn't anticipate"* Cheney, *In My Time*, p. 433; Ricks, "Cheney Stands by His 'Last Throes' Remark."

337 *"what we are doing is not working"* Rice, *No Higher Honor*, p. 515.

338 *"we pretended it wasn't happening," "some of my colleagues"* Greg Jonsson, "Shift the Burden," *St. Louis Post-Dispatch*, December 8, 2006.

338 *"The United States is losing* "Colin Powell on Iraq: Study Group Was Right," *Star Tribune*, December 19, 2006.

338 *the Republicans could lose control of Congress* Bush, *Decision Points*, p. 355.

338 *"This time, the president didn't wait around"* Cheney, *In My Time*, p. 443.

339 *"I could barely contain my joy"* Rice, *No Higher Honor*, p. 540.

339 *"Cheney? . . . only one voice"* Gates, *Duty*, p. 7.

339 *"Colin not only knew the Pentagon well* Ibid., p. 22.

339 *"the outlier," "I know I'm alone on this"* Ibid., p. 584, p. 98.

340 *at the instruction of the president* Cheney, *In My Time*, p. 456.

341 *"I am not persuaded" . . . the U.S. Army was "about broken"* Interview with Colin Powell, CBS News, December 17, 2006, https://www.cbsnews.com/htdocs/pdf/F12-17-6.pdf; David Johnson, "Powell Doubts Need to Raise Troop Levels," *New York Times*, December 18, 2006.

342 *"I believed"* Cheney, *In My Time*, p. 468.

342 *Cheney had been dealing with the North Korea issue* Author interview with Carl W. Ford Jr., March 26, 2003.

342 *rewrote the State Department's instructions* Rice, *No Higher Honor*, pp. 161–62.

343 *"Hill and Rice made concession after concession"* Cheney, *In My Time*, p. 474.

343 *"I marched over with her"* Burns interview.

343 *a military attack on Iran* Gates, *Duty*, p. 182.

344 *Gates was speaking only for himself* Cheney, *In My Time*, p. 478.

344 *"not just any Israeli point of view, but usually the most right-wing"* Burns interview.

344 *special friend . . . his own private conversations* Rice, *No Higher Honor*, pp. 134, 490.

345 *"demonstrate our seriousness," "enhance our credibility"* Cheney, *In My Time*, pp. 468–71.

345 *"I was convinced Americans were tired of war"* Gates, *Duty*, p. 182.

345 *"Does anyone here agree with the vice president?" . . . "Not a single hand went up"* Cheney, *In My Time*, p. 471.

345 *Bush was unwilling to confront Olmert* Dennis Ross, *Doomed to Succeed* (New York: Farrar, Straus and Giroux, 2015), p. 334.

346 *"President of the United States Senate Richard B. Cheney"* Robert Barnes, "Cheney Joins Congress in Opposing D.C. Gun Ban; Vice-President Breaks with Administration," *Washington Post*, February 9, 2008.

346 *worked only for the vice president* Cheney, *In My Time*, p. 495.

346 *"So?"* Interview with Vice President Cheney, *Good Morning America*, ABC, March 19, 2008.

347 *"He really didn't give a damn"* Friedberg interview.

350 *"It has moved more to the right than I would like to see it"* Interview with Colin Powell, *Meet the Press*, NBC, October 19, 2008.

350 *"You are leaving a good man wounded"* Cheney, *In My Time*, p. 410.

351 *"I wish that pardoning Scooter Libby had been one of them"* Ibid.

Epilogue

354 *"could well be catastrophic"* Passages from Cheney's speech are taken from author notes and from the American Enterprise Institute transcript of the speech, Dick Cheney, "The Nuclear Deal with Iran and the Implications for U.S. Security," September 8, 2015, http://www.aei.org/press/prepared-remarks-former-vice-president-dick-cheney-on-the -nuclear-deal-with-iran-and-the-implications-for-us-security.

355 *"on a superhighway," "standing on the sidelines"* Colin Powell interview on *Meet the Press*, NBC, September 6, 2015.

355 *"Once you pull out the top"* Ibid.

356 *"People asked me"* . . . *"We're still there"* Powell 2018 interview.

356 *"We didn't need a war at that time"* Ibid.

357 *"Hee, hee, he won't"* Eric Geller, "Emails Show Powell Unloading on Clinton, Rumsfeld and Trump," *Politico*, September 14, 2016. The emails were made public by a website with Russia connections that had hacked Powell's account. Powell later confirmed that they were genuine.

357 *"I'll freely admit"* Dick Cheney speech to American Enterprise Institute, May 21, 2009.

358 *"unpleasant things"* Ibid.

358 *"It worked"* Mike DeBonis, "Speaking Out on Torture and Trump Nominee, Ailing McCain Roils Washington," *Washington Post*, May 12, 2018.

358 *"I have better things to do in life than grind my molars"* Author's phone conversation with Colin Powell, June 8, 2016.

359 *"I insist on punctuality"* Powell, *It Worked for Me*, p. 144.

359 *"damage that Barack Obama has done," "realistic and credible threat of military force"* Dick Cheney and Liz Cheney, *Exceptional: Why the World Needs a Powerful America* (New York: Threshold Editions, 2015), pp. 259, 254.

359 *"They are idiots and spent force"* Andrew Kaczynski, Christopher Massie, and Tatal Ansari, "Colin Powell Called the Cheneys Idiots," BuzzFeed, https://www.buzzfeednews .com/article/andrewkaczynski/colin-powell-called-the-cheneys-idiots.

359 *"we could finish each other's sentences"* Powell, *My American Journey*, p. 554.

360 *"get them together on the same stage"* Crocker interview.

360 *"They were all hiding behind their newspapers"* Ibid. Crocker wasn't on the flight himself but was told about it by others who were. His account of the plane ride was corroborated by another, unrelated source who was involved in these events.

360 *"an almost chummy rapport"* Elisabeth Bumiller, "'Band of Brothers' Mark Gulf War Anniversary," *New York Times*, January 20, 2011.

360 *"how much they loathed each other"* Crocker interview.

361 *He claimed that he had always been against it* See Michelle Lee, "Fact Check: Yes, Trump Did Support the Iraq War," *Washington Post*, September 26, 2016, https:// www.washingtonpost.com/politics/2016/live-updates/general-election/real-time-fact -checking-and-analysis-of-the-first-presidential-debate/fact-check-yes-trump-did -oppose-the-iraq-war/?utm_term=.ab99b6548e70.

361 *"He sounds like a liberal Democrat"* Nick Goss, "Cheney: Trump 'Sounds Like a Liberal Democrat,'" *Politico*, February 16, 2016.

361 *"torture works"* Jenna Johnson, "Donald Trump on Waterboarding: 'Torture Works,'" *Washington Post*, February 17, 2016, https://www.washingtonpost.com/news/post-politics/ wp/2016/02/17/donald-trump-on-waterboarding-torture-works/?utm_term= .9de773946c12.

361 *he announced that he would support Trump* Nick Gass, "Dick Cheney Will Support Trump," *Politico*, May 16, 2016.

362 *DCLeaks had Russian connections . . . hacking operations* Geller, "Emails Show Colin Powell Unloading on Clinton, Rumsfeld and Trump"; Mark Mazzetti and Katie Benner, "12 Russian Agents Indicted in Mueller Investigation," *New York Times*, July 14, 2018. See also Robert S. Mueller, *Report on the Investigation into Russian Interference in the 2016 Presidential Election,* U.S. Department of Justice, Vol. 1, March 2019, p. 36.

362 *"a national disgrace"* Powell emails as quoted in Eric Geller, "Emails Show Colin Powell Unloading on Clinton, Rumsfeld and Trump," *Politico*, September 14, 2016, https://www.politico.com/story/2016/09/colin-powell-emails-clinton-trump-rumsfeld-228158.

362 *"insults us every day"* Robert Brodsky, "Colin Powell Endorses Hillary Clinton for President," *Newsday*, October 25, 2016, https://www.newsday.com/news/nation/colin-powell-endorses-hillary-clinton-for-president-1.12504956.

362 *"C'mon, Rick," "They left me years ago"* Powell emails as quoted in Robert Samuels and Aaron Blake, "Obama's Former VA Secretary Pleaded with Colin Powell to Make Late Entry into the 2016 GOP Race," *Washington Post*, September 14, 2016, https://www.washingtonpost.com/news/the-fix/wp/2016/09/14/obamas-former-va-secretary-pleaded-with-colin-powell-to-make-late-entry-into-the-2016-gop-race/?utm_term=.05ef17180125. In a 2018 interview with the author, Powell said he was still asked almost daily why he hadn't or didn't run for president.

363 *"President Trump righted this wrong"* Peter Baker, "President Trump Pardons Scooter Libby in a Case That Mirrors His Own," *New York Times*, April 14, 2018, p. A-11.

363 *"act of war"* Morgan Chalfont, "Cheney: Russian Election Interference Could Be 'Act of War,'" *The Hill,* March 27, 2017, http://thehill.com/policy/cybersecurity/325928-cheney-russian-election-interference-could-be-act-of-war.

364 *Cheney repeatedly pressed Vice President Mike Pence* Robert Costa and Ashley Parker, "Former Vice President Cheney Challenges Pence at Private Retreat," *Washington Post*, March 11, 2019, https://www.washingtonpost.com/politics/former-vice-president-cheney-challenges-pence-on-trumps-foreign-policy/2019/03/11/ecddbff6-4436-11e9-aaf8-4512a6fe3439_story.html?utm_term=.7c8be8b3098e.

ACKNOWLEDGMENTS

My first expression of thanks for help in writing this book goes to the institution that has served as a home base for me during the research and writing of it: Paul H. Nitze School of Advanced International Studies (SAIS) at Johns Hopkins. This is now the fifth book I have written while based at SAIS. Although the school doesn't choose the subjects of the books or even know what's in them before they are published, it nevertheless supports the books and my work in countless ways, above all through the library, which is invaluable for my research, and through the faculty and students with whom I interact.

I am especially grateful to a number of individuals in the SAIS community. Dean Vali Nasr has helped by reinvigorating SAIS in general and by carrying forward the school's traditions of open inquiry. Within the Department of European and Eurasian Studies, where my office is located, I am thankful to Erik Jones and the late Kathryn Knowles, who provided help, support, and friendship both in Washington and at the SAIS campus in Bologna, where they gave me a chance to escape from Washington for several weeks to pull the book together. Kathryn Knowles passed away at a tragically young age as this book was being finished. Cristina Benitez provided the cheerful, superbly efficient administrative help in Washington necessary to keep things running. I also was fortunate to have the support of SAIS's Foreign Policy Institute, ably led by Carla Freeman and Christine Kunkel.

On the research side, the entire SAIS Library deserves thanks. I need to single out Stephen Sears, who flawlessly handled my endless questions; and Jenny Gelman, who did likewise on days when Stephen wasn't around. Finally, I was aided by three excellent SAIS students who each served for an academic year as my researchers for this book: Michael O'Donnell, Christoph Erber, and Michael Fedynsky.

While researching the book, I spent a couple of weeks at the George H. W. Bush Presidential Library in College Station, Texas, and also at the Ronald Reagan Presidential Library in Simi Valley, California. To cover my travel to and my stay at the Bush Library, I received support from the Peter and Edith O'Donnell Endowment of the Scowcroft Institute of International Affairs. Andrew Natsios, the director of the Scowcroft Institute, and Don W. Bailey, its assistant director, provided assistance during my week at the library. Meanwhile, for my visit to the Reagan Library, I had the invaluable help of Derek Shearer of Occidental College, who arranged housing in Los Angeles so that I did not have to stay in Simi Valley again, and who, in general, provided the same sort of advice and friendship on this project as he has on several previous books.

Peggy Cifrino, the principal assistant to Colin Powell, was especially helpful in arranging an interview with him. Susan Lemke of the National Defense University Library also provided kind assistance in arranging access to archival material collected by Powell.

I am grateful to the many people I interviewed for the book. I will not provide a list of them here because almost all are already named in the notes to the specific passages in which they are quoted. I also want to thank the other people who, at one time or another during the research, offered various thoughts, insights, or leads for further research: Richard Allen, Bill Burr, Seth Center, Eliot Cohen, Karen DeYoung, Jeffrey Engel, Carl Ford, Jack Matlock, Bob Woodward.

My agent, Andrew Wylie, provided wise counsel on the book. My superb editor at Holt, Paul Golob, was an invaluable contributor to this book all the way through, from helping to conceive the book in its earliest days and supporting it during the research to giving it the best, most thoughtful line-editing I can ever recall. Paul's assistant, Fiora Elbers-

Tibbitts, also supplied important help on numerous occasions toward getting the book out.

Finally, I want to thank my wife, Caroline Dexter, who as always served as a sounding board for ideas and a steadying influence during an author's moments of impatience or frustration; and my family, including Elizabeth and Micah, Ted and Kristin, and my five grandchildren, for keeping me happy even when I was swearing at the word processor.

Washington, D.C.
May 2019

INDEX

ABOUT THE AUTHOR

JAMES MANN is the author of six books on American politics and national security issues, including *Rise of the Vulcans: The History of Bush's War Cabinet* and *The Obamians: The Struggle Inside the White House to Redefine American Power.* A longtime correspondent for the *Los Angeles Times*, he is currently a fellow in residence at the Johns Hopkins University Paul H. Nitze School of Advanced International Studies. He lives in Washington, DC.